# CORPORATE

# SECRETARY'S

## BOOK OF

# AGREEMENTS, CORRESPONDENCE, FORMS, AND RESOLUTIONS

# CORPORATE

# SECRETARY'S

## BOOK OF

# AGREEMENTS,
# CORRESPONDENCE,
# FORMS, AND
# RESOLUTIONS

# DANA SHILLING

**PRENTICE HALL**
Englewood Cliffs, New Jersey 07632

Prentice-Hall International (UK) Limited, *London*
Prentice-Hall of Australia Pty. Limited, *Sydney*
Prentice-Hall Canada, Inc., *Toronto*
Prentice-Hall Hispanoamericana, S.A., *Mexico*
Prentice-Hall of India Private Limited, *New Delhi*
Prentice-Hall of Japan, Inc., *Tokyo*
Simon & Schuster Asia Pte. Ltd., *Singapore*
Editora Prentice-Hall do Brasil, Ltda., *Rio de Janeiro*

©1991 *by*
PRENTICE-HALL, Inc.
Englewood Cliffs, NJ

10   9   8   7   6   5   4   3   2   1

**Library of Congress Cataloging-in-Publication Data**

Shilling, Dana.
   Corporate secretary's book of agreements, correspondence, forms,
and resolutions / by Dana Shilling.
     p.  cm.
   Includes index.
   ISBN 0-13-174764-9
   1. Corporation law—United States—Forms.  2. Corporation
secretaries—United States—Handbooks, manuals, etc.  I. Title.
KF1411.S47   1990
346.73′066′0269—dc20
[347.306660269]                               90-37526
                                                    CIP

ISBN 0-13-174764-9

**PRENTICE HALL**
**BUSINESS & PROFESSIONAL DIVISION**
**A division of Simon & Schuster**
**Englewood Cliffs, New Jersey 07632**

Printed in the United States of America

# CONTENTS

# WORDS FROM THE AUTHOR ABOUT THE CORPORATION AND THE CORPORATE SECRETARY

The modern corporation is a powerful entity that is tailored to the needs of modern business. By incorporating (becoming a corporation), a business gains the advantage of "limited liability": except in unusual circumstances, only the corporation is liable for the corporation's debts and obligations. The shareholders cannot be held personally responsible for corporate obligations. Although the stockholders risk the loss of value of their shares, they do not risk indefinite liability the way sole proprietors and partners do.

## LAWS OF CORPORATE GOVERNANCE

This privilege is not without its price. For one thing, corporations have to pay taxes (unless they are organized as Subchapter S corporations, with the stockholders responsible for tax payments). For another thing, the corporation is subject to a great deal of regulation. A corporation cannot exist unless it is granted a charter by a state; before granting the charter, the state will require filing of Articles of Incorporation setting out the basic structure under which the corporation will be organized and governed. The new corporation will probably have to pay state taxes on its "franchise" (privilege of doing business in the state), its income earned within the state, or both, and will have to apply for a sales tax number and remit sales tax on its retail sales.

If the corporation does business in states in addition to the state in which it is originally incorporated, it will have to qualify in those states as a foreign corporation and will probably have reporting and tax paying obligations in those states as well.

*Practice Tip*: Sometimes business owners want to incorporate in Delaware, or some other jurisdiction that is considered to be probusiness, instead of the state in which they will be located. This is almost always inadvisable for the small corporation, because it will then have to qualify as a foreign corporation in the state of actual operations and will be responsible to at least two states.

Furthermore, a corporation is required to maintain a certain level of formality. It must keep books and records that are appropriate and sufficient to complete its federal and state tax forms and to keep stockholders informed of the corporation's financial conditions. The corporation must hold meetings. Unless it is a small, closely held corporation that has chosen to do without a Board of Directors, it must hold an annual meeting of stockholders to elect a Board of Directors. The directors must then vote and pass resolutions that become the official policy of the corporation. (Depending on state law and the political situation within the corporation, it may be necessary for the stockholders to vote on certain transactions and policies as well.) If the corporation adopts a seal, use of the corporate seal is evidence that the document to which the seal is attached has been officially adopted by the corporation.

Typically, state corporation law will require that a corporation have at least four officer titles (president, vice-president, secretary, and treasurer), and there must be at least two officers sharing the titles.

The corporate secretary is the person with the basic responsibility for making sure that the corporation's actions are properly authorized and properly documented. The corporate secretary usually is the secretary of all Board of Directors and stockholders' meetings, responsible for preparing resolution forms and maintaining the corporate minute and record books.

## RESPONSIBILITIES AND DUTIES OF THE CORPORATE SECRETARY

Generally speaking, the corporate secretary prepares resolutions and brings them to the meeting, so that the resolution can be read and voted on; if it is approved, the secretary notes that fact and the number voting for and against the resolution and the number abstaining. The resolution (and any dissents to the resolution filed by a director or stockholder) then becomes part of the corporation's minute book.

*Practice Tip*: A computerized or card index of corporate resolutions adopted, and separate annual volumes or annual tabs within the minute book, make it much easier to find the references to adoption of a particular action or policy when it is called for.

Frequently, the corporate secretary maintains the records of who is a shareholder (records that are crucial in notifying stockholders to attend annual meetings or vote by proxy for the directors) and makes the official notations that transfer ownership from the seller of the corporation's stock to the buyer. The usual practice is for the corporate secretary to prepare a list of registered stockholders (usually in alphabetical order), their addresses, and stockholdings, so that this list can be used to notify them of the meeting.

*Practice Tip*: A corporation's failure to maintain the required books and records is powerful evidence to "pierce the corporate veil"—disregard the corporation's legal status and make the stockholders personally responsible for corporate obligations.

The corporate secretary also acts as the liaison between corporate management and the stockholders, giving them notices of meetings, informing them of corporate transitions and transactions, and giving them access to corporate records if they choose to exercise their statutory privilege to inspect them.

## LEGALLY REQUIRED RECORD MAINTENANCE

Last, but by no means least, the corporate secretary is also the corporation's historian and archivist, responsible for maintaining records in accessible form. The corporate secretary should get legal advice and set up a "records retention" plan, under which some records are maintained in full paper form at headquarters; some are maintained in paper form, but transferred to offices away from the home office or to back office or warehouse space; others are preserved in electronic form (e.g., on computer tapes) or "microform" (microfilm or fiche) and the papers are destroyed; and others are discarded, shredded, or destroyed outright. Some records can be transferred to the corporation's attorney or accountant for maintenance (e.g., workpapers used to complete a tax return). Some state and federal statutes mandate retaining certain records for a certain amount of time (e.g., one year, four years, six years). Even if there is no legal requirement, it may be a practical necessity to retain certain information indefinitely, for instance to demonstrate to a prospective buyer of the business how much was invested in plant and equipment, or for use in valuing the stock repurchased by the corporation from a retiring stockholder, or the estate of a deceased stockholder.

If the corporation keeps full copies of all records (especially the multiple copies that proliferate when photocopying machines are available), it will be impossible to find anything in the raft of paper, and the corporation will have to devote a great deal of valuable space to maintaining the records. On the other hand, destroying records that are needed later can be anything from embarrassing (if the corporation has to pay a bill a second time, because it can't prove the original payment), to a factor in losing a major lawsuit, to outright contempt of court. Therefore, the corporation must set and enforce a records retention policy after getting legal advice.

DANA SHILLING

# HOW TO USE THIS BOOK

Every corporation, and every situation confronting the corporation, is individual and requires the best judgment of the corporation and its advisors. However, there are many situations that arise frequently, and it is possible to prepare useful model agreements, resolutions, and forms that the corporate secretary can use as a starting point in drafting and negotiating.

The forms in this book are not designed to be incorporated without changes into a real corporation's minute book. Instead, they are meant to spark the imagination, and give the corporate secretary insight into the drafting possibilities. If you use forms in a negotiation, of course, the agreement that is finally adopted will reflect the give and take of negotiations. (The people and corporations used in the forms are fictitious, and are not intended as a portrait of real individuals or businesses; and the fictional states of Adams, Madison, Monroe, Roosevelt, and Tyler are used to show the variations in state practice, but are not intended to represent actual states of the United States.) Adapt them based on your own corporation's situation—and be sure to get legal and accounting advice as required. This book is not supposed to replace professional advice; instead, it is aimed at making you, the corporate secretary, a better informed client who can make the most efficient and economical use of your advisors' time.

In these forms, blanks are left for "fill-ins." If there are several possibilities, the possibilities are separated by a slash ("plurality/simple majority/supermajority of 60%") or set out with boxes to check ("[ ] common stock only [ ] common stock and 5% cumulative preferred stock [ ] common stock, 5% cumulative preferred stock, and 7% noncumulative preferred stock subordinated to the 5% cumulative preferred stock"). Optional provisions are set off in brackets; either remove the brackets to adopt the provision, or strike the provisions out if they are not wanted.

The basic purposes of drafting are definition and control of risk. The perfect document defines all the things that are intended to happen under the agreement, resolution, notice, or other type of document; explains who must make payments to whom, and who must perform in other ways (e.g., by constructing a factory, delivering chrome-plated trailer hitches); gives a schedule for performance; sets out all the things that could go wrong; explains who takes the risk of something going wrong; explains who can cancel the agreement, when, and why; and explains what a party that believes it has been injured can do to enforce the document. Needless to say, few documents are perfect! Maybe the document as drafted does not express what the parties really wanted; maybe one party didn't foresee a potential problem, and failed to provide for it; maybe one party took advantage of the other by including a subtle provision that provides a benefit that the other party was not aware of.

Documents frequently contain standard or "boilerplate" provisions, such as arbitration clauses (providing that disputes will go to arbitration, not litigation, to save time and expenses), "choice of law" clauses (explaining which state's laws will be used to interpret the document), "successorship" clauses (stating that any heir, assignee, or other successor is just as bound by the document as the original parties), and "cumulative remedies" and "nonwaiver" clauses (saying that an injured party that ignores one default can still pursue remedies for other defaults, and that injured parties can enforce all their legal rights, not just rights specifically set out in the document). In these forms, various "boilerplate" clauses are included in some documents, but omitted from others to save space and avoid duplication.

With tools such as these forms, with adequate professional advice, and armed with a personal knowledge of the corporation's operations, needs, and objectives, the corporate secretary can prepare the documents needed to carry out and document the work of the corporation.

# LIST OF AGREEMENTS, FORMS, MEMORANDA, CORRESPONDENCE, AND ALTERNATIVE AND OPTIONAL CLAUSES

## Chapter 3: CORPORATE GOVERNANCE, MEETINGS, AND RESOLUTIONS 57

# Chapter 1

# ORGANIZATION OF THE CORPORATION

## ARTICLES OF INCORPORATION

All too often, entrepreneurs (and even their attorneys) setting up corporations treat the drafting of the Articles of Incorporation as a boring, trivial task best accomplished by signing a stock form from a corporate kit or "filling in the blanks" in a form book. They don't realize that the Articles of Incorporation (also called Certificate of Incorporation or Charter in some jurisdictions) set the basic terms on which the corporation operates and is governed. Including a seemingly routine provision, or failing to include a necessary provision, can lead to serious political difficulties within the corporation; it can even lead to litigation.

Drafting a corporation's Articles of Incorporation requires more than a form book—even this form book! The drafter must make an accurate assessment of the balance of power within the corporation's founding group, predict future political battles, think about how the corporation will behave in the future and whether it is a likely takeover target, and set up the conditions on which the corporation will be passed on to a new generation when the founders die or retire.

Experts differ about how real "shareholder democracy" really is in the large public corporation, and whether stockholders want to participate in the running of the corporation, or are just interested in their dividends and the price they can get for their shares. The dynamics of the small close corporation are entirely different. In fact, the corporation's officers and Board of Directors—usually overlapping if not identical groups—often find out that they have more "shareholder democracy" on their hands than they ever wanted! Before the corporation is formed, while the provisions of the Articles of Incorporation are being hammered out, the stockholders who will serve on the Board of Directors often want to increase the powers given to the Board (for instance, by making the Board of Directors the only people who can adopt or amend bylaws or call a special meeting of stockholders). The other stockholders typically want to expand their own powers, for instance, by getting the right to call special meetings, or the right to veto corporate actions unless all the stockholders, or a very high percentage ("supermajority"), agree. The drafter should be aware, however, that a provision adopted to make minority shareholders happy may later backfire if a would-be raider buys some stock in the corporation and then calls a special meeting or tries to oust the Board of Directors. (Adopting transfer restrictions can cope with this problem by making it much less likely that a raider will be able to buy any stock and "get the camel's nose in the tent.")

### Handling Director's Conflicts

Conflicts within the close corporation are very typical. Sometimes there is a serious disagreement about how the corporation should be run, or the business directions it should take. Another pattern (especially common in the second generation) is for one group of stockholders to have active management of the corporation and receive salaries, while other stockholders do not get salaries. They get dividends on their stock—*if* the "in group" decide to declare them. They may find it impossible to sell their stock to anyone except the "in group" (because there is little demand for close corporation stock), or may have a willing buyer but be limited by transfer restrictions. Or, on the other hand, the harmony of a smoothly running close corporation can be disrupted if a disgruntled minority shareholder who is not subject to transfer restrictions sells his or her shares to a raider.

### Governing State Corporation Law

The drafter should also study the state's corporation law. Maybe cumulative voting for directors (a provision that tends to help minority shareholders by making it easier for them to get at least one seat on the board of Directors) is required by state law. But if it is optional, it's a matter of corporate politics to determine whether the majority group will eliminate cumulative voting, or if the minority group will be in a position to demand it. State law may also determine who can adopt and amend bylaws and who has the right to amend the Articles of Incorporation. The power to amend makes it possible to remedy omissions and mistakes. But if there's a serious conflict between the Board and the minority shareholders, and if a heavy shareholder vote is required to amend, the Board is likely to lose, or to have to make, important concessions to the minority shareholders to get their votes.

Most state corporation codes include a "laundry list" of powers that all corporations have automatically. It's not necessary to include these powers in the Articles of Incorporation (unless it's desirable to inform the corporation's shareholders and creditors of these powers). However, it's important to decide which additional powers, permitted but not automatic under state law, should be included in the Articles of Incorporation: matters such as borrowing power and power to invest in real estate.

## Tax Effects

The drafter must also consider the tax effects of the provisions of the Articles of Incorporation. For instance, if the corporation elects Subchapter S status under the Internal Revenue Code, but does not adopt transfer restrictions, an angry shareholder can cause the corporation to lose Sub S status (and incur heavy additional tax liability) just by selling shares to a few too many buyers, or to any buyer (e.g., a corporation) who cannot be a Sub S shareholder.

Many of the most powerful "shark repellant" devices to keep away raiders are only effective for public corporations, because they depend on the existence of a large number of shares and an active public market. However, close corporations should seriously consider transfer restrictions (for this as well as many other reasons explored throughout this book); giving the Board of Directors broad discretion to amend the Articles or even to reincorporate in another state that allows stronger defensive measures; denying shareholders the right to call special meetings, and making sure that directors can only be removed for good cause such as proof of bad faith or conflict or interest (because raiders can use such powers to call a special meeting, increase the number of directors on the Board and elect their own puppets, or remove incumbent directors and substitute pro-raider candidates).

In short, the Articles of Incorporation are important documents. Mistakes *can* be remedied by amendment, but it is better to do the job right the first time and select the options permitted by state law that most accurately represent the political balance of the corporation and the wishes of the corporate management and the stockholder-"voters."

---

## AGREEMENT TO INCORPORATE A PARTNERSHIP

The Parties are James Milton III, Bernard Nadeau, and Walter Ashberry, who are partners in a general partnership doing business as Window Decor Designs [as governed by a partnership agreement dated _____ , 199____]. They intend to continue the business in corporate form, by incorporating in the state of Roosevelt, under the name Window Decor Designs, Inc.

All interests in the partnership's tangible and intangible assets and business will be transferred to the corporation, for example, inventory, fixtures, equipment, and goodwill. The corporation will assume and agree to pay all obligations and liabilities of the partnership and will indemnify the partners and hold them harmless against partnership liabilities and obligations.

The parties agree to transfer their partnership interests to the corporation in exchange solely for shares of stock, with 1 share of stock to be issued for each $100 of value of a partner's interest (as evidenced by the partnership's books of record as of the close of business on _____ , 199 ___ ).

The parties will serve as the corporation's initial Board of Directors and will devote full time, effort, and loyalty to the affairs of the new corporation. If any partner ever ceases to serve as an employee or director of the corporation, he agrees not to compete with the corporation—that is, he will not engage in the same or a similar business of designing and selling window treatments for residences, offices, and commercial buildings within 25 miles of the corporation's offices, for a period of five years.

The parties agree to execute all legal instruments required for the change from partnership to corporate form and to give notice of the partnership's dissolution and intention to incorporate wherever required to divest themselves of personal liability for the business' liabilities and obligations.

Date: _____ , 199_____
Signed: _____

# PREINCORPORATION AGREEMENT WITH PROMOTER

**1. *Parties:*** The *incorporators* are Allan Dix, Charles Garrison, and Michelle Garrison. The *promoter* is Arthur Lipscombe.

**2. *Purpose:*** The incorporators intend to incorporate a business to be known as MASON-LIKE PREFAB CONSTRUCTION, INC. in the state of Lincoln, for corporate purposes including but not limited to prefabricated construction and erection of residences, offices, and commercial buildings, using a patented process involving the use of processed corn stalks as a building material.

**3. *Promoter's Role:*** The promoter is experienced in the promotion of the stock of new corporations and is licensed as a securities dealer, investment advisor, and financial planner in the states of Lincoln, Adams, and Roosevelt. The incorporators and promoter enter into this agreement so that the promoter can use his experience, skills, and connections to secure subscriptions to the stock to be issued by Mason-Like.

**4. *Incorporation:*** The incorporators will use their best efforts to incorporate in the state of Lincoln, to secure ratification of this agreement by the corporation's Board of Directors as soon as incorporation is completed, and to carry out any applicable requirements of the Securities Act, Securities Exchange Act, and the blue-sky laws of each state in which the stock will be offered for sale. It is contemplated that Mason-Like will be authorized to issue 25,000 shares of common stock with a par value of $10 per share and 5,000 shares of preferred stock with a par value of $25 per share. It is contemplated that the initial offering will consist of 20,000 shares of common stock at an estimated offering price of $60 per share and 4,000 shares of preferred stock at an estimated offering price of $100 per share, to be sold in the state of Lincoln. It is contemplated that the issue will be public/intrastate only in compliance with Regulation A/in compliance with Regulation D.

**5. *Disclosure to Promoter:*** The incorporators will give the promoter full information about the progress of the offering and will promptly give the promoter at least 25 copies of the required disclosure documents such as registration statements, preliminary prospectuses, and prospectuses.

**6. *Promoter's Duties and Compensation:*** The promoter will use his best efforts to secure valid, written subscriptions, on forms approved by the incorporators, for the sale of up to 20,000 shares of common stock at an estimated offering price of $60 per share and up to 4,000 shares of preferred stock at an estimated offering price of $100 per share. The promoter agrees to abide by all applicable federal and state laws and regulations during the process of soliciting subscriptions and agrees not to make any statement, representation, or promise that is untrue or inconsistent with the disclosure documents issued by the corporation and to disclose all material facts.

   If Mason-Like is incorporated as contemplated, and if the promoter secures valid subscriptions for at least $1 million worth of stock on or before _____ , 199_____ , the promoter will be compensated solely by receiving 1 share of Mason-Like's common stock for every 50 shares for which he has obtained subscriptions. The incorporators are obligated to issue such stock as soon as possible after the corporation's organization meeting.

7. *Failure of Agreement:* If Mason-Like is not in fact incorporated in the state of Lincoln on or before _____ , 199_____ , this agreement will expire, and the incorporators will reimburse the promoter for his documented out-of-pocket expenses in soliciting subscriptions for the stock. Furthermore, if the failure to incorporate is caused by the incorporators' wrongdoing or negligence, they will pay the sum of $25,000 to the promoter as liquidated damages (not as a penalty). The incorporators' liability for expenses or liquidated damages will be joint and several.

   However, if the failure to incorporate is due to causes beyond the control of the incorporators, their liability to the promoter will be limited to out-of-pocket expenses.

   If incorporation takes place as contemplated, but the promoter fails to obtain valid subscriptions totaling at least $500,000 within 60 days of the first date on which sale of stock first becomes permissible, this agreement will expire on that date unless the incorporators and promoter agree on an extension. Unless $500,000 worth of stock has been subscribed to by the close date (as extended), the amounts paid by subscribers will be returned to them. The corporation will reimburse the promoter for documented out-of-pocket expenses, but will have no other or further obligations to the promoter.

## PREINCORPORATION AGREEMENT (One Signatory Finances the Corporation, the Other Manages It)

### Introduction

Luther Paulsen has developed a process of casting plastic industrial components. He needs capital to develop the process for commercial use. Alexander LeMoyne has capital to invest. Therefore, it is mutually agreed that Luther Paulsen will form a corporation to develop and exploit his process and that Alexander LeMoyne will invest in the new enterprise.

### A. Corporate Nature and Identity

*1.* As soon as possible, the parties will form a corporation, to have perpetual duration, under the laws of the state of Adams and headquartered in that state. If the name "Cast Plastic Components, Inc." is available in the state of Adams, the parties will reserve and register that name and use it; if it is not available, the nearest available name will be selected and used.

*2.* The corporation will have a five-member Board of Directors.

*3.* The corporation will be capitalized at 1,000 shares of preferred stock with a par value of $10 per share and 10,000 shares of no-par common stock. The preferred stock will be entitled to cumulative dividends at the rate of 7% per year; preference will extend to dividends and distribution of the corporation's assets if and when it is dissolved.

*4.* Alexander LeMoyne agrees to make an initial investment of $250,000 in return for 800 shares of the corporation's preferred stock and 4,500 shares of its common stock.

## STOCK SUBSCRIPTION ROADMAP

- Date
- Name, address of subscribers—note if subscriber is an incorporator or promoter of the corporation
- Name of corporation—include alternate(s) if chosen name is unavailable
- Number, type of shares subscribed for
- Consideration for subscription (e.g., subscriptions by others)
- Conditions on subscriptions
- Closing date—when subscriptions are executed by paying for and receiving the stock
- Special conditions (e.g., preferred stock is redeemable)

## PREINCORPORATION AGREEMENT
### ("Inside Man" and "Outside Man")

### Introduction

This document, dated _____ , 199____ , represents the entire agreement between John Brinkmore and Andrew McLauren, who wish to enter into an agreement regulating the terms under which Brinkmore will provide the capital to develop McLauren's novel system for retailing books, magazines, records, compact disks, audio- and videocassettes, and other entertainment media.

*1. Corporate Formation:* The parties intend, as soon as possible after signing this agreement, to form a corporation under the laws of the state of Adams, having perpetual duration, under the name Entertainment at the Brink Corporation. If this name is not available for corporate use, or if a trademark search discloses that trademark registration would be unavailable, the parties will select another name by mutual consent.

*2. Corporate Purposes:* The corporation will be formed and operated to retail, wholesale, and produce entertainment media of all types, and for other lawful corporate purposes. It will have the powers granted to corporations by the laws of the state of Adams, plus any other lawful powers chosen by the parties.

*3. Corporate Operations:* The corporation will have a Board of Directors consisting of five directors/as permitted by Section 413.202 of the consolidated laws of the state of Adams, the corporation will dispense with a Board of Directors and will be managed directly by its stockholders.

*4. Headquarters:* The corporation's headquarters will be Suite 202, The Entertainment Office Condominium, 2219 Spring Drive, Adams.

**5. *Capitalization:*** The corporation will begin business with an initial capital of $650,000. Its initial capitalization will consist of 10,000 shares of voting, no-par common stock and 10,000 shares of nonvoting, 6% cumulative preferred stock, preferred as to dividends and to distribution of the corporation's assets on liquidation.

**6. *Subscriptions:*** As soon as the corporation is organized, McLauren agrees to subscribe for 6,500 shares of common stock, paying $50 per share, and for all 10,000 shares of the preferred stock, paying $30 per share. Brinkmore agrees to subscribe to 3,500 shares of common stock, paying a total of $25,000 plus the services he has already rendered in developing a marketing system and methodology and providing management services during the organization period.

**7. *Supplementary Capital:*** McLauren agrees to contribute up to $500,000 if additional capital is required during the first two years of operation; if necessary, the corporation will issue additional common and/or preferred stock to be distributed to McLauren representing his additional contribution; price per share will be either book value or $30 per preferred, $50 per common share, whichever is lower.

**8. *Corporate Officers and Directors:*** The corporation's officers will be a President and a Secretary. The initial Board of Directors, serving until the first annual meeting, will be Brinkmore, McLauren, Michael Petty, Jeffrey Slade, and Carolyn Schmidt [omit if corporation has no board of directors].

**9. *Employment Agreement:*** Brinkmore agrees to sign an employment agreement, obligating him to devote his full time, attention, and efforts exclusively to the corporation for a term of five years from the date of incorporation, at an annual salary of $75,000 plus performance bonuses.

**10. *Transfer Restrictions:*** Neither party (nor their executors, administrators, or assigns) may sell, transfer, or otherwise dispose of any of their shares without first offering the other party a right of first refusal on the shares. Price will be set by Arthur Lodge, of Lodge & Company, whom the parties agree is a qualified neutral appraiser; if he is unavailable, by the person assuming his title and functions at Lodge & Company. The right of first refusal lasts for 30 days; if, by that time, the prospective purchasing party has not agreed to purchase and secured financing, the prospective seller is free to offer the stock elsewhere.

Date: _____ , 199____

Signed: _____

# OPTIONAL CLAUSES FOR PREINCORPORATION AGREEMENT

**1. *Close Corporation:*** It is the intention of the parties that the corporation be closely held at all times; therefore, there will be no public market for the corporation's shares. The tax planning of the corporation and its shareholders would be furthered by Subchapter S and Section 1244 status for the corporation. All the parties to this agreement consent to the adoption of a buy-sell agreement by the shareholders, and its adoption by the corporation once it is formed. All the parties to this agreement agree to sign the necessary consents to the corporation's Subchapter S election [and its state counterpart under Section _____ of the laws of the state of _____ ] and to refrain from any activity that would terminate the Subchapter S election (e.g., sale of shares to an impermissible shareholder or to an excessively large number of shareholders), unless corporate action is taken to terminate the election.

**2. *Letter Stock:*** Each signatory hereby states that his/her motive for subscribing to and purchasing stock in the corporation to be formed is personal investment for his/her own account, not resale. He/she has no present intent to resell or distribute the shares. S/he also states that s/he is a bona fide resident of the state of _____ ; as all of the subscribers are bona fide residents of that state, the offering is made entirely within a single state, and thus the intrastate offering exemption is available.

**3. *Property for Stock:*** Of the parties to this preincorporation agreement, Martha Latymer will pay cash for the stock of the newly formed corporation that she will receive as soon as issuance of stock is legally permissible. The other parties, Jerome Steinmetz and Lloyd Walsh, will receive their stock in exchange for tangible and intangible personal property to be contributed to the corporation for use in its business. Steinmetz will contribute property with a fair market value of $235,000, consisting of machinery and materials suitable for use in the business to be conducted. Walsh will contribute property with a fair market value of $100,000, consisting of trade secrets, know-how, and a U.S. patent application number _____ for a process crucial to the success of the business to be conducted. The fair market value of the property disclosed above is accepted by all parties to this agreement and is the value that the newly formed corporation will assign to the property in its books of account.

## ARTICLES OF INCORPORATION

**1. *Name:*** These Articles of Incorporation are intended to create and regulate the corporate existence of a corporation to be known as CHOCO-MENTHE CUPCAKES, INC. ("the Corporation"). This corporate name has already been reserved/if this corporate name is unavailable, the corporation will be known as CUPCAKES A LA CHOCOLAT, INC.

**2. *State of Incorporation:*** The Corporation will be incorporated in the state of Monroe, although it may do business in other states and countries.

**3. *Duration:*** The Corporation's existence will be perpetual. [If state law requires, use instead: The Corporation's existence will be 30 years/50 years/or other maximum term permitted by state law.]

**4. *Corporate Purposes:*** The Corporation is organized and will operate to develop, manufacture, and market single-serving baked desserts of chocolate flavor, and for other legally permitted purposes. However, at no time will the Corporation provide banking or insurance services, or hold itself out as providing such services.

**5. *Incorporators:*** The incorporators of the Corporation are Edward Loomis, Tara Spicer, and George O'Flaherty. [If state law requires, add: each is an adult citizen of the United States and of this state; AND/OR each has purchased 100 shares of the capital stock of the Corporation; AND/OR together, the incorporators have invested an aggregate of at least $1,000 in the capital stock of the Corporation.]

**6. *Corporate Governance:*** The Corporation will be managed by its Board of Directors. The initial Directors, who will serve until the organization meeting, are Edward Loomis, Dorothy Loomis, and Stuart Mittleman. The Board of Directors will consist of seven people, who will serve three-year terms. [If a classified Board of Directors is desired, add: of the seven directors, three will serve an initial term of three years, two will serve an initial term of two years, and two will serve an initial term of one year. All directors subsequently elected to the Board of Directors will serve a two-year term.] OR The corporation will have a "sliding scale" Board of Directors: that is, the initial number of

Directors will be seven, but the number can be decreased (but not to fewer than three) or increased (but not to more than twenty-five) by vote of the shareholders holding a majority of the Corporation's common stock, provided that the number of directors at all times must be an odd number.

The power to adopt and amend Bylaws will be held solely by the Board of Directors OR Bylaws may be adopted or amended either by the Board of Directors or by the shareholders. [OR, see below, vis-à-vis provisions protecting the minority shareholders.]

**7. *Indemnification of Directors:*** The Corporation agrees to indemnify the [outside] directors for any monetary liability incurred for breach of fiduciary duty of care. However, indemnification will not be available when directors are found liable for intentional misconduct or illegal acts.

**8. *Officers:*** The Corporation's officers will be a President, Vice-President, Secretary, and Treasurer. The duties of the Board of Directors include appointing the corporation's officers OR The officers will be elected by the stockholders at the annual meeting. Any person can hold any combination of offices [if state law requires, add: except that no person can serve as both President and Secretary at the same time].

**9. *Capitalization:*** The Corporation is authorized to issue shares of stock as follows:
*a.* 10,000 shares of common stock. The common stock will be no-par stock/have a par value of $1.00 per share.
*b.* 2,000 shares of [convertible] [cumulative] preferred stock. The preferred stock will be no-par stock/have a par value of $1.00 per share.

Holders of preferred stock will not be entitled to vote for directors and on other corporate issues [unless four quarterly dividends in a row have been omitted]. However, the consent of holders of at least two-thirds of the preferred shares (one vote per share) will be required for adoption of any amendment to these Articles of Incorporation that affects the rights of the holders of preferred stock; or for adoption of a plan of liquidation, merger, or reorganization; or the sale, lease, or other disposition of all or substantially all of the Corporation's property.

The preferred stock will carry a dividend rate of at least 6 ½%, and no dividends on common stock will be paid until the preferred stockholders have received a dividend. [For cumulative preferred, add: and all dividends previously passed.] [For convertible preferred stock, add: Shares of preferred stock can be converted to common stock by surrender of the share certificate; stockholders will receive three shares of common stock for every two shares of common stock surrendered.] If, at any time, the Corporation is voluntarily liquidated, dissolved, or wound up, the preferred stockholders will be entitled to a payment of $75 per preferred share held out of the corporate assets remaining after its debts have been paid, and before any distribution of assets is made to the common shareholders. At any time that the Corporation undergoes involuntary liquidation, the preferred shareholders will be entitled to a distribution equal to the par value of the preferred shares, plus any dividends accrued but unpaid, before any distribution of assets is made to the common shareholders.

The Board of Directors has the power, at any time, to redeem all or part of the Corporation's preferred stock, on 60 days' written notice to all the preferred stockholders, by paying them $115 per share plus any accrued but unpaid dividends. Once preferred stock is redeemed, it will be canceled and may not be reissued. In order to fund the redemption of preferred stock, the Corporation shall/may, on vote of a majority of the Board of Directors, establish a sinking fund out of net profits or net assets legally available for payment of dividends. The sinking fund payment shall/may be declared as of the date of the annual meeting of shareholders, in the amount of either $15,000 or 6 ½% of net earnings, whichever is greater. The sinking fund can be funded either in cash or in shares of preferred stock already redeemed. Shares to be redeemed with sinking fund money will be chosen by lot. However, no shares may be redeemed with sinking fund money at any time that dividends are in arrears.

Shares of stock can be issued for cash, notes, property (provided that the fair market value of property is at least equal to the fair market value of the shares at the time of the exchange), or for services actually provided to the Corporation. Shares cannot be issued in return for future services to the Corporation. Once consideration has been received (if the consideration is in the form of notes, once the amount due has been paid in full), the shares will be considered fully paid and non-assessable.

**10. Dividend Policy:** Dividends on common stock may only be declared out of profits of the preceding year, not out of accumulated profits from earlier years OR Dividends on common stock may only be declared if the corporation's surplus account contains sufficient net earnings to pay preferred dividends for the year [for this year and the preceding year]. [Note: Before declaring a dividend, the Corporation should consult the provisions of any outstanding mortgages on its real property—the mortgagor may have restricted dividend declaration to increase the funds available to pay debt service.]

**11. Shareholders' Personal Property:** Shareholders' personal property will be immune to all claims against the Corporation OR As provided by Section 229.B7 of the laws of the state of Monroe, shareholders are hereby placed on notice that their personal property will be subject to claims against the Corporation under the following circumstances: _____

**12. Registered Office/Registered Agent:** The Corporation's registered office and headquarters will be located at 1703 Amarillo Boulevard, Future City, Monroe. Its registered agent for service of process at this address will be Stanley Reed.

**13. Corporate Powers:** [Omit powers provided in state's corporation statute] In addition to the powers provided by the corporation laws of the state of Monroe, the Corporation shall have the following powers, to the extent that they do not violate the laws of Monroe or other states in which the Corporation is doing business:

*a.* To enter into partnerships.

*b.* To sell or otherwise dispose of corporate property, provided that a fair price is received.

*c.* To acquire, redeem, hold, pledge, and transfer its own shares.

*d.* To make grants and charitable contributions to tax-exempt organizations, provided that such grants and contributions do not involve self-dealing on the part of the Corporation's officers or directors.

*e.* To establish and maintain reserves of funds to be expended later for legitimate corporate purposes.

*f.* To enter into contracts with the Corporation's directors, or with other corporations having directors in common with the corporation, provided that all such contracts benefit the Corporation, full disclosure of the interest is made, and the contracts are entered into terms no less favorable to the corporation than arm's-length contracts that do not involve interested parties. Interested directors may be counted in determining whether a quorum is present at a Board of Directors' meeting, but they are not permitted to vote on transactions in which they have an interest.

*g.* To form committees of the Board of Directors to investigate and report to the full Board on matters of corporate interest such as potential mergers and acquisitions or possible future litigation.

*h.* To determine when and to what extent the corporation's books and records may be examined, and by whom.

*i.* To establish incentive and deferred compensation plans (e.g., bonus, profit-sharing, and stock option plans) to reward and motivate the Corporation's officers, directors, and employees.

*14. **Preemptive Rights:*** Preemptive rights will not be granted OR shareholders will have a preemptive right to purchase shares of stock that are authorized by these Articles (as amended) and newly issued by the Corporation. Preemptive rights will be granted to shareholders in proportion to their ownership of the Corporation's outstanding capital stock as of the time the new issue of stock is announced.

*15. **Meetings:*** Meetings of the Board of Directors will be held at least annually; a special meeting can be called by the Chairman of the Board at his or her own instance, or on request of at least two directors, on two weeks' written notice to the Directors. In an emergency, special meetings can be held by notifying the Directors by telephone, telegram, or fax, giving them as much notice as the situation permits. Directors' meetings can be held by conference call as well as in person, and the Board of Directors can also legitimately take actions by unanimous written consent of all Directors without holding a meeting.

Meetings of the stockholders will be held at least annually, on the eighth of March (or the next business day, if March eighth is a Saturday, Sunday, legal, or religious holiday).

Shareholders may take any action that would be appropriate at a meeting without a meeting, on signed consent of all shareholder/the number of shareholders required to take the action if a meeting had been held. OR Shareholders may only take action or signal their consent to a corporate action by voting at the corporation's regular annual or special meetings. No corporate action can be taken or ratified on written consent of the shareholders without a meeting. Special meetings can be called only by resolution adopted by a majority of the Board of Directors, not at the instance of stockholders. [Note: Before adopting provisions that give shareholders the right to call meetings or to take action on consent without a meeting, consider whether the provision will facilitate the job of a raider who wants to take over the corporation.]

Directors' and stockholders' meetings may be called to take place either inside or outside the state of incorporation.

*16. **Cumulative Voting:*** Shareholders will be permitted to cumulate their votes for Directors; that is, each shareholder's total voting power will equal one vote times each share he or she owns, but these votes can be allocated among the candidates for Director however the stockholder wishes. OR Cumulative voting for directors will not be permitted.

*17. **Amendments:*** These Articles of Incorporation may be amended or repealed as provided by the laws of the state of Monroe, and on the affirmative vote of at least two-thirds of the common shareholders (and two-thirds of the preferred shareholders, if the proposed amendment affects the rights of the preferred shareholders).

## SPECIAL ARTICLES OF INCORPORATION PROVISIONS
## FOR CLOSE CORPORATIONS

*1. **Existence as Close Corporation:*** The Corporation is intended to operate as a [statutory] close corporation [as described in Section _____ of the Statutes of the state of _____ ], and to this end will not have more than _____ shareholders.

**2. Subchapter S Status:** The Corporation will apply for Subchapter S status under federal law [and for corresponding state status under Section _____ of the Statutes of the state of _____] and will not issue its stock, or permit transfer of its stock, to anyone who is not qualified to be a Subchapter S stockholder.

As long as the Corporation maintains its Subchapter S status, it will not actually issue any stock other than one class of common stock, even if issuance of other kinds of stock is authorized by its Articles of Incorporation as amended. However, the Corporation has the power to issue common stock whose shares have identical rights with respect to the corporation's assets, but whose voting rights differ.

**3. Transfer Restrictions:** Certificates for all the Corporation's shares of stock will carry a printed endorsement or sticker alerting all actual and potential owners, holders and transferees that the shares are subject to transfer restrictions under an agreement entitled "Shareholder Agreement Dealing with Transfer Restrictions," dated _____ , 199____ and signed by all persons who were shareholders on that date.

**4. Operation Without a Board of Directors:** The Corporation will be managed directly by its stockholders; there will be no Board of Directors. Instead, the stockholders will perform all the functions normally assumed by a corporation's Board of Directors (except _____ , which is delegated to the officers of the corporation).

## CLAUSES FOR PROTECTION OF MINORITY SHAREHOLDERS

**1. Amendment of Articles of Incorporation:** Only the shareholders have the power to amend the Articles of Incorporation, which may be done by a simple majority/75% majority/unanimously either of votes taken at an annual or special meeting, or on written consent of the stockholders. The Board of Directors has no power to amend the Articles of Incorporation.

**2. Bylaws:** Same, substituting the word "bylaws" for "articles of incorporation."

**3. Limits on Borrowing Powers:** The prior written consent of each [5%, 10%, 20%] shareholder, given in person or by proxy, will be required for the corporation to borrow a sum exceeding $____ from a bank, or from any person or organization who is not a shareholder.

**4. Mandatory Dividends:** Except as restricted by law, the corporation must declare a dividend of at least $____ per common share per year. If the corporation's earnings and profits fall below that level, the corporation must distribute $____ per common share per year of its capital surplus (or the maximum amount of capital surplus that the law will permit it to distribute).

## OPTIONAL CLAUSES

**1. Purchase of Stock:** The corporation will have the power, at the discretion of the Board of Directors, to purchase its own stock. Repurchased stock shall have no voting rights, and dividends will not be paid on such stock/repurchased shares will be treated as treasury stock.

Such purchase may be made for any legitimate corporate objective/for any purpose permitted by state law/to retire preferred stock, and for no other purpose/to carry out the buy-sell agreement entered into on _____ , 199_____ between the corporation and its stockholders/only to retire preferred stock or effectuate a buy-sell agreement between the corporation and a key employee or its shareholders/for use in an ESOP, or incentive stock option plan/to eliminate fractional shares.

The Board of Directors may repurchase the corporation's own stock out of earned surplus at their own discretion; however, consent of the holders of a majority/two-thirds of the outstanding common shares, obtained at a special meeting of stockholders, will be required for the use of capital surplus to repurchase shares/repurchase can be made out of earned surplus, capital surplus, or paid-in surplus; however, no repurchase may be made at any time that such use of funds would impair the corporation's capital/repurchase will not be permitted at any time that the effect of the purchase would be to reduce the corporation's net assets so far as to jeopardize the preference to which the corporation's preferred shareholders are entitled in case of liquidation of the corporation.

*2. Debt Limitation:* At no time may the corporation's indebtedness exceed $ _____ /the par value of the corporation's outstanding stock [unless a majority of the shareholders have affirmatively voted to permit a higher level of debt].

The corporation's Board of Directors will have the power to purchase property subject to mortgages and assume such mortgages, to secure mortgage financing for purchases of property, and to mortgage corporate property [provided that a majority/two-thirds vote of shareholders at a special meeting, or written consent without a meeting, is required for any mortgage transaction bringing the aggregate mortgage debt of the corporation over $ _____ /over _____ % of the corporation's outstanding capital stock].

The Board of Directors will have the power to authorize, by resolution, borrowing from banks, other corporations, or individuals with or without security [provided that consent of the holders of a majority/two-thirds of the corporation's common stock will be required to ratify any debt that brings the aggregate debt of the corporation over $ _____ /over _____ % of the corporation's outstanding capital stock].

*3. Power to Guarantee:* The Board of Directors, by resolution, shall have the power to guarantee the obligations of others [provided that there is a legitimate corporate purpose for the guarantee]. In this context, "obligations" includes contracts, loan notes, bonds, and dividends/contracts only/loan notes only, with a limit of $ _____ . The Board of Directors may guarantee the obligations of the corporation's subsidiaries only/its customers, suppliers, and subsidiaries/personal obligations of officers, directors, and key employees on a vote by a quorum of disinterested directors/other: _____

*4. Dividends:* In order to determine the presence of a surplus so that dividends may be declared and paid, the value of the corporation's capital stock shall equal the par value of its outstanding shares, times the number of shares; however, if at any time the corporation issued shares for less than their par value, the amount received shall be used to calculate the corporation's capital stock. OR The corporation's capital stock shall equal the consideration received for its no-par shares. OR The corporation's capital stock shall equal $ _____ per no-par share.

Dividends can be declared only from a surplus deriving from current earnings/from current earnings and/or accumulated surplus; a dividend can legitimately be declared from accumulated surplus in a year in which there is no current surplus/from surplus deriving from any source, for example, an increase in asset value, a reduction of capital stock, a sale of capital stock, settlement of a debt or claim at a discount.

The preferred stock of the corporation shall be nonparticipating as to dividends/after a regular dividend has been declared on both common and preferred stock, including payment of any accrued but unpaid dividends on cumulative preferred stock, the Board shall have discretion to declare an additional dividend in which common and preferred stock will participate equally/after a regular dividend has been declared and paid on both common and preferred stock, including bringing cumulative preferred stock up to date, the preferred stock shall participate in any additional dividends declared, but only after the common shareholders have received an additional $ ____ per share/but only a ratio of $1 of special dividend for the preferred shareholders to $2/$3 of special dividend for the common shareholders.

## BYLAWS (For-Profit Corporation)

### General Matters

*1. Corporate Name:* The corporation's name will be _____ , Inc. OR The corporation's registered name will be _____ , Inc., but it will do business under the artificial name of _____ .

*2. Registered Address:* The corporation's registered address will be _____ , although it will have the power to do business at other locations inside and outside this state.

*3. Registered Agent:* The corporation's registered agent for service of process will be _____ .

*4. Business Year:* For financial and tax purposes, the corporation will operate on the basis of: ☐calendar year ☐initial 52/53-week year, then calendar/fiscal year beginning _____ of each year and ending the following _____ ☐ fiscal year beginning _____ of each year and ending the following _____ .

*5. Corporate Seal:* ☐The corporation will not adopt a seal.
☐The corporation hereby adopts a corporate seal, described as follows:
Affixation of the corporate seal to a document is prima facie evidence that the document has been duly adopted by the corporation, which will therefore be bound by the terms of the document.

## BYLAWS RELATING TO THE CORPORATION'S STOCK

*1. Capitalization:* The corporation's initial capitalization will be as follows:
☐ ____ shares of stock; all stock will be voting common stock.
☐ ____ shares of voting common stock; ____ shares of nonvoting common stock with dividend rights as described here: _____ ; ☐ ____ shares of cumulative/noncumulative preferred stock with dividend rights as described here: ____
Shares of preferred stock will be ☐nonconvertible ☐convertible to common stock on the following terms: _____ .
A share of the corporation's stock will be considered fully paid and nonassessable when it has been paid for in money, tangible or intangible property, or services that have actually been provided to the corporation before the shares were issued to the person performing the services. Stock issued to reimburse those who have advanced money for the corporation's organizational expenses will be treated as fully paid and nonassessable.

The decision of the Board of Directors will be final with respect to whether the consideration paid for shares was adequate or not (except in cases of fraud committed against the corporation and its directors, in which cases the decision of the Board of Directors can be challenged). Services that will be provided to the corporation in the future do not constitute adequate consideration for fully paid, nonassessable shares of the corporation's stock.

*2. Stock Certificates:* All stockholders will receive certificates, signed by the corporation's President and Secretary, and carrying the corporate seal, to prove their ownership of shares.

*3. Transfer Restrictions:* There are restrictions on the transfer of □the corporation's shares □corporate shares of the _____ class. Certificates for restricted shares will be endorsed with the transfer restrictions, either printed directly on the certificate or attached to the certificate in sticker form.

*4. Replacement of Certificates:* Stockholders whose stock certificates are lost, destroyed, or stolen can get replacement certificates by signing an affidavit that the certificates have been lost, destroyed, or stolen and by posting bond indemnifying the corporation against losses caused by reissuance of the certificates. However, the corporation will not reissue certificates if the corporation is aware that the original certificates have been acquired by a bona fide purchaser who did not have notice of the claims of the original owner.

*5. Registration of Transfers:* A record owner of the corporation's shares who wants the corporation to register a transfer of the shares on the corporation's books must
*a.* Pay any required stock transfer taxes.
*b.* Endorse the stock certificates (or have them endorsed by an authorized representative).
*c.* Have the endorsement witnessed by at least _____ individuals who sign an affidavit—unless the corporation's Secretary has given written permission to waive this requirement.

If the corporation has notice that the proposed transfer is subject to adverse claims, it will not register the proposed transfer—but the corporation has no obligation to check to see if any adverse claims exist.

## Shareholder's Meetings

*1.* The corporation will hold its regular annual meeting of shareholders, to elect the Board of Directors and carry out other corporate business, on the _____ day of the _____ month of every year (or on the next business day, if that day is a Saturday, Sunday, or legal holiday).

*2.* Special meetings (in addition to the regular annual meeting) can be held on request from the corporation's President, if the Board of Directors passes a resolution calling such a meeting, or if the holders of _____% or more of the corporation's stock request the meeting.

*3.* Unless otherwise specified, all meetings of the corporation's stockholders will be held at its headquarters, located at _____ , but it is permitted to hold the meetings at other places, whether inside or outside the state of _____ .

*4. Shareholders of Record:* One of the Secretary's duties is to maintain a list of the shareholders of record, that is, those who are entitled to vote at the annual meeting. The list will be updated regularly, based on transfers recorded on the corporation's books. The list of shareholders will be kept at the corporation's headquarters; shareholders and their authorized representatives can inspect it at any time during normal business hours.

*5. Notice of Annual Meeting:* The shareholders of record as of _____ days before the annual meeting—that is, the people who are entitled to vote at the corporation's regular annual meeting—will receive at least _____ days' notice of the time and place of the meeting. Notice will be sent by first-class mail to the address given in the corporation's books and records.

*6. Notice of Special Meeting:* Those who are shareholders of record _____ days before the date scheduled for a special meeting will be given at least _____ days' notice of the time, place, and purpose of the meeting. Notice will be sent by ☐first-class mail ☐overnight delivery service ☐mail and fax to the name, address, and fax number (if any) in the corporation's books and records.

*7. Waiver of Notice:* Any shareholder can waive the requirement of receiving written notice of meetings. Waiver can be done either explicitly, in writing, or implicitly, by appearing and voting at a meeting (unless it is indicated in the minutes of the meeting that the appearance was made only to protest the absence of notice) or by voting at a meeting by proxy.

*8. Quorum:* A simple majority of the issued voting shares constitutes a quorum for a meeting— whether the holders of those shares are present or are represented by proxies. If a quorum is present at the beginning of a meeting, the meeting can legally continue, and actions can legitimately be taken based on the vote at the meeting, even if some shareholders leave before the end of the meeting, and even if their departure results in one or more votes being taken at a time when a quorum is not present.

## Arbitration of Shareholder Disputes

Arbitration by a panel of three arbitrators pursuant to the rules of the American Arbitration Association shall be used to resolve deadlock if, at any time, the Board of Directors is so divided that it is unable to pass resolutions with respect to material matters affecting the management of the corporation. Any director may make a written request for arbitration. Each of the equally divided factions on the Board will select an arbitrator; the two arbitrators will select a third arbitrator.

The decisions of the arbitrators as to a matter of corporate policy on which the Board of Directors was deadlocked shall be final, and shall have the same force and effect as if the Board had so voted unanimously.

The stockholders shall not have the right to seek dissolution of the corporation for deadlock until and unless the arbitration procedure has been completed. This provision shall be included in the Shareholder Agreement signed by all present and future shareholders, and a reference to the Agreement as amended will be endorsed on all certificates for shares of the corporation's stock.

## Board of Directors

*1. Size:* The corporation will maintain a _____-member Board of Directors. [All directors must be stockholders/all directors must be stockholders, except for outside directors, persons of exceptional achievement and standing in the community. The corporation will make every effort to recruit qualified women and minority group members to serve as outside directors.]

*2. Election:* The entire slate of Directors will be up for reelection at each year's annual meeting/the corporation's Board of Directors will be classified, with _____ directors to be elected in each year.

*3. Voting:* Voting for directors will be done by secret ballot at the annual meeting, in person or by proxy.

*4. Removal:* Directors can be removed from office [for good cause only] by the corporation's President/by vote of the holders of ____ % of the corporation's outstanding common stock.

*5. Replacement:* Upon the death, resignation, or removal of any director, the appointments committee of the Board of Directors/the President will appoint a successor, who will serve until the next annual meeting OR a Special Meeting of stockholders will be called on not less than 14 days/not more than 30 days' notice to elect a replacement.

**6. *Compensation:*** Directors will receive $ \_\_\_\_ compensation for each regular meeting of the full Board of Directors and $ \_\_\_\_ for each committee meeting they attend, but will not be compensated for attendance at special meetings.

**7. *Committees:*** The Board of Directors shall have the power to divide into committees of less than the entire board; the committees shall investigate, and report to the full Board, on major issues of significance to the corporation, for example, litigation, compensation, and mergers and acquisitions.

**8. *Quorum:*** A quorum of _____ Directors shall be required to transact business, unless all the Directors give their unanimous consent to action in lieu of a meeting. A simple majority of Directors [actually voting on the matter, not abstaining] shall be sufficient to bind the corporation at any meeting at which a quorum is present.

**9. *Meetings:*** In addition to the regular annual meeting held one month before the stockholders' meeting/quarterly/monthly meetings, special meetings of the board may be called on two weeks' written notice, which can be waived in an emergency, by any director or officer of the corporation.

## Officers

**1. *Titles:*** The corporation's officers shall be a President, Vice-President, Treasurer, and Secretary, all of whom must be shareholders in the corporation.

**2. *Replacement:*** The corporation's initial officers shall be: _____ .
If any officer dies, retires, resigns, or is removed by the Board of Directors for a serious offense against the corporation or its stockholders (e.g., misappropriation of corporate funds or business opportunity; engaging in intentional or negligent conduct which subjects the corporation to liability or a significant risk of liability), his or her successor will be appointed by the corporation's highest remaining officer and submitted to the Board of Directors for ratification. If not ratified by a simple majority of Directors (other than the candidate, if he or she is a Director, or the candidate's spouse or other immediate relative), another appointment will be made.

**3. *Compensation:*** Each year, the President will prepare a schedule of proposed compensation for officers and senior managers, which must not exceed reasonable compensation or be dividend-equivalent. This schedule will be submitted to the Board of Directors, which can either ratify it or, by simple majority vote, reduce the compensation to be paid to some or all of the officers and senior managers.

## Corporate Documents and Obligations

**1. *Contracts:*** Any manager or department head may bind the corporation by entering into a contract in the ordinary course of business involving an amount up to $ \_\_\_\_ .

**2. *Board Approval:*** Any larger contract, or any loan secured by corporate property, or any unsecured loan over $ \_\_\_\_\_ , must be authorized by a resolution of the Board of Directors passed at a regular or special meeting.

**3. *Checks:*** All corporate checks must be signed by the Treasurer or his or her delegate; checks over $ \_\_\_\_ must be personally signed by the Treasurer and countersigned by an officer at or above the level of Vice-President.

## Indemnification

The corporation shall/may, by simple majority vote of disinterested Directors, indemnify to the fullest extent permitted by law any person who is or is threatened with becoming a party to any suit or proceeding arising out of service as an officer or director of the corporation [while acting in good faith to further what were reasonably believed to be the best interests of the corporation] and may pay or reimburse such person for all sums he or she must expend as fines, judgments, or legal fees in any such action or proceeding except amounts due to the corporation itself and those attributable to intentional misconduct. The corporation shall/may, by simple majority vote of disinterested directors, advance litigation and other expenses to a person presumptively entitled to indemnification, subject to his or her written agreement to reimburse the corporation if indemnification is later found improper. The corporation may maintain and pay premiums on D&O liability insurance.

## MINUTES OF ORGANIZATION MEETING

An organization meeting was held on _____ , 199 ____ at ____ P.M., at the offices of the law firm of Fowler and Novak, 145 Midway Boulevard, Lake City, Adams, in order to take the official steps necessary to organize a corporation known as Simmons-Lacey Consultants, Inc., which is being organized for the purpose of rendering financial advice, financial planning, pension consulting, and other permissible and valid business objectives.

The nominal incorporators and the organizers and promoters of the corporation were present:

| Name | Address | Status |
|------|---------|--------|
| Robert Simmons | 209 Blake St., Borden | Incorporator |
| James D. Lacey | 1530 W. 8 St., Borden | Incorporator |
| Kitty Morgan | 1219 Avenue L, Lake City | Incorporator |
| Ian Stewart | The Estates Tower, Borden | Promoter |

Those present elected Robert Simmons as Chairman of the meeting and James D. Lacey as its Secretary; these minutes were taken by the Secretary.

The Chairman announced the purpose of the meeting: to organize a corporation to be known as Simmons-Lacey Consultants, Inc. (or, if that name is unavailable, as Borden City Financial Advice, Inc.), under the laws of the state of Adams [and with authorization to do business as a foreign corporation in the states of Madison and Tyler], with an authorized capitalization of $175,000 and an authorized capital stock of 2,500 shares of common stock.

It was moved, seconded, and unanimously voted that the document annexed to these minutes as Exhibit A be adopted as the corporation's Certificate of Incorporation; the incorporators then signed and duly acknowledged this document.

It was moved, seconded, and unanimously approved that James D. Lacey be directed to file the Certificate of Incorporation with the Secretary of the State of the state of Adams as soon as possible and to pay any necessary fees (to be reimbursed by the corporation after its formation) and take all steps necessary to bring the corporation into being.

Each person present signed a subscription agreement in the form given in Exhibit B, agreeing to purchase shares of the corporation's stock as soon as it can lawfully be issued.

It was moved, seconded, and unanimously approved that the Chairman of the meeting would have the right to call additional meetings of the organizers on at least 24 hours' notice; meetings will be held at the same place as the initial meeting.

That concluded the business of the meeting, and a motion to adjourn was made, seconded, and unanimously approved.

Signed, _____ Robert Simmons, Chairman of the meeting; _____ James D. Lacey, Secretary of the Meeting

## PREINCORPORATION CONTRACT
### (Acquisition of Stock/Assets of Existing Corporation)

The intent of this agreement is that the incorporators, Sandra Dumas, Thomas Spingarn, and Michael Smyrnov, will buy all the stock of Bentonia Corporation, or all its assets (at the discretion of the incorporators), for a price of not more than $765,000 [as provided for in the option/sale agreement of _____ , 199 ___ between Bentonia Corporation and the incorporators/promoters of the corporation to be formed].

After the acquisition, and after the new corporation, to be known as Twenty-third Century Nonferrous Metals, Inc., has been formed, the incorporators/promoters will transfer such stock or assets, subject to any existing purchase money mortgage(s), to the newly formed corporation, in exchange for shares in the new corporation as follows:

| Name | Total # of Shares | Description |
|------|-------------------|-------------|
| Sandra Dumas | 5,000 shares | 4,000 common, 1,000 pref. |
| Thomas Spingarn | 4,000 shares | 3,000 common, 1,000 pref. |
| Michael Smyrnov | 1,000 shares | 1,000 common |

## AGREEMENT BETWEEN PROMOTER AND PROPERTY OWNER (Exchange of Property for Cash and Stock)

*1.* Leo Maldonado, the promoter, and Steven Blair, sole owner of real property located at 92–108 Mockingbird Lane, city of Wynona, county of Salmon River, state of Lincoln (block number 15, lot number 239), hereby agree that the property owner will sell, and the promoter will buy, the real property described above and all its improvements and appurtenances, for the account of a corporation to be formed under the laws of the state of Lincoln. The corporation will be known as Sweet Wynona Fashions, Inc.

*2.* The total purchase price for the property is $628,000, payable as follows:

*a.* $63,000 already paid by the promoter, receipt of which is acknowledged.

*b.* $65,000 payable in cash by the promoter at the closing, which is to occur on or before _____ , 199 ___ .

*c.* 10,000 shares of common stock to be issued by Sweet Wynona Fashions, Inc., after its incorporation; it is agreed that this stock is valued at $40 per share and that the capital structure of the corporation will consist entirely of 50,000 shares of voting common stock.

*d.* assumption of the first mortgage, held by the Farmers & Ranchers Bank, in the amount of $75,000 (due date, March 9, 1997), bearing interest at the rate of 10%, and of the second mortgage, held by the Integrity Trust Co. in the amount of $25,000 (due date, July 18, 1992), bearing interest at the rate of 11%. By their terms, both these mortgages are assumable.

**3.** The property owner will provide, at his own expense, a title insurance policy in a form acceptable to the promoter with a face amount equal to or greater than the purchase price.

**4.** After Sweet Wynona Fashions, Inc., has been duly incorporated, shares in satisfaction of the balance of the purchase price will be issued and delivered to the property owner or his nominee at the closing, at which time the property will be transferred to the corporation and conveyed by a deed in a form acceptable to the corporation's legal counsel. The corporation will also assume the mortgages. The promoter will pay the cash balance due at the closing in return for shares of Sweet Wynona Fashions, Inc., stock having a value equal to the cash downpayment and cash balance advanced by the promoter.

**5.** If the corporation is not formed as intended, or if the closing is not held on or before _____ , 199____ (unless the time for the closing has been extended by mutual consent of the promoter and the property owner), then this agreement will expire, and the promoter will deliver to the property owner his signed quitclaim releasing all interest in the property. The property owner will return all sums paid by the promoter, except for the sum of $10,000 to be retained as liquidated damages to compensate for loss income and opportunity to sell the property, not as a penalty.

Date: _____ , 199____
Signed:_____

## APPLICATION FOR CERTIFICATE OF AUTHORITY TO TRANSACT BUSINESS AS A FOREIGN CORPORATION

To the Secretary of State of the State of Adams: Dai-Ichi Genmai Kogyo, Inc., a Madison corporation, hereby applies for a Certificate of Authority that would qualify it to do business in the state of Adams as a foreign corporation, using the name of Dai-Ichi Genmai Kogyo, Inc., if that name is available in Adams; otherwise, under the name of Seven Tigers Trading Corp, carrying out the business of importing and marketing the products of Southeast and East Asia.

Dai-Ichi Genmai Kogyo, Inc., was incorporated in the state of Madison on _____ , 199 ____ as a corporation with perpetual duration; it has been duly registered, in good standing, and doing business in Madison since that date. Its principal office is located at 3247 Downtown Business Tower, Perkinsville, Madison. Its intended registered office within the state of Adams is located in the Penthouse of the Fitzpatrick Building (172 Welch Avenue), Bailey's Landing, Adams; its intended registered agent for service of process is Walter Carmody/the corporation consents to the appointment of the Secretary of State of the state of Adams as its agent for service of process within the state of Adams.

The names and addresses of officers and directors of Dai-Ichi Genmai Kogyo, Inc., are as follows: _____ .

The corporation's stated capital is $ ____ . Under its Articles of Incorporation, the corporation is authorized to issue 50,000 shares of common stock and 5,000 shares of cumulative preferred stock, all of which are now issued and outstanding. All such shares are without par value/have a par value of $____ per common, $____ per preferred share.

For the year 199_____ , it is estimated that Dai-Ichi Genmai Kogyo, Inc., if permitted to do business within the state of Adams, will own property worth an aggregate of $_____ wherever held, of which $_____ worth will be within the state of Adams. For the same year, it is estimated that the corporation's gross volume of business will be $_____ , of which it is estimated that $_____will be attributable to activities within the state of Adams.

Roger Miuki, President of Dai-Ichi Genmai Kogyo, Inc., hereby applies for authority to transact business within the state of Adams and attaches an authenticated copy of the Corporation's Articles of Incorporation (as amended) to the application.

Date: _____ , 199_____
Dai-Ichi Genmai Kogyo, Inc., by
Roger Miuki
State of Madison
County of Berklee ss
I, Linda Berman, a notary public, certify that Roger Miuki appeared before me on _____ , 199 _____ ; swore to tell the truth; and stated that he is the President of Dai-Ichi Genmai Kogyo, Inc., that he signed this document in his role as President, and that all statements made within the document are true.

_____ Linda Berman, Notary Public Commission
No. 34719, commission expires _____ , 199 _____ .

## FOREIGN CORPORATION'S CERTIFICATE OF AUTHORITY

**State of Monroe**
**Office of the Secretary of State**
**Certificate of Authority of Lucinda Lavender & Co., Inc.**

I, Paul Thelwell, Secretary of State of the state of Monroe, hereby certify that I have received an application from Edward Costellano, president of Lucinda Lavender & Co., Inc., for a Certificate of Authority to transact business within the state of Madison; that this application was prepared in proper form, was duly signed, and was accompanied by the statutory filing fee and by a certified copy of Lucinda Lavender & Co., Inc.'s Articles of Incorporation in the state of Roosevelt. Therefore, the application of Lucinda Lavender & Co., Inc., to transact business within this state, under that style and title, is hereby GRANTED.

Date: _____ , 199_____
Signed: Paul Thelwell, Secretary of State

## APPLICATION FOR CERTIFICATE OF WITHDRAWAL OF A FOREIGN CORPORATION

**Application for Certificate of Withdrawal of Masonic Maize Products, Inc.**

To the Secretary of State for the state of Lincoln: MASONIC MAIZE PRODUCTS, INC., a Tyler corporation, is the recipient of a Certificate of Authority (dated _____ , 199_____ ) permitting it to transact business within the state of Lincoln. Masonic Maize Products, Inc.'s authorized capitalization consists of 100,000 common shares $1 par value, of which 50,000 are issued and outstanding. As of the date of this application, its stated capital is $ ____ .

However, it is no longer true that Masonic Maize Products, Inc., actively transacts business within the state of Lincoln, and therefore it hereby surrenders its authority to do business as a foreign corporation within Lincoln and revokes the designation of Parker LeMoyne as its agent for service of process within the state of Lincoln. Should any process be served upon the Secretary of State for the state of Lincoln in any action or proceeding against Masonic Maize Products, Inc., such process can be forwarded to the corporation at Route 19K, Tallewegga, Tyler.

Date: _____ , 199____
Masonic Maize Products, Inc., by
Lewis Geraghty, President
State of Tyler
County of PineTree ss

Robert Fischer, notary public hereby certifies that, on _____ , 199____ , a person whom he knew to be Lewis Geraghty appeared before him and swore that he signed this application in his capacity as president of the corporation and that every statement contained within the application is true.

Signed: _____ Robert Fischer, Notary Public
Date: _____ , 199____

# Chapter 2

# STOCK AND DIVIDENDS

## INTRODUCTION

One of the most basic characteristics of the corporation is that ownership in the corporation is evidenced by the corporation's issuance of stock certificates. Stockholders are owners of the corporation; yet, except in extraordinary circumstances, they have no personal responsibility for the corporation's debts or liabilities. Their stock can become valueless, but they can't be forced to make further contributions to the corporate treasury once their stock has been paid for.

The fundamental type of stock is common stock, and the basic common stock is voting stock, each share entitling the holder to one vote on significant corporate issues such as election of the Board of Directors. The Board is legally responsible for managing the corporation, and most significant corporate actions must be authorized by a resolution duly passed by the Board. Depending on state law and the corporation's charter and bylaws, it may also be necessary for a majority (or a "supermajority," more than a simple majority) of the stockholders to vote to ratify the Board's action in especially important matters such as a merger or a sale of all of the corporation's assets.

State corporation laws require the designation of stock as either "no-par" stock, with no stated value, or "par" value; stock cannot legally be issued for less than its par value, so the stated value is usually a nominal amount such as $1 or $5 a share.

### Types of Stock

Some corporations have both common stock and "preferred" stock: preferred stock is preferred because its dividends are paid before the common stock dividends are. Preferred stock can be issued with an entitlement to a specific level of dividends (which must be paid in full before any dividend is declared on the common stock). If preferred stock is "cumulative," any dividends that were not paid as scheduled must be made up before the common stock can receive a dividend. Usually, preferred stock does not carry voting privileges, but vote of the preferred stockholders may be required on fundamental corporate transactions such as mergers, or preferred stockholders may be given a vote if the dividends are not paid as required.

*Practice Tip:* The "preferred stock recapitalization" used to be a method of ensuring corporate succession while getting significant tax benefits. That is, when a business founder was ready to retire, the corporation would be recapitalized, giving the preferred stock to the retiree, the common stock to his or her successors. The effect was to provide retirement income for the business founder, while the new generation got the voting power to make further corporate decisions and got the benefit of increasing value of the common stock. The tax benefits have been removed by amendments to the Internal Revenue Code, but this can still be a practical strategy for passing along corporate control, if the tax cost is affordable. Check with your lawyer and accountant about the effect of the 1990 budget bill.

The dramatic battles for business control fought out every night on *Dallas* and *Dynasty* reruns often have their real-life counterparts. A small business usually has a small circle of stockholders. It's not uncommon for there to be dramatic disputes about the direction corporate policy should take. Stockholders who do not receive a salary from the corporation often want to place tight limits on employee compensation—because each dollar paid out in salary reduces the amount available for dividends. In a common situation, one or a group of two or three stockholders hold a majority of the voting shares, or a solid plurality, and can control elections for the Board of Directors. That can leave the other stockholders out in the cold—a situation that they can avoid by entering into a voting agreement or voting trust, under which they agree to vote as a bloc to gain greater power within the corporation.

## Rules Governing Purchase vs Sale

Any time you want to buy or sell shares of a major corporation like General Motors, you can do it by contacting any stockbroker. There's a constant market for shares of such companies, and the value of the stock can be determined at any time by consulting the stock quotes published in the press. The situation is very different when it comes to the stock of small corporations.

From the stockholder's point of view, it may be impossible to sell the stock because nobody wants it, or the only buyer could be the corporation itself, or fellow stockholders seeking to increase their holdings, but unwilling to pay a fair price because they know the market is limited.

## Transfer Restrictions

The problem becomes more acute over time. A stockholder dies with the stock in his or her estate; frequently, the stock is divided among several beneficiaries. They, in turn, have stock that may pay little or no dividends, is hard to sell, and carries little practical political power within the corporation. (In family businesses, a common development is that one "branch" of the family ends up running the corporation, while the cousins glare at them and plot revenge.) The problem is especially acute if much of the deceased's estate was tied up in the business, and the survivors need money for living expenses. Or a conflict leads the business' founders to split up, with one or more wishing to leave the corporation but get a fair price for their stock, or an older stockholder wants to fund retirement, or a disabled stockholder needs money for living expenses but is unable to work.

In all these situations, the "buy-sell" agreement comes to the rescue: the stockholders enter into an agreement under which the corporation itself or the other stockholders agree to buy the stock. That way, the political situation stays the same, and the stockholder or stockholder's estate can get cash for the value of the interest in the corporation. Sometimes the agreement sets the price that will be paid for the stock, or includes a formula for valuation; other buy-sell agreements state that the valuation will be based on contemporary factors at the time the valuation is made, or state that an arbitrator or appraiser will set the price. (The valuation of closely held business stock is considered one of the most difficult valuation problems; so many subjective and speculative factors are involved.) If the "triggering event" for the buy-sell is death or disability, the purchasers usually use insurance to fund the purchase. However, if the triggering event is retirement or dissension, the corporation or other stockholders may need a lot of cash at an unexpected, or especially unwelcome, time, and must be prepared to save up and maintain a reserve, or borrow the money if necessary.

The risk of conflict doesn't go in only one direction. From the corporation's point of view, unhappy stockholders are like loose cannons: they can destroy a tax-saving Subchapter S election by selling their stock to an ineligible stockholder; they can cause trouble by selling to a competitor (who will then have access to corporate information) or to an unfriendly family member. Corporations protect themselves by imposing transfer restrictions on the stock, perhaps giving the corporation or the other shareholders a right of first refusal, or forbidding certain transfers (such as transfers that jeopardize an S election).

In addition to transfer restrictions voluntarily imposed, federal and state law regulate the transfer of corporate shares. Before shares can be generally sold on the open market, they must be "registered"; that is, the corporation must go through a complex and very expensive process of gathering financial information and making it available to the public in the form of a "prospectus." In addition to the federal securities laws, the states have their own securities laws, called blue-sky laws (because nineteenth-century entrepreneurs—or buccaneers—would have sold the blue sky itself if someone didn't stop them). In many circumstances, complying with the federal securities laws also counts as complying with the state laws (this is called "registration by coordination").

## Private Placements

However, there are many small or start-up corporations that must issue and sell stock, but can't afford the cost or delays inherent in an "IPO" (initial public offering). The federal and state laws allow the sale of stock by "private placement" without registration, as long as the stock is not generally advertised or sold to the public without adequate disclosure of relevant information. There are many federal statutes regulating private placements, and there is no explicit definition in the statute of what constitutes a public offering or private placement. Instead, a number of factors must be considered:

○ The number of offerees (persons contacted and asked to purchase securities).

○ The nature of the offerees (are they institutions, sophisticated investment experts, or the proverbial "widows and orphans" who must be protected against losing their life savings?).

○ The financial size of the offering—if less than $250,000 is raised, the offering will almost certainly be considered a private placement; under the right circumstances, up to $5 million can be raised in a private placement, and one of the federal securities law rules allows a sale in any amount as long as there are only 35 offerees who are not "accredited investors" (qualified by investment sophistication, knowledge, and wealth).

○ The number of investment units offered—an offering purchased by a few very large investors is more likely to be considered a private placement.

○ How the offering is made. It's not illegal to use an investment banker to organize a private placement, but use of an investment banker is more commonly associated with a public offering. If the offering is advertised, it will almost certainly be treated as a public offering.

Stock that is purchased in a private placement must carry transfer restrictions. The stock certificate must say that the shares are unregistered and can only be sold or transferred if they are registered, or if the transfer conforms to an exemption from registration. The corporation must either note on its transfer books that transfer is restricted or inform its transfer agent of the restrictions. The corporation must also get the buyers' agreement that they won't resell the stock in violation of the securities laws, and the corporation has an obligation to try to find out if the buyers are buying for their own account, to make a long-term investment, instead of purchasing for the hidden interest of other speculators.

## SECURITY PURCHASE AGREEMENT ROADMAP

○ The type of securities being sold (common stock, preferred stock, bonds, rights, warrants, options, etc.)

○ The percentage of ownership in the corporation to be transferred

○ How the issuing corporation will use the money to be raised by selling the securities

○ What and how the buyers will pay (cash? notes? securities of other corporations?)

○ The scheduled date of the closing; provisions for extending the date (for instance, if more time is needed to complete financial statements)

○ Conditions required for the closing to take place (e.g., that all representations and warranties are true, that the issuer's counsel provides a written opinion that the transaction is valid and lawful)

○ Representation and warranties made by the seller (e.g., that it is duly organized; what its capitalization consists of; that it is authorized to enter into the transaction; that the transaction does not violate any law or agreement; that the financial statements are accurate)

○ Representations and warranties made by the buyer (for instance, that no broker is entitled to a fee, that the securities are purchased for investment, not resale, and will not be resold in violation of securities laws)

○ Affirmative and negative covenants (things the buyer and seller promise to do—such as inform the other of material adverse changes in their financial condition—or promise not to do—such as enter into a merger or merger agreement)

○ Put and call provisions, under which the corporation has a right to buy back the securities, or the holders have a right to require that the corporation repurchase the securities

---

## INVESTMENT AGREEMENT FOR PRIVATE PLACEMENT

### Preamble

This agreement governs a private placement transaction under which a group of otherwise unaffiliated parties, each an accredited and sophisticated investor, agrees to purchase securities issued by Danstix Limited, Inc. This private placement is exempt from federal registration under Regulation D and is also exempt from state regulation under the laws of the state of Roosevelt/and all blue-sky requirements under the laws of the state of Roosevelt either have been complied with or will be timely complied with.

### Part One: Securities to Be Issued

*1. Principal Securities:* The principal securities to be issued are _____ shares of common stock at $ ____ per share/ _____ shares of [cumulative] preferred stock, at $ ____ per share, with preference as follows: _____ /a series of ____ % debentures, with an aggregate face

value of not more than $ \_\_\_\_ , sold at par/a discount of _____ /a premium of _____ ,
subordinated as follows: _____ .
The entire issue is to be allocated among the investors as follows: _____ .

*2. Warrants:* As an additional incentive to the investors, each investor will be issued one warrant for
every hundred dollars' worth of securities purchased under this private placement. Investors will
pay $1 per warrant. Each warrant can be redeemed at any time after _____ ,
199 \_\_\_\_ for \_\_\_\_ shares of the issuer's common stock at $ \_\_\_\_ per share [provided that the issuer's
common shares are publicly traded at that time].

*3. Puts and Calls:* The provisions of this section apply only if none of the issuer's securities is
registered and publicly traded. The issuer shall have the right to repurchase the principal securities
and warrants from their holders ("call") and the holders shall have the right to obligate the issuer to
purchase the principal securities and warrants ("put") at any time beginning _____ ,
199 \_\_\_\_ and ending _____ , 199 \_\_\_\_ , on \_\_\_\_ days' written notice. The price of securities
will be set by _____ , hereby designated as arbitrator (or by his/her successor, assign, or
designee if s/he is unavailable). Arbitration expenses will be paid by the issuer (for call transactions)
or by the holder (for put transactions). The issuer will pay for securities subject to put or call either in
cash or by its \_\_\_\_ -month note, bearing interest at a rate of \_\_\_\_ %.

*4. Issuer's Right of First Refusal:* At all times when the issuer is a private company (none of whose
securities are registered or publicly traded) the investors under this Agreement consent to give the
issuer and its principal stockholders, Lloyd Garber, Dennis MacKenzie, and Arthur Dougald, a right
of first refusal. That is to say, 30 days before consummating a sale of securities issued as part of this
private placement, the investor must notify the issuer and principal stockholders of the intent to sell
and the price demanded for the securities. If the issuer and stockholders do not offer within the 30-day
period, the investor may sell the principal securities and/or warrants provided that the resale is
permissible under federal and state securities laws and the price is at least as high as that demanded
in the notice of intent to sell.


## Part Two: Parties

*1. Issuer:* The issuer is Danstix Limited, Inc., a corporation duly incorporated and doing business in
the state of Roosevelt. Issuance of the principal securities and warrants is permissible under the
issuer's Articles of Incorporation and bylaws, and has been approved by the issuer's Board of
Directors [and ratified by its stockholders]. The relevant resolution[s] is/are attached to this
agreement.

*2. Investors:* The investors, and the reason for their status as accredited investors, are:

○ Haulers & Carters Pension Fund: A pension fund with assets over $5 million.

○ Fleming Family Trust: A trust with assets over $5 million.

○ James Tisman: Income for the past two years has exceeded $100,000; expected income for this
year is over $100,000.

○ Marsha Gaile and Stephen Gaile: Each spouse is a purchaser. Their joint income for the past two
years, and expected income for this year, all exceed $200,000.

○ Caroline DePuyster: An individual with net worth in excess of $1 million.

In addition, each individual has either received investment advice from a financially sophisticated purchaser representative or has been apprised of the usefulness of such advice but has decided to forgo it.

## Part Three: Closing

*1. Scheduled Date:* The closing, at which time the investors will be issued and will pay for principal securities and warrants, is scheduled for _____ , 199 ____ at M in the offices of _____ , or such adjourned date as agreed by the parties to complete the conditions required as a condition of the closing.

*2. Conditions:* The closing cannot take place until and unless

○ The issuer's counsel provides a favorable opinion on the transaction to the investors.

○ The issuer's President issues a certificate to the investors that the issuer is not in default under any note, mortgage, agreement, or other document or instrument to which it is a party, nor would closing the private placement transaction operate as an instance of default.

○ The closing of the transaction does not violate any applicable law, regulation, decision, or interpretation made by a regulatory agency.

○ As of the scheduled closing date, the issuer's indebtedness of all types and to all creditors does not exceed $ ____ , nor is there any indebtedness except as has already been disclosed to the investors.

○ The issuer has provided a disclosure to the investors of all its material contracts, and is not in default under any such contract; consummation of the private placement transactions does not constitute a default under any such contract.

○ Releases in a form acceptable to the investors must be delivered to the investors, indemnifying them against any and all claims made by brokers and others for finders' fees, brokerage fees, and expenses of this private placement transaction.

○ The issuer has obtained, and paid for, single-premium term life insurance policies on the lives of its officers and its two managers holding the title of Vice-President, each in the amount of $ ____ . If any of these key persons dies during the term, the insurance will be paid to the corporation and serve as security for the value of the principal securities and warrants.

○ The issuer has not, and in the future will not, issue dividends on any of its stock in an amount that is unreasonable or impairs the value of the principal securities and warrants.

○ The issuer has given the investors copies of its certified balance sheet and income statements for a five-year period, prepared by Rachel Sealey, CPA.

## Part Four: Issuer's Representations and Warranties

The issuer represents and warrants that, as of the date of this Agreement, each of these statements is true; the issuer will notify the investors of any material changes (whether adverse or favorable) between the date of the Agreement and the date of the closing (as adjourned). This Agreement neither contains any materially untrue statement nor omits any material fact that must be disclosed to prevent the statements from being misleading.

*1. Use of Proceeds.* All proceeds of the private placement will be used for general corporate purposes/working capital/explain: _____ .

**2. *Continued Business:*** The issuer will continue to engage in the business of biological and chemical research, adding business activities involving development of organic and chemical pesticides and insecticides.

**3. *Common Control:*** The issuer has no subsidiaries, is not a subsidiary of another company, and is not part of a controlled group of corporations. It is not a successor in interest or liabilities to any other company.

**4. *Financial Statements:*** The financial statements provided to the investors are accurate, complete, prepared in accordance with GAAP, and fairly represent the corporation's financial condition as of the time of rendition of the statement. The issuer had no material contingent liabilities at any time other than those disclosed, and there has been no material adverse change in any aspect of the issuer's financial condition since the date of the last statement except as disclosed. The issuer maintains adequate reserves for all reasonable corporate purposes for which reserves should be maintained. No dividend or payment has been made outside the ordinary course of business. All dispositions of corporate assets have been made at or above fair market value.

**5. *Litigation:*** The issuer is not in default under any judicial or administrative order, is not a plaintiff in or contemplating instituting litigation or administrative proceedings [except as follows: _____ ], and is not a defendant and is not aware of pending or threatened litigation or administrative proceedings [except as follows: _____ ].

**6. *Title.*** The issuer has good marketable title to all the assets disclosed to the investors; all assets used in the issuer's business and operations are properly maintained and in good condition. There are no liens or encumbrances on any such asset except as disclosed, and the issuer will not materially encumber or subject to lien any such asset without consent of the investors.

**7. *Other Obligations:*** The issuer is in material compliance with all its contracts and agreements [except insofar as there is a legitimate dispute/except as follows: _____ ]. The issuance of the principal securities and warrants does not violate any agreement to which the issuer is a party. All taxes on the corporation's business and assets have been paid [except for matters legitimately in dispute, that is, _____ ].

## Part Five: The Issuer's Affirmative Covenants

The issuer agrees to do all these things as long as there are any outstanding principal securities or warrants, unless the investors or other holders of the securities unanimously consent to an exemption from the requirements.

**1. *Payments:*** The issuer agrees to pay timely all obligations to the investors under notes payable to them [and all interest and principal payments required under any debt securities issued].

**2. *Normal Operations.*** The issuer agrees to maintain operations and carry on business in all respects as a law-abiding and well-managed corporation, for example, payment of all taxes and obligations as they accrue; maintenance of all corporate property in good condition; preparation and maintenance of complete, accurate, and current financial records in conformity with GAAP; and maintenance of insurance coverage adequate in type and amount, including life insurance on the life of key persons.

**3. *Board Representation.*** The investors will have the right to elect _____ directors of the issuer, and these directors will be entitled to the same compensation and indemnification as the issuer's other directors.

**4. *Disclosure to Investors*.** Each investor will receive quarterly balance sheets and profit and loss statements, which will be summarized annually, and will be promptly notified of all material changes in the issuer's business, including all pending litigation (whether the issuer is plaintiff or defendant). All investors will be entitled (in person by representative) to inspect the issuer's books, records, and operations at any time during normal business hours.

## Part Six: Issuer's Negative Covenants

The issuer agrees not to do any of these things without express unanimous consent of all investors at any time when any principal securities or warrants are outstanding:

**1. *Change in Business:*** Stop operating in the normal course of business or make a material change in its type of business or business methods; enter into any merger, consolidation, acquisition, or agreement for any of these.

**2. *Liens and Loans:*** Enter into any loan, mortgage, or security agreement; enter into or permit any lien or encumbrance on corporate property; make any loan to a corporate key person; enter into any leasing transaction.

**3. *Changes in Corporate Structure:*** Issue, cancel, redeem, or repurchase any new securities or otherwise alter the issuer's capital structure or the rights or preferences of any of the issuer's outstanding securities; amend the charter or bylaws.

**4. *Compensation:*** Pay to any employee any salary, bonus, deferred compensation, or other compensation in excess of what is reasonably earned as current compensation and would be payable by a reasonable corporation in the issuer's financial condition; pay to any officer, director, or stockholder any amount alleged to be compensation although it is actually dividend-equivalent.

**5. *Securities Laws:*** Commit any direct or indirect violation of federal or state securities laws in connection with the issuance, sale, or transfer of any of its securities.

## Part Seven: Default

**1. *Incidents of Default*.** Failure to comply with any term or condition of this Agreement, or the terms of any principal securities or warrants issued under this Agreement, or violation of any affirmative or negative covenant contained in this Agreement, shall constitute an incident of default.

**2. *Remedies:*** On default, any investor may accelerate payment of principal and interest owed to that investor under any note or debt security; demand rescission; or pursue any other remedy available under state or federal law. If at any time, any investor attempts to pursue any default remedy, the issuer is obligated to notify all investors of this fact and of their remedies.

## Part Eight: Securities Law Issues

**1. *Transfer Restrictions:*** The principal securities and warrants issued pursuant to this Agreement are unregistered, and until and unless they are registered, all investors agree not to make any transfer of the securities that would require registration; all investors agree to abide by the call provisions of this Agreement.

**2. *Legend and Stop-Transfer:*** At all times preceding the effective date of any registration, the securities issued pursuant to this Agreement will bear a legend stating that they have been acquired for investment only, not for resale; that they are unregistered; and that they are subject to transfer restrictions. The issuer will impose a "stop transfer" instruction on its records, and will inform its transfer agent(s) not to permit any transfer in violation of federal or state securities laws or of this Agreement.

**3. *Investors' Right to Mandate Registration:*** On or after _____ , 199 ____ , the holders of ____ % or more of the securities issued under this Agreement will have the right to demand that the issuer register the securities held by the investors. After such a demand the issuer must seek registration as expeditiously as possible, at its own expense. The investors agree to give the issuer any information reasonably requested by the issuer about their financial condition and plans for disposition of the securities. The issuer also agrees to register securities (at its own expense) if the issuer issues any other securities that would be integrated with the securities issued pursuant to this Agreement under federal securities laws.

**4. *Mutual Indemnification:*** The issuer agrees to indemnify all investors and hold them harmless against liability resulting from the issuer's false statements or nondisclosures of material facts. All investors jointly and severally agree to indemnify the issuer and hold it harmless against liability resulting from any investor's transfer of securities in violation of securities laws and/or this Agreement.

## Part Nine: Standard Provisions

**1. *Choice of Law.*** Insofar as state law questions arise, this Agreement shall be interpreted according to the laws of the state of Roosevelt, and the precedent of the Fourteenth Federal Circuit, and specifically of the Western District of Roosevelt within that circuit, shall be applied.

**2. *Integration.*** This written Agreement sets out the entire agreement between the parties and cannot be varied or supplemented orally. All modifications must be negotiated, then expressed in a writing signed by all parties and authorized by resolution of all corporate parties' Board of Directors [and stockholders].

**3. *Substitute Parties:*** The heirs, successors, and assigns of all parties shall be equally bound with the original parties.

Date: _____ , 199____
Issuer by: _____
Investors: _____

# FORM D

<table>
<tr><td colspan="2" align="center">UNITED STATES<br>SECURITIES AND EXCHANGE COMMISSION<br>Washington, D.C. 20549</td><td>OMB APPROVAL</td></tr>
</table>

| | |
|---|---|
| UNITED STATES<br>**SECURITIES AND EXCHANGE COMMISSION**<br>Washington, D.C. 20549 | **OMB APPROVAL** |
| | OMB Number:    3235-0076 |
| | Expires:    March 31, 1991 |
| | Estimated average burden<br>hours per response . . . 16.00 |

## FORM D

**NOTICE OF SALE OF SECURITIES
PURSUANT TO REGULATION D,
SECTION 4(6), AND/OR
UNIFORM LIMITED OFFERING EXEMPTION**

| SEC USE ONLY | |
|---|---|
| Prefix | Serial |
| DATE RECEIVED | |

Name of Offering   (☐ check if this is an amendment and name has changed, and indicate change.)

Filing Under (Check box(es) that apply):   ☐ Rule 504   ☐ Rule 505   ☐ Rule 506   ☐ Section 4(6)   ☐ ULOE

Type of Filing:   ☐ New Filing   ☐ Amendment

### A. BASIC IDENTIFICATION DATA

1. Enter the information requested about the issuer

Name of Issuer   (☐ check if this is an amendment and name has changed, and indicate change.)

| Address of Executive Offices   (Number and Street, City, State, Zip Code) | Telephone Number (Including Area Code) |
|---|---|
| Address of Principal Business Operations (Number and Street, City, State, Zip Code)<br>(if different from Executive Offices) | Telephone Number (Including Area Code) |

Brief Description of Business

Type of Business Organization
☐ corporation                    ☐ limited partnership, already formed          ☐ other (please specify):
☐ business trust                 ☐ limited partnership, to be formed

Actual or Estimated Date of Incorporation or Organization: ☐☐ Month ☐☐ Year   ☐ Actual   ☐ Estimated

Jurisdiction of Incorporation or Organization: (Enter two-letter U.S. Postal Service abbreviation for State:
CN for Canada; FN for other foreign jurisdiction)   ☐☐

## GENERAL INSTRUCTIONS

**Federal:**

*Who Must File:* All issuers making an offering of securities in reliance on an exemption under Regulation D or Section 4(6), 17 CFR 230.501 et seq. or 15 U.S.C. 77d(6).

*When To File:* A notice must be filed no later than 15 days after the first sale of securities in the offering. A notice is deemed filed with the U.S. Securities and Exchange Commission (SEC) on the earlier of the date it is received by the SEC at the address given below or, if received at that address after the date on which it is due, on the date it was mailed by United States registered or certified mail to that address.

*Where to File:* U.S. Securities and Exchange Commission, 450 Fifth Street, N.W., Washington, D.C. 20549.

*Copies Required:* Five (5) copies of this notice must be filed with the SEC, one of which must be manually signed. Any copies not manually signed must be photocopies of the manually signed copy or bear typed or printed signatures.

*Information Required:* A new filing must contain all information requested. Amendments need only report the name of the issuer and offering, any changes thereto, the information requested in Part C, and any material changes from the information previously supplied in Parts A and B. Part E and the Appendix need not be filed with the SEC.

*Filing Fee:* There is no federal filing fee.

**State:**

This notice shall be used to indicate reliance on the Uniform Limited Offering Exemption (ULOE) for sales of securities in those states that have adopted ULOE and that have adopted this form. Issuers relying on ULOE must file a separate notice with the Securities Administrator in each state where sales are to be, or have been made. If a state requires the payment of a fee as a precondition to the claim for the exemption, a fee in the proper amount shall accompany this form. This notice shall be filed in the appropriate states in accordance with state law. The Appendix to the notice constitutes a part of this notice and must be completed.

─────────── **ATTENTION** ───────────
**Failure to file notice in the appropriate states will not result in a loss of the federal exemption. Conversely, failure to file the appropriate federal notice will not result in a loss of an available state exemption unless such exemption is predicated on the filing of a federal notice.**

## A. BASIC IDENTIFICATION DATA

2. Enter the information requested for the following:

- Each promoter of the issuer, if the issuer has been organized within the past five years;
- Each beneficial owner having the power to vote or dispose, or direct the vote or disposition of, 10% or more of a class of equity securities of the issuer;
- Each executive officer and director of corporate issuers and of corporate general and managing partners of partnership issuers; and
- Each general and managing partner of partnership issuers.

Check Box(es) that Apply:  □ Promoter   □ Beneficial Owner   □ Executive Officer   □ Director   □ General and/or Managing Partner

Full Name (Last name first, if individual)

Business or Residence Address    (Number and Street, City, State, Zip Code)

Check Box(es) that Apply:  □ Promoter   □ Beneficial Owner   □ Executive Officer   □ Director   □ General and/or Managing Partner

Full Name (Last name first, if individual)

Business or Residence Address    (Number and Street, City, State, Zip Code)

Check Box(es) that Apply:  □ Promoter   □ Beneficial Owner   □ Executive Officer   □ Director   □ General and/or Managing Partner

Full Name (Last name first, if individual)

Business or Residence Address    (Number and Street, City, State, Zip Code)

Check Box(es) that Apply:  □ Promoter   □ Beneficial Owner   □ Executive Officer   □ Director   □ General and/or Managing Partner

Full Name (Last name first, if individual)

Business or Residence Address    (Number and Street, City, State, Zip Code)

Check Box(es) that Apply:  □ Promoter   □ Beneficial Owner   □ Executive Officer   □ Director   □ General and/or Managing Partner

Full Name (Last name first, if individual)

Business or Residence Address    (Number and Street, City, State, Zip Code)

Check Box(es) that Apply:  □ Promoter   □ Beneficial Owner   □ Executive Officer   □ Director   □ General and/or Managing Partner

Full Name (Last name first, if individual)

Business or Residence Address    (Number and Street, City, State, Zip Code)

Check Box(es) that Apply:  □ Promoter   □ Beneficial Owner   □ Executive Officer   □ Director   □ General and/or Managing Partner

Full Name (Last name first, if individual)

Business or Residence Address    (Number and Street, City, State, Zip Code)

(Use blank sheet, or copy and use additional copies of this sheet, as necessary.)

## B. INFORMATION ABOUT OFFERING

|  | Yes | No |
|---|---|---|
| 1. Has the issuer sold, or does the issuer intend to sell, to non-accredited investors in this offering?................ | ☐ | ☐ |

Answer also in Appendix, Column 2, if filing under ULOE.

2. What is the minimum investment that will be accepted from any individual? .................................... $ _____

|  | Yes | No |
|---|---|---|
| 3. Does the offering permit joint ownership of a single unit? .................................................. | ☐ | ☐ |

4. Enter the information requested for each person who has been or will be paid or given, directly or indirectly, any commission or similar remuneration for solicitation of purchasers in connection with sales of securities in the offering. If a person to be listed is an associated person or agent of a broker or dealer registered with the SEC and/or with a state or states, list the name of the broker or dealer. If more than five (5) persons to be listed are associated persons of such a broker or dealer, you may set forth the information for that broker or dealer only..

Full Name (Last name first, if individual)

Business or Residence Address (Number and Street, City, State, Zip Code)

Name of Associated Broker or Dealer

States in Which Person Listed Has Solicited or Intends to Solicit Purchasers

(Check "All States" or check individual States) ............................................................. ☐ All States

| [AL] | [AK] | [AZ] | [AR] | [CA] | [CO] | [CT] | [DE] | [DC] | [FL] | [GA] | [HI] | [ID] |
|---|---|---|---|---|---|---|---|---|---|---|---|---|
| [IL] | [IN] | [IA] | [KS] | [KY] | [LA] | [ME] | [MD] | [MA] | [MI] | [MN] | [MS] | [MO] |
| [MT] | [NE] | [NV] | [NH] | [NJ] | [NM] | [NY] | [NC] | [ND] | [OH] | [OK] | [OR] | [PA] |
| [RI] | [SC] | [SD] | [TN] | [TX] | [UT] | [VT] | [VA] | [WA] | [WV] | [WI] | [WY] | [PR] |

Full Name (Last name first, if individual)

Business or Residence Address (Number and Street, City, State, Zip Code)

Name of Associated Broker or Dealer

States in Which Person Listed Has Solicited or Intends to Solicit Purchasers

(Check "All States" or check individual States) ............................................................. ☐ All States

| [AL] | [AK] | [AZ] | [AR] | [CA] | [CO] | [CT] | [DE] | [DC] | [FL] | [GA] | [HI] | [ID] |
|---|---|---|---|---|---|---|---|---|---|---|---|---|
| [IL] | [IN] | [IA] | [KS] | [KY] | [LA] | [ME] | [MD] | [MA] | [MI] | [MN] | [MS] | [MO] |
| [MT] | [NE] | [NV] | [NH] | [NJ] | [NM] | [NY] | [NC] | [ND] | [OH] | [OK] | [OR] | [PA] |
| [RI] | [SC] | [SD] | [TN] | [TX] | [UT] | [VT] | [VA] | [WA] | [WV] | [WI] | [WY] | [PR] |

Full Name (Last name first, if individual)

Business or Residence Address (Number and Street, City, State, Zip Code)

Name of Associated Broker or Dealer

States in Which Person Listed Has Solicited or Intends to Solicit Purchasers

(Check "All States" or check individual States) ............................................................. ☐ All States

| [AL] | [AK] | [AZ] | [AR] | [CA] | [CO] | [CT] | [DE] | [DC] | [FL] | [GA] | [HI] | [ID] |
|---|---|---|---|---|---|---|---|---|---|---|---|---|
| [IL] | [IN] | [IA] | [KS] | [KY] | [LA] | [ME] | [MD] | [MA] | [MI] | [MN] | [MS] | [MO] |
| [MT] | [NE] | [NV] | [NH] | [NJ] | [NM] | [NY] | [NC] | [ND] | [OH] | [OK] | [OR] | [PA] |
| [RI] | [SC] | [SD] | [TN] | [TX] | [UT] | [VT] | [VA] | [WA] | [WV] | [WI] | [WY] | [PR] |

(Use blank sheet, or copy and use additional copies of this sheet, as necessary.)

## C. OFFERING PRICE, NUMBER OF INVESTORS, EXPENSES AND USE OF PROCEEDS

1. Enter the aggregate offering price of securities included in this offering and the total amount already sold. Enter "0" if answer is "none" or "zero." If the transaction is an exchange offering, check this box ☐ and indicate in the columns below the amounts of the securities offered for exchange and already exchanged.

| Type of Security | Aggregate Offering Price | Amount Already Sold |
|---|---|---|
| Debt . . . . . . . . . . . . . . . . . . . . . . . . . . . . . . . . . . . . . . . . . . . . . . . . . . . . . . . | $_____ | $_____ |
| Equity . . . . . . . . . . . . . . . . . . . . . . . . . . . . . . . . . . . . . . . . . . . . . . . . . . . . . . | $_____ | $_____ |
|           ☐ Common    ☐ Preferred | | |
| Convertible Securities (including warrants) . . . . . . . . . . . . . . . . . . . . . . . . . . . . . | $_____ | $_____ |
| Partnership Interests . . . . . . . . . . . . . . . . . . . . . . . . . . . . . . . . . . . . . . . . . . . | $_____ | $_____ |
| Other (Specify _____) . . . . . . . . . . . . . . . . . . . . . | $_____ | $_____ |
|     Total . . . . . . . . . . . . . . . . . . . . . . . . . . . . . . . . . . . . . . . . . . . . . . | $_____ | $_____ |

Answer also in Appendix, Column 3, if filing under ULOE.

2. Enter the number of accredited and non-accredited investors who have purchased securities in this offering and the aggregate dollar amounts of their purchases. For offerings under Rule 504, indicate the number of persons who have purchased securities and the aggregate dollar amount of their purchases on the total lines. Enter "0" if answer is "none" or "zero."

| | Number Investors | Aggregate Dollar Amount of Purchases |
|---|---|---|
| Accredited Investors . . . . . . . . . . . . . . . . . . . . . . . . . . . . . . . . . . . . . . . . . . . | _____ | $_____ |
| Non-accredited Investors . . . . . . . . . . . . . . . . . . . . . . . . . . . . . . . . . . . . . . . . | _____ | $_____ |
|     Total (for filings under Rule 504 only) . . . . . . . . . . . . . . . . . . . . . . . . . . . | _____ | $_____ |

Answer also in Appendix, Column 4, if filing under ULOE.

3. If this filing is for an offering under Rule 504 or 505, enter the information requested for all securities sold by the issuer, to date, in offerings of the types indicated, in the twelve (12) months prior to the first sale of securities in this offering. Classify securities by type listed in Part C - Question 1.

| Type of offering | Type of Security | Dollar Amount Sold |
|---|---|---|
| Rule 505 . . . . . . . . . . . . . . . . . . . . . . . . . . . . . . . . . . . . . . . . . . . . . . . . . | _____ | $_____ |
| Regulation A . . . . . . . . . . . . . . . . . . . . . . . . . . . . . . . . . . . . . . . . . . . . . . . | _____ | $_____ |
| Rule 504 . . . . . . . . . . . . . . . . . . . . . . . . . . . . . . . . . . . . . . . . . . . . . . . . . | _____ | $_____ |
|     Total . . . . . . . . . . . . . . . . . . . . . . . . . . . . . . . . . . . . . . . . . . . . . . . | _____ | $_____ |

4. a. Furnish a statement of all expenses in connection with the issuance and distribution of the securities in this offering. Exclude amounts relating solely to organization expenses of the issuer. The information may be given as subject to future contingencies. If the amount of an expenditure is not known, furnish an estimate and check the box to the left of the estimate.

| | | |
|---|---|---|
| Transfer Agent's Fees . . . . . . . . . . . . . . . . . . . . . . . . . . . . . . . . . . . . . . . . . . | ☐ | $_____ |
| Printing and Engraving Costs . . . . . . . . . . . . . . . . . . . . . . . . . . . . . . . . . . . . | ☐ | $_____ |
| Legal Fees . . . . . . . . . . . . . . . . . . . . . . . . . . . . . . . . . . . . . . . . . . . . . . . . . | ☐ | $_____ |
| Accounting Fees . . . . . . . . . . . . . . . . . . . . . . . . . . . . . . . . . . . . . . . . . . . . . | ☐ | $_____ |
| Engineering Fees . . . . . . . . . . . . . . . . . . . . . . . . . . . . . . . . . . . . . . . . . . . . | ☐ | $_____ |
| Sales Commissions (specify finders' fees separately) . . . . . . . . . . . . . . . . . . . . . | ☐ | $_____ |
| Other Expenses (identify) _____ . . . . . . . . . . . . . . . . | ☐ | $_____ |
|     Total . . . . . . . . . . . . . . . . . . . . . . . . . . . . . . . . . . . . . . . . . . . . . . . . | ☐ | $_____ |

---

#### C. OFFERING PRICE, NUMBER OF INVESTORS, EXPENSES AND USE OF PROCEEDS

---

b.   Enter the difference between the aggregate offering price given in response to Part C - Question 1 and total expenses furnished in response to Part C - Question 4.a. This difference is the "adjusted gross proceeds to the issuer." ............................................................   $_____

5. Indicate below the amount of the adjusted gross proceeds to the issuer used or proposed to be used for each of the purposes shown. If the amount for any purpose is not known, furnish an estimate and check the box to the left of the estimate. The total of the payments listed must equal the adjusted gross proceeds to the issuer set forth in response to Part C - Question 4.b above.

|  | Payments to Officers, Directors, & Affiliates | Payments To Others |
|---|---|---|
| Salaries and fees ....................................................... | ☐ $_____ | ☐ $_____ |
| Purchase of real estate ................................................. | ☐ $_____ | ☐ $_____ |
| Purchase, rental or leasing and installation of machinery and equipment ........... | ☐ $_____ | ☐ $_____ |
| Construction or leasing of plant buildings and facilities ......................... | ☐ $_____ | ☐ $_____ |
| Acquisition of other businesses (including the value of securities involved in this offering that may be used in exchange for the assets or securities of another issuer pursuant to a merger) ............................................ | ☐ $_____ | ☐ $_____ |
| Repayment of indebtedness .............................................. | ☐ $_____ | ☐ $_____ |
| Working capital ........................................................ | ☐ $_____ | ☐ $_____ |
| Other (specify): _____ | ☐ $_____ | ☐ $_____ |
| _____ ..... | ☐ $_____ | ☐ $_____ |
| Column Totals ......................................................... | ☐ $_____ | ☐ $_____ |
| Total Payments Listed (column totals added) ................................. | ☐ $_____ | |

---

#### D. FEDERAL SIGNATURE

---

The issuer has duly caused this notice to be signed by the undersigned duly authorized person. If this notice is filed under Rule 505, the following signature constitutes an undertaking by the issuer to furnish to the U.S. Securities and Exchange Commission, upon written request of its staff, the information furnished by the issuer to any non-accredited investor pursuant to paragraph (b)(2) of Rule 502.

| Issuer (Print or Type) | Signature | Date |
|---|---|---|
| Name of Signer (Print or Type) | Title of Signer (Print or Type) | |

---

## ATTENTION

**Intentional misstatements or omissions of fact constitute federal criminal violations. (See 18 U.S.C. 1001.)**

## E. STATE SIGNATURE

1. Is any party described in 17 CFR 230.252(c), (d), (e) or (f) presently subject to any of the disqualification provisions of such rule? .................................................................................................

   Yes  No
   ☐   ☐

   See Appendix, Column 5, for state response.

2. The undersigned issuer hereby undertakes to furnish to any state administrator of any state in which this notice is filed, a notice on Form D (17 CFR 239.500) at such times as required by state law.

3. The undersigned issuer hereby undertakes to furnish to the state administrators, upon written request, information furnished by the issuer to offerees.

4. The undersigned issuer represents that the issuer is familiar with the conditions that must be satisfied to be entitled to the Uniform limited Offering Exemption (ULOE) of the state in which this notice is filed and understands that the issuer claiming the availability of this exemption has the burden of establishing that these conditions have been satisfied.

The issuer has read this notification and knows the contents to be true and has duly caused this notice to be signed on its behalf by the undersigned duly authorized person.

| Issuer (Print or Type) | Signature | Date |
|---|---|---|
| Name (Print or Type) | Title (Print or Type) | |

*Instruction:*
Print the name and title of the signing representative under his signature for the state portion of this form. One copy of every notice on Form D must be manually signed. Any copies not manually signed must be photocopies of the manually signed copy or bear typed or printed signatures.

**APPENDIX**

| 1 | 2 | | 3 | 4 | | | | 5 | |
|---|---|---|---|---|---|---|---|---|---|
| | Intend to sell to non-accredited investors in State (Part B-Item 1) | | Type of security and aggregate offering price offered in state (Part C-Item1) | Type of investor and amount purchased in State (Part C-Item 2) | | | | Disqualification under State ULOE (if yes, attach explanation of waiver granted) (Part E-Item1) | |
| State | Yes | No | | Number of Accredited Investors | Amount | Number of Non-Accredited Investors | Amount | Yes | No |
| AL | | | | | | | | | |
| AK | | | | | | | | | |
| AZ | | | | | | | | | |
| AR | | | | | | | | | |
| CA | | | | | | | | | |
| CO | | | | | | | | | |
| CT | | | | | | | | | |
| DE | | | | | | | | | |
| DC | | | | | | | | | |
| FL | | | | | | | | | |
| GA | | | | | | | | | |
| HI | | | | | | | | | |
| ID | | | | | | | | | |
| IL | | | | | | | | | |
| IN | | | | | | | | | |
| IA | | | | | | | | | |
| KS | | | | | | | | | |
| KY | | | | | | | | | |
| LA | | | | | | | | | |
| ME | | | | | | | | | |
| MD | | | | | | | | | |
| MA | | | | | | | | | |
| MI | | | | | | | | | |
| MN | | | | | | | | | |
| MS | | | | | | | | | |
| MO | | | | | | | | | |

| **1** | **2** | | **3** | **4** | | | | **5** | |
|---|---|---|---|---|---|---|---|---|---|
| | Intend to sell to non-accredited investors in State (Part B-Item 1) | | Type of security and aggregate offering price offered in state (Part C-Item1) | Type of investor and amount purchased in State (Part C-Item 2) | | | | Disqualification under State ULOE (if yes, attach explanation of waiver granted) (Part E-Item1) | |
| **State** | **Yes** | **No** | | **Number of Accredited Investors** | **Amount** | **Number of Non-Accredited Investors** | **Amount** | **Yes** | **No** |
| MT | | | | | | | | | |
| NE | | | | | | | | | |
| NV | | | | | | | | | |
| NH | | | | | | | | | |
| NJ | | | | | | | | | |
| NM | | | | | | | | | |
| NY | | | | | | | | | |
| NC | | | | | | | | | |
| ND | | | | | | | | | |
| OH | | | | | | | | | |
| OK | | | | | | | | | |
| OR | | | | | | | | | |
| PA | | | | | | | | | |
| RI | | | | | | | | | |
| SC | | | | | | | | | |
| SD | | | | | | | | | |
| TN | | | | | | | | | |
| TX | | | | | | | | | |
| UT | | | | | | | | | |
| VT | | | | | | | | | |
| VA | | | | | | | | | |
| WA | | | | | | | | | |
| WV | | | | | | | | | |
| WI | | | | | | | | | |
| WY | | | | | | | | | |
| PR | | | | | | | | | |

**APPENDIX**

## STOCK CERTIFICATE ROADMAP

- ○ Name of corporation, state of incorporation
- ○ Certificate number
- ○ Par value or statement that stock is no-par
- ○ Owner's name
- ○ Whether shares are fully paid and nonassessable
- ○ Statement or summary of the respective rights of various classes of stock (if more than one is authorized); existence or absence of preemptive rights
- ○ Statement of how the stock can be transferred
- ○ Transfer restrictions—printed on certificate or in the form of a sticker
- ○ Date of issue
- ○ Officers' signatures, corporate seal

---

## STOP TRANSFER NOTICE

Please be advised that stock certificates of the WebNet Corporation have been reported lost/stolen/destroyed and replacements have been issued:

*Cert. #    Class of Stock    # of Shares    Registered Owner*

Please place a stop order against the original certificates; do not accept them for sale, assignment, or pledge; and notify WebNet if they are offered to you.

RiverView Trust Co., Transfer Agent

## PROVISIONS, CLAUSES, AND RESOLUTIONS PERTAINING TO STOCKS

### Stock Certificate Provision: No Preemptive Rights

The holder of this stock certificate knowingly waives all preemptive rights and is aware that the corporation's Board of Directors has the right to issue additional shares of stock without giving then-current stockholders the right to subscribe to the stock.

### Articles of Incorporation: Residual Preemptive Rights

If stock is offered to the shareholders under their preemptive rights, but some of the shares are not purchased, a residual preemptive right will come into play. A further offering will be made to those shareholders who exercised their preemptive rights to purchase additional shares; this offering will give them the right to purchase additional shares proportionate to their stockholdings. After one reoffering, the corporation will be free to sell the shares free of all preemptive rights, or to retain them as treasury shares.

## Resolution

Section ____ of the laws of the state of _____ and/or Section ____ of the Articles of Incorporation of this corporation grant preemptive rights to [all/common/preferred] shareholders.

This corporation now has ____ shares of authorized but unissued common stock (par value $ ____ per share), subject to these preemptive rights.

Therefore, it is RESOLVED that all ____ shares of unissued common stock now be issued and offered to those individuals who are shareholders of record as of the close of business on _____ , 199 ____ . Those who are shareholders of record as of that date will have the right, until _____ , 199 ____ , to subscribe to the unissued stock proportionate to their shareholdings on that date. The shares will be offered for par value/$ ____ per share, which must be paid in cash at the time of subscription.

It is further RESOLVED that the _____ Bank and Trust Company be appointed as agent to receive subscriptions, collect payment and remit it to the corporation, and distribute shares under the subscriptions.

Any shares remaining unsold on _____ , 199 ____ may be sold by the corporation, free of preemptive rights, for the same price as shares subscribed for under shareholders' preemptive rights.

## Notice to Stockholder

Dear                   :

According to our corporation's stock transfer books, you own ____ shares of common [ ____ shares of preferred stock]: that is, ____ % of the oustanding shares.

During the period from _____ , 199 ____ to _____ 199 ____ , the Corporation will make ____ shares of common/preferred stock available for subscription at $ ____ per share.
□ These shares are not subject to preemptive rights under Section ____ of the Laws of the state of _____ /Section _____ of the Articles of Incorporation/ an agreement of all the corporation's shareholders signed _____ , 199 ____ . Of course, you will have the same right to subscribe for these shares as any other investor.
□ These shares are subject to preemptive rights. You have the right to maintain your current percentage ownership of the corporation's stock by subscribing for up to ____ shares of stock. Payment in cash must accompany the subscription. You may also assign part or all of your preemptive right to subscribe to another person [subject to the transfer restrictions set out in Section ____ of this corporation's Articles of Incorporation/Bylaw adopted _____ , 199 ____ /shareholders' agreement dated _____ , 199 ____ and endorsed on the share certificates.

## Notice of Redemption

By order of the Board of Directors of Filigree Corporation, you are hereby NOTIFIED that all/ ____ shares of the corporation's 6% [cumulative] preferred stock have been called for redemption on _____ , 199 ____ . The redemption price is $ ____ per share, plus dividends from the last payment date ( _____ , 199 ____ ) until the redemption date [plus any earlier dividend accrued but not paid].

[Add, if less than the entire class is being redeemed: Shares represented by the following numbered certificates have been chosen for redemption by random drawing/proportionate to each shareholder's interest/at the discretion of the Board of Directors, bearing in mind the respective rights of the corporation's majority and minority shareholders and its creditors].

Certificate Numbers to be Redeemed: Holders of the above-numbered certificates/shares of the corporation's 6% [cumulative] preferred stock are notified that they have an obligation to surrender these certificates to the Harmonia Trust Company, the corporation's transfer agent, on or before _____ , 199 ____ . When they surrender their certificates, they will be paid the redemption price immediately. Filigree Corp. has deposited sufficient funds with the Harmonia Trust Company to make all such payments.

After the scheduled redemption date, the 6% [cumulative] preferred shares will be canceled, and will no longer be shares of Filigree Corporation bearing rights and generating dividends. Shareholders who fail or refuse to surrender their/the above-designated certificates on or before the redemption date will have no rights as to these shares other than the right to receive the redemption price, without interest, upon surrender of certificates to the Harmonia Trust Company.

Filigree Corp., by Petra Malone, Secretary

## CLAUSES IN ARTICLES OF INCORPORATION COVERING STOCK

### Protection of Preferred

The vote (in person or by proxy) of the holders of at least two-thirds of the preferred shares outstanding at that time will be required before the Corporation can issue any stock having preference or priority over the Preferred Stock as authorized by Section ____ of these Articles of Incorporation, or to issue, assume, or guarantee any bonds, notes, or other evidences of indebtedness with a term of one year or more, if at any time the aggregate of all long-term debt exceeds 50% of the corporation's capital and surplus, thus endangering the payment of dividends on the preferred shares.

The vote of the Preferred shareholders must be taken at a special meeting of Preferred shareholders called for that purpose on at least ____ days' notice.

### Consideration for Stock

The Board of Directors has the discretion to set the consideration to be paid for shares of the corporation's stock. Payment of the price set by the Board makes shares fully paid and nonassessable. Absent fraud, the Board's judgment as to the value of property or services paid for shares will be conclusive. However, shares may not, at any time, be issued for less than their par value, and the Corporation shall not commence its corporate existence and operations until it has received at least $1,000 (the minimum stated capital required by Section 30-14-22 of the Revised Statutes Annotated of the State of Monroe) as consideration for shares of its stock.

## Stock Bonuses/Dividends Permitted

The Board of Directors also has the power to issue any authorized shares for use as bonuses for the corporation's employees or as dividends payable to the holders of the corporation's common stock.

## Deduction of Expenses

Shares of par-value common and preferred stock may still be treated as fully paid and nonassessable if the corporation exercises its election to deduct the reasonable expenses of corporate organization and stock underwriting from the consideration received for the stock.

## CLAUSES FOR SUBSCRIPTION AGREEMENT

The subscriber may prepay any such installment at any time without penalty; a certificate for the shares subscribed to will be issued as soon as payment of the full subscription price has been made.

On default by the subscriber (i.e., 30 days have passed since the due date of an installment) the corporation will have the right to sell all or part of the stock subscribed for to someone else, applying the sale proceeds to the subscriber's obligation, and returning any surplus to the subscriber. No notice to the defaulting subscriber is required before any such sale.

## RESOLUTION AFTER RESIGNATION OF OFFICER

RESOLVED that the corporation be permitted to continue the use of and that the transfer agent be permitted to continue to authenticate, issue, and register stock certificates (including certificates for authorized but unissued shares) signed by _____ while s/he was in office.

## BYLAW (Replacement of Stock Certificate)

When a stockholder alleges that a certificate has been destroyed, stolen, or lost, the Board of Directors can issue a replacement certificate (clearly identified on its face as a duplicate), provided that the stockholder produces satisfactory evidence of the loss, theft, or destruction of the certificate. At the discretion of the Board of Directors, a waiting period can be imposed before issuance of replacement shares, in case the certificate has merely been misplaced and could be located.

The Board of Directors has the discretion to require the stockholder to post an indemnity bond of up to twice the value of the shares of stock represented by the missing certificate, or the Board of Directors can waive the bond requirement but require the stockholder to furnish an affidavit of the circumstances requiring the certificate to be replaced. The number, date of issuance, and registered owner of the duplicate certificate shall be duly entered in the corporation's books.

## BOARD RESOLUTION AUTHORIZING ISSUANCE OF NEW STOCK CERTIFICATE

William Barker, a stockholder who resides at 19B Magnolia Court, Schermahorn, Tyler, has provided his affidavit stating that he is the record owner of 250 shares of this corporation's common/preferred stock and that the certificate evidencing his ownership was lost/stolen from his desk during a burglary occurring _____ , 199_____ /destroyed by fire/flood/other [describe] on _____ , 199_____ /other [describe] and therefore is unavailable and unlikely to be recovered.

Barker has/is directed to/furnish[ed] bond in the amount of $10,000 [to be] issued by the Columbia Surety Co. indemnifying and saving harmless the RiverView Trust Company in its role as Transfer Agent for this corporation's stock against all liabilities and claims arising out of its issuance of a replacement stock certificate. OR Given the stockholder's credible assurance that the certificate is irrevocably destroyed, the requirement of a bond is waived.

Therefore, it is RESOLVED that RiverView Trust Co. be authorized to issue and register a replacement certificate in the name of William Barker, and that the certificate be described on its face as a duplicate.

## AFFIDAVIT COVERING LOSS OF CERTIFICATE

State of Tyler
County of Bernardsville ss:

William Barker being duly sworn deposes and says that, to his knowledge, information, and belief the following statements are true;

○ He is the lawful owner of Certificate #219, evidencing his ownership of 250 shares of WebNet Corporation's common stock

○ The certificate was lost/stolen/destroyed under the following circumstances: removed from a locked desk in his home, during a burglary occurring April 5, 1991.

○ He has not sold, assigned, transferred, or pledged this stock certificate.

○ He will indemnify and hold harmless the RiverView Trust Company against any claims or liability arising out of its issuance of a duplicate certificate.

○ If, at any time after issuance of a duplicate certificate, the original is recovered, he will surrender one of the certificates to the transfer agent for cancellation.

## VOTING AGREEMENT

John Tenuta and Roger Staunton have invested, and intend to continue to invest, significant time, effort, and money in the success of Boysenberry Reserves, Inc., in which they are major stockholders. In order to promote the smooth and harmonious operation of the corporation, Tenuta and Staunton each agrees as follows:

*1.* As long as he remains a stockholder, and as long as the other remains a stockholder, and otherwise eligible to serve, that he will vote all of his shares for the election of the other as director of the corporation.

*2.* As long as he is a stockholder, and otherwise eligible to serve, Tenuta agrees to serve as President and Treasurer of the corporation; Staunton agrees to vote for him for these offices. Staunton agrees to serve as Vice-President and Secretary, and Tenuta agrees to vote for him for these offices.

Date: _____ , 199____
Signed: _____

John Tenuta
Roger Staunton

## VOTING TRUST AGREEMENT

Blaine Geary, Michael Donnethorpe, Helene Pimm, and Justo Martinez are minority stockholders in Moseley Artistic Management, Inc. However, when their holdings are combined, they hold a majority of the corporation's shares. In order to prevent oppression by the corporation's other stockholders, and in order to secure the benefits of majority voting power, Geary, Donnethorpe, Pimm, and Martinez agree to enter into a voting trust on this ____ day of _____ , 199 ____ ; as required by the laws of the state of Tyler, the voting trust will have a duration limited to ten years. Eustachio Cabral, Esq., has agreed to serve as trustee of the voting trust.

*1.* Geary, Donnethorpe, Pimm, and Martinez (and any other Moseley Artistic Management, Inc., stockholder who wishes to participate in the voting trust) agree to deposit the certificates for all their shares of Moseley common stock with the trustee, accompanied by a duly signed and stamped instrument sufficient to complete the transfer of the shares to the trustee.

*2.* The trustee will provide each depositing shareholder with a voting trust certificate in a form satisfactory under Section 913-26(c) of the Consolidated Statutes of the state of Tyler, representing the number of shares deposited pursuant to this voting trust agreement.

*3.* The voting trust certificates are freely transferrable by the depositing shareholders on notice to the trustee and by endorsement of the voting trust certificate. The transferee becomes bound by all terms of this voting trust agreement to the same extent as the original signatories.

Although voting trust certificates are assignable and transferrable, the stockholders participating in this voting trust agree not to assign, transfer, or sell their voting trust certificates to a person who is not a depositing stockholder unless they first give the other depositing stockholders at least ____ days' notice of the intended sale and of the highest bona fide offer made by an offeror who is not a depositing stockholder. If no offer has yet been made, the depositing stockholder must disclose the lowest bona fide price he or she will accept from an offeror who is not a depositing stockholder. The depositing stockholder who wishes to sell a voting trust certificate must accept the highest bid from a participant that equals or exceeds the outside bid or price sought by the offeror.

*4.* The trustee will deposit a duplicate original of this voting trust agreement with the corporation as soon as possible after this agreement is signed. All deposited shares will be listed on the corporation's records as the property of the trustee, who will have all rights of a stockholder, including voting on all corporate issues for which the vote of common stockholders is solicited. The trustee will vote according to his best judgment, after consulting the depositing stockholders. The depositing stockholders will have no rights or cause of action against the trustee for any vote or other corporate action that the trustee takes in good faith, on information and inquiry, using reasonable professional judgment, and in the absence of any negligence or willful misconduct.

5. The depositing stockholders agree to contribute equally to reimburse the trustee for all reasonable expenses encountered and attributable to his service as trustee. If they fail to do so, the amounts in question will operate as a lien on the deposited shares of stock. The trustee will not be compensated for service as trustee/will receive quarterly payments of $____ each for service as trustee; the depositing stockholders will contribute equally to the trustee's compensation.

6. If the trustee delivers a written resignation to each of the depositing stockholders, or if the trustee dies, becomes disabled, or is removed from office on unanimous vote of the depositing stockholders, the depositing stockholders will elect a new trustee and will notify the corporation of the election. The new trustee will succeed to all rights and obligations of the original trustee.

7. The trustee will promptly deliver each depositing stockholder's share of all dividends that he receives in his role as trustee.

8. At any time before the effectiveness of this voting trust agreement expires, it can be terminated on vote of the depositing stockholders holding 75% of the deposited shares, by giving notice to the trustee, making payment of any amount due to the trustee but unpaid, notifying the corporation, and paying any required stamp or transfer taxes as a condition of having their stock certificates returned. When the corporation is notified of the termination of the voting trust, it will correct its book entries to name the depositing shareholders, not the voting trustee, as owners of the formerly deposited stock certificates.

IN WITNESS OF THE ABOVE, THE DEPOSITING STOCKHOLDERS AND THE TRUSTEE HAVE SIGNED THIS AGREEMENT, ON THE ____ DAY OF _____ , 199____ .

TRUSTEE: _____

DEPOSITING STOCKHOLDERS: _____

ASSIGNMENT FORM (to be printed on the reverse of the voting trust certificate)

_____ , holder of this voting trust certificate, hereby sells, transfers, and assigns all rights and interest in the corporation issuing the underlying stock to _____ for value received. The transferor hereby authorizes and directs the voting trustee to note the transfer on the books and records of the trust.

## VOTING TRUST CERTIFICATE

*Certificate No.:* _____    *Date of Deposit:* _____

This Certificate certifies that a stockholder, _____ , has deposited certificates evidencing ownership of ____ common and ____ preferred shares of the stock of Wingate Medical Products, Inc., pursuant to a Voting Trust agreement entered into by certain of Wingate's stockholders on _____ , 199 ____ , with Martin Zasloffsky, Trustee under this agreement. A duplicate original of the Voting Trust agreement is kept on file at Wingate's registered office, 9319 Acacia Terrace, Randolph, Adams, and can be inspected at any time during normal business hours by any stockholder or the designee of any stockholder.

As long as the Voting Trust agreement remains in force, the stockholder who deposits shares with the Trustee is entitled to receive dividend payments passed through the Trust (with a deduction for taxes on the dividends paid by the Trustee, stamp or transfer taxes paid by the Trustee on transfers of shares, and a deduction not to exceed $ _____ per quarterly dividend payment representing payment of Zasloffsky's expenses as Trustee).

The depositor, who is registered on Wingate's record books as the owner of the shares deposited under this Certificate, retains the right to transfer the Certificate by notifying the Trustee of the transfer. Until such notification, the Trustee will treat the depositor as the registered owner of the shares.

If and when the Voting Trust agreement terminates according to its terms or is canceled, the Trustee will cease to exercise the rights of a stockholder (e.g., voting the deposited shares) and will return the stock certificates to the shareholders who deposited them.

If and when Wingate is dissolved or undergoes total or partial liquidation, the Trustee will receive the funds paid on account of the certificates held under the Voting Trust; but the proceeds will be passed through to the depositing stockholders when they deliver this Voting Trust Certificate when the corporation is dissolved, or when they present this Certificate for a notation to be made of the effect of partial liquidation.

Date: _____ , 199____
Signed: _____                                                                              Martin Zasloffsky, Trustee

## STOCKHOLDERS' AGREEMENT

HUFFABIG, INC., a corporation duly organized and doing business under the laws of the state of Lincoln, is a closely held Subchapter S corporation. Its entire authorized capitalization of 15,000 shares of no-par common stock has been issued and is held as follows:

| | |
|---|---|
| George Grody | 4,000 shares |
| Matthew Huffman | 3,000 shares |
| Frederick Bigelow | 3,000 shares |
| Leonard Bickel | 2,000 shares |
| Dorothy Goff | 2,000 shares |
| Peter Chong | 1,000 shares |

The shareholders believe that maintenance of the corporation as a closely held S corporation that is independent of ownership by other corporations promotes the long-term best interests of the shareholders, corporation, employees, and community. Therefore, the stockholders have entered into a buy-sell agreement embodying transfer restrictions.

### A. Transfer Restrictions

*1.* No voluntary transfer of any kind (e.g., sale, gift, pledge, exchange) may be made by any shareholder except as provided by this agreement or with the unanimous advance written consent of all shareholders. If any transfer in violation of this agreement is made to a bona fide purchaser or other party who takes in good faith and without knowledge that the transfer violated this agreement, the transferee will be bound by this agreement to the same extent as the transferor. [Transfers by gift,

gift to minors, exchange, trust, will, or durable power of attorney to members of the stockholder's immediate family will be exempt from this restriction.]

*2.* Every stock certificate for the corporation's stock will bear a legend referring to the fact that the stock is subject to transfer restrictions imposed by this agreement.

*3.* No transfer of stock is valid or conveys the rights of a stockholder on the transferee until and unless the transfer has been recorded in the corporation's stock transfer records (whether maintained in book or electronic form). The corporation will not enter any transfer that violates this agreement in its stock transfer records, and will inform any transfer agent not to enter violative transfers in the stock transfer records.

*4.* All stockholders agree not to do or permit any act that would jeopardize the validity of the corporation's Subchapter S election.

## B. Voting Agreement

*1.* In order to prevent the domination of shareholders by other shareholders with larger holdings, and also to prevent corporate deadlock, Frederick Bigelow, Leonard Bickel, Dorothy Goff, and Peter Chong agree at all times to vote their shares as a bloc for all directors and with respect to all corporate transactions on which a stockholder vote is required. The vote of the bloc will be determined:

☐ By a vote—Bigelow will have three votes, Bickel and Goff will have two votes, and Chong will have one vote.

☐ By a trustee: the minority shareholders will transfer their shares to a voting trust.

☐ By any three of the minority stockholders, whose vote will bind all four of the minority stockholders.

## C. Right of First Refusal

*1.* Any stockholder who wishes to sell part or all of his or her stock, and who has received a bona fide offer to purchase the stock, is not permitted to sell (or otherwise transfer) the stock until these right of first refusal provisions have been complied with.

*2.* The stockholder who wants to transfer stock must give the corporation and each of the other stockholders 30 days' written notice of intent to transfer and of the terms of the bona fide offer. No offer whose acceptance would impair the Subchapter S election can be deemed bona fide.

*3.* During this 30-day period, the corporation and/or stockholders have a right to acquire the shares that the stockholder wants to transfer. If the corporation and/or stockholders express an interest in acquiring more shares than the stockholder wishes to transfer, the shares will be allocated as follows:

☐ First, all the shares the corporation wishes to acquire, then all the shares each stockholder wishes to acquire, in order of their stockholdings prior to the transfer, until all the shares have been acquired.

☐ First to the corporation, then to the other stockholders who wish to acquire shares, in proportion to their initial holdings.

☐ Proportionate to the percentage of shares offered that he, she, or it expressed a willingness to acquire.

☐ By auction, with price determining stock acquisition.

*4.* ☐ The shares must be acquired for cash, payable within _____ days.

☐ The shares may be acquired for cash and/or an unsecured month note bearing interest at _____ %, with a present value at or above the bona fide offer.

**5.** If the corporation or other stockholders fail to acquire the entire number of shares to be transferred, the stockholder can sell or otherwise dispose of the balance to the offeror at or above the bona fide offering price as soon as the 30-day period has elapsed.

## D. Reacquisition on Death of a Stockholder

**1.** All signatories agree not to dispose of their shares in the corporation by will, trust (other than an inter vivos voting trust), or durable power of attorney. [Note: Omit this provision if the option relating to transfers to the immediate family was adopted.]

**2.** If a stockholder dies, the corporation/corporation and stockholders in this proportion: _____ /the other stockholders, in proportion to their original holdings agree to acquire the deceased stockholder's shares, paying cash and/or giving a \_\_\_\_ month unsecured note bearing interest at \_\_\_\_ % to the deceased's estate no later than three months after the death.

    In the interim, the deceased's executor or personal representative will be entitled to vote the shares at any annual or special meeting to the extent that the deceased could have voted them; the executor or personal representative is bound by any voting trust or voting agreement to the same extent as the deceased.

**3.** To fund this obligation, the potential acquirors agree to maintain a life insurance policy on the life of each of the other stockholders in an amount of at least \$ \_\_\_\_ . Purchases by individuals are to be made at their own personal expense; purchase of insurance on stockholders by the corporation is hereby expressly declared to be an appropriate use of corporate funds. Any insurance proceeds payable to the corporation and remaining after a deceased stockholder's shares have been repurchased can be used for general corporation purposes.

**4.** The price to be paid for the shares will be determined by a licensed appraiser familiar with valuation of closely held business stock, to be selected by vote of the acquirors. The appraiser's fee will be paid by the estate of the deceased shareholder.

## BUY-SELL AGREEMENT (Provision re Confidential Information)

The stockholders acknowledge that their status as such may give them access to valuable, confidential, proprietary information about and belonging to the corporation (e.g., customer and client lists, trade secrets). They agree not to disclose this information at any time, except to authorized representatives of the corporation or with its consent. In case of breach or threatened breach of this provision, the corporation will be entitled to an injunction against disclosure, in addition to its other common law, statutory, and contractual remedies.

## BUY-SELL (Noncompete)

All stockholders agree that, while they are stockholders and for five years after termination of their holdings in ownership, they will not compete with the corporation, within 25 miles of any of the corporation's places of business, by: _____ . If, at any time, the laws of the state of Monroe deem this restriction excessive in space or time, this provision will be reformed to specify the maximum permitted restriction. OR

Stockholders agree, within these space and time limitations, not to approach any customers/ clients of the corporation and directly or indirectly suggest or advise that they stop doing business with the corporation or its successors. Nor will they directly or indirectly solicit or induce the corporation's clients/ customers to patronize any other business (whether or not the stockholder has an interest in the business) or voluntarily disclose all or part of the corporation's customer/client list to any person or organization. They also agree not to attempt to induce or solicit any of the corporation's employees to leave the corporation's employ and accept employment with any other business organization.

## NOTICE OF CASH DIVIDEND DECLARATION

To the Stockholders of Griggout Corporation:
At its meeting held _____ , 199 ____ , the Board of Directors of Griggout Corporation declared a regular/special dividend of $ ____ per share on common stock and $ ____ per share on preferred stock [$ ____ of which consists of a payment of amounts owed but not paid earlier to holders of cumulative preferred stock]. The dividend is payable out of the corporation's earned surplus.

To speed up dividend payment, please use the form on the back of this notice to inform Griggout Corp. of any changes of address.
[Reverse]
I, _____ am a holder of common/preferred shares of Griggout's stock. Please correct the corporation's record books to reflect my change of address from _____ to _____ .

Date: _____ , 199____
Signed: _____

## RESOLUTION RESCINDING DIVIDEND DECLARATION

On _____ , 199 ____ , at a special/regular meeting, the Board of Directors declared a regular/special dividend of $ ____ per common, $ ____ per preferred share. However, the declaration of dividend was motivated by a belief that the corporation had capital surplus in the amount of $ ____ /that declaration of a dividend was required to avoid the imposition of the personal holding company penalty tax. This belief is erroneous.

Therefore, it is RESOLVED that the resolution declaring the dividend be rescinded, and that all stockholders be informed that the dividend has been rescinded, and that they must return to the corporation all amounts received pursuant to the mistaken declaration of the dividend.

# PERMANENT NOTICE RE DIVIDENDS

To Bennett Foundry Equipment Co.: _____ Date: _____
    Until I revoke this order in writing, please remit all dividend checks which may later become due on all the shares of Bennett Foundry Equipment Co. which I now own or may later acquire:

☐ Payable to my order, to me at _____

☐ Payable to the order of _____ , at _____

Date:_____ , 199____
Signed, exactly as signature appears on the stock certificate: _____
Add notariat if dividend payments are assigned.


# NOTICE TO STOCKHOLDERS RE TAX STATUS

Dear Stockholders of Rhiannon Dental Supplies, Inc.:
During the year ending 12/31/9 ____ , the corporation made distributions to stockholders totaling $ ____ per share. The corporation estimates that ____ % of this amount represents a return of stockholders' capital. Therefore, you should use this percentage of the distributions you received to reduce your cost or other basis for your shares—it is not dividend income. If your basis has already been reduced to zero, this part of the distribution should be reported on your tax return as capital gain.
    The other ____ % of the distributions for this year constitutes dividend income and should be reported that way on your tax return.


# DIRECTORS' DISSENT RE DIVIDEND DECLARATION
## (Append to Resolution)

However, the resolution was passed over the dissent of Director(s) _____ , who claimed that declaration of the dividend was improper because the corporation was insolvent/did not have adequate earned surplus for this purpose/other [explain]: _____ . This/these director(s) requested that his/her/their dissent be made official by entering it in the minutes of the meeting and on the corporation's books.

## Notice from Director

At the meeting of _____ , 199 ____ , Luxor Luminous Tiles, Inc.'s Board of Directors voted to declare a dividend of $ ____ per common, $ ____ per share of preferred stock.

☐ I was present at the meeting and voted against the declaration of the dividend.

☐ I was absent from the meeting and wish to place my dissent from this action on the record.

I dissent from the declaration of the dividend because:

Date: _____ , 199____
Signed: _____

## STATEMENT OF CANCELLATION OF REDEEMABLE SHARES

To the Secretary of State of the State of Madison:
Ionic Oscillation, Inc., is a corporation organized under the laws of the state of Madison. Its incorporation became effective _____ , 19 _____ .
Ionic Oscillation, Inc., has canceled certain of its redeemable shares by redemption or purchase, as permitted by Section 13-2-102 of the laws of Madison.
Cancellation occurred as follows:

   shares of [class][series] _____ were redeemed
   shares of [class][series] _____ were purchased by the corporation.
After the cancellation, the corporation's stated capital is $ _____ , and a total of _____ shares [itemize by class and series if necessary] remain issued.
[Add only if the Articles of Incorporation provide that canceled shares will not be reissued: After the cancellation, the corporation has authority to issue shares, itemized as follows by class and series:

Date: _____ , 199_____ Ionic Oscillations, Inc., by Gerald Mandino,
President _____ [Seal]
Acknowledgment
State of MADISON
County of Clare _____ ss:
On _____ , 199 _____ , Gerald Mandino, whom I know to be the President of Ionic Oscillations, Inc., appeared before me and was duly sworn. He swore that:

□ Ionic Oscillations, Inc., has not adopted a corporate seal.
□ The seal attached to the document is the seal of Ionic Oscillations, Inc., and signifies that the document was voluntarily executed as an official act of the Corporation and approved by its Board of Directors.

Date: _____ , 199_____                     Helga Siemens, Notary Public
                                                    Seal


## NOTICE TO SHAREHOLDERS ABOUT REPURCHASE

Dear Stockholder:
At its _____ , 199 _____ meeting, the Board of Directors resolved that it was in the corporation's best interest to invest up to $ _____ in order to repurchase the corporation's own stock.
   Anyone who is a stockholder of record of the corporation's common stock as of _____ , 199 _____ can sell stock back to the corporation.

□ We will pay $ _____ per share, and will buy stock on a "first-come, first-served" basis until we have purchased _____ shares/we will accumulate all offers to sell until _____ , 199 _____ ; if, at that time, stockholders have offered to tender more than a total of _____ shares, we will accept each tender proportionate to the number of shares tendered/proportionate to stockholdings before the tender.
□ We will accept offers in reverse price order: that is, we will accept the lowest tenders first, until shares costing a total of $ _____ have been purchased. (Our estimate of the fair market value of the

stock is $ ____ per share.) However, the Board of Directors has discretion to reject any tender whose price it deems excessive, and the Board of Directors is not required to purchase the entire $ ____ worth of stock whose purchase has been authorized.

If you want to tender your stock for repurchase, complete the form enclosed with this notice, and send the form, and the certificates for the stock you want to tender (endorsed to the Transfer Agent) to the Fredonia Trust Company, 9219 Bay Boulevard, Principia, which is the corporation's transfer agent.

If your tender is not accepted (either because the price you ask is too high or because too many shares have been tendered) the certificates for the stock that is not repurchased will be reendorsed and returned to you promptly.

## Certificate

To the Spaeth Service Co., Inc.:
I hereby tender to you certificates representing ____ shares of Spaeth Service Co. common stock for repurchase by the corporation at $ ____ per share.

## OFFER TO BUY OUT SMALL SHAREHOLDERS

Dear Holder of 50 or Fewer Shares of Stock:
We have discovered that the administrative costs of tracking, handling, and paying dividends on holdings of 50 or fewer shares are disproportionately high. At the same time, many holders of such small "odd lots" would like to be able to receive cash for their stock, which is hard to sell on the open market.

The Board of Directors voted, at a regular/special meeting held _____ , 199 ____ to offer $ ____ per share in cash to all holders of 50 or fewer shares of our common stock who wish to sell their shares; a total of ____ shares are held in lots of 50 shares or under. The Board of Directors is willing to devote up to $ ____ to repurchasing these shares, which will then be canceled and retired/held as treasury shares/used as part of the corporation's ESOP, stock option, or stock bonus plan. The offer to purchase the shares if valid only until _____ , 199 ____ .

Since its last Annual Report to the Stockholders, the corporation's net asset value has increased/decreased from $ ____ to $ ____ ; its net investment income for this period is $ ____ , or $ ____ per share. There have been no significant changes in business or operations since the Annual Report [other than: _____ ].

This offer is made purely as a convenience to the corporation and its stockholders; there is no penalty if you decide not to accept this offer. The corporation neither recommends nor refrains from recommending acceptance of the offer. The tax consequences of the sale will be the same as if you sold to an individual. We do recommend that you consult your financial and tax advisors to determine if selling your stock is advisable under your own particular circumstances.

If you wish to accept this offer, fill out the enclosed card and sent it with your stock certificate, by registered mail, to the corporation's transfer agent. It is not necessary to endorse the stock certificates or have your signature on the acceptance card guaranteed.

## Acceptance Card

I accept the corporation's offer to purchase my _____ shares of its common stock for $ _____ a share. I enclose my stock certificate. Please send the check in payment for my shares to _____

Date: _____ , 199_____
Signed: _____ (The signature must be exactly as your name appears on the stock certificate; if the stock is jointly owned, all the joint owners must sign.)

    Note: This offer expires _____ , 199 ____ ; no payment will be made for certificates received after the close of business on that date.

## CONTRACT TO BUY OUT A STOCKHOLDER

James Piraki is a Vice-President and Director of Aegean General Contractors, Inc., and is the owner of 2,500 shares of its common stock. He has reached an age at which he contemplates retirement and wishes to ensure his own postretirement financial security and a smooth transition in corporate management. OR

    Differences have arisen between Piraki and the rest of the corporation's officers and directors to the extent that it is mutually agreed that he should withdraw from all participation in the conduct of the corporation and its business.

    Piraki and the corporation have reached an agreement on the terms of his withdrawal.

*1.* He will sell, and the corporation will buy, all right, title, and interest in his 2,500 shares of stock, for $50 per share (a total of $125,000). He expressly warrants and represents that he has title to these shares, free and clear of all claims and encumbrances.

*2.* On execution of this agreement, he will surrender certificates representing his entire stockholding and will tender a written resignation from all offices and directorships in Aegean General Contracting, Inc.

*3.* The corporation will pay for the stock in cash on execution of this agreement/$ ____ on execution, plus ____ annual/quarterly/monthly installments of $ ____ each, beginning _____ , 199 ____ , secured by the corporation's note bearing interest on the unpaid balance at the rate of ____ %APR. The note will be payable to Piraki or his estate.

*4.* This agreement binds and benefits the parties, heirs, personal representatives, successors, and assigns.

## RESOLUTION PASSING A DIVIDEND

No reason given
RESOLVED, that no dividend be declared on the common stock of this corporation for the ____ quarter of 199 ____ .

    Business reason given _____ .

    Based on the report given by _____ , and incorporated by reference into the minutes of this meeting, the corporation needs funds to expand operations/increase its work force/devote to research and development/clean up improperly disposed hazardous waste/settle a case now pending in the _____ Court of _____ , under index number ____ /other [explain]:

The total needed for this purpose has been estimated as $ ____ .

Examination of this corporation's financial records shows that it would be in the best interests of the corporation to use its surplus for the purpose given above and to omit payment of a dividend on the common stock for the quarter of _____ .

## LETTER TO SHAREHOLDERS (Passing a Dividend)

Dear Shareholder:

We, the Board of Directors, have examined the corporation's financial situation and have made plans for its future. In our judgment, it is best for the corporation and its stockholders, in the long run, if we do not pay a dividend to the common shareholders this quarter, even though the corporation does have a surplus available which could be used to pay a dividend on the common stock.

Instead, we will use the funds that could have been used to pay a dividend for research and development/corporate expansion/to add new employees/to clean up toxic waste/to settle a claim or lawsuit against the corporation/other: _____ . We believe that building a stronger corporation will mean a higher stock price in the long run and higher dividends in the future.

# Chapter 3

# CORPORATE GOVERNANCE, MEETINGS, AND RESOLUTIONS

## INTRODUCTION

One of the secretary's most important tasks is to make sure that adequate notice is given of meetings; to take minutes at those meetings; and to make sure that a record is kept, in proper form, of all resolutions adopted by the corporation at its meetings.

State law has a major role in prescribing how much notice board members and stockholders must be given of regular and special meetings, and who can be permitted to call a meeting (and for what purposes). Note that the broader the power of stockholders to call special meetings, the easier it is for a would-be raider to buy a few shares of stock or work with dissident stockholders to call a meeting when it suits the raider's timetable—a reason why many corporations either refuse from the outset to let stockholders call meetings or amend their charter or bylaws to limit or eliminate this right. In addition to state law requirements, the corporate secretary must consult the corporation's charter and bylaws to see whether the corporation has limited or expanded the statutory powers.

### Notice of Meetings

The notice of any meeting must state that the meeting has been called on proper authority. The notice of a special meeting must state the purpose of the meeting. Some corporations whose bylaws permit the stockholders to call special meetings also include a requirement that the notice of such a special meeting must include the name of the person calling it. If, for some reason, the regular meeting is not held, the board of directors usually passes a resolution authorizing the call of the meeting and ordering the corporate secretary to give notice of the meeting.

Routine corporate governance also includes preparing and circulating the annual report to stockholders and any quarterly or event-oriented reports that are required by the SEC or state securities regulators.

The usual practice is for the corporation to hold a directors' meeting before the annual meeting of stockholders; at this meeting, the board will pass resolutions to be submitted for the approval of the stockholders. In most close corporations, the election of directors is as undramatic a process as can be imagined, with the sitting board of directors returned to office year after year until they choose to retire. However, a takeover bid or a political struggle within the corporation can lead to a robust battle for control of the board of directors or to amend the corporation's charter and bylaws in the direction favoring the insurgents.

The corporate secretary's premeeting tasks in preparation for the annual meeting of stockholders include

- ☐ Consulting the corporation's attorney and accountant to discuss requirements for soliciting proxies and providing related disclosure to stockholders. If the corporation has any securities registered under Section 12 of the Exchange Act, the entire proxy process given in Section 14 of the Exchange Act must be followed.
- ☐ Working with the team preparing the annual report.
- ☐ Gathering information needed for proxy disclosure, such as the employment and financial history of the corporation's board of directors and the compensation they receive from (and debts they owe to) the corporation.
- ☐ Hiring a proxy solicitation firm.
- ☐ Making arrangements with the corporation's stock transfer agent to mail proxies and tabulate them once they have been returned by the stockholders.
- ☐ Getting the proxies printed; having them delivered to the transfer agent. A proxy form should
  * Identify the stockholder who grants the proxy.
  * Appoint the holder of the proxy as the shareholder's agent and attorney in fact, with all the voting rights the shareholder would have if present in person.
  * Make it clear what the shareholder's directions are: whether the proxy should be voted only in a particular way stated on the proxy, in any way the proxyholder sees fit to vote, or according to the stockholder's known or expressed wishes.
  * Identify the duration of the proxy—only for this meeting, only for this meeting and any adjournments, or for all meetings until the proxy is revoked? (The general rule is that a proxy lasts until it is revoked—but check state law; they may be good only for a year, or only for 11 months.)
  * Clarify how and when the proxy can be revoked (usually revocations must be filed with the corporate secretary); proxies coupled with an interest cannot be revoked.
- ☐ If a 10-K form must be submitted to the SEC, cooperating with the form's auditors in preparing the 10-K.
- ☐ If shareholders have submitted questions to be raised at the annual meeting, or proposals to be submitted for a vote, reviewing the corporation's response with the board of directors, the other officers, and top management; having information necessary to respond to questions and give the management side of the questions.

- □ Determining if state law, or the corporation's charter and bylaws, requires that inspectors must be appointed to conduct the election, or stockholders may have the right to demand election inspectors if they are dubious about the fairness of the coming election. Usually, if inspectors are required, either one or three inspectors will be appointed (a small number, to be efficient—and an odd number, so there won't be any tie votes). Officers and those running for corporate office can't serve as inspectors.
- □ Making arrangements for communications at the meeting—arrange for clearing of the appropriate-sized room if the meeting will be held on corporate premises, or for rental of outside space (e.g., at a local hotel or conference center), arrange for public address system, microphones, overhead projectors, refreshments, parking, etc.
- □ If the corporation's securities are listed on a stock exchange, notifying the exchange of the record date for the meeting.
- □ If appropriate, publishing a notice of the meeting in the financial press.
- □ Getting ballots printed for the meeting, including blank space for voting on unscheduled motions.
- □ Drafting resolutions for the board meeting dealing with routine meeting matters such as employment of proxy solicitors, approval of proxy materials, and appointment of auditors.

## After the Meeting

- □ Prepare a report to the stockholders about the meeting and resolutions adopted at the meeting.
- □ Meet with the public relations staff or outside public relations firm to decide if press releases are required and, if so, what they should contain.
- □ If required by the SEC, prepare and submit a Form 8-K after conferring with counsel and accountants.

*Practice Tip:* Did you have to adjourn a meeting because there was no quorum present? Corporations in this situation often adopt a bylaw that sets the quorum for an adjourned meeting at a lower level than that required for the original meeting; the notice of the adjourned meeting should state that the meeting could not be held as originally scheduled because of failure to obtain a quorum.

## Order of Business at Meetings

Many corporations' bylaws include a provision stating the order of business at meetings. If your bylaws do not specify this, the conventional order of business for board meetings is

- □ Reading and correction of the minutes of the last meeting (this is not necessary if the minutes have already been circulated)
- □ Reports from the corporation's officers
- □ Report of the Executive Committee, if there is one

☐ Reports from other standing committees

☐ Reports from special committees

*Practice Tip:* A convenient way to inform the entire board and keep complete corporate records is to have committees circulate the minutes of committee meetings to the full board before the board meeting; the secretary files a copy of the committee meeting minutes with the minutes of the last meeting.

☐ Unfinished business from the last meeting

☐ New business.

The basic function of meetings is to adopt corporate policies. In formal terms, a motion is a proposal; a resolution is an official policy adopted by the corporation. A motion is made to adopt the resolution, the motion is seconded, a vote is taken, and if the appropriate majority is secured, the resolution is adopted and binds the corporation. Generally, the corporation's attorney, the corporate secretary, or the person proposing the resolution drafts a text in advance, to be discussed at the meeting and amended as needed. The board can transact business and pass binding resolutions even if there are one or more vacancies on the board—as long as a quorum is present. (A resolution is just as legally binding on the corporation as a bylaw.) Of course, it's good policy to fill vacancies as soon as possible—state laws usually provide that the board can appoint new board members to sit until the next annual meeting, unless the corporation's charter and bylaws provide another method (e.g., a special meeting and election). Interested directors can't vote on matters in which they have an interest—so the minutes should indicate which directors were interested, that they left the room during the discussion or voting, and that the necessary quorum or majority of disinterested directors voted for the transaction.

The corresponding agenda for stockholder meetings is

☐ Introduction and opening remarks by a management representative

☐ Preelection discussion of candidates for board of directors, selection of auditors, and resolutions submitted for stockholder approval

☐ Ballotting

☐ Report by management to the stockholders on the corporation's status and financial performance

☐ Questions from the floor, general discussion among stockholders

☐ Report of the election results

*Practice Tip:* Stockholder meetings can get pretty wild and woolly if stockholders disagree with management, or among themselves. To prevent disruption, the corporation can use its bylaws to adopt reasonable rules such as a three-minute limit on speeches (or five minutes for someone introducing a motion or resolution, two minutes for comments on someone else's proposal); requiring speakers to be recognized by the chair before speaking; requiring them to get a number from an usher or election inspector before speaking, and then speaking only in turn; and limiting discussion at the open meeting to matters of general corporate interest by giving access to stockholders after the meeting to discuss their own personal, individual concerns. Time limits can be placed on discussion of any one motion or resolution (e.g., one hour) or to any item on the agenda. Some companies have a large clock on the podium to make it clear when time limits have run out; some even shut off the microphones when time limits have been exceeded.

## Minutes of Meetings

The minutes of a meeting usually start with a formal recital of

- ☐ The type of meeting: board or stockholder, regular or special.
- ☐ The time and place the meeting was held.
- ☐ How it was called: if it was a regular meeting, for which no notice is required; if notice was given as required by state law and the corporation's own charter and bylaws; or if notice of the meeting was waived.
- ☐ Who was present in person or by proxy. (If a stockholder who has granted a proxy appears at the meeting in person, the general rule is that the proxy is revoked.) Indicate that a quorum was present. Note if people came in after the meeting began, or left while it was still in progress—and make sure that departures did not bring attendance below a quorum.
- ☐ Any objections placed on the record—in today's litigious climate, stockholders and (especially) directors often want to indicate their objection to actions that they believe to be improper or illegal.
- ☐ Who presided at the meeting, and who kept the minutes.

The corporate secretary should take minutes at both board and stockholders' meetings, then have the minutes typed up or word processed and filed in the corporation's minute book in chronological order. Check to see if your state statute makes it mandatory to keep the corporation's minute books at its headquarters (this may be required to make it easier for stockholders to inspect the corporation's records). If this is not required, and if the corporation's charter and bylaws do not specify some other place, it's conventional to keep the minute books in the office of the corporation's attorneys.

Significant corporate actions should be memorialized in the minutes. This includes changes in the corporation's charter (Articles of Incorporation or bylaw amendments); matters of internal management (such as opening a bank account, delegating authority—e.g., by appointing special committees of the board of directors); entering into significant business contracts; and taking steps for tax reasons such as accumulating earnings, setting the compensation of directors, setting up a retirement plan, and reorganizing or liquidating the business.

These major actions are the most likely to be challenged by stockholders, dissident directors, corporations seeking a takeover, or third parties; the corporation must be able to show that the actions were taken at meetings that were held on proper notice, with a quorum present, and adopted with the necessary margin of votes. As discussed shortly, the "business judgment rule" means that courts will not attempt to run a normal corporation, or to second-guess the business decisions adopted by its board of directors. But when the directors defend against charges of impropriety, or seek indemnification if they are ordered to pay damages, they must be able to show that they attended meetings, took care to inform themselves of relevant facts, and explored the issues thoroughly before voting or abstaining from a vote. Properly drafted minutes make this burden much easier.

The corporate secretary is frequently required to certify that the documents appearing in the corporation's minute book are complete and accurate. Check with the corporation's lawyer to see if you are required to certify the minutes, and if so, whether the certificate must be sworn or can be unsworn.

*Practice Tip:* Make your corporation's records easier to use by creating an index to the minutes, and cross-references to matters that often arise (e.g., compensation of officers and directors, indemnification of directors). Depending on corporate needs and resources, this can be as simple as a handwritten index and a box of file cards or as complex as a computer database program. The typical card system identifies actions by subject matter and states the date of the meeting at which the action (e.g., amending the bylaws, adopting a resolution) was taken.

*Practice Tip:* It's a good idea to circulate the minutes of board meetings to the members and have them sign or initial the minutes to show their approval. That way, they can't complain that their opinions and statements were misrepresented if a stockholder (or anyone else) complains about a corporate action.

If state law and the corporation's governing instruments allow action to be taken without a meeting on the unanimous consent of the board or the stockholders, the proposals adopted on consent should be drawn up in the form of resolutions and included in the minute book as if a meeting had been held on the date of the consent action.

---

## SECRETARY'S CERTIFICATE (Shareholder List)

I, Phillip Barnes, am Secretary of Harper Woodwind Instruments, Inc., a corporation organized under the laws of the state of Tyler. I certify that the attached list is a true and accurate list of all the corporation's shareholders, their addresses, and respective stockholdings, all of whom were shareholders and entitled to vote as shown by the corporation's books and records as of the record date/date books were closed for transfer, _____ , 199 ____ . In evidence of this, I have signed this certificate and attached the corporation's seal today, _____ , 199 ____ .
Signature: _____

## NOTICE OF SPECIAL MEETING DEALING WITH RESOLUTION

Dear Stockholder:

A special meeting of the Bright Day Ltd.'s stockholders will be held at the corporate headquarters, 3904 Industrial Park Terrace, at _____ M. on _____ , 199 ____ . The meeting has been called by the Board of Directors pursuant to their resolution adopted_____ , 199 ____ so that the stockholders can consider and vote on the following resolution adopted by the Board of Directors on 199 ____ : [insert text of resolution]

The meeting may also involve any other business that might properly come before a meeting of stockholders.

## SECRETARY'S AFFIDAVIT THAT NOTICE OF ANNUAL MEETING WAS MAILED

State of Monroe
County of Lemoine ss:
Michelle Marmor Fielding, duly sworn, deposes and says:
I am the Secretary of Cured Marble Products, Inc., a corporation duly organized and doing business in the state of Monroe.
On _____ , 199 ____ , I caused notice of the corporation's annual meeting to be mailed first-class to every stockholder of record of Cured Marble Products, Inc., as of_____ , 199 ____ . Mailing was done to the last known address for the stockholder appearing in the corporation's books of record. A copy of the notice of meeting as mailed to the stockholders is attached to this affidavit and incorporated into it by reference.

Date: _____ , 199____
Signed: _____
Subscribed and sworn to before me on _____ , 199 ____

_____ , Notary Public

## SECRETARY'S AFFIDAVIT OF PUBLICATION OF NOTICE OF STOCKHOLDER'S MEETING

State of Madison,
County of Columbia ss:
After swearing to tell the truth, Edgar Milsap deposes and says that he is the Secretary of Emmanelle Corporation, which is duly organized and doing business in the state of Madison. He further deposes that, acting on orders from the corporation's Board of Directors, he caused a notice of the corporation's regular annual/special meeting of stockholders to be held _____ , 199 ____ to be published _____ time(s) each in the *Madison Courier-Herald* and *Columbia Times-Bee*, two newspapers of general circulation published in and circulating in the county of Columbia. A copy of the advertisement is attached to and incorporated by reference in Mr. Milsap's affidavit.

Publication began on _____ , 199 ____ and continued until _____ , 199 ____ , thus giving shareholders _____ days' notice, but not more than ____ days' notice, as required by state law/the corporation's charter and bylaws.

Date: _____ , 199____
Signed: _____
  On _____ , 199 ____ , a person known to me as Edgar Milsap appeared before me and swore, under penalty of perjury, that the above statement was true to the best of his knowledge.

Date: _____
Signed, Notary Public: _____


## PROOF OF SERVICE OF NOTICE OF
## STOCKHOLDERS' MEETING ON STOCKHOLDER

State of Roosevelt
County of Winteralia ss:
Mitchell Drullyan, being duly sworn, deposes and says that he is Secretary of Dillworth Relishes & Preserves, Inc., and that he made personal service of notice of a stockholder's meeting on Thomas Parkment, holder of 1,500 shares of Dillworth common stock. Personal service was made on _____ , 199 ____ by delivering to Parkment and leaving with him a true copy of the notice of meeting of stockholders to be held _____ , 199 ____ . A true copy of the notice of meeting is attached to this affidavit and made part of the affidavit.
Signed, _____ Secretary
Sworn to before me this _____ day of _____ , 199 ____ :

                                                                              Notary Public


## NOTICE OF ADJOURNED SPECIAL MEETING OF THE
## BOARD OF DIRECTORS

To the Directors of Marchbanks Electrical Co.:
Please be informed that on _____ , 199 ____ , the special meeting of the board of directors called for ____ M. at corporate headquarters, 193 Browning Terrace, could not be held because a quorum was not present. In this situation, the corporation's bylaws provide that another special meeting be called and that in this special situation, the presence of five directors will constitute a quorum.
  Accordingly, a meeting is called for _____ , 199 ____ , at ____ M., at corporate headquarters, to consider the possible purchase of E. M. Rosenzweig's electrical contracting business (now operated in sole proprietorship form) and other business that may properly come before a board of directors meeting.

## WRITTEN CONSENT OF DIRECTOR

I am a member of the Board of Directors of Beaverman's General Stores, Inc., and hereby consent to the following resolution:

Date: _____ , 199\_\_\_\_

Signature: _____

[Add Secretary's certificate as above]

## PROXY

I, Paul deKuyper, own 500 shares of the common stock of Jerri Fay, Inc. I hereby appoint Linda Travers as my proxy

☐ until I revoke this proxy or appear at a meeting and vote my shares personally

☐ for a period of 2 years

☐ for a period of 11 months

☐ only for the regular/special meeting of the shareholders scheduled to be held _____ , 199 \_\_\_\_ , or on the adjourned date of that meeting

☐ Linda Travers has full power to vote my shares as, in her discretion, she sees best

☐ Linda Travers is hereby directed to vote as follows:

☐ This proxy is given in connection with the sale/pledge of my shares, and hence is coupled with an interest and is irrevocable.

Date: _____ , 199\_\_\_\_

Signed: _____

## REVOCATION OF PROXY

I hereby REVOKE the proxy dated _____ , 199 \_\_\_\_ , under which I named Dale Sperling as my proxy with power to vote my shares of Lilac Tyme, Inc.'s common stock.

Date: _____ , 199\_\_\_\_

Signature: _____

## POSTCARD PROXY WITH NOTICE OF MEETING

### Proxy of Standish Lace Co. Solicited on Behalf of Management

By signing this proxy, the shareholder appoints Lloyd Standish, Arthur Collyer, and Frederick T. Liston as proxies with full power to vote all of his or her shares at the corporation's annual meeting to be held _____ , 199 \_\_\_\_ .

They intend to vote on behalf of management: to elect the management slate of directors (Jeremy Standish, Walter Hanlon, and Gregory Baylor), in favor of the amendments to the corporation's Articles of Incorporation favored by management, to ratify transactions taken by the board of directors in the preceding year, and other business properly brought before the meeting.

Date: _____ , 199____
Signed: _____
Number of Shares: _____

## PROXY OF VOTING TRUSTEE

The Abbotsford Bank and Trust Co. acts as Trustee under a voting trust agreement dated _____ , 199 ____ between the Bank and eleven shareholders including members of the Stine and Gordon families. The Bank hereby appoints George Russell as its proxy to attend the annual meeting/special stockholders' meeting of the DeLouria Electronics & Lasers, Inc., company to be held _____ , 199 ____ at the corporation's headquarters, 1119 Guadalcanal Boulevard, Shay's Landing, Roosevelt, or as adjourned.

Mr. Russell has full standing and power to vote all the shares of DeLouria Electronics & Lasers covered by the voting trust agreement, provided that he votes consistently with the provisions of the voting trust agreement.

## BALLOT FOR NONCUMULATIVE VOTING

Stenellida Corp., Inc., a Tyler Corporation
Annual meeting held _____ , 199 ____ .

I, [proxy for] the holder of ____ shares of common stock hereby cast my votes for the directors who will serve from this annual meeting until successors are elected at the next annual meeting.
☐ Management's slate of _____ directors
☐ The following persons: _____

_____          _____
Stockholder in person                                              Proxy for shareholder

## CUMULATIVE VOTING BALLOT

As the [proxy for] the holder of ____ shares, I am entitled to a number of votes equal to the number of shares times the number of directors to be elected, for a total of ____ votes which may be allocated in any way I choose among the candidates.

As directors to serve until the election of successors at the next annual meeting, I choose: _____
Candidate: _____
Number of votes for him/her: _____
Total: _____

_____                    _____
Stockholder in person                                                      Proxy for stockholder

## SHAREHOLDER CONSENT TO ACTION TAKEN BY BOARD OF DIRECTORS

I am a shareholder of Battaille-Lorrimer Corp., a Lincoln corporation. I own _____ shares of its common/preferred stock. I hereby give my consent to the following corporate action, although no meeting was held: _____

Date: _____ , 199_____
Signed: _____

## Or:

## SHAREHOLDER'S RESOLUTION RATIFYING ALL ACTIONS OF THE BOARD OF DIRECTORS

RESOLVED, that we approve and ratify all resolutions, activities, and proceedings by the corporation's Board of Directors and officers entered into or performed since the last annual meeting to promote the corporation's purposes and in its best interests.

## SECRETARY'S CERTIFICATE (Action on Consent)

I, _____ , Secretary of Battaille-Lorrimer Corp., hereby certify that these 38 numbered pages dated _____ , 199 _____ to _____ , 199 _____ contain and constitute the consent of all of the corporation's shareholders to the corporate action described therein. Therefore, I have signed this certificate and attached the corporation's seal as evidence of the shareholders' consent to the corporate action.

Date: _____ , 199_____
Signature: _____
Seal: _____

## EIGHTY-NINE SAMPLE RESOLUTIONS OF BOARD DIRECTORS AS REPORTED IN MINUTES OF CORPORATE MEETINGS

### No. 1: Resolution Adopting Promoter Contract

On _____ , 199_____ , the incorporators of this corporation signed a contract with _____ , whose address is _____ , to serve as promoter to obtain subscriptions for stock and undertake other requirements necessary to create a corporation under the laws of the state of _____ . It is hereby RESOLVED that the incorporator-promoter contract of _____ , 199 _____ be adopted by the corporation and become an obligation of the corporation itself, including the obligation to pay the sum of $_____ to the promoter to compensate him for his services.

### No. 2: Fixing the Record Date

RESOLVED that anyone who is a stockholder of record as of the close of business on _____ of each year (or, if this date is a Saturday, Sunday, or holiday, on the next business day) will be entitled to vote at the annual meeting for that year and will be entitled to notice of the meeting.

### No. 3: Resolution Authorizing Officers to Sign Checks, etc.

It is RESOLVED that any check, draft, bill of lading, contract, or document obligating the corporation in the ordinary course of business, other than a transaction requiring approval by the Board of Directors or stockholders, will be presumed valid if signed by the corporation's President or Vice-President and countersigned by its Treasurer or Assistant Treasurer.

### No. 4: Resolution re Bank Accounts

It is RESOLVED that the Corporation's Treasurer is authorized to open bank accounts in the Corporation's name, and make deposits to, and withdrawals from, such accounts on the Corporation's behalf. The number and type of accounts, and the bank(s) in which they are opened, is a matter for the Treasurer's own discretion. For this purpose, the Corporation's President will draw and sign checks, to be countersigned by the Treasurer and deposited by the Treasurer.

In addition to these accounts, it is RESOLVED that, at the President's discretion, s/he may open a special checking account to handle payroll and petty cash and the Corporation's President, Vice-President, and Treasurer can endorse checks on this account with no requirement for countersignature. The President is also authorized to rent a safe deposit box for the corporation, and corporate securities and books and records can be stored there; the person then serving as President and the members of the Executive Committee can have access to the box from time to time.

### No. 5: Board of Directors' Resolution re Expense Accounts

RESOLVED, that engaging in the corporation's business and marketing its products and services requires that, from time to time, its officers and executives incur expenses, for example, for travel, entertainment, office equipment and decoration, dues in social and professional organizations, books and publications, charitable contributions and events, and continuing education and training.

It is RESOLVED that the persons listed below be granted an expense account for the calendar/fiscal year of 199 ____ up to the amount endorsed against their names; that they use this expense account only for the corporation's legitimate business purposes; that no corporate funds be used to pay dues for any organization that practices racial, religious, or sex discrimination; that the recipients will not be entitled to any balance remaining in the account at the end of the year (the balance will revert to the corporate treasury); that expense account funds do not constitute compensation and will not be taxed as such; that each recipient of an expense account maintain records showing use and application of expense account funds for at least three years; that recipients of expense account funds produce these records when required by the corporation's treasurer, CPA, tax counsel, or the staff of any of these; and that each recipient, before his or her initial receipt of expense account funds, signs an undertaking to repay the corporation any expense account funds later determined by the corporation to have been obtained or used improperly.

RESOLVED, that the corporation's treasurer have discretion to administer expense account funds and determine the form in which they will be made available, for example, by issuing company credit cards, opening accounts, making cash advances, and/or reimbursing expenditures.

Person Receiving Expense Account: ____

Title: ____

Maximum Amount: ____

## No. 6: Board of Directors' Resolution to Qualify in Another State

The volume of orders/anticipated orders/potential transactions to be obtained in the state of Tyler makes it commercially feasible to open an office, employ sales staff, make purchases and sales, and engage in other activities constituting "doing business" in the state of Tyler. However, the advice of Janet Baumgarten, Esq., is that, prior to doing business in Tyler, this corporation must qualify there as a foreign corporation.

Therefore, it is RESOLVED that this corporation's officers consult Ms. Baumgarten and take all steps she recommends for this corporation to qualify as a foreign corporation in Tyler, including reserving its corporate name for use in that state; filing a certificate of qualification; paying the initial qualification fee and any continuing franchise, income, and sales taxes; obtaining a sales tax number; and appointing Jesse Woodhull, whose office address is 2319 The Groves, Lake Peak Point, Tyler, as this corporation's agent for service of process in the state of Tyler. That address will also serve as this corporation's Tyler office, and all necessary books and records of Tyler operations will be maintained there.

## No. 7: Board of Directors' Resolution Authorizing Issuance of a New Series of Stock

Article II, Section 5, of this corporation's Articles of Incorporation and Bylaw #22 give the Board of Directors the right and power at any time to issue Class B nonvoting common stock, up to an aggregate of 10,000 outstanding Class B shares. At this time, no Class B shares have been issued. In the judgment of the directors, it is now appropriate to issue 2,000 Class B nonvoting common shares, with a par value of $5 per share, and bearing all the rights and obligations of common shares (including treatment on liquidation of the corporation and entitlement to dividends), except that holders of Class B shares will only be entitled to vote on the terms and conditions on which holders of the corporation's preferred shares are permitted to vote.

It is RESOLVED that 2,000 Class B nonvoting common shares be issued; that the corporation's Secretary instruct its outside counsel, the firm of Gertner, Thomassy, and LaDeau, to prepare stock certificates; and that the corporation's President and Secretary file the certificates under the corporation's seal and perform any requirements under state and federal securities law for the issue and sale of such shares for cash; their exchange for patents, trade secrets, or other things of value; or for their use under the corporation's stock bonus plan.

## No. 8: Board of Directors' Resolution Authorizing Call of Preferred Stock

The capitalization of this corporation includes 5,000 shares of 8% cumulative preferred stock, with a par value of $20 per share. Four thousand shares of this stock are outstanding and held by members of the public; 1,000 shares are held by the corporation as treasury shares which cannot be reissued. Under Section 22.9 of this corporation's Articles of Incorporation, the powers of the Board of Directors include calling the corporation's preferred stock for redemption at any time that the Board sees fit in order to effectuate legitimate corporate objectives.

The Board has now reached a consensus that the corporation's capital structure and financial position would be improved by calling the 4,000 outstanding shares of preferred stock. The corporation has adequate funds which can be used to purchase this stock without imperilling corporate financial soundness.

It is RESOLVED that the 4,000 outstanding shares be called for redemption on _____ , 199_____ ("call date") at a price of $38 per share plus any unpaid dividends from the period _____ , 199_____ until the call date. It is also RESOLVED that the corporation's Secretary issue a notice of redemption (in a form acceptable to the corporation's legal counsel) giving at least 15, but not more than 45, days' notice of the call, by mail to everyone who was a holder of record of the preferred stock on _____ , 199_____ , and also by publication in a newspaper of general circulation in Wildflower County.

It is also RESOLVED that the Cold Spring Trust Company act as the corporation's agent for redemption of the preferred stock and that the corporation deposit sufficient funds on or before _____ , 199_____ to pay the redemption price plus accrued but unpaid dividends. The Cold Spring Trust Company is authorized to cancel the preferred stock certificates it receives in return for the appropriate payment, and also to cancel the certificates of preferred stock now held as treasury stock when such certificates are surrendered by the corporation's officers. It is further RESOLVED that the corporation reimburse the Cold Spring Trust Company for expenses of the redemption and cancellation and pay it a fee of $_____ for its services in this connection.

It is also RESOLVED that the corporation's officers execute, file, and acknowledge all forms and documents necessary to evidence the retirement of the shares and that the corporation's Articles of Incorporation be amended to eliminate all references to the preferred shares so retired.

## No. 9: Board of Directors' Resolution Authorizing Offer to Stockholders to Buy Newly Issued Common Stock

This corporation's Articles of Incorporation authorize the issuance of 25,000 shares of common stock. Fifteen thousand shares are already issued and outstanding. In order to raise additional capital, it is now deemed useful and in the corporation's best interests to issue an additional 5,000 shares of no-par common stock, to be sold to those who are already shareholders of the corporation, for $45 per share, payable in cash or cash and notes, subject to the preemptive rights provision of Article II,

Section 4, of this corporation's Articles of Incorporation. Such shares will have the same voting rights and rights on liquidation as the common shares already issued and outstanding.

It is RESOLVED that the Board of Directors issue 5,000 additional shares of no-par common stock and have subscription warrants and transfers mailed to everyone who is a stockholder of record as of _____ , 199____ , informing them of their right to purchase the newly issued shares by pro-rata subscription proportionate to their shareholdings in the already issued common stock, either by immediate cash payment or by payment of a ____ % cash deposit and executing a note to the corporation calling for payment in not more than eight quarterly installments at a ____ % APR.

It is further RESOLVED that the Board of Directors have stock certificates prepared for the new shares, to be issued when subscribing shareholders have paid [the first installment] of the consideration for the shares, and that the Board take any other action necessary and proper to effectuate the issuance of new common stock, including the appointment of the Cattleman's and Farmer's Trust Company as subscription agent to handle and process subscription warrants for the newly issued shares.

## No. 10: Board Resolution—Use Factoring as Financing Device

After hearing reports by this corporation's Treasurer and its accountant, Bernard Todd, CPA, and on examination of the corporation's books and records, this Board concludes that the corporation is fiscally sound and transacts a volume of business with creditworthy customers sufficient to meet the corporation's obligations. However, it is also the conclusion of this Board that collection of accounts receivable can be a time-consuming activity and that despite its basic financial soundness the corporation is subject to periodic cash flow difficulties.

Therefore, it is RESOLVED that the corporation adopt a policy of factoring [ ____ %] of its accounts receivable [aged over ____ days] by entering into transactions with McGurk & Sons or other factoring firm of comparable or better size, stature, and reputation.

## No. 11: Board of Directors' Resolution Declaring Dividend

This corporation's efforts for the first/second/third/quarter of fiscal 199 ____ have been crowned with financial success, and it is the intention of the Board of Directors to share this financial success with the corporation's shareholders. Therefore, it is RESOLVED that a dividend of $3 per common share/2% of the par value of the corporation's capital stock/7% on the preferred stock be declared for this quarter. This dividend will be payable on or before _____ , 199 ____ , to those who were stockholders of record on _____ , 199 ____ .

## No. 12: Board of Directors' Resolution Increasing Stated Capital

A special meeting of the corporation's stockholders was held on _____ , 199 ____ . At that meeting, the stockholders adopted a resolution by a vote of _____ to _____ (the text of which is annexed to this resolution) permitting the Board of Directors to issue up to _____ shares of additional common stock, in order to raise an additional $ ____ of capital to be used for corporate purposes such as research and development, adding new employees to the payroll, replacing obsolete equipment and adding new equipment, improving the manufacturing process, and enhancing the corporation's marketing efforts.

To implement this resolution, it is hereby RESOLVED by the Board of Directors that the Board authorize the issuance of ____ shares of common stock [which is already authorized but unissued], to be sold for $ _____ per share, that the issue be completed on or before _____ , 199 _____ , and that [in furtherance of their preemptive rights as provided by statute/this corporation's Articles of Incorporation/a resolution dated _____ , 199 _____ ], everyone who is a stockholder of record on _____ , 199 _____ (on which date the corporation's transfer books will be closed until _____ , 199 _____ ) be permitted to subscribe to these additional shares of common stock [as he or she desires/proportionate to his or her holdings of the common stock outstanding before the passage of this resolution]. The right to subscribe will extend until _____ , 199 _____ . Full payment must accompany each subscription.

## No. 13: Board of Directors' Resolution Decreasing Stated Capital

Eddie's Prime Meats, Inc., has a total stated capital of $400,000, consisting entirely of 10,000 shares of no-par common stock. The earned surplus account is currently in deficit to the extent of $69,235. The Board of Directors has studied the situation and determined that the best interests of the corporation would be served by eliminating the deficit by reducing the corporation's stated capital. Therefore, it is RESOLVED that the Board of Directors propose to the stockholders that the corporation's stated capital be reduced by $75,000 by means of debiting that amount against the stated capital account and transferring it to a newly created "reduction surplus account."

It is further RESOLVED that a special meeting of the stockholders be held at the corporation's headquarters on _____ , 19 _____ at _____ o'clock to consider this proposal, and that the Secretary promptly notify all stockholders of the meeting as required by state law.

RESOLVED, that, if the stockholders agree to this reduction of stated capital, that the corporation's President and Secretary will promptly notify the Secretary of State of the state of Monroe of the reduction, and the Treasurer will promptly reflect the change on the corporation's books by charging the reduction to the stated capital account, crediting the reduction to a newly created reduction surplus account, and then charging the reduction surplus account with the amount of $75,000, which will then be used to pay corporate liabilities and reduce the deficit.

## No. 14: Dispensing with the Regular Order of Business

RESOLVED, that the regular order of business be dispensed with, and that the meeting of _____ , 19 _____ instead be devoted to consideration of the following issues: (explain).

## No. 15: Dissent from Board Decision or Action

I, _____ , am a Director of _____ , Inc., and was present at the meeting of the Board of Directors held on _____ . After discussion, a vote was taken on the issue of _____ , and by a vote of _____ to _____ , the Board adopted a resolution. Mine was one of the dissenting votes. I am opposed to the decision/action taken by the Board because: _____ .

Therefore, I dissent from the Board's decision/action and require that my dissent be entered into, and made part of, the minutes of the meeting.

Date: _____ 19 _____
Signed: _____

## No. 16: Resolution re Salary (establishing reasonable compensation)

_____ has served as _____ of the _____ Corporation since _____ , 19\_\_\_\_ . During that time, s/he has rendered services that were invaluable in securing the corporation's success and its development as a prosperous corporation.

_____'s commitment to the success of the corporation has been so great that s/he has been willing to work unusually long hours, undertake tasks that, in a larger organization, would be divided among several well-paid employees, and work for a salary significantly below the market range for a highly trained executive performing the functions of Chief Executive Officer/Chief Operating Officer/Chairman of the Board/President/Vice-President/Secretary/Treasurer/Comptroller/Director of Marketing/Director of Research and Development [etc.].

Thanks in large part to _____'s efforts, the corporation has now achieved unprecedented levels of success and has a higher level of financial resources than in the past. Therefore, it is RESOLVED that _____'s salary be increased from \$\_\_\_\_ to \$\_\_\_\_ a year, in order to bring it into line with free market salaries for comparable positions in other companies and to acknowledge his/her efforts in earlier years that increased the corporation's prosperity. The increased salary level represents reasonable compensation for past services, the quantity and quality of services currently rendered, and motivation to continue serving the corporation faithfully and well. However, if, at any time, it is determined by a state or federal taxing authority that any portion of this salary is unreasonable and therefore not deductible by the corporation, _____ agrees to refund to the corporation any portion of his or her compensation adjudged to be unreasonable.

## No. 17: Board of Directors' Resolution Compensating Officers with Salary Plus Net Profit Share

This corporation was founded by, and depends for its success on the technical, marketing, and operational knowledge of its officers, Robert Rickman, George Czolgocz, and Peter Lorton, each of whom has provided unstinting and effective service to the corporation, although each could find many high-paid jobs outside the corporation. Therefore, it is RESOLVED that the compensation of each officer include salary and a bonus based on the corporation's net profits. Rickman's salary, for serving as President of the corporation, will be \$85,000 per year. Czolgocz's salary, for serving as Vice-President and Treasurer, will be \$79,000 per year, and Lorton's salary, for serving as Secretary, will be \$70,000 per year.

In addition, each will receive a bonus based on the corporation's net profits. The bonus will be paid in a lump sum, within 90 days of the end of the corporation's fiscal year. For this purpose, "net profits" are defined as gross profits minus an amount equal to 5% of the corporation's capital (to be set aside as further capital for expansion) and minus 10% depreciation on fixtures and equipment, 6% depreciation on buildings. Each year, Rickman's bonus will be 10% of net profits; Czolgocz and Lorton's bonus will equal 6% of net profits each. These bonus amounts are not cumulative, and no adjustment will be made to bonuses in later years to compensate for any year in which net profits are insufficient to permit the payment of bonuses.

## No. 18: Board of Directors' Resolution Authorizing Reimbursement of Money Advanced by an Officer, Director, or Employee

Acting on a request by [a duly authorized officer of] the corporation, on _____ , 199\_\_\_\_ , John Burbage, an officer/director/employee of the corporation advanced the sum of \$12,000 from his personal funds to Albert Sloan for the purpose of securing an option on real property owned by Sloan, to be purchased by the corporation/settling a claim by Sloan against the corporation/purchasing a trade secret owned by Sloan, for use in the corporation's business/other [describe]. Both Burbage and the corporation intended that this use of personal funds was for the corporation's benefit and would be reimbursed at the appropriate time.

It is hereby RESOLVED that the corporation appropriate, and the corporation's Treasurer pay, the sum of $12,000 to John Burbage (without interest), as reimbursement for the sum advanced for corporate purposes.

## No. 19: Board of Directors' Resolution Making Loan to Corporate Officer

Carol Benson Shellhammer, Vice-President of Operations, requests that the corporation lend her the sum of $25,000 at an annual percentage rate of prime plus 2% for a term of ten years, secured by a second mortgage on her home/her stock in the corporation/her future salary and bonuses/as an unsecured personal loan. This money is required to pay educational expenses for her children/for personal and family medical expenses/to buy/remodel a home/to pay capital gains taxes on the sale of her former home occasioned by her acceptance of her current job, and the relocation involved.

Providing this loan will reward Ms. Shellhammer for her contributions to the corporation and motivate her to work better and remain in the corporation's employ longer, by relieving some of her financial anxieties. The loan can be made as just described from corporate surplus, and without excessive financial risk to the corporation. The loan is bona fide; it is not dividend equivalent and is made on terms approximating an arm's-length loan. Because repayment is required, a loan rather than compensation is involved.

Therefore, it is RESOLVED that the corporation's counsel prepare a Loan Note and Agreement embodying the terms described and that the corporation lend the sum of $25,000 to Ms. Shellhammer on those terms.

## No. 20: Board of Directors' Resolution Adopting a Policy of Indemnification

The best interests of the corporation demand that it be able to attract, retain, and motivate individuals of the highest qualifications, talents, and ethical standards to serve as its officers and directors. Yet recruitment and retention are difficult in a litigious age in which directors and officers, or potential directors and officers, fear that they will be subjected to liability for actions or omissions taken honestly and conscientiously—and in which even eventual vindication is obtained only at high cost in time, effort, resources, and loss of reputation.

The corporate law of the state of _____ recognizes, in Sections _____ , that it is appropriate for corporations to indemnify their officers and directors for damages incurred in the course of their service to the corporation, and for litigation expenses. Therefore, it is RESOLVED that this corporation's bylaws be amended to permit indemnification of officers and directors in cases not involving moral turpitude, self-dealing, or conflict of interest and that, in cases in which indemnification is proper, it extend to litigation expenses as well as to damages. It is also RESOLVED that the Board of Directors recommend to the stockholders that they adopt the proposed amendment.

## No. 21: Board of Directors' Resolution Awarding Bonuses

Awarding bonuses to [high-performing] employees has the effect of encouraging hard work and excellent results. Furthermore, from time to time, the corporation conducts surveys to see how its compensation of officers, directors, and employees compares to compensation provided by other similar companies including the corporation's competitors; payment of competitive salaries also encourages recruitment and retention of a superior work force.

Therefore, it is RESOLVED that everyone who has completed one year/six months of service for the corporation be awarded a bonus equal to _____% of his or her base compensation for the year and that the bonus be paid in the form of a single check distributed at the same time as the paycheck for the pay period ending _____ , 199____ OR it is RESOLVED that the persons listed on the attached schedule be paid a one-time bonus in the amount given on the schedule, in gratitude for their superior performance this year and to motivate them to continued excellent work and results/to bring their compensation into line with the compensation of those performing similar services for other companies.

It is further RESOLVED that the Treasurer charge these bonuses to the corporation's salary account.

## No. 22: Board of Directors' Resolution Adopting a Stock Bonus Plan

In the judgment of the Board of Directors, the adoption of a stock bonus plan, and the award of stock bonuses from time to time to qualified employees, is an appropriate and cost-effective way to motivate employees to better performance and thus to enhance corporate profits and the value of the corporation's shares. To this end, it is RESOLVED that a stock bonus plan be adopted in the form attached to this resolution (and incorporated into it by reference), on condition that it is ratified by the stockholders at the special meeting to be held _____ , 199____ .

## No. 23: Board of Directors' Resolution Authorizing Payment of Club Dues for Officer(s)

It has come to the attention of the Board of Directors that many business and civic leaders of our community belong to the University Club/Commercial & Civic Club/Clear Lake County Club, that the premises of this club provide a suitable location for corporate entertaining and press conferences, and that valuable business contacts can be made there. Thus, providing the corporation's President and Vice-President with club membership would promote the corporation's goodwill and public image and would likely lead to expansion of its business and supplier relationships. Former Mayor Laurence Naismith has agreed to nominate the President and Vice-President for membership. Our investigation discloses that the Club does not, by policy or practice, discriminate on the basis of race, sex, or national origin.

Therefore, it is RESOLVED that the corporation's President and Vice-President apply for membership in said Club and that the corporation reimburse them for their application fee, annual fees, locker fees, greens fees, equipment rental, meals, and bar bills actually used for corporate entertaining as distinct from personal and social use of club facilities.

## No. 24: Board of Directors' Resolution to Investigate Adoption of a Group Term Life Insurance Plan

In light of the motivating effect on employees obtainable on favorable tax terms for the employer by establishing a program of employer-paid group insurance, it is hereby RESOLVED that the corporation's treasurer investigate the terms offered by various insurance companies and negotiate with them to secure favorable terms for providing a life insurance policy in the amount of $5,000 pursuant to a program of group term life insurance, for all employees with a year or more of service. It is further

RESOLVED that the Treasurer report to the Board of Directors on the terms offered by the various insurance companies and that the Board of Directors select an insurer by majority vote.

## No. 25: Board of Directors' Resolution Adopting a Group Term Life Insurance Plan

After considering the report of Alvin Dennis, Treasurer, it is our judgment that the terms offered by the Constantia Insurance Co. are the most favorable; it is RESOLVED that the corporation enter into a plan of group term life insurance with Constantia, that a policy in the amount of $5,000 be purchased for every full-time corporate employee who has completed one year of service, and that the policy be maintained as long as the employee remains an active employee.

## No. 26: Board Resolution Authorizing Purchase of Life Insurance on the Life of an Officer

In order to make provision for the corporate losses likely to ensue after the untimely death of the corporation's President/Vice-President/Secretary/Treasurer until a replacement can be selected and can begin effective work, OR

In order to motivate the corporation's President/Vice-President/Secretary/Treasurer by demonstrating that the financial welfare of his/her family is important to the corporation.

It is hereby RESOLVED that the corporation purchase a term/whole life policy carrying a death benefit in the amount of $_____ on the life of _____ , the corporation's President/ Vice-President/Secretary/Treasurer from the _____ Life and Casualty Company/from the insurer recommended by _____ , the corporation's insurance broker/from the company offering the best terms for a policy on the life of the officer, and that the corporation maintain the policy in force and pay the premiums as long as he or she continues to serve in that office, and as long as the premiums constitute an ordinary and necessary business expense deductible as such by the corporation.

The corporation will at all times be the owner of the policy, possessing all incidents of ownership (e.g., beneficiary designation, loans against any cash value the policy possesses). The corporation will [irrevocably] be designated as the beneficiary of such policy/the officer's spouse/ child _____ will be named as beneficiary.

## No. 27: Resolution Authorizing Sale of Policy

_____ , the insured under policy #_____ issued by _____ Life & Casualty Co., in the amount of $_____ and with the corporation as beneficiary, serves/served as the corporation's President/Vice-President/Secretary/Treasurer from _____ , 19_____ to _____ , 199_____ /to the present, but has tendered his/her resignation effective _____ , 199_____ / but intends to retire on _____ , 199_____ /has been removed from office effective _____ , 199_____ . Hence, it is no longer necessary or desirable that the corporation maintain insurance on his/her life after that date. Therefore, it is RESOLVED that the corporation sell this insurance policy to _____ for the sum of $_____ , to be paid in a lump sum/in _____ equal quarterly/monthly installments, and that the appropriate corporate officers execute any assignment or other document necessary to sell, assign, and transfer the corporation's entire interest in the policy to the insured.

## No. 28: Beneficiary Designation Under a Split Dollar Plan

Seaman's Rest Life Insurance Co. Beneficiary Designation Policy 86-2322-IV49-3047
Insured: Paul Kramer

Baffin Bay Waterproofs, Inc. (Paul Kramer's employer), and Grace Kramer (Paul Kramer's wife) are hereby designated as beneficiaries under this policy to receive benefits under the policy, subject to policy provisions and any loans or assignments outstanding against the policy at the time of the insured's death.

On the death of the insured, policy proceeds will be payable as follows:

To Baffin Bay Waterproofs, the cash value that would have been payable on the policy anniversary following the insured's death, plus unpaid dividends and the dividend for the year of death, minus outstanding policy loans. Baffin Bay will also be entitled to a refund of any premium it has paid for any time after the end of the policy month in which the insured's death occurs.

Any remaining policy proceeds will be paid to Grace Kramer if she survives Paul Kramer; otherwise, to Paul Kramer's executor(s) or administrator(s).

Paul Kramer's consent is required for any change of beneficiary designation.
Signed: Paul Kramer                                                                     Baffin Bay

## No. 29: Board of Directors' Resolution Authorizing Gift to Widow

We note with sorrow that Stanley Germaine, who served for many years as Treasurer of this corporation, passed away on _____ , 199____ . We extend our sympathy to his family, and in gratitude for his many years of devoted and effective service to the corporation, it is hereby RESOLVED that the sum of $25,000 be paid to his widow, Eleanor Germaine in ten equal monthly installments, beginning _____ , 199____ /that the corporation assume payments of the tuition of Stanley Germaine, Jr., as long as he remains an undergraduate student in good standing at the University of Chicago/that the corporation purchase a single-premium annuity making monthly payments for the period of ten years to his widow, Eleanor Germaine, or her heirs. This payment will be made irrespective of whether it is determined that the payment will be deductible by the corporation.

## No. 30: Board of Directors' Resolution Adopting a Profit-Sharing Plan

Due in large part to the successful efforts of its work force, this corporation has achieved a measure of financial security and profits can be anticipated in all or virtually all future quarters. In order to reward past loyal services and motivate continued performance and innovation, the Board wishes to adopt a profit-sharing plan that will offer tax benefits to the corporation as well as benefits to the employees. Therefore, it is RESOLVED that the profit-sharing plan drafted by Ralph Douglass, Esq., of the firm of Siebald & Douglass (the corporation's outside counsel) be adopted, subject to approval of the stockholders, and that the corporation grant Ralph Douglass its power of attorney to secure an IRS ruling that this profit-sharing plan qualifies under Internal Revenue Code Sections 401(a) and 404. Once this ruling has been approved, the Board will call a special meeting of the stockholders and request that they approve adoption of the plan.

It is also RESOLVED that the corporation's Secretary be authorized and directed to sign the Trust Agreement between the corporation and the Federal Amalgamated Bank & Trust Company as Trustee, to affix the corporation's seal to the trust agreement, and take other steps necessary to bring the agreement into operation.

## No. 31: Board of Directors' Resolution Establishing a Self-insured Medical and Dental Plan for Key Employees

It is recognized that the high cost of medical and dental care is a major challenge for those seeking to make useful and practical financial plans. In order to motivate certain key employees of the corporation by relieving them of a degree of anxiety, it is hereby RESOLVED that a medical and dental expense reimbursement plan be adopted covering those individuals serving as President, Vice-President, Secretary, Treasurer, and General Manager and their dependents, during their tenure in such offices.

It is further RESOLVED that the plan become effective as of _____ , 199____.

The plan will provide either direct payment or reimbursement (evidenced by bills and proof of payment) of medical and dental expenses incurrent on behalf of current key employees and their dependents, up to a maximum of $5,000 per year per key employee. Expenses qualifying under this plan are those defined under Internal Revenue Code Section 213 and not paid by insurance, government programs, liability insurance, or other third-party payors.

Each covered key employee will be given a copy of this resolution; the copy is to be signed, dated, and placed in the employee's personnel file.

## No. 32: Board of Directors' Resolution Setting Up a Scholarship or College Loan Plan

The Board of Directors recognizes that financing a child's college education is one of the more difficult challenges facing families today and takes notice of the fact that student grants and loans are harder to get than in prior years, and bear a higher interest rate. The Board also acknowledges that relieving financial anxiety motivates employees to work harder and that the corporation must attract a new generation of highly trained and skillful employees. Therefore, it is in the corporation's best interests to provide scholarships and student loans for deserving students and their families who are corporate employees.

It is hereby RESOLVED that the corporation adopt the Model Corporate Scholarship Program developed by the University Aid Foundation (a copy of the program is attached and hereby incorporated by reference) and that the corporation appropriate a sum of money each year (determined with reference to the corporation's financial status and the number of scholarship applications submitted by employees and employees' children) to provide scholarships. Scholarships will be awarded without regard to race, sex, or national origin, based on demonstrated financial need, standardized test scores, and high school and college grades. The parents' status within the company and stock ownership will not be used as positive determining factors in the award of scholarships.

RESOLVED that the corporation adopt the Model Student Loan Program developed by the University Aid Foundation (a copy of which is attached to and incorporated by reference in, this resolution), and that the corporation appropriate a sum of money each year to provide student loans at an interest rate of prime plus 2%, with payment deferred until six months after the student graduates or otherwise ceases to be a college student in good standing. Loans will be awarded on a nondiscriminatory basis premised on demonstrated financial need and unavailability of other financing sources; parents' corporate status and stock ownership will not be factors in the award of student loans.

## No. 33: Board of Directors' Resolution on Plan Termination

Under Section _____ of this corporation's Articles of Incorporation/of the Pension Plan and Trust adopted by this corporation on _____ , 199_____ , termination of the pension plan is permissible under certain named circumstances, including a change in ownership of the corporation. Inasmuch as this company is in the process of undergoing a sale to/merger with _____ Corp., as detailed in the Minutes of the Board of Directors meeting(s) held _____ , 199_____ and as set forth in resolutions adopted by the Board on those dates, it is hereby RESOLVED that the Pension Plan and Trust known as _____ be terminated as of _____ , 19_____ , provided that the Internal Revenue Service and Pension Benefits Guarantee Corporation have ruled favorably on the termination of the plan. Once the favorable rulings have been obtained, it is RESOLVED that the plan's trustees distribute the plan's assets to the participants, that the trust terminate, and that any surplus revert to the corporation.

It is further RESOLVED that the corporation's officers be directed to take all actions reasonably necessary to obtain the Treasury and PBGC approval as soon as possible.

## No. 34: Resolution Appointing a General Counsel

It is hereby RESOLVED that _____ , Esq., of the firm of _____ be appointed as outside General Counsel to the corporation for the period _____ – _____ , and that s/he be paid a retainer of $_____ per year (in equal quarterly/monthly installments) to cover all advice and legal work normally performed by outside general counsel, but not including litigation, which will be billed to the corporation at _____ 's then-prevailing hourly rates or subject to his/her then-prevailing contingent fee structure.

## No. 35: Resolution Engaging an Auditor

It is RESOLVED by the Board of Directors/Stockholders that the CPA firm of _____ , whose address is _____ , be hired to audit the corporation's books and records for the calendar year 199_____ , for a fee of $_____ under a written retainer agreement executed by the corporation's Board of Directors.

## No. 36: Appointment of Purchasing Agent

RESOLVED that _____ be designated as Purchasing Agent for _____ Corporation, authorized to make purchases of [explain] _____ and obligate the Corporation up to a total of $_____ outstanding at any one time, and that this authority will continue until expressly revoked by the Board of Directors.

## No. 37: Appointment of Renting Agent

_____ Corporation owns a factory/office/commercial residential/mixed-use building located at _____ . Successful operation of such a building depends on maintaining a low vacancy rate and performing many managerial tasks outside the corporation's normal range of expertise but not requiring the addition of full-time corporate staff. Therefore, it is RESOLVED that _____ Realty be appointed as rental agent for the building, for the period running from _____ , 199_____ to carry out the normal functions performed by a rental agent, such as performing any maintenance or repairs needed to maintain the building in good tenantable condition, to sign rental leases in the Corporation's name and on its behalf, to find suitable tenants when vacancies occur, and to collect rents and remit them to the Corporation less a commission of _____ % of the gross rent roll and less any allowable expenses documented in a monthly report prepared in a form satisfactory to the Corporation.

## No. 38: Resolution Approving Proposed Contract

Negotiations between this Corporation and _____ , Inc., have been successfully concluded, and both corporations have agreed in principle to the terms of a _____-year contract dealing with _____ . The President of this Corporation has fully informed the Board of Directors about the course of the negotiations, the proposed contract terms, and the advantages and disadvantages of adopting such a contract. In the judgment of the Board of Directors, adoption of the contract is in the corporation's best interests, and it is RESOLVED that the President is authorized and empowered to enter into the contract and sign the contract on behalf of and binding the Corporation.

## No. 39: Board of Directors' Resolution Authorizing Purchase of Real Estate

Demographic and economic studies show that the East Wychwood area is likely to undergo continued expansion of population and increase in real estate values for at least the next decade. Furthermore, East Wychwood has easy access to highways and rail and air transportation. In light of these advantages, it is our judgment that purchase of a plant and office building in East Wychwood would be advantageous to the corporation, and it is RESOLVED that the corporation make an offer to Joseph Helmond to purchase the land and buildings located at Highway 43 and Route 19A, block 75, lot B, in East Wychwood, Lancelot County, Tyler, for the sum of $850,000. This plot contains two buildings, a two-story factory building and a six-story office building, zoned appropriately for manufacturing and commercial activities.

It is also RESOLVED that the offer be made to purchase the land and buildings with a deposit of $50,000 to be paid at the signing of the contract of sale; $50,000 to be paid at closing in return for a warranty deed conveying good and marketable title; the balance to be paid by assuming the mortgage on the property now held by the Squires National Bank/on execution of a purchase money mortgage with a 20-year term, bearing interest at an APR of prime plus 1%/conditional on the corporation's securing a 20-year mortgage at a fixed interest rate no higher than 11%; if no such mortgage is obtainable, the corporation will have the right to withdraw from the contract of sale and receive its deposit back.

It is further RESOLVED that the corporation's President and Secretary enter into all documents necessary to effectuate the purchase and secure any necessary mortgage financing and to set the corporation's seal on such documents.

## No. 40: Board of Directors' Resolution Authorizing Purchase of a Business

On examination of the business plan and disclosure documents submitted by Steven Nazorino, a sole proprietor doing business as Downtown General Contracting and Remodeling/the partnership of Rawson and Patrick/Craigmuire Ltd. Inc., we believe that purchase of this entire business by this corporation would be a simple and cost-effective method of acquiring valuable assets, trade secrets, inventory, and goodwill and access to profitable business sites. Therefore, it is RESOLVED that this corporation offer to purchase the entire business so described, for the sum of $1.2 million cash and notes/$250,000 in cash and 20,000 shares of this corporation's common stock/35,000 shares of this corporation's common stock, contingent on opinion of our counsel, Jumel & Tandini, that the purchase can be consummated with favorable tax treatment for this corporation. It is further RESOLVED that, if the business to be purchased accepts our offer, or that the course of negotiations leads to a mutually acceptable modified offer, that a special meeting of this corporation's stockholders be held as soon as it can conveniently be called, to ratify the purchase transaction.

## No. 41: Resolution of Authorization re Tax Compromise

On _____ , 199____ , this corporation requested that the Internal Revenue Service enter into an agreement respecting the final determination of its income taxes for the calendar/fiscal year(s) _____-_____ . Because a corporation's President requires authorization to sign such an agreement, it is RESOLVED that the President of this corporation be authorized to sign an agreement with the Commissioner of Internal Revenue with respect to such taxes.

## No. 42: Resolution Authorizing Reimbursement of Relocating Employees' Moving Expenses

Corporate employees _____ and _____/the employees listed on the attached Schedule A have relocated themselves and their families to corporate headquarters/to the branch office located at _____ /to the plant located at _____ / to _____ on temporary assignment to [describe]: _____ and have undergone extensive expenses for finding new housing, placing their previous homes on the market, traveling to the new job location, moving their furniture and household goods, and taking temporary or hotel accommodations until their new homes are ready for occupation. It is hereby RESOLVED that, on submission of receipted bills showing payment of such expenses or copies of canceled checks used to pay such expenses, employees be reimbursed for legitimate moving expenses, up to a maximum of $____ per employee.

## No. 43: Board of Directors' Resolution Appointing Branch Manager

_____ Corporation has qualified to do business as a foreign corporation in the state of _____ , effective as of _____ , 199____ . It is RESOLVED that the corporation open a branch office in that state to transact business, to be located at _____ . It is further RESOLVED that _____ be appointed to serve as branch manager for a term of ____ years, at a base salary of $____ plus deferred compensation as provided by the resolution adopted _____ , 199____ and bonuses as voted by the Board; and that such branch office serve as the corporation's registered office, and the branch manager as the registered agent for service of process, in the state of _____ .

## No. 44: Board of Directors' Resolution Authorizing Acceptance of an Offer to Sell Property

In the judgment of this corporation's officers and managers, operation of one particular line of its business, manufacture of _____ /operation of a store/office/restaurant/other at

_____ /marketing and sale of _____ is unprofitable, and there is no prospect of its becoming profitable in the foreseeable future. However, the corporation owns tools, equipment, and inventory associated with this line of business (as described on Schedule A attached to this resolution), which could be converted to cash usable in other corporate endeavors or provide other valuable consideration if a buyer can be found at a reasonable price.

Paragon/Exemplar Corporation, whose headquarters is located at 4992 Detroit Avenue, Marbury, Madison, has offered to purchase the assets associated with this line of business for the sum of $85,000/in exchange for 2,000 shares of its common stock, carrying a current fair market value of $47 per share/in exchange for machinery, equipment, and inventory as described in Schedule B, appraised by Edward Compton, ASA, as having a fair market value of $86,500. The Paragon/Exemplar offer is set out in a Resolution adopted by its Board of Directors on _____ , 199_____ ; a copy of this resolution is attached to this resolution.

In the judgment of this corporation's directors, based on advice of counsel and its independent auditor, it is in this corporation's best interests to accept the offer, which will have favorable economic and tax consequences. Therefore, it is RESOLVED that the offer by Paragon/Exemplar to purchase the listed assets be accepted according to its terms. The sale does not constitute a Bulk Sale as defined by Chapter 38, Section 504, of the Laws of the State of Madison, nor does it constitute a sale of all or substantially all of this corporation's assets such as would require consent of the shareholders.

## No. 45: Board of Directors' Resolution or Stockholders' Resolution—Lease of Corporate Property

The corporation, acting on advice from its counsel and auditors, has determined that it is financially advisable for the corporation to lease certain unused assets to Quinella Corporation for a term of five years, beginning _____ , 199 _____ . Such assets do/do not constitute substantially all of the assets of this corporation.

Quinella Corporation has agreed to pay $ _____ per year [escalating to $ _____ per year over the lease term/ plus _____ % of Quinella Corporation's gross/net profits] for lease of these assets and to assume payment of taxes and insurance premiums on the leased assets. The terms of the proposed lease are set out in Attachment A, which is incorporated by reference into this resolution.

RESOLVED that the Resolution of the Board of Directors to enter into this lease adopted at their meeting of _____ , 199 _____ be ratified/that in that the shareholders have approved this lease transaction at a special meeting on _____ , 199 _____ by a vote of _____ to _____ , that this corporation enter into the leasing transaction on terms specified in Attachment A [subject to approval by the holders of a majority/two-thirds of this corporation's stock].

## No. 46: Resolution of Lessor's Board of Directors Enforcing a Lease

This corporation entered into a lease agreement with Burton Sammish, Inc., on _____ , 199 _____ , covering certain property of this corporation. The terms of this lease provide for continuing lease payments and also provide that, when any payment is in default for more than _____ days after the scheduled payment date, this corporation, as lessor, is entitled to issue a notice of default. If default has not been cured within _____ days of notice, this corporation as lessor has the right to declare the lease terminated and retake the leased property.

Burton Sammish, Inc., has been in default since _____ , 199 ____ in that: _____
RESOLVED that this corporation issue a notice of default to Burton Sammish, Inc., specifying that if default is not cured on or before _____ , 199 ____ , this corporation will vacate the lease, retake the leased property, and, if necessary, bring suit for the unpaid balance under the lease and other damages.

## No. 47: Board of Directors' Resolution: Enter into a Sublease of a Commercial Lease

This corporation is the lessee of ____ square feet of store/office space located at Patriot Plaza Mall, 3914 Acacia Lane, 2 Silicon Towers, Suite 919 under a lease dated _____ , 199 ____ , commencing _____ , 199 ____ for a term of ____ years [with an option to renew for a further ____ years]. The lessor is Circle in the Star Realty Corporation.

This corporation no longer needs this space/cannot operate the space profitably/no longer wishes to maintain a business presence in the city of _____ /other:

Negotiations with the Gilmartin Corporation have led to Gilmartin's offer to sublease [ ____ square feet] of this space from this corporation on terms set out in Attachment A, which is incorporated by reference into this Resolution. The officers of this corporation have agreed in principle to the terms of the sublease agreement set out in Attachment A.

Under Article C, Section 5, of this corporation's lease of the space, Circle in the Star's consent is required for all subleases; however, such consent may not be unreasonably withheld.

It is RESOLVED that the officers of this corporation request Circle in the Star's consent for the sublease to Gilmartin Corporation; it is further RESOLVED that this corporation's officers adduce proof that Gilmartin Corporation is an appropriate subtenant, that is, in good corporate and financial standing, creditworthy, engaged in a line of business substantially identical to that of this corporation, but not violative of Circle in the Star's promises of exclusivity to other tenants. It is also RESOLVED that, if Circle in the Star consents to the sublease, this corporation enter into a sublease agreement with Gilmartin Corporation on the terms set out in Attachment A.

## No. 48: Board of Directors' Resolution to Sublease Commercial Space Under Another Corporation's Lease

This corporation requires [further] store/office space.

_____ square feet of space located at Patriot Plaza Mall/3914 Acacia Lane/2 Silicon Tower, Suite 919 are available by sublease from Wirebird Entertainment Company, lessee under a lease dated _____ , 199 ____ , having Circle in the Star Realty Corp. as lessor.

This corporation and Wirebird have reached an agreement in principle, set out in Appendix I attached to this resolution and incorporated into it by reference.

Wirebird's officers have agreed to seek a resolution from Wirebird's Board of Directors authorizing the adoption of this agreement and a request to Circle in the Star Realty Corp. that it consent to the sublease of this space for a term of ____ years commencing _____ , 199 ____ .

RESOLVED that, if Wirebird obtains this consent and proper corporate authorization, this corporation enter into the sublease on terms set out in Appendix I and that this corporation furnish any information needed to demonstrate its suitability as a subtenant.

## No. 49: Board of Directors' Resolution: Assign a Commercial Lease

It is the judgment of this Board that the best interests of this corporation would be served by assignment of the balance of the lease term and that all rights under the lease, to Barkman & Bergman Corp. Inc., which will then assume all rights and obligations of tenancy. This corporation will pay Barkman & Bergman Corp., Inc./Barkman & Bergman Corp., Inc., has agreed to pay this corporation _____ the sum of $ _____ to motivate it to enter into the assignment.

Therefore, it is RESOLVED that this corporation seek the lessor's consent to assignment of the balance of the lease term [and that the payment of $ _____ be made to induce Barkman & Bergman Corp., Inc., to enter into the assignment transaction].

## No. 50: Consent by Board of Directors of Lessor to Assignment or Sublease

Wirebird Entertainment Corp., lessee of a property described as _____ , under a lease dated _____ , 199 _____ , commencing _____ , 199 _____ for a term of _____ years, has requested permission to assign the balance of the lease term/sublease _____ square feet of the space for a term of _____ years to Gilmartin Corp. On investigation, this Board has found that the financial status of Gilmartin is at least equal to that of Wirebird; that its proposed use of the space is appropriate, does not violate the rights of other tenants or any law or ordinance; and that consenting to the assignment/sublease would not be financially injurious to this corporation/would tend to mitigate this corporation's losses [and is likely to be financially more advantageous than exercising our right under the lease to reenter and relet the premises].

In light of these considerations, it is RESOLVED that this corporation consent to the sublease/ assignment, effective _____ , 199 _____ , on the terms requested by Wirebird.

## No. 51: Resolution of Lessor's Board of Directors Calling for Termination of a Lease

Mandall Manufacturing Ltd., lessee of certain property of this corporation under an agreement dated _____ , 199 _____ has been in default on lease payments since _____ , 199 _____ .

RESOLVED that the President of this corporation instruct its attorneys, Stanshall, Borley and Mays, to serve a notice to return leased property/vacate the leased premises on the lessee, as provided by Section IV.3 of the lease agreement, and that the President of this corporation instruct the law firm to negotiate with the lessees for payment of the amounts in default and, if necessary, to bring suit on behalf of the corporation to recover the amounts in default plus any applicable damages.

## No. 52: Resolution by Lessor's Board of Directors Consenting to Assignment of a Lease

RESOLVED that the request of Amalfitano Corp., lessee of certain property belonging to this corporation under a lease agreement dated _____ , 199 _____ , that the lease agreement be assigned to Saturday Night Fun Entertainment, Inc., be GRANTED. RESOLVED that this corporation's President and Secretary execute a new lease agreement with Saturday Night Fun Entertainment, Inc., as lessee.

## No. 53: Board of Directors' Resolution Authorizing Sale-Leaseback of Real Estate

This Board has concluded that this corporation requires additional working capital and that, if such capital is secured, the corporation's prospects for profits (and funds to make continuing payments) are excellent. After receiving advice on the legal and tax consequences, this Board has decided that a sale-leaseback of real property owned by this corporation would be prudent and in the best interests of the corporation and its stockholders.

A tentative agreement, subject to corporate [and shareholder] approval, has been reached with Emantee Copper Co./Seaman's Rest Insurance Co./this corporation's employee benefit plan and trust under which it will purchase real estate now owned by this corporation: a 600' by 200' plot, with two buildings located on it, located at Block 18, Lot 22, in the County of Manfred, for the sum of $1.25 million.

After the purchase, it has been tentatively agreed that this corporation continue to use this real property, leasing it back from the purchaser for 25 years at an annual net rental of $100,000 [escalating to $150,000 a year]. RESOLVED that the corporation enter into a sale-leaseback transaction with the potential buyer, on terms set out in Exhibit A (contract of sale) and Exhibit B (lease agreement), which are hereby incorporated by reference, and that the President and Secretary of this corporation execute all required documents, including a deed to the property, and affix the corporate seal to them.

## No. 54: Classification of Directors

[Consult state law, articles of incorporation, and bylaws to see if this can be done by the Board of Directors or whether it requires a stockholders' resolution.]

The Board of Directors of _____ Corporation consists of _____ Directors. The current system of corporate governance calls for an annual election of the entire Board of Directors. However, this can result in an entirely new Board each year, with no carry-over of experienced Directors from earlier years.

In order to promote efficiency, the Board of Directors/stockholders of _____ Corporation wish to divide the Board of Directors into three classes, each class consisting of _____ directors. The term of office of the first class of directors will expire at the next annual meeting of the corporation, the term of office of directors of the second class will expire at the annual meeting in the following year, and the term of office of the third class of directors will expire at the annual meeting two years after the next annual meeting. Directors in each class will be elected for a three-year term.

## No. 55: Date of Regular Board Meeting

RESOLVED that the Board of Directors will hold regular monthly meetings, on the (date/first, second, third, fourth Monday, Tuesday, Wednesday, Thursday, Friday) of each month, at _____ M. If any regular meeting is scheduled for a national or religious holiday, the meeting will be held on the next business day that is not a holiday after the scheduled meeting date. These meetings will be in addition to the regular annual meeting of the Board of Directors. The monthly directors' meetings will be held at (the corporation's headquarters/ _____ ). It is not required that directors be notified of each meeting; this resolution serves as official notice.

## No. 56: Changing the Place of a Board Meeting

RESOLVED that (because the space normally used is unavailable/for the convenience of certain Board members/for the convenience of non-Board members invited to address the meeting/[explain]), the Board of Directors meeting scheduled for _____ at _____ M. will be held at _____ rather than the usual location. The Secretary is responsible for notifying all Board members and those invited to the meeting of the change.

## No. 57: Inviting an Expert to a Board Meeting

_____ , of [give firm or other credentials] has important information relevant to a matter under consideration by the Board of Directors: [explain the matter]. So that the Board can use this information and experience in evaluating the matter to be decided, it is RESOLVED that _____ be invited to attend the Board meeting to be held on _____ at _____ M. and that the Secretary notify him/her of the invitation.

## No. 58: Resolution Creating Committee of Board of Directors

In order to assist the full Board of Directors to obtain the information and expert advice necessary to carry out its functions, it is hereby RESOLVED that a permanent standing/temporary committee of the Board of Directors be created to deal with the issue of potential litigation involving _____ / compensation of officers and directors/environmental issues affecting or potentially affecting the corporation/search for a new President/CEO for the corporation/selection of investments for the corporation/source and nature of optimal insurance coverage for the corporation/possible merger or acquisition of or by the corporation/investigation of an alleged inventory shortage/investigate the possibility of hiring a management consultant, and selecting such a consultant/other [explain]; [Note: A litigation committee appointed when shareholder derivative action is threatened should include only outside, noninterested directors, who must be prepared for a heavy time commitment: perhaps 2–3 weeks of full-time work.]

The committee will consist of _____ persons: the first _____ members of the Board who volunteer for the task/the corporation's treasurer, comptroller, and outside auditor/the _____ members of the Board getting the largest number of votes in a special ballot of the Board to be held on _____ , 199_____ .

The committee will investigate its issue and report to the entire Board, verbally and in writing, on or before _____ , 199_____ /at the March meeting of the Board of Directors/at the annual directors' meeting/as requested by the full Board.

The committee is authorized to retain on the corporation's behalf and to submit invoices for payment of corporate funds to compensate, independent counsel, CPAs, scientific experts, and others who can assist the committee in its work.

Committee members who are not also employees of the corporation will be paid an attendance fee of $_____ for each committee meeting (as distinct from meetings of the entire Board) attended and will be reimbursed for documented expenses of attending committee meetings. [Note: Presumably, the salary paid to employee directors is set to include tasks such as serving on committees.]

## No. 59: Resolution Directing Distribution of Committee Report

On _____ , 199_____ , the _____ Committee rendered its final report to the entire Board by way of an oral presentation and written report. Because the committee's conclusions and supporting data are of vital interest to the corporation and its stockholders, it is RESOLVED that the Secretary distribute a copy of the committee report to everyone who was a stockholder of record on _____ , 199_____ , with a copy of this resolution attached.

## No. 60: Resolution Disbanding Special Committee

On _____ , 199_____ , this Board passed a resolution creating a standing/temporary special committee to deal with and to report to the full Board on or before _____ , 199_____ . The committee rendered its [final] report to the Board on _____ , 199_____ ; the written report is hereby entered into the corporate records and made part of the minutes of this meeting. In that the committee has performed the task for which it was created, it is hereby RESOLVED that the committee be disbanded and that any sums due and owing to nonemployee directors or to experts rendering services to the committee, be paid. It is further RESOLVED that the corporation acknowledges, with gratitude, the services performed by the committee members.

## No. 61: Resolution re Interested Directors

It is RESOLVED that the corporation enter into a contract with _____ / purchase the following asset from _____ /enter into a contract with _____ Corp., whose Board of Directors includes _____ , despite the fact that _____ is a Director of this corporation. The terms of the contract are at least as favorable to this corporation as an arm's-length contract with a nonrelated party would be. The interested director has made full disclosure of his own interest and the advantages and disadvantages of the proposed contract to both parties.

## No. 62: Board of Directors' Resolution Disavowing a Contract Entered into by an Officer

On _____ , 199_____ , _____ , then serving as this corporation's President/ Vice-President/Secretary/Treasurer/other [explain] entered into a contract with _____ , purporting to bind the corporation and to obligate the corporation to _____ .

However, in the judgment of the Board of Directors, such a contract is not in the best interests of the corporation because _____ , and therefore it is RESOLVED that the contract (and any action taken in compliance with it except on instruction of the corporation's in-house or outside counsel) is hereby disavowed and disapproved. It is hereby directed that the corporation so inform the other party to the purported contract, and the officer who entered into the contract; it is further directed that the corporation return to the other party anything of value it has received from the other party and that the corporation demand return of anything of value paid to the other party under the purported contract.

## No. 63: Resolution re Disqualification of Director: New Appointment

As of _____ , 199_____ , _____ ceased to be qualified to serve as director of _____ Corporation, in that s/he ceased to be a stockholder of the corporation/became involved in a conflict of interest because of his/her position with/stockholdings in _____ , a competitor of _____ Corp./ came under investigation for alleged breach of fiduciary duty/ other [explain]: Therefore, it is RESOLVED that s/he be notified by _____'s Secretary that s/he is disqualified as director, that the office of director formerly held by _____ is declared vacant, and that the Board of Directors appoints _____ to serve as a Director for the unexpired portion of _____'s term. [Note: Sometimes corporations that fear a hostile takeover adopt a provision in their Articles of Incorporation or Bylaws that forbid removal of directors (for instance, by a raider who wants control of the board) unless due cause has been shown. This type of resolution is important when the corporation wants to remove a director and needs to show that there was due cause for the removal.]

## No. 64: Removal of Director for Cause

_____was elected as a Director of this Corporation on _____ , 19_____ and has served since that time. It has come to the attention of the Board of Directors that s/he is guilty of misconduct/his/her conduct is not in the best interests of the corporation, in that [describe]:

Therefore, it is RESOLVED that removal of this Director is justified and is in the best interests of the corporation. Removal of a director for cause is authorized by Part _____ , Paragraph _____ of the Corporation's Articles of Incorporation and Part _____ , Paragraph _____ of its Bylaws, on the vote of at least _____ Directors. A vote was taken on _____ , 199_____ , at a time when a quorum was present or had tendered their proxies; of the _____ Directors, _____ , equaling at least a simple majority/two-thirds as required by the Articles of Incorporation and/or Bylaws, voted for removal of _____ . Therefore, it is RESOLVED that _____ be removed from office as Director, that _____ serve as Director in his/her place, and that the Secretary notify _____ that s/he has been removed from the Board of Directors.

## No. 65: Resolution Requesting Resignation of an Officer

RESOLVED that _____ , who now serves as President/Vice-President/Secretary/Treasurer/ [other] of this corporation is no longer able to continue effectively in that capacity because: _____. Therefore, s/he is requested to resign this office. The Secretary of the Corporation (or _____ , if the Secretary's resignation is sought) is hereby requested to notify the officer of the call for his/her resignation.

## No. 66: Resolution Accepting Resignation

_____ , duly elected and serving as President/Vice-President/Secretary/Treasurer of _____ Corporation, has tendered his/her resignation from this office orally/in a letter dated _____ , 19_____ . It is hereby RESOLVED that the resignation be accepted, effective _____ , 19_____ .

At the Board meeting held on _____ , 19_____ , an election was held. _____ of the _____ Directors, constituting a quorum, were present; _____ Directors had submitted their proxies. By a vote of _____ to _____ (constituting at least a simple majority), _____was elected to replace the resigning officer. S/he has indicated willingness to accept the office, and thus will assume the office of President/Vice-President/Secretary/Treasurer as soon as the resignation of the incumbent becomes effective.

## No. 67: Officer Must Reimburse Corporation for Its Loss Due to Officer's Acts

It is the judgment of the Board of Directors that _____ , a corporate officer serving as _____ , has caused injury to the corporation's reputation, financial position, stock price, and/or exposed the corporation to the risk of litigation through his/her action/inaction/negligence, by [describe]:

The officer in question admits to the wrongdoing so charged, and wishes to reimburse the corporation for the losses he/she has caused, in the amount determined by the Board of Directors.

RESOLVED that the officer in question reimburse the corporation in the sum of $____ , to be debited from his/her current, incentive, and deferred compensation, and which will remain as a debt to the corporation until paid in full.

## No. 68: Denial of Derivative Suit

On _____ , 199____ [a] [a committee of] stockholder[s], _____ , notified the corporation that s/he/they believed the corporation has a legitimate and enforceable claims against [a] member[s] of the Board of Directors, based on the director'[s]' action/inaction in _____ , allegedly resulting in loss or damage to the corporation to the extent of $____ .

Pursuant to a resolution of the Board of Directors dated _____ , 199____ , a ____-member committee was appointed to investigate these charges, including retaining the law firm of Riggs, Schnell & Bandini as independent counsel, and to report to the Board as a whole no later than _____ , 199____ . The report was duly rendered and has been presented in both written form and oral form with opportunities for questions by the Board members.

It is the decision of the Board, taken after full consideration of the committee report and the information provided by independent counsel, that the accused director acted reasonably, in good faith, and in the best interests of the corporation, without conflict of interest or self-dealing. Therefore, it is RESOLVED that the stockholder's demand to bring suit is hereby denied unless and until the holders of the majority of the corporation's common stock so demand; on written demand of any stockholder, the corporation's President will call a special stockholder's meeting to vote on the propriety of bringing such a suit.

## No. 69: Resolution Authorizing Bringing Suit Against a Director or Officer

Based on allegations brought by stockholder _____ and based on a full investigation by a committee of the Board of Directors appointed by resolution dated _____ , 199____ undertaken with the cooperation of independent counsel from the firm of Starkweather and Combie, the full Board of Directors has determined that the accusations against _____ , officer[s] and/or director[s] of this corporation serving in the capacity[ies] of _____ are justified, and that the corporation has a legitimate and enforceable cause of action against him/her/them. Therefore, it is RESOLVED that the corporation approach the officer[s]/director[s] in question informing them of the allegations, hearing his/her/their side of the story, and demanding that the officer[s]/director[s] reimburse the corporation in the sum of $____ and/or take other action to eliminate and make up for the alleged impropriety. If the matter can be settled without litigation, the corporation is authorized to settle and compromise the claim on equitable terms; otherwise, the corporation is authorized to institute a suit against the accused person[s], seeking damages in the amount of $____ and other relief that can be granted by the court of appropriate jurisdiction.

## No. 70: Directors' Resolution Settling a Claim or Suit

This corporation is the plaintiff/defendant in a federal/state civil suit, identified as #_____ and captioned as _____ v. _____ , pending in the_____ Court of the State of _____ /_____ District of _____ . OR

This corporation has a claim against _____ for _____ / _____ alleges that he/she/it/they has a claim against this corporation for _____ , in the amount of $_____ .

Both parties wish to avoid litigation/settle the litigation now pending on terms that are fair and mutually agreeable to both parties. Both parties are represented by counsel, and negotiations have taken place in good faith and with full disclosure of relevant facts. Acting on advice of counsel, both parties have agreed to settle the pending claims and counterclaims by the payment of $_____ by _____ to _____ , on or before _____ , 199_____ and by the performance of _____ by _____ on or before _____ , 199_____ .

It is not necessary that approval of the proposed settlement be granted by any person, entity, or organization/consent of _____ to the proposed settlement is required and has been obtained in the form of a resolution/letter/order/other [explain] dated _____ , 199_____ /will be obtained by _____ on or before _____ , 199_____ and if it is not obtained, the litigation will be instituted/will proceed.

Therefore, it is RESOLVED that the corporation settle the claim/lawsuit now pending on the terms and conditions detailed above and that the corporation enter into a stipulation of settlement, make payments as described above in return for a full release of all related claims/accept the payments as described above and grant a full release of all related claims provided that payments are made as stipulated.

## No. 71: Board of Directors' Resolution Refusing to Pay Dissenting Shareholders the Amount They Demand

We, the directors of Minagault Corporation, have received a timely notice in proper form from Jennifer Tillson, owner of 1,000 common shares, and from Donald Graebell, owner of 2,500 common shares, that they dissent from the proposed sale of all of Minagault's assets to The Tyndall Property Group Ltd. They demand the sum of $89.50 per share for their holdings.

In accordance with Chapter 213 of the Revised Statutes Annotated of the state of Monroe, we hereby notify Tillson and Graebell that we do not accept their estimate of the value of their shares, although we acknowledge their appraisal right and right to receive the fair value of their shares from the corporation. It is hereby RESOLVED that a written offer of $76 per common share, effective until _____ , 199_____ be made to Tillson and Graebell by the corporation's Treasurer, in satisfaction of their appraisal right.

## No. 72: Notice to Dissenting Stockholders

Dear Stockholder:

We have received your notice of dissent to the proposed purchase of all Minagault Co. assets by Tyndall Property Group Ltd. and acknowledge that your demand is timely and that the laws of this state provide that dissenting shareholders have the right to demand payment of the fair cash value of their shares by the corporation itself. However, we reject your demand of $89.50 per share as excessive and disproportionate to the value of your shares. Instead, we offer the sum of $76 per share for all of your shares of Minagault Co. common stock.

## No. 73: Board of Directors' Resolution Directing Distribution of Stock Received for the Corporation's Assets

On _____ , 199____ , pursuant to a resolution of this Board of Directors adopted _____ , 199____ and ratified by a majority of the stockholders on _____ , 199____ , all of the assets of this corporation were transferred to the purchasing corporation, SouthSide Venture Capital Group, Inc., in exchange for 1,000 shares of its common stock. Two of this corporation's shareholders, Simon Lathrop and Marshall T. Pattmore, dissented from this transaction; they have already been paid the fair value of their stock, pursuant to the Corporate Code of the state of Tyler. With respect to the corporation's other shareholders, it is hereby RESOLVED that the 1,000 shares of SouthSide Venture Capital Group common stock received by this corporation in exchange for its assets be distributed as a dividend, proportional to each shareholder's holdings of this corporation's stock as evidenced by its books and records as of _____ , 199____ , conditional on the remaining shareholders' surrender of their certificates for the stock of the corporation, endorsed for transfer, in exchange for their SouthSide shares.

## No. 74: Board of Directors' Resolution Calling for Filing of a Voluntary Bankruptcy Petition

On review of the corporation's books and records, and after hearing the report prepared by Jason Tilghman, CPA, the Board of Directors has determined that the corporation is now unable to pay its debts, and can be expected to continue so in the foreseeable future. The best interests of the corporation, its stockholders, employees, and creditors can best be reconciled by the corporation's filing of a voluntary bankruptcy petition and its reorganization under Chapter 11 of the Bankruptcy Code. Therefore, it is RESOLVED that the law firm of Lundeen & Toretski be retained as bankruptcy counsel to represent this corporation; that Ernest Gallagher, Vice-President of this corporation, is directed to execute and file a Chapter 11 petition on behalf of the corporation in federal court; and that all corporate officers take the necessary steps (including execution of instruments) needed to reorganize the corporation in bankruptcy.

## No. 75: Board of Directors' Resolution in Response to an Involuntary Petition

On _____ , 199 ____ , this corporation was served with a subpoena and petition for involuntary bankruptcy, duly filed in Bankruptcy Court on _____ , 199 ____ by Galesburg Fittings, Inc., in its status as creditor/trustee.

The judgment of this Board of Directors is that a reorganization if this corporation in bankruptcy is desirable, but that a voluntary reorganization is preferable and can be arranged on terms equitable to all parties. Therefore, it is RESOLVED that the officers of this corporation be authorized to admit the jurisdiction of the Bankruptcy Court and to admit the allegations of Galesburg Fittings' petition except as to grounds for relief.

It is further RESOLVED that the officers of this corporation enter into negotiations with the petitioner and take all other steps necessary for the creation and implementation of a plan of reorganization under Chapter 11 of the Bankruptcy Code.

## No. 76: Board of Directors' Resolution to Participate in Another Corporation's Reorganization Plan

Minton-DeBale, Inc., is a corporation suffering financial difficulties. It is the judgment of the management of Minto-DeBale, Inc., that the operation of the corporation as an independent entity is no longer financially feasible, and the corporation has resolved (by a Board resolution dated _____ , 199___ and a stockholder resolution dated _____ , 199___ ) to seek reorganization by having a financially sound corporation issue shares of its stock in exchange for all of Minton-DeBale's assets, with the sound corporation assuming all of Minton-DeBale's liabilities.

This corporation's officers, auditors, and legal counsel have visited Minton-DeBale, Inc.'s headquarters and business location and have fully investigated the corporation's facilities, customers, and financial statements. Their conclusion is that Minton-DeBale has assets that would be extremely useful to this corporation; that its liabilities do not exceed sums that could be furnished by this corporation; and that Minton-DeBale's accounts and client relationships are such that, given new sources of capital and sound management, the business could be operated profitably.

A plan of reorganization has been prepared and agreed to in principle by the management of both corporations. The plan calls for this corporation to issue 15,000 shares of its common stock (an action permissible under the laws of this state and this corporation's charter and bylaws) in exchange for all of Minton-De Bale's assets, including its corporate name and goodwill. Such stock, when issued, will be fully paid and nonassessable; the value of Minton-De Bale's assets, net of liabilities, is at least equal to the value of this corporation's common shares to be issued in exchange for them.

In light of the above considerations, it is RESOLVED that this corporation and its officers undertake all necessary actions to adopt and implement the plan of reorganization, including issuance of an additional 15,000 shares of common stock and distribution of this stock to Minton-De Bale shareholders, and RESOLVED that a special meeting of this corporation's shareholders be called for _____ , 199___ at _____ M. at this corporation's headquarters, to ratify the Board of Directors' action.

## No. 77: Board of Directors' Resolution Authorizing a General Assignment for the Benefit of Creditors

At the present time, this corporation is unable to pay its debts by use of the proceeds of its ordinary course of business, and this condition is expected to continue for the foreseeable future. Certain creditors have sued the corporation to enforce its debts, and others have threatened to bring such suits. These suits, if successful, could result in judgments against corporate assets.

The judgment of the Board of Directors, acting on reports made by the corporation's Treasurer, Walter Limone, and Judith Kessler-Blaine, CPA, is that the best solution to the serious financial problems besetting the corporation is for the corporation to make a general assignment for the benefit of its creditors.

This would be done pursuant to a plan under which the corporation would assign all income and its assets to a creditor's committee comprising representatives from the corporation's three largest creditors, Tyler Realty, Inc., Jeffreys Materials Corp., and Bainbridge Fabrication and Machining Corp. The creditors' committee would then assume operation and control of the business and would also sell the corporate assets listed on Schedule A. The creditors' committee would remain operational until all claims of the creditors in existence when the plan went into operation had been paid in full, at which time the creditors' committee would reconvey any remaining assets to the corporation. RESOLVED that this corporation's officers be authorized to retain legal counsel to develop such a plan of general assignment and that, once the plan is developed, they execute any and all necessary documents on behalf of the corporation and affix the corporate seal.

It is also RESOLVED that a Special Meeting of stockholders be called for _____ , 199 ____ at _____ M., to be held at corporate headquarters, to obtain the stockholders' approval of the adoption of the general assignment, and RESOLVED that the corporation's Secretary notify all stockholders of record as of _____ , 199 ____ of this impending Special Meeting.

## No. 78: Board of Directors' Resolution Appointing a Trust Company as Liquidator

On a petition by stockholders Lawrence Barlow and Stuart Lifton dated _____ , 199 ____ , the Recorders' Court of Roosevelt has rendered an order dated _____ , 199 ____ in the case of In re Sheppard Loom and Shuttle Corporation, Index #Civ-H-2207-91, directing the liquidation of the corporation and sale of all its assets on or before _____ , 199 ____ , and for payment of all its debts and distribution of any remaining assets or funds to the stockholders.

However, it is not administratively feasible for the corporation's own personnel to identify, marshall, and sell all its assets within the time allotted for the liquidation to be completed. Therefore, it is RESOLVED that the Dickinsonville Trust Co. be appointed as liquidator, with the following powers:

o To conduct the business from _____ , 199 ____ , the effective date of the appointment, until the liquidation process begins.

o To make a comprehensive listing of the corporation's assets and liabilities, and to send each stockholder a copy of this list by first-class mail.

o To advertise the sale of the corporation's assets by open auction for cash, certified check, or major credit card.

o To employ an auctioneer and any necessary staff.

o To keep complete and detailed records of the auction and its proceeds and send each stockholder a copy of the records by first-class mail.

o To pay the corporation's debts out of the proceeds, using records supplied by the corporation and claims filed by its creditors.

o To distribute any remaining cash, after all debts have been satisfied [and after reservation of $ ____ to be held for six months to cover late-filed and contingent claims] to the stockholders in proportion to their holdings.

## No. 79: Stockholder's Resolution Increasing Stated Capital

At this special meeting of the stockholders of _____ Corp., held _____ , 199 ____ at _____ M. at the corporate headquarters, the meeting was properly called, on appropriate notice to the stockholders, and a quorum was present. Based on a report by the corporation's Treasurer indicating that its corporate purposes would be served by an increase in the corporation's stated capital, because funds are needed for research, development, improvement in manufacturing techniques, and marketing, a vote was taken. By a vote of _____ to _____ , it is hereby RESOLVED that the corporation's capital stock be increased from $ ____ to $ ____ ; that the increase be implemented by permitting the issuance of ____ shares of common stock already authorized but not issued/in addition to the shares of stock already authorized; and that the Board of Directors be given the discretion to issue common stock in amounts and on a schedule it believes appropriate, up to the new limit on authorized capital stock.

## No. 80: Stockholders' Resolution of Removal

In the judgment of the holders of at least a majority of _____ , Inc.'s shares, _____ is/are unfit to serve as President/Vice-President/Secretary/Treasurer/Director of the corporation, in that s/he has acted improperly by _____/has failed to take necessary actions in the corporation's best interests by _____ . Therefore, it is RESOLVED that he/she/they be removed from office effective as of the date of this Resolution and that a replacement be appointed/elected by _____ not later than _____ , 199____ to fill the removed officer/director's remaining term of office. In the interim, until the election is held/appointment is made and the substitute assumes the duties of office, _____ will serve as substitute with all the powers of the removed officer/director.

## No. 81: Stockholders' Resolution Approving Adoption of Retirement Plan

RESOLVED that it is in the best interests of the corporation and employees that the corporation provide incentives for recruitment and continued high performance by offering a reasonable and competitive compensation package, including both current and deferred compensation arranged to maximize favorable tax treatment of the employee.

At its meeting of _____ , 199____, this corporation's Board of Directors approved and adopted a Retirement Plan, a copy of which is attached to this resolution and hereby made part of the books and records of the corporation.

IT IS FURTHER RESOLVED that the plan be ratified, approved, and confirmed as adopted and that the corporation's officers and directors carry out any steps required to bring the plan into operation on the terms described in the Board of Directors' resolution.

## No. 82: Stockholders' Resolution Ratifying Adoption of Profit-Sharing Plan

We have studied the proposed profit-sharing plan (a copy of which is attached to this resolution) and heard reports about its advantages and costs, and, in our judgment, it is in the best interests of the corporation that a profit-sharing plan be adopted in this form. Therefore, it is RESOLVED that the profit-sharing plan be adopted as given and that the corporation's Secretary execute a trust agreement with the Federal Amalgamated Bank & Trust as trustee, as provided in the plan.

## No. 83: Stockholders' Resolution Approving Stock Bonus Plan

We have considered the stock bonus plan adopted by resolution of this corporation's Board of Directors on _____ , 199____ , and believe that adoption and implementation of such a plan is in the best interests of the corporation, its stockholders, and its work force. Therefore, at a special meeting called on proper notice and held on _____ , 199____ at which a quorum was present, and by a vote of ____ shares in favor to ____ shares opposed, we approve and ratify the stock bonus plan.

## No. 84: Stockholders' Resolution Ratifying Sale-Leaseback

We have reviewed the contract of sale, warranty deed, and 25-year lease that, by resolution dated _____ , 199_____ , the Board of Directors has determined to enter into. At a special meeting held on proper notice _____ , 199_____ , at which a quorum was present, we have heard the arguments presented by the directors in favor of this transaction, and the objections raised by stockholder Laura Dill, and have decided that the transaction as proposed by the Board of Directors would redound to the corporation's long-term financial security and advance its tax planning objectives. Therefore, it is RESOLVED that the sale-leaseback transaction be implemented and that we ratify the decision of the Board of Directors to enter into this transaction.

## No. 85: Stockholders' Resolution Ratifying Purchase of a Business

This corporation, acting pursuant to a resolution adopted by the Board of Directors on _____ , 199_____ , has entered into negotiations with a sole proprietor/partnership/ corporation doing business under the name of _____ . The negotiations have resulted in the drafting of a plan of purchase under which this corporation seeks to purchase the other business and all its tangible and intangible assets, on terms accepted in principle by the business to be purchased. A copy of this plan of purchase, and the proposed plan of reorganization of the business to be purchased, are attached to this resolution.

We have examined this material; heard presentations from the special Acquisitions Committee of this corporation's Board of Directors and from the potentially acquired business; and are satisfied that acquiring the subject business, on the terms given in the plan, would be in the best interests of this corporation and its stockholders. So we RESOLVE to ratify the Board of Directors' decision to purchase the business on terms outlined in the plan.

## No. 86: Stockholders' Resolution Ratifying Refusal to Bring Suit

We have examined the evidence submitted by _____ , the stockholder seeking corporate action, by the accused director, and by the Board of Directors and its independent counsel, and, in our judgment, there is no legitimate grounds for a suit against the accused director, and it would not be in the best interests of the corporation to bring such a suit. Therefore, it is RESOLVED that the Board of Directors' resolution, dated _____ , 199_____ , refusing to bring suit against the accused director, is hereby ratified and approved.

## No. 87: Shareholders' Resolution Ratifying a General Assignment

At a special meeting held _____ , 199 _____ , at _____ M., at the corporation's headquarters, a quorum was present in person or by proxy. The Board of Directors reported to those present that it was not anticipated that the corporation would be able to meet its financial obligations in the ordinary course of its business now and in the foreseeable future. The Board of Directors explained that its recommendation was that the corporation make a general assignment for the benefit of its creditors: that is, turn over all its assets and income to a committee of creditors, who would sell off certain assets and manage the corporation until the corporation's debts have been paid in full, at which time the assets would be returned to the corporation.

By a vote of ____ shares to ____ shares/unanimous vote, it was RESOLVED to adopt the recommendation of the Board of Directors.

## No. 88: Consent by Stockholders to Sale of All or Substantially All Assets of the Corporation

This corporation has had seven successive loss quarters, and no plausible plan for returning the corporation to profitability at an attainable capital cost has been proposed. However, a bona fide offer to purchase all the corporation's assets has been made by Fleming Corporation of Kannawonda Lake, Tyler, for the sum of $750,000 cash and 10,000 shares of its common stock, currently selling over the counter for $32 per share; Fleming also agrees to assume this corporation's debts and liabilities.

We are the holders of all/at least a majority of this corporation's outstanding shares, and we believe that acceptance of Fleming's offer gives us the best chance to achieve a fair return on our investment in this corporation's stock. Therefore, we grant our consent and approve the purchase of all this corporation's assets [with the specific exception of _____ , which will be sold and distributed to the shareholders/distributed to the shareholders] by Fleming, on the terms as offered and as embodied in a resolution of this corporation's Board of Directors, dated _____ , 199_____ .

## No. 89: Stockholder's Objection to Sale of All Assets

I was present at the special meeting of stockholders held on _____ , 199_____ , at which the holders of the majority of this corporation's common stock voted to accept the offer of Ramsay Foods, Inc., to purchase all of this corporation's assets. However, I dissent from this offer, believing that the consideration offered for the corporation's assets is unreasonably low and that sale of all assets is less favorable to the interests of the corporation's shareholders than continued corporate existence and operation would be. Under the laws of this state, I am entitled to an appraisal of my shares and payment for the cash value of the shares at the rate of $_____ per share; I am the owner of _____ shares and therefore am entitled to a payment of $_____ .

# Chapter 4

# FINANCING THE CORPORATION

## INTRODUCTION

Once the corporation has attained its initial capitalization and begins operations, the need for funds is far from over. In time, of course, corporate operations will generate enough funds to pay salaries, buy raw materials, pay rent or mortgage payments, and otherwise meet the expenses of doing business. But there is a period of time when the corporation is incurring expenses but has not yet made sales, or the sales have not been paid for, or expenses temporarily exceed income.

In order to succeed, a corporation must be aware of a variety of financing devices, employing the ones that best suit its needs. For instance, a "venture capitalist" can provide funds, whether for a corporate start-up or when a growing business needs expansion capital—usually a combination of loans and an "equity kicker" that lets the venture capitalist become a stockholder with the right to acquire a certain type of stock at a certain date or dates, at a defined price. Venture capitalists often want convertible preferred stock, so that they can get income with the prospect of profiting by the increasing stock price as the corporation develops.

*Practice Tip:* The corporation will want the stock to be callable so the venture capitalist can be bought out when the corporation gets some extra funds; the venture capitalist wants a "call protection period" during which calls are forbidden. Who wins? It's a matter of bargaining power.

## VENTURE CAPITAL ROADMAP

- ○ Loan agreement or agreement about the venture capitalist's purchase of bonds or notes

○ Private placement memorandum and subscription agreements detailing the purchase of unregistered securities

○ (Optional) An agreement governing the rights, options, or warrants that constitute the "equity kicker"

○ (Optional) A voting trust or shareholder agreement giving the venture capitalist control or a significant say in corporate policy

○ (Optional) Mortgage or security agreement binding the corporation's assets

○ (Optional) Personal guarantees of the corporation's debt from the corporation's officers, directors, or shareholders

If no venture capitalist is available, or if the corporation decides that a venture capital transaction would require the surrender of too much control, loans may be available from a bank or from private individuals.

*Practice Tip:* Don't rely too heavily on the possibility of Small Business Administration financing; the SBA has only a limited amount of money, which must be divided among many applicants (including bail-out situations). However, your state of incorporation may have incentive financing for new businesses or businesses that increase local employment.

It's important to understand the distinction between "unsecured" loans (where the lender relies solely on the credit of the borrower) and "secured" loans (where collateral is provided). If the borrower defaults on the loan, the lender can seize and sell the collateral. If the lender has a "purchase money security interest" (if the loan was used to purchase the collateral itself), the creditor is entitled to an extra degree of priority over other creditors. It's common for lenders to demand that the management of small, closely held corporations give personal guarantees of corporate loans. If you do so, be aware that your own assets may be seized for corporate debts.

### Events of Default

Also be aware that loan and commercial sale agreements are frequently written so that "default" includes much more than simple failure to make payments on time. Loan and security agreements are frequently written so that the borrower is in default if it becomes insolvent, if a guarantor dies or becomes bankrupt or insolvent, or even if the lender "deems itself insecure." Creditors have many remedies in case of default, such as "acceleration" (the right to declare the entire remaining balance of the debt due at once). Acceleration is permitted so that creditors can enforce their remedies at one time, instead of having to bring multiple lawsuits when each installment comes due and remains unpaid. This will probably seem much fairer when you include acceleration provisions in contracts in which you are a creditor than when you are subject to these provisions as a buyer or borrower!

*Practice Tip:* Watch out for the interaction of different credit arrangements. A business may have many loans or credit sale relationships—each with a default clause—and default under any agreement may constitute default under the others, forcing the business to satisfy many creditors immediately. Furthermore, the "fine print" of a credit arrangement may make it an instance of default to enter into other loans or credit purchases, or to enter into more than a certain amount of other debt.

## Secured Loan Transactions

A secured loan transaction involves several documents, for example, a loan agreement (also called a loan note) and a security agreement (spelling out the lender's rights in the collateral), and a "financing statement" under the Uniform Commercial Code is frequently filed by the lender to prove its interest in the collateral.

In addition to simple term loans (in which a sum of money is borrowed for a term such as five years, with regular monthly repayments), lenders have developed many other forms of business financing. The borrower may be entitled to a revolving line of credit, under which it can borrow only as needed.

*Practice Tip:* Check the agreement—is advance notice to the lender required before drawing on the line of credit? Must a fee be paid each month or each quarter based on the unused part of the credit line? Does the lender have the right to reduce the amount of credit available under the credit line? Or, in a "credit facility loan," a fixed sum is reserved for the borrower, which the borrower can take all at once or in installments, but every amount borrowed reduces the amount that can be borrowed later, even if it is repaid.

"Floor plan" financing is a method under which a bank or manufacturer advances a retailer money to buy items (usually big-ticket items such as cars or major appliances), to be repaid when the items are sold. "Accounts receivable" financing is a method under which a business uses its accounts receivable (obligations owed to the business by customers) as security for a loan. "Factoring" is a type of accounts receivable financing in which the business, in effect, sells its accounts receivable to a "factor" (usually at a deep discount); the factor then collects the accounts receivable and gets to keep the proceeds. The discount is both an interest charge and a form of insurance against the risk that some of the accounts will be uncollectable.

## Letters of Credit

A "letter of credit" is a centuries-old arrangement for financing (in fact, letters of credit were developed long before there was a banking system). A letter of credit specifies the terms on which a bank or other party will honor demands for payment (usually called drafts). A letter of credit can be revocable or irrevocable, general or addressed to a specific person, and unconditional or dependent on presentation of title documents, invoices, certificates, or other documents. (This last type of demand for payment under a letter of credit is called a "documentary draft.") The bank or other payor is the "issuer," a "confirming bank" agrees to honor another bank's letter of credit, the person who causes issuance of the letter of credit by depositing funds with the issuer is called the "customer," and anyone who can draw on the letter is a "beneficiary." In effect, a letter of credit is a fancy money order: the beneficiary doesn't have to trust the customer to pay, because the customer has already deposited funds in (or arranged to borrow funds from) a bank or other source that the beneficiary trusts. Letters of credit are especially useful in import-export situations, where the beneficiary is not familiar with U.S. banks or is unable to perform a credit check on the customer.

## Leasing Agreements

Leasing is another financing method. A business that has regular income but lacks large amounts of capital may want to lease assets used in the business instead of buying them outright (especially if buying them would call for borrowing, or a credit purchase, at high interest rates). Or, if the corporation has excess assets which it is inadvisable to sell (for instance, because they may be needed later), the assets can be leased to other businesses to gain extra income. In a "single-investor" lease, the lessor finances 100% of the cost of the leased property. In a "leveraged lease," the lessor borrows part of the cost of the property and then uses lease payments to repay the lender. In a "full-payout" lease, the combined present value of the rentals, residual value (the value of the leased property at the end of the lease), and tax benefits is at least as great as the cost of repaying the purchase price at current interest rates. In a "net" lease, the lessee assumes the obligations of ownership (such as paying taxes and maintaining the leased property); in a "gross" lease, the lessor would be responsible for these obligations. In a "hell-or-high-water" lease, as the name suggests, the lessee is required to make lease payments regardless of any claims, setoffs, or defenses against anyone; the claims can still be pursued, but only after lease payments have been made.

## NET LEASE ROADMAP

- ○ Certificate of delivery and acceptance showing that the lessee has received the leased property in good condition.
- ○ Amount and timing of lease payments.
- ○ Interest to be paid on late payments.
- ○ Lessee's obligation to maintain the leased property in good condition, making repairs when necessary, or even replacing leased property that has been destroyed or

damaged beyond repair; the lessee may have to maintain a service contract on the property.

○ Disclaimer of warranties; the lessee states that it did not enter into the lease on the basis of warranties or statements by the lessor.

○ Lessee must indemnify the lessor if the leased property causes injury to any third parties.

○ Either a prohibition on subleases or conditions under which the property can be subleased.

○ A "quiet enjoyment" provision preventing the lessor or the lessor's creditors from seeking to take back the property as long as the lease is not in default.

○ Cancellation provisions—can the lessee terminate the lease before the scheduled expiration date? Doing so will probably require payment of a "termination value" approximately equal to the projected resale value of the property plus recaptured tax benefits.

○ Opinion of counsel from the lessee's lawyer, stating, for example, that the lessee is a validly organized corporation in good standing, not in default under any of its obligations to anyone, and authorized to enter into the lease.

Another possibility is a "sale-leaseback" if a large sum of cash is needed: the assets are sold to someone else; then your company leases them back, continuing to use them in exchange for lease payments.

*Practice Tip:* Leases and sale-leasebacks can also have tax advantages, because a current tax deduction is available for lease payments paid in the ordinary course of business, but the purchase price of a newly purchased asset must usually be deducted over several years (so that the deduction in each year is smaller). Get tax advice before entering into a lease transaction as either lessor or lessee.

## LOAN AGREEMENT ROADMAP

○ Definitions (who is the borrower; who is the lender; amount of borrowing or encumbrances from other sources the borrower can incur without being in default).
   *Practice Tip:* Watch out—some loan documents include definitions of accounting terms such as "current liabilities" which are contrary to the usual definitions and which have the effect of hampering corporate financing and operations.

○ Lender's agreement to lend a certain amount (or to advance credit up to a limit, based on the borrower's needs).

○ Borrower's agreement to borrow.

○ Purpose(s) for which the borrower will use the loan proceeds.

○ If a separate loan note will be used to legally obligate the borrower, a description of the loan note.

○ Interest rate, or method of calculating the rate (e.g., 2% over prime, a rate based on Treasury bill rates on certain dates.)

*Practice Tip:* Make sure there are no ambiguities in the calculation of a floating rate—even the phrase "prime rate" can be interpreted many different ways.

○ How the funds will be made available to the borrower (e.g., deposit into a bank account, in cash, wire transfer).

*Practice Tip:* A bank lender may force the borrower to maintain "compensating balances"—to keep a portion of the outstanding balance of the loan in an account with the bank, which can be used if the borrower defaults. (This is called the "right of setoff.")

○ Closing date for the loan transaction.

○ Place of the loan transaction closing—usually the offices of the lender's law firm.

○ Collateral or other security given.

○ Any guarantees from officers or stockholders of borrower.

○ Payment terms (e.g., 24 monthly payments, payment on demand).

○ Commitment fee or other fee to the lender (usually payable at the closing).

○ The borrower's representations and warranties (for instance, that it is a validly organized corporation, that borrowing is a valid corporate transaction, that this loan does not constitute default under any other agreement).

○ The borrower's "affirmative covenants" or promises of things it will do (e.g., keep the collateral in good condition, pay all its debts, pay its taxes, maintain a certain level of working capital and easily realized assets).

○ The borrower's "negative covenants" or things it promises it will not do (such as merge with another corporation, sell or lease its property, or let its pension plan violate the tax or labor laws).

○ Conditions on the loan (e.g., that the borrower's representations and warranties are true, that the borrower has completed and submitted all necessary documents).

○ What constitutes default (failing to make payments, becoming bankrupt or insolvent, violating a covenant, etc.).

○ Standard provisions or "boilerplate" (such as which state's law will govern, a provision that the lender does not waive its rights by ignoring a default).

---

## BANK COMMITMENT LETTER FOR LOAN

From: Corn Chandlers & Merchants Bank
To: Sebastian Anders, President, Poly-Anders Polymers, Inc.

In response to your _____ , 199 ____ letter requesting a letter of credit $1.2 million for the purpose of securing a patent on a new manufacturing process, and to expand your manufacturing and marketing capabilities to exploit the patent, and pursuant to negotiations between your firm and this Bank, we have agreed to loan Poly-Anders Polymers the sum of $1,000,000 (one million dollars) on the following terms:

○ The loan will be a ____ -year term loan, bearing interest at a fixed rate of ____ %/at a variable rate equal to the prime rate plus ____ %, with an initial rate of ____ % and adjustments every year/six months/quarter with a "cap" of ____ %. Payments [initially] of $ ____ [then as adjusted to reflect interest rate changes] will be due on the ____ of every month for ____ months/quarterly throughout the loan term.

○ At the loan closing, the Bank will deduct a commitment and closing fee of $ ____ from the amount payable to you. The closing is scheduled to take place _____ , 199 ____ at ____ M. at the main office of this Bank.

○ The loan will be secured by your unconditional personal guarantee and by a first mortgage lien on all Poly-Anders' business and commercial real property including the factory located on Route 23 near Exit 17 (and any real property purchased under the expansion program to be financed by this loan) and a security interest as set out in a Form UCC-1 Financing Statement on all the personal property used by Poly-Anders in its business.

In addition to this commitment for permanent financing, the Bank agrees to provide interim financing for up to ____ months, in an amount not to exceed ____ $ ____ , at an interest rate of ____ %.

This commitment is effective until _____ , 199 ____ , provided that there is no material adverse change in your company's financial condition or obligations before the closing date. This commitment can be accepted only by signing below and returning a copy of this letter to the Bank before the commitment expires.

## BUSINESS LOAN AGREEMENT

*1.* Manciple City Bank & Trust Co. ("Lender") agrees to lend the amount of $1,000,000 to Chivalry Sportswear ("Chivalry"), in return for Chivalry's promise to repay on or before _____ , 199 ____ , secured by its Note and Security Agreement. The loan bears interest at a rate of ____ %/a variable rate of interest computed each quarter and equivalent to the prime rate for one week before the due date plus ____ %/at a rate of ____ %, plus contingent interest equal to 5% of the corporation's pretax earnings for the previous year, with a minimum contingent interest of $ ____ per year, a maximum of $ ____ ; contingent interest will be paid in four equal quarterly payments.

A fully executed Security Agreement will be filed and indexed in the appropriate county or counties.

To induce the Lender to make this loan, Chivalry makes certain representations and warranties set out below.

2. Closing of the loan will take place on _____ , 199 ____ , at ____ M. at the Lender's headquarters (or on such other date or place as agreed to by Lender and Chivalry). At the closing, Lender will deliver funds in the form of a certified check payable to Chivalry, in an amount equal to the principal of the loan less closing costs and expenses as itemized and set forth on Schedule A annexed to this Loan Agreement.

At the closing, Chivalry will deliver its Note(s) evidencing an obligation to repay the loan. Chivalry will be responsible for payment of Lender's costs incurred with respect to the loan transaction (even if it is not consummated), including costs of investigation, printing, legal fees, and transfer and stamp taxes. The obligation to pay such costs survives payment of the Note.

Closing of the loan transaction is contingent on Chivalry's delivery of an officers' certificate and opinion of counsel in a form satisfactory to the Lender, evidencing

○ Chivalry's proper organization and good standing

○ The legality of its entering into the loan transaction

○ The propriety of the loan as a corporate transaction

○ The absence of other contractual commitments that would bar this loan transaction.

*3.* Regularly scheduled payments of principal and interest will be made quarterly (on January 2, April 1, July 1, or October 1 of each year, or the next business day if such day is a Sunday or legal holiday) in equal amounts of $ _____ each, plus any applicable late charges (a late charge of $ _____ / _____ % of the outstanding unpaid balance will be assessed whenever a payment is _____ days or more late), or the lesser amount specified by the amended amortization schedule provided by the Lender after a prepayment of principal.

*4.* On at least 30, but not more than 60, days' notice to the Lender, Chivalry may prepay the principal of the loan:

○ Without prepayment penalty, if prepayment accompanies a timely regular payment, and the prepayment is not greater than the principal component of the regularly scheduled payment

○ At any other time, or in any amount, subject to a prepayment penalty equal to a percentage of the amount prepaid, on a sliding scale, as follows: [insert scale]; no prepayment penalty will be required for prepayments made after _____ , 199 _____ /200 _____ .

    If any prepayment is made at a time when Chivalry has more than one outstanding Note payable to the Lender, the prepayment will be allocated among all the Notes proportionate to the amounts outstanding under each.

*5.* At all times when any Note to the Lender is outstanding, Chivalry covenants that it will

○ Provide regular financial statements to the Lender four times a year (within 45 days at the end of the first three quarters of its fiscal year, within 60 days of the end of the fiscal year), consisting of balance sheet, income statement, and consolidated statement of changes in financial position, all prepared in reasonable detail, in conformity with Generally Accepted Accounting Principles, by a CPA firm retained by but otherwise independent of Chivalry; plus a statement from the CPA firm at the end of each fiscal year to the effect that the CPA firm has no knowledge of any default under this Agreement or the accompanying Security Agreement, except as disclosed in the letter; plus any other document or financial information reasonably requested by the Lender.

○ Provide an annual Officers' Certificate, dated as of the end of the fiscal year, in which Chivalry's officers certify that, to their knowledge, Chivalry is not in default under the Loan Agreement and/or Security Agreement, or, if default does exist, what action Chivalry has taken or proposes to take to cure the default.

○ Maintain proper books of record and maintain appropriate reserves as required by GAAP; permit the Lender to examine and copy the books during normal business hours.

○ Remain a corporation in good standing and pay all applicable taxes; be and remain in compliance with all applicable statutes and regulations.

○ Obtain, pay for, and maintain in good standing, in commercially reasonable amounts (but in no case less than the amount then due under the Note), covering

    ○ ○ Workers' Compensation as required by law

    ○ ○ Liability insurance on Chivalry's products and premises

    ○ ○ Business interruption insurance covering an interruption of up to one year

    ○ ○ Casualty and fire insurance against risks as normally maintained by a prudently managed comparable business

○ It has no debt except existing debt as disclosed in Schedule B annexed to this Loan Agreement, debt in an amount not greater than $ _____ incurred and used to purchase inventory or equipment used in the business, debt in an amount not greater than $ _____ / _____ % of the corporation's Accounts Receivable and used for operating purposes, and existing mortgages as disclosed in Schedule C.

○ It will not engage in sale-leaseback transactions affecting corporate property without Lender's advance approval, nor will it factor its accounts receivable without Lender's advance approval.

○ It will maintain a tangible net worth at least equal to $ _____ , and current assets at least equal to 125% of current liabilities, at all times.

○ It will perform all its obligations under the Security Agreement and will not engage in or permit any events or conditions that would constitute default under the Security Agreement. Default shall include failure to make timely payment of any required payment under the Note; failure to live up to any of the representations given in this Loan Agreement 30 days or more after receipt of written notice to cure; falsity of any material representation in this Agreement or the Security Agreement; insolvency, bankruptcy, receivership, assignment for benefit of creditors, or filing of a voluntary or involuntary petition for bankruptcy or liquidation; entry of final judgment by a court against the corporation in an amount greater than $ _____ , if the judgment is not discharged within 60 days of the expiration of any stay of execution pending appeal; the corporation's merger; its acquisition by another corporation; _____ ceasing to be the majority stockholder of the corporation; the ouster of _____ as President and Chairman of the Board of Directors of the corporation.

   All representations and warranties made by Chivalry will survive the execution and delivery of this Loan Agreement and Note. This agreement binds and benefits the successors and assigns of both Chivalry and the Lender.

**6.** Chivalry makes the following representations and warranties:

○ It is a corporation validly organized and in good standing and has obtained any and all necessary licenses and permits for its business activities.

○ It is and will remain in compliance with all contracts, loan agreements, security agreements, notes, et cetera; it is not and will not be in default on any tax payment.

○ There is no material accumulated funding deficiency or PBGC liability under any ERISA plan maintained by Chivalry.

○ Chivalry is not directly or indirectly controlled by, or acting on behalf of, any "Investment Company" as defined by the Investment Company Act of 1940.

○ No litigation materially jeopardizing Chivalry's ability to repay is in progress or, to the best knowledge of Chivalry and its officers, pending or threatened.

○ Chivalry has made full disclosure of its financial condition in a form satisfactory to the Lender, in documents accurately prepared in conformity with GAAP and which do not omit or misstate any material facts

○ Chivalry has no subsidiaries.

○ Chivalry has good and marketable title to the real and personal (tangible and intangible) assets used in its business, including but not limited to those named as collateral in the Security Agreement.

○ Chivalry's business has not undergone any material adverse changes since preparation of its financial statements.

○ Proceeds of this loan transaction will be used as working capital and to purchase materials and equipment for use in Chivalry's business.

**7.** On occurrence of default, Lender will have the right to give Chivalry written notice that the note (including matured interest) is due and payable. The Lender will have the right to sue for payment of the Note and/or specific performance of the covenants. Chivalry will be liable for the reasonable cost of collecting defaulted or accelerated obligations, including reasonable attorneys' fees.

# GUARANTY AGREEMENT

Manfred Falls Bank and Edna's Boutique, Inc. have entered into a term loan agreement/revolving credit line relationship/mortgage agreement/secured loan/inventory financing arrangement/accounts receivable financing arrangement. However, the Borrower is a closely held business with limited assets. Therefore, as further security, the Bank requires a personal guaranty by the principals of Edna's Boutique, Inc., as a condition of advancing credit.

Edna Steptoe (President), Robert Steptoe, Jr. (Vice-President), and George Peacham (principal stockholder) each and all jointly and severally agree that, as long as Edna's Boutique, Inc., owes any amount to the Bank under any agreement or arrangement, if, on the due date (as accelerated) for any obligation of Edna's Boutique, Inc., to the Bank, Edna's Boutique, Inc., is in default or is unable to pay the full amount owed to the Bank (including penalties and interest), they will pay the amount owed. The Bank has the right to seek the entire amount owed from any one of them, or to seek repayment from them in any proportion. Furthermore, all personal assets held by any guarantor as separate or marital property, whether owned at the time this guaranty is signed or later acquired (except for property protected by a homestead exemption) shall serve as security and shall be subject to attachment, levy, or seizure under this guaranty.

The guarantors agree not to enter into any other or further guaranty, or to agree to or suffer any subsequent lien or encumbrance, that would impair enforcement of this guaranty.

This guaranty binds and benefits the heirs, successors, and assigns of the Bank, of Edna's Boutique, Inc., and of each guarantor.

Date:_____ , 199____
Signed: _____ Manfred Falls Bank, by: _____
Edna Steptoe: _____
Robert Steptoe, Jr.: _____
George Peacham: _____

# CONSTRUCTION LOAN

*1. Parties:* The Lender is the Cattleman's Trust and Security Company. The Borrower is Kanewha Meter and Calibration Company. Both Lender and Borrower are duly chartered Tyler corporations in good standing.

*2. Loan:* This Loan Agreement sets out the terms under which the Lender will extend a construction loan with two components (secured and unsecured) in the amount of $4,500,000 to the Borrower.

*3. Secured Loan:* The secured loan(s), in an aggregate amount not to exceed $3,000,000, will be secured by Exhibit A, Collateral Note, dated on the closing date of this loan agreement, maturing _____ , 199 ____ , bearing interest at a rate of ____ % until maturity and ____ % after maturity. The collateral note, in turn, will be secured by a first/second mortgage and mortgage note in the amount of $____ payable to the order of the lender and covering all of the Borrower's real property currently owned or acquired while any portion of the Construction Loan (as extended) remains in effect. The Borrower agrees to obtain a mortgage guarantee policy issued by a reputable title company in an amount at least equal to $____ and to deliver proof of such insurance at the closing. Any default under the Construction Loan will also constitute a default under the mortgage and mortgage note.

**4. *Unsecured Loan:*** The unsecured component of the loan, in an amount of $ ____ , will be evidenced by unsecured notes executed by the Borrower as Exhibit B. The Exhibit B unsecured notes will be dated as of the closing date of the Construction Loan transaction and will bear interest at a rate of ____ % until maturity ( _____ , 199 ____ as extended) and ____ % subsequent to maturity. Payments on the unsecured note will be made monthly/quarterly in the amount of $ ____ each.

**5. *Representations and Warranties:*** In order to induce the Lender to make the Construction Loan, the Borrower makes the following representations and warrants that each is true:

*a.* The borrower owns in fee simple a ____ -acre parcel of real estate, Block No. ____ , Lot No. ____ , in Sassafras County in the State of Tyler, subject to restrictions and easements as follows: _____ and free and clear/subject to mortgage(s) and lien(s) as follows: The company's title is insured by Policy No. ____ , issued by the _____ Title Company on _____ , 199 ____ .

*b.* The purpose of the Construction Loan is to build a mixed-use, manufacturing and office complex on the land, in accordance with the plans and specifications prepared by Jonathan Mitwald, AIA. The Borrower agrees to follow these plans and specifications and will not alter them in any way that decreases the use, rental, and/or sale value of the complex. Advance written consent of the Lender is required for all modifications, even if the modifications do not so decrease the value.

*c.* Entering into the Construction Loan Agreement is within the Borrower's corporate powers, does not violate the terms of its charter or bylaws or any agreement entered into with any other party, and has been approved by the Borrower's Board of Directors [and ratified by its stockholders].

*d.* The financial statements (e.g., balance sheet, profit and loss statement) prepared by Dennis Blegen, CPA, and submitted by the Borrower as part of the application process are complete, accurate as of the date prepared, and were prepared in conformity with GAAP. There has been no material adverse change in the interim. The Borrower has no contingent liabilities other than those disclosed in these statements [and the following: _____ ]. The Borrower will continue to furnish financial statements from the closing date of this transaction for as long as the loan is in effect. Although unaudited statements will be acceptable for this purpose, the CFO of the Borrower corporation must certify each statement as true and correct.

*e.* The Borrower's real and personal property is unencumbered and free from mortgages, liens, and charges [except as disclosed in its financial statements/except for: _____ ].

*f.* The Borrower is not a subsidiary of any other corporation, does not have any subsidiaries, and is not part of any group of controlled corporations.

*g.* The Borrower is not a party to any litigation, administrative proceeding, or arbitration proceeding [except as disclosed: _____ ] and is not aware of any such action or proceeding to be commenced in the future [except as follows: _____ ].

*h.* On or before _____ , 199 ____ , the Borrower will furnish a favorable opinion of independent counsel of all matters contained in these Representations and Warranties, and any other matter of legal import with respect to which Lender has demanded an opinion of independent counsel on or before _____ , 199 ____ .

**6. *Covenants:*** As long as there is any outstanding secured or unsecured loan balance, the Borrower covenants as follows: _____

*a.* Its net working capital, calculated under GAAP (current assets, including the land on which construction will be done, valued at $ ____ , minus current liabilities, NOT including the construction loan balance) will equal or exceed $ ____ at all times.

*b.* The Borrower will at all times maintain insurance coverage reasonable in type and amount as judged by prevailing standards within the Borrower's industry. Property insurance covering the construction project will be made payable to the Borrower and Lender proportionate to their respective interests in the construction project. The Borrower will turn over all insurance policies and certificates covering the construction project and its other property and business to the Lender, which will be entitled to hold them as long as there is any balance outstanding under the Construction Loan.

*c.* The Borrower agrees not to undertake or permit to occur any mortgage, lien, pledge, borrowing, or encumbrance on itself or its business without advance consent of the Lender, at any time during which there is an outstanding balance under the Construction Loan as extended, other than current borrowings from the Lender in amounts up to $ ____ and real estate liens and encumbrances which do not materially impair the use of the construction site. To this end, the Borrower agrees to pay all taxes as they come due (other than taxes being contested in good faith) and to promptly pay all claims, demands, and debts (other than those being contested in good faith) that, if unpaid, would or might be given priority over the construction loan in a bankruptcy or insolvency proceeding.

*d.* The Borrower agrees not to repurchase or redeem any of its stock or declare a cash dividend on any class or series of its stock/its common stock without advance consent of the Lender.

*e.* The Borrower agrees not to participate in any voluntary merger or consolidation or to convey, sell, lease, or exchange all or substantially all of its business assets without advance written consent of the Lender.

*f.* The Borrower agrees to maintain at all times an account with the Lender, titled as the Borrower Corporation Construction Account. All proceeds of the Construction Loan will be deposited in this account which will be used only for purposes approved by the Lender, for example, payment of construction costs and fees.

*g.* The Borrower agrees to proceed diligently and in good faith to hire acceptable and bondable contractors and to see that they carry out construction in accordance with the plans and with any applicable building codes. The construction contracts will call for completion on or before _____ , 199 ____ . The Borrower agrees to include in each prime contract a 10% retainage factor against completion of the contract.

*h.* If at any time when there is any outstanding balance on the construction loan, the Lender determines that the loan proceeds still unused are insufficient to complete the project on time and in conformity with the plans and specifications, the Borrower agrees to pay to the Lender the amount of the deficiency as determined by the Lender. The Lender will place these funds in a segregated account where they can be released only to complete the project. Any segregated funds remaining after completion of the project will be returned to the Borrower.

**7. *Default:*** Any one or more of these will constitute a default by the Borrower, entitling the Lender immediately to cease advancing or disbursing construction funds. On default, all outstanding notes under the Construction Loan agreement will immediately become due and payable without further notice or demand to the Borrower. On default, the Lender will have the right to enter the construction site and have any necessary work done to complete the project on schedule according to the plans and specifications. The expenses of doing so will be charged to the Borrower. The Lender will also have any other remedy available to creditors, and the choice of remedy is entirely discretionary with the Lender. The Borrower will be responsible for reimbursing the Lender for any costs incurred in enforcing these default provisions, including attorneys' fees, judgment searches, and the fees of an architect and/or engineer.

*a.* Falsity or materially misleading nature of any representation or warranty made in this agreement.

*b.* Failure to make any installment payment (including interest) of any Note under the Construction Loan agreement, within ten days of its due date, whether or not the Lender has made a formal demand for payment.

*c.* Breach or violation of any covenant or condition in this agreement or any loan note that is part of the Construction Loan transaction.

*d.* The building to be constructed is substantially injured or destroyed while it is after construction, or after construction while there is an outstanding balance under the Construction Loan agreement, or the relevant governmental agency precludes or halts construction based on its disapproval of the plans, or because any law, regulation, or ordinance has been violated in the course of construction, and the Borrower has not promptly corrected the violation.

*e.* The Borrower is voluntarily or involuntarily adjudged bankrupt; is placed in receivership; undergoes a judicial proceeding for reorganization, liquidation, or dissolution; or makes an assignment for benefit of its creditors.

**8. *Prepayment:*** The Borrower has the right to prepay part or all of any note that is part of the Construction Loan agreement, without penalty, at any time.

**9. *Extension:*** The Lender agrees to a reasonable extension of loan note maturity if completion of the building is delayed for reasons beyond the control of the Borrower.

## Exhibit A   Secured Note

FOR VALUE RECEIVED, the Borrower (Kanewha Meter & Calibration Co.), a Tyler corporation, promises to pay to the order of Lender (Cattleman's Trust and Security Co.) the sum of $ ____ with interest at the rate of ____ % on the unpaid balance until maturity, ____ % thereafter, in equal monthly payments of $ ____ each that will completely amortize the loan in ____ years.

This Secured Note evidences the Construction Loan arrangement set out in an agreement dated _____ , 199 ____ between Borrower and Lender, to which this Secured Note is attached as an exhibit.

Payment of the Borrower's obligations under this Note is secured by a mortgage note executed by the Borrower on _____ , 199 ____ payable to the order of the Lender and by a first mortgage deed on the property on which the building is to be constructed, naming the Lender as mortgagee. The mortgage deed has been recorded under Number ____ in the office of the Registar of Sassafras County, Tyler.

Date: _____ , 199____        Kanewha Meter & Calibration Co. by _____
                                    Lillian Baxter Poole, President

## Exhibit B   Unsecured Note

FOR VALUE RECEIVED, the Borrower agrees to make regular monthly payments of $ ____ each, representing the principal plus interest at ____ % on the unpaid balance of the sum of $ ____ lent by the Lender on _____ , 199 ____ as part of the Construction Loan arrangement set out in the Construction Loan agreement to which this Note is attached as an exhibit.

Date: _____ , 199____        Kanewha Meter & Calibration Co., by _____
                                    Lillian Baxter Poole, President

## LETTER OF CREDIT

In this document, the issuer is Minagault Stream Bank & Trust, which agrees to pay checks/sight drafts signed by the customer, West Minagault Apparel [and made payable to Chang Liu Gray Goods

Mill, Singapore, also known as the beneficiary] [up to a total amount of outstanding checks/sight drafts of $ ____ U.S.] [and provided that the check/sight draft is signed in the presence of the beneficiary/a correspondent banker of the issuing bank], by the authorized signer, Clancy McHugh, and that the signature conforms to the specimen signature included in the letter of identification made available with this letter of credit.

This letter of credit is confirmed and irrevocable/revocable by _____ on ____ days' notice given by _____ to _____ . [The customer may only draw on this letter of credit by presenting the following documents:

* A full set of "On Board" ocean bills of lading dated on or before _____ , 199 ____ , evidencing shipment to the port of Boston

* Abstract of invoice/commercial invoice

* Certificate of marine and war-risk insurance

* Export documentation from the country of origin (e.g., sanitary and weight certificates)

* Documentation permitting importation of the merchandise into the United States]

This letter of credit is usable for any lawful transaction/only for the purpose of purchasing 45″ wide cotton muslin gray goods.

We promise all drawers, endorsers, and bona fide holders of drafts drawn in accordance with the terms of this letter of credit while it remains valid and in force that the drafts will be honored when they are duly presented to us. Drawers, endorsers, and bona fide holders of drafts will have no liability with respect to forged or altered shipping documents or as to the quantity and/or quality of merchandise delivered.

When the funds available under the letter of credit are exhausted, cancel the letter of credit and attach it to the final draft.


## WHOLESALE FLOOR PLAN SECURITY AGREEMENT

*1. Introduction:* The purpose of this Agreement is to induce Willow Pond National Bank ("Bank") to enter into a long-term relationship with Nate 'n' Benny's Appliance Barn ("Dealer") under which the Bank provides financing for the acquisition of appliances to serve as inventory. Dealer agrees to give the bank a security interest in its current inventory and in all future and replacement inventory as long as this agreement remains in force, and the security interest will be a purchase money security interest to the extent that Bank funds are used to purchase collateral. A list of current inventory of household appliances (e.g., washing machines, refrigerators, stoves, dishwashers) is attached to this agreement as Exhibit A.

*2. Financing:* The Bank agrees to provide financing subject to the terms and conditions of this agreement sufficient for the Dealer to maintain an adequate inventory of appliances.

*3. Repayment:* Subject to the terms and conditions of this agreement, the Dealer agrees to pay to the Bank on demand the amount of each payment made by the bank to finance the Dealer's inventory, plus interest and any premiums incurred by the Bank to insure the inventory.

*4. Security Interest in the Collateral:* The Dealer hereby gives the Bank a security interest in all the inventory described in Schedule A, all inventory later acquired as additional or replacement inventory while this agreement is in force, as well as the proceeds of the sale of any such inventory.

Inventory and proceeds will be known collectively as the collateral. The security interest in the collateral secures all existing and future obligations of the Dealer to the Bank under this and any other agreement of any type. To this end, the Dealer agrees to execute and deliver to the Bank any and all documents that the Bank demands as further evidence of the Dealer's obligations, such as notes, trust receipts, and security agreements. The Dealer agrees to offer to the Bank all chattel paper executed by its customers as part of the sale of the collateral; the Bank has the discretion to accept or reject the chattel paper.

**5. *Bank's Power with Respect to Documents:*** To expedite financing of its inventory, the Dealer hereby grants its irrevocable authorization to the Bank to make, execute, and file (in the Dealer's name) all notes, wholesale instruments, financing statements, chattel mortgage statements, and other documents commonly used in the banking industry in connection with inventory financing and to complete incomplete portions of any documents executed by the Dealer on or on the Dealer's behalf.

**6. *Dealer's Treatment of Inventory:***

*a.* Unless the Bank gives its consent to a different treatment, the Dealer agrees to keep and use all inventory financed under this agreement solely for resale to the public at retail, at prices equal to or greater than the amount owed to the Bank for that item of collateral.

*b.* All risk of loss or damage to the collateral will be on the Dealer at all times.

*c.* When any item of collateral is sold, the Dealer is obligated to account to the Bank for the proceeds, to the extent the Bank advanced financing for that item of collateral; to deliver such portion of the proceeds to the Bank, accompanied by assignments and endorsements as requested by the Bank; and to pay interest to the Bank at the rate of _____ % running from the date funds were advanced for the Dealer to purchase the collateral until the date the collateral was sold at retail to a consumer. Until the proceeds (defined to include all cash and noncash sales proceeds, trade-ins, chattel paper, notes and drafts, and repossessed items of collateral) are turned over to the Bank, the Dealer holds the proceeds in trust for the Bank, at the Dealer's risk.

*d.* The Dealer is required to maintain insurance on the collateral at its own expense, in type and amount as required by the Bank, in the form of policies issued by a carrier acceptable to the Bank and payable to the Bank and Dealer in proportion to their respective interests in the insured collateral items. The Dealer agrees to turn over the policy documents to the Bank. If the Dealer fails to insure the collateral adequately, the Bank has the right (but not the obligation) to secure insurance on the collateral and demand reimbursement from the Dealer for any premiums paid.

*e.* There is no other lien or security interest in the inventory. The Dealer agrees to give the Bank ten days' written notice before entering into any other floor plan or inventory financing arrangement.

*f.* The Dealer agrees to make its books and records available for the Bank's inspection at any commercially reasonable time, insofar as these books and records relate to the sale, disposition, and proceeds of the collateral.

**7. *Default:*** The Dealer will be in default at any time when

○ The Dealer fails to perform any obligation under this agreement, including failure to make payments when due.

○ A substantial portion of the collateral is damaged or destroyed.

○ Any key person within the Dealer's organization dies.

○ The Dealer enters voluntary or involuntary bankruptcy or receivership or makes an assignment for the benefit of its creditors.

○ The financial condition of the Dealer deteriorates to the extent that the Bank deems itself insecure.

*8. Bank's Rights on Default:* On default, the Bank has and can exercise all the rights granted by the Uniform Commercial Code, for example, the right to:

○ Demand that the Dealer assemble the collateral and make it available to the Bank at a mutually convenient location.

○ Enter on the Dealer's premises and repossess the collateral.

○ Take exclusive control of the Dealer's premises (rent free) for the purpose of storing and/or selling the collateral.

○ Sell repossessed collateral by public or private sale, or retail any item or items of collateral.

The Dealer will remain responsible for any deficiency remaining after sale of repossessed collateral.

All the Bank's remedies are cumulative; choice of one remedy does not bar the subsequent use of other remedies, and the Bank's failure to pursue remedies as to one event of default does not operate as a waiver with respect to other events of default.

Date: _____ , 199____
Signed, Bank, by: _____
Dealer, by: _____

## TRUST RECEIPT FOR INVENTORY FINANCING

### Heaston Valley Bank Trust Receipt

The Heaston Valley Bank, as Entruster, has a security interest in all of Pavonia Hardware's present and after-acquired inventory of stoves, sinks, refrigerators, and other household appliances. Pavonia Hardware acknowledges that it holds such inventory as Trustee for the Heaston Valley Bank and that all risk of loss or damage to the inventory falls on the Trustee. The Trustee agrees to keep the inventory at its place of business; to maintain it in good condition; and to pay all taxes, costs, liens, and insurance premiums on the inventory. The Trustee agrees not to permit the inventory to be mortgaged, pledged, encumbered, or moved from the Trustee's business premises unless it has been sold in the ordinary course of business or repossessed by the Entruster, which has the right to enter into the Trustee's premises for this purpose.

Exhibit A, attached to this Trust Receipt, gives a description of each item of current inventory and the amount to which the Trustee is obligated to the Entruster for that item (plus interest accruing at the Bank's then-prevailing prime rate of interest).

Whenever it sells an item of inventory financed by the Entruster, the Trustee agrees to pay the amount of the obligation for such item to the Entruster. The amount of the obligation becomes the property of the Entruster immediately on sale of the item of inventory. The Trustee agrees to keep all such sums of money in a separate account (not commingled with the Trustee's own funds) until the funds have been submitted to the Entruster.

The Entruster is a secured party and has all the rights as such provided by the Uniform Commercial Code. The Trustee agrees to pay all costs incurred by the Entruster, including a reasonable attorney's fee, that the Entruster is forced to pay to vindicate its rights upon default.

The Trustee acknowledges that it has received a true and complete copy of this Trust Receipt.

# FACTORING AGREEMENT (Security Agreement with Respect to Accounts Receivable)

*1. A/R Financing:* The First Federal Bank ("Bank") and Haeberle Swiss Embroidery Mill, Inc. ("Borrower"), wish to enter into a continuing agreement under which the Bank will advance funds from time to time, up to a total of $ ____ in any single advance, $ ____ outstanding at any one time, to the Borrower. The Borrower, in turn, will execute a note or notes payable to the Bank, using forms acceptable to the Bank. The Borrower agrees to grant a security interest in all of its current and future accounts receivable ("A/R") as collateral to secure repayment of the note(s).

*2. Other Collateral:* The Borrower also agrees to give the Bank a security interest in its present and future inventory and raw materials, in order to secure all amounts borrowed from the Bank under this or any other loan agreement or arrangement.

*3. Financing Statement:* Before the Bank advances any money to the Borrower, the Borrower agrees to submit to the Bank an executed Financing Statement. The Borrower also agrees to execute continuation statements on request of the Bank at any time that this Security Agreement remains in effect.

*4. A/R Invoices:* The Borrower agrees to assign its accounts receivable (A/R) to the Bank as they are created. The Borrower will deliver to the Bank, as part of each assignment, supporting documentation as required by the Bank, for example, invoices stamped to indicate that the underlying A/R has been assigned to the Bank to secure loans, bills of lading, waybills, freight bills, and delivery receipts. The Bank can examine the Borrower's books and records without notice at any commercially reasonable hour and can contact the Borrower's customers directly to ascertain the state of the account.

*5. Bank as Successor:* The Bank succeeds to, and can enforce or have enforced for its own benefit, any and all of the Borrower's rights, interests, security, and liens with respect to the assigned accounts receivable, including the right of stoppage in transitu, and can collect the assigned A/R as they come due and treat the proceeds as security for the underlying loan.

*6. Borrower's Representations:* Any assignment of an A/R acts as and constitutes a representation by the Borrower that

○ The A/R arises from a bona fide sale to a customer.
○ A balance is owed by the customer, but is not past due.
○ The A/R accurately states the amount so owed.
○ The merchandise has been duly delivered and accepted.
○ There is no other legal or equitable claim (e.g., financing statement, judgment, security interest, lien) on the A/R.

*7. Borrower's Treatment of the A/R:* The borrower agrees not to compromise, settle, discount, or extend the time for payment of any assigned A/R without the Bank's advance written permission.

*8. Agency:* The Borrower collects all assigned A/R as agent for the Bank and must deliver them to the Bank in the form in which they are received (plus any required endorsements by the Borrower). Until delivery, the A/R will be kept separate and not commingled with Borrower's own funds. Delivery will take place by the deposit of the A/R into a collateral account with the Bank named as assignee. The Borrower can make withdrawals from this account only with consent of the Bank, and at times when the Borrower is not in default under this agreement.

**9. *Release:*** If the Borrower is not in default on any note payable to the Bank, or on this Security Agreement, and if the collateral account exceeds _____ % of the amount then outstanding under all of the Borrower's notes payable to the Bank, the Bank will release the difference between the collateral account balance and _____ % of the outstanding notes to the borrower on a quarterly basis (January 2, April 1, July 1, October 1 or the next business day in the event of a holiday).

**10. *Customer Problems:*** The borrower will make a monthly report to the Bank of all merchandise whose sale creates an assigned A/R where the goods are returned by the customer or if delivery is stopped in transitu. The Borrower agrees to keep such merchandise separate and to hold it in trust for the Bank until the Borrower submits substitute A/R to the bank, at least equal in amount and collection potential to the A/R originally covering the merchandise.

**11. *Borrower's Default:*** The Borrower will be in default whenever

○ Any obligation under this agreement is unperformed, including failure to make payments as and when due.

○ The Borrower becomes insolvent, makes an assignment for benefit of its creditors, or is involved as a potential bankrupt in a voluntary or involuntary bankruptcy proceeding.

○ Any officer, manager above the level of Vice-President, or guarantor or surety under this agreement dies, is adjudged incompetent, or becomes bankrupt or insolvent.

○ Any customer whose A/R represents 10% or more of the outstanding A/R at any time becomes bankrupt or insolvent or makes an assignment for benefit of its creditors.

○ The financial condition of the Borrower worsens to the extent that the Bank deems itself insecure.

On occurrence of any default, the Bank has the right (but not the obligation) to accelerate the due date of all notes executed by the Borrower to the Bank; collect the assigned A/R directly from the Borrower's customers; sell anything that serves as collateral under the note(s) or this Security Agreement; or all of them.

## Assignment of A/R

For value received, and to secure its payment of indebtedness under certain loan notes and under the Security Agreement that constitutes part of this document, Haeberle Swiss Embroidery Mill, Inc. (Borrower), hereby assigns and transfers to the First Federal Bank (Bank) all of its right, title, and interest in accounts receivable with an aggregate balance of $ _____ , evidenced by Borrower's invoices numbered _____ through _____ , and in subsequent and replacement accounts receivable. The accounts receivable are assigned to the bank to secure a line of credit under which the Bank will disburse funds as requested by the Borrower, with a maximum single disbursement of $ _____ at any one time, and with a maximum aggregate outstanding balance of $ _____ existing at any one time.

The Borrower represents and warrants that each and every account receivable now assigned or to be assigned in the future arises out of a bona fide sale of merchandise to a customer reasonably believed to be creditworthy; that the amount stated on the account receivable is the amount owed by the customer; that there is no assignment, lien, judgment, or other encumbrance on accounts receivable so assigned; and that the Borrower will not create or suffer to be created any assignment, lien, judgment, or other encumbrance in the future on any account receivable assigned to the Bank.

Date: _____ , 199_____
Signed, Bank, by: _____
Borrower, by: _____

## EQUIPMENT LEASE

In consideration of the sums paid and to be paid, and the benefits received and to be received, the Lessor, Simpkins Industrial Heavy Machinery, Inc., and the Lessee, Windsmuir Basic Processes & Processing Co., enter into a lease arrangement under which the Lessee shall have use of certain machinery belonging to the Lessor.

*1. Term:* For the term beginning _____ , 199 ____ , and extending for five years (unless extended by mutual agreement, or terminated pursuant to this agreement), the Lessee agrees to lease the equipment described on Schedule A attached to this agreement. The equipment so described shall include all replacement parts, accessories, additions, and repairs during the lease term. The Lessor agrees either to deliver the leased equipment on or before the commencement date or to contract with an appropriate licensed carrier to have delivery made. Installation shall be the responsibility of, and at the expense of, the lessee.

*2. Net Lease Payments:* Beginning on the commencement date, and on or before the _____ day of each month during the entire term, the Lessee agrees to make a lease payment of $ ____ per month, payable in U.S. dollars by check drawn on a bank within the state of Tyler, to the Lessor at its offices located at Building B, Industrial Plaza, Mockingbird Village, Tyler, or to such assignee of the Lessor or other party to whom the Lessor directs that payments be made. Payments that are more than ten days late will be subject to a late charge of $25.00.

Lessor and Lessee agree that this will be a net lease, with the Lessee assuming the obligation to pay all taxes related to the use or ownership of the leased machinery.

*3. Title and Return:* Title to the leased machinery will, at all times, remain in the Lessor, and the Lessee agrees that it will not claim that it has title to the leased machinery, nor will it remove labels, plates, license numbers, or other evidence of the Lessor's ownership. The Lessor is authorized to file this lease agreement, or any other relevant related document, such as UCC financing statements, in any appropriate governmental office, at the expense of the Lessee (who is also responsible for paying any license fees or tax stamps required).

On termination of this lease, the Lessee is obligated to return the leased machinery and will have no right under this lease to buy or otherwise acquire the leased machinery.

*4. Maintenance and Care:* The Lessee is obligated to maintain the leased machinery in good condition, to keep it at the location specified in Schedule A unless the Lessor gives its advance written consent to moving the machinery, to perform or have performed any necessary repairs, and to add accessories or replacement parts as required for efficient and safe operation of the leased machinery, all at its own expense; and to maintain in effect and pay for a service contract covering the leased machinery. The Lessee is forbidden to customize, modify, or adapt the leased machinery or to add any accessories not required for safe and efficient operation, without the advance written consent of the Lessor (which is not to be unreasonably withheld). The leased machinery will, at all times, have the legal status of personal property and will not be converted into a fixture or realty no matter what use the Lessee makes of the leased machinery.

*5. Risk of Loss:* The Lessee shall bear the entire risk of loss, damage, or destruction of the leased machinery by or from all causes during the entire term of the lease, and, should the leased machinery become damaged, the Lessee must repair or replace it at its own expense. The Lessee will maintain insurance on the leased machinery throughout the term of the lease, covering at least the replacement cost of the leased machinery (computed without allowance for depreciation), against all commercially reasonable risks, and will maintain liability insurance in commercially reasonable amounts covering liability to any individual for personal injury or property damage arising out of the use or operation of the leased machinery. Such insurance will be maintained at the expense of the Lessee.

**6. *Indemnification:*** The Lessee agrees to indemnify the Lessor, hold it harmless, and provide defense counsel for all liability of all types arising out of Lessee's use of the leased machinery during the lease term, or out of the resale, reuse, or releasing of the leased machinery after default by the Lessee and repossession of the leased machinery. All claims arising out of improper condition, delivery, or installation of the leased machinery shall be made against the equipment's manufacturer or the delivery agent, not against the Lessor, and the obligation to make payments to the Lessor shall continue irrespective of the existence or progress of such claims.

**7. *Lessor's Representations, Covenants, Warranties, and Disclaimers:*** The Lessor guarantees quiet enjoyment during the lease term on condition that the Lessee performs its obligations under the lease. The Lessor represents and warrants that it is legally entitled to lease the equipment and that entering into this lease is an appropriately authorized corporate act that is not ultra vires.

The Lessor has not undertaken any attempt to induce the Lessee to lease specific items of equipment; the lease is a response to demand by the Lessee, based on the Lessee's prior decision about the equipment it needed, and not based on any representation or warranty made by the Lessor as to the nature, condition, purpose, suitability, or fitness for any particular use of the leased machinery. The Lessor hereby disclaims all warranties with respect to the leased machinery, which is accepted and used in an "as is" condition. The Lessor and its assignees will have no liability for any direct or consequential damages caused to anybody by the Lessee's selection, installation, use, or operation of the leased machinery.

**8. *Lessee's Representations, Covenants, and Warranties:*** The Lessee agrees to make all payments called for under this lease, regardless of whether it asserts any claim of any type against any person. The Lessee warrants that the financial statements submitted to induce the Lessor to enter into this agreement are complete and accurate, and are prepared in accordance with GAAP, and that it will promptly furnish the Lessor with notice and documentation of any material change in the Lessee's financial condition. The Lessee warrants that entering into this lease is a properly authorized corporate act that is not ultra vires and that does not conflict with or constitute an act of default under any other agreement or transaction.

**9. *Performance by Lessor:*** In order to safeguard the value of its property, the Lessor will have the right (but not the duty) to perform any of the Lessee's obligations other than making lease payments (e.g., securing and paying for insurance); the cost of doing so will be added to the next lease payment when it becomes due.

**10. *Default:*** Any or all of these will constitute default:

○ The Lessee fails to make any payment when due, unless the payment is made, plus late charge, within ten business days of the due date.

○ Any representation made by the Lessee is false.

○ The Lessee breaches any covenant or warranty contained in this agreement.

○ The Lessee fails to meet its obligations to the Lessor under any agreement or transaction other than this lease.

○ The Lessee becomes insolvent, makes an assignment for benefit of its creditors, is placed in receivership, or is the subject of a voluntary or involuntary bankruptcy petition.

**11. *Default Remedies:*** The Lessor has the option of declaring the lease terminated and accelerating the entire remaining balance due under the lease if and when any event of default occurs. The Lessor may enter into the Lessee's premises and repossess the leased machinery, the Lessor can sue the Lessee for damages in any court having jurisdiction over the Lessee, or any combination of these. Failure to pursue remedies upon one event of default does not constitute a waiver of remedies with respect to other or future acts of default. If, after repossession and resale or releasing of the property, a balance remains, the Lessee will remain responsible for the balance. All default remedies are cumulative, and the remedies listed in this clause are in addition to any other creditors' remedies provided by state law.

**12. *Return of Property:*** When the lease expires or is terminated, the Lessee is required to return the leased machinery promptly, intact and in good condition, to the Lessor or to the next Lessee, as stipulated by the Lessor. Return shall be at the expense of the Lessee, and risk of loss or damage to the leased machinery shall be on the Lessee until the Lessor or next Lessee has received the machinery, and the Lessor has had an opportunity to inspect the leased machinery or have it inspected.

**13. *Assignment:*** The Lessee may not sublease the machinery, or assign this lease, without advance written consent of the Lessor. The Lessor, however, may freely assign the lease without consent of or notice to the Lessee; if such an assignment is made, the Lessor will inform the Lessee where and to whom all further lease payments must be made.

Date: _____ , 199____

Lessor, by: _____

Lessee, by: _____

# LEASE OF ALL CORPORATE ASSETS

## Preamble

Dignum Enterprises, Inc., a corporation validly organized and in good standing in the state of Adams, has determined that it is in the best interests of the corporation to raise funds by entering into an agreement with the Blaine Company under which the Blaine Company agrees to lease all the corporate assets belonging to Dignum Enterprises, Inc.

Dignum's Articles of Incorporation require ratification by a 60% supermajority of any lease of all or substantially all of the corporation's assets. At a special meeting held on _____ , 199 ____ , the holders of 12,000 of the corporation's 15,000 shares of authorized and issued voting stock voted to ratify the resolution of Dignum's Board of Directors, dated _____ , 199 ____ , calling for the lease agreement with Blaine. Hence, the transaction is proper and has received proper authorization and ratification.

*1.* Blaine agrees to lease the entire Dignum business, its real and personal, tangible and intangible property, goodwill, brands, trademarks and trade names, trade secrets, processes, and inventions and to assume Dignum's obligations under the following commercial leases _____ and the following equipment leases— _____ —for a term of ten years commencing on _____ , 199 ____ , provided that Blaine can terminate the lease at any time on six months' written notice to Dignum.

*2.* This lease shall not terminate Dignum's corporate existence, powers, or franchise.

**3.** Dignum agrees, represents, warrants, and covenants that it will maintain corporate existence in good standing throughout the lease term, undertaking any action required to do so; that it has good and unencumbered title to all of the assets covered by this leasing arrangement (except encumbrances as disclosed to Blaine); that Blaine will have full and free use and quiet enjoyment of the leased assets during the lease term provided that Blaine is not in default; and that it will not sell, assign, transfer, or encumber any property covered by the lease during the lease term.

**4.** Blaine agrees, represents, warrants, and covenants that it will make 12 equal monthly payments of $ _____ throughout the lease term/pay _____ % of its gross income/ _____ % of its gross income attributable to the use of the leased assets/ _____ % of its net income, defined as follows: _____ , with the first payment due on _____ , 199 _____ ; that during the lease term, it will maintain the leased property in good condition (except for normal wear and tear) and will undertake all necessary acts of maintenance, preservation, and repair that a prudent owner would undertake; that, pursuant to this net lease, it will pay all real estate taxes, occupancy taxes, and water and sewer charges on leased property (and will have the right to protest and appeal tax assessments/ demand that Dignum protest and appeal tax assessments); and that it will not purport or attempt to sell, assign, or transfer this lease or any rights under it, and will not sublease any leased property, without advance written consent from Dignum.

**5.** If any lease payment remains unpaid ten business days after its due date, or if Blaine violates any portion of this agreement, Dignum shall have the right to terminate this lease and resume possession and use of all leased assets, or accelerate all remaining lease payments and declare them immediately due and payable.

Dated: _____ , 199 _____

Dignum, by: _____                                          [Seal]

Blaine, by: _____                                           [Seal]

## SALE-LEASEBACK AGREEMENT

**1.** The Maremount Companies, Inc., is the owner in fee simple, free and clear, of a parcel of real estate located at Block 19, Lot 2429 in Salmontail County, Roosevelt. A 22-story office building has been constructed on this plot. The building, currently owned by Maremount Companies, Inc., in fee simple, free and clear of all encumbrance, is used by Maremount as its headquarters.

**2.** The Maremount Companies, Inc., is in need of further capital for current operations, expansion, research, and development.

**3.** Castenetta Property Development, Inc., a Tyler corporation licensed to do business in the state of Roosevelt, has offered to purchase the real estate and building from Maremount for the sum of $5.5 million, and to lease ten floors of the building to Maremount for an annual rental of $100,000.

**4.** A special committee of the Board of Directors of Maremount was appointed to study the advisability of entering into a sale-leaseback transaction with Castenetta Property Development. At a special meeting of Maremount's Board of Directors held on _____ , 199 _____ , the special committee rendered its report (which was positive), and the corporation's attorney and CPA, Michael Costantinos and Roger Symmes-Bradley, answered questions posed by the Board members and rendered their opinions that the sale-leaseback transaction would be lawful and would provide financial advantages to the corporation. In light of this information, and on review of the written reports rendered by the special committee, attorney, and accountant, Maremount's Board of Directors voted unanimously to authorize the sale-leaseback transaction, and passed a resolution to this effect.

**5.** By resolution dated _____ , 9 of Castenetta's 11 directors voted to enter into the sale-leaseback transaction (there was 1 dissent, and 1 interested director abstained).

THEREFORE,

**6.** Maremount agrees to sell and convey the property to Castenetta in return for $2 million cash and a $3.5 million purchase money mortgage bearing an interest rate of 10%; Maremount also agrees to lease floors 12–22 of the building for a term of 20 years, with an initial rent of $100,000 per year (with rent and adjustments to be made every 5 years, corresponding to changes in the Department of Labor's Producers' Price Index), pursuant to a commercial lease in a form approved by both corporations and their counsel.

Date: _____ , 199____

Maremount, by: _____             [Seal]

Castenetta, by: _____             [Seal]

## COMMERCIAL LEASES

Depending on the corporation's ventures and style of doing business, the corporation will probably require office space, one or more retail stores, warehouse space, manufacturing space, or some combination of all of those. The corporate secretary, drawing on past experience of renting apartments, may *think* that he or she already understands commercial leases—but there are many differences between commercial and residential leases.

One of the most significant differences is that residential tenants have a high degree of protection. Landlords are often compelled to disclose many interesting (and perhaps embarrassing) facts to residential tenants. States and cities often protect residential tenants against eviction without due process and excessive rent increases; if tenants continue to occupy the premises peacefully and pay their rent, they may be entitled to indefinite occupancy, and to pass the tenancy of the apartment along to their heirs.

The situation for commercial tenants is far more precarious. Many successful businesses have gone under because they lost their leases, or because the rent demanded for a renewal lease was more than the business could afford to pay. Even if comparable space is available elsewhere at a reasonable price, moving is very disruptive and causes loss of valuable business time.

Furthermore, determining the "rent" under a residential lease is a very simple process: the lease spells out how much the tenant must pay, and the rent usually includes heat and hot water and sometimes includes utilities. The typical residential lease is a "gross" lease, with the landlord responsible for repairs and many other building expenses. Commercial landlords try to make their leases as "net" as possible: that is, to make the tenants assume most or all of the burdens of operating expenses and taxes.

Commercial rent is a very complex calculation, and landlords use many varieties of formulas (so that what appears to be a bargain-basement rent can turn out to be very high indeed). The typical office lease is based on a yearly rent per square foot of office space. However, this figure is only a starting point: the landlord will be entitled to various "escalators" used to pass along cost increases (or the full amount of costs) to tenants. Furthermore, landlords have different ways of calculating the square footage included under the lease. The square footage may include everything from the outside of the building, or everything from the inside walls; elevators, corridors, and stairwells may be either included or excluded. Tenants end up paying for far more square feet than they think they need, because only a portion of the space they rent is usable.

If the office lease includes a "porter's wage increase," the rental per square foot will go up (usually 1¢–1½¢ for every dollar increase) whenever the wages of janitors and other building employees go up. Sometimes the definition of wages includes Social Security taxes and benefits as well as straight salary. Depending on the lease, the tenant may be billed directly by the utilities for gas and electric use, may pay a dollar amount or a percentage of the landlord's usage, or may pay the landlord for usage as measured by a separate meter. Real estate taxes are another controversial area. Leases usually require the tenants to pay the entire tax increase over a base year (or the entire amount of the tax)—a provision that, tenants charge, prevents landlords from challenging unfairly high tax assessments (after all, the tenants pay them, not the landlord). So tenants may want the right to force landlords to challenge tax increases—or the right to go to court directly to protest the assessment.

## Store Leases

Retail tenants (especially those in shopping centers) frequently pay a base rent (either a dollar figure or an amount per square foot) plus a percentage of their sales. The definition of "sales" is crucial. The landlord, of course, wants to include as many things as possible, and wants the payments as soon as possible; the tenant wants to exclude as much as possible and delay the payments. Many controversies have arisen over questions such as how tenants must maintain records; whether items such as lottery tickets and gift-wrapping count as "sales" and whether mail orders and sales made at another location are included in the calculation. Shopping center tenants often are required to pay dues to a merchants' association that takes care of things like sanitation, security, and promotion of the shopping center.

Shopping center leases may include two other distinctive clauses: an "exclusive" (promising a tenant that no other tenant in the shopping center will compete by offering the specified products or services) and a "radius clause" (obligating the tenant not to limit the amount of sales subject to the landlord's percentage by opening another location within a specified radius of the shopping center). These provisions, too, can give rise to many disagreements, and the tenant must review them carefully to see that they are drafted the way the tenant wants. (Tenants must also make sure that what they plan to do will not conflict with exclusives already granted to other tenants.)

Many commercial leases are signed before the office building or retail store has been constructed. This gives the tenant maximum flexibility in making design changes, but creates a risk that the space will not be ready on the date the tenant is supposed to move in. The lease must spell out (in terms acceptable to the tenant) who is responsible for performing and paying for various phases of construction (tenants are often responsible for finish work once the landlord has provided a roof, wiring, plumbing, walls, and floors); who has the right to approve of designs and changes in designs; and when the tenant's obligations under the lease officially "commence."

For example, shopping center leases frequently provide that tenants do not have to move in and start paying rent until the "anchor tenants" (commercial magnets such as major department stores) and a certain percentage of the other tenants have opened for business. The tenant may have to pay the basic rent, but not the "percentage rent" (percentage of tenant's sales) until the center is fully operational.

Commercial tenants must also consider other kinds of risks. Remember, commercial landlords try to pass along as many risks as possible, so the tenant may have an obligation under the lease to maintain a certain amount of insurance. Tenants will also want to consider whether they need insurance to protect their stock in trade and to provide coverage against business interruption. A well-informed insurance agent or broker will be able to explain the various coverages available and which are suitable for the tenant.

## Transferring the Lease

There are many reasons why a tenant would want to give up a lease. The tenant could be unsuccessful, and unable to meet the rent payments, or, on the contrary, the tenant could be so successful that much more space, or space in a more elegant neighborhood, is necessary. Or the tenant could have made a spectacularly right guess about the future of gentrification in a neighborhood with the result that space leased for $10 a square foot can now be subleased for $100 a square foot.

Thus, the tenant's attorney must review the proposed lease carefully to see if tenants have the right to sublease or assign freely (an assignment is a transfer of all of the tenant's obligations, for the balance of the lease term; a sublease is anything less), and if there are any limitations on the use the subtenant or assignee can make of the space (for instance, in a shopping center, the other tenants' exclusives must be considered) and whether the landlord has the right to terminate the original tenant's lease and make a deal directly with the subtenant or assignee.

## Reviewing the Lease

In light of all these considerations and potential problems, businesses must be very careful before they sign a commercial lease. Luckily for tenants, many cities have an abundance or overabundance of office and retail space, so landlords may have to make concessions (such as lower rent, one or more months of free rent) or renegotiate leases to relax provisions that are unfavorable to tenants.

Various leases must be compared, to see which is the most cost effective in light of the tenant's actual business practices and what it can anticipate for the future. The business may want an option to rent additional space in the same building or other buildings owned by the landlord, and may also want an option to buy the entire development or the space covered by the lease.

In short, reviewing a commercial lease calls for the best judgment of the corporate secretary and other top management, aided by advice from professionals such as real estate professionals, appraisers, attorneys, accountants, and tax counsel.

## OFFICE LEASE

*1. Parties:* The "landlord" is Pumpkin Leasing and Real Estate Enterprises, a Madison corporation; the "tenant" is Smitherman Import/Export Co., Inc., a Madison corporation.

*2. Premises:* The "premises" are _____ square feet constituting Suite 1912A of the Pegasus Building, [to be] located at 411 Japonica Boulevard, Remsen, Madison. The dimensions of this space, its ventilation, doors, windows, and access to stairs and elevators are as shown on the plan attached to this lease and described as Exhibit A. For purposes of this lease, base rent will be calculated on the assumption that the premises contain _____ rentable square feet, whether or not all of this space is usable by the tenant for its office purposes. The premises to be rented by the tenant constitute _____ % of the total rentable area of the building, and this figure will be used in all calculations of rent escalators.

Payment of the rent entitles the tenant to the use of _____ square feet of storage space in the basement, and to reasonable use of the lobbies, loading docks, elevators, hallways, and restrooms by its personnel, customers, and individuals doing business with the company.

**3. *Condition of Premises:*** Before commencement of the lease, tenant has had/will have an opportunity to have the premises, and the building as a whole, inspected by an architect and engineer of its choice, at its own expense. Tenant either accepts the premises and building as is, or has had an opportunity to determine that the premises and building are structurally and mechanically sound and free from chemical contamination. The landlord disclaims all warranties of fitness of the space for the tenant's intended use.

**4. *Commencement of Term:*** □ The Pegasus Building has been completed, inspected by all officials required to do so, has been issued a Certificate of Occupancy and a fire protection certificate and is ready for immediately occupancy/is ready for finish work to be performed by the tenant at its own expense, and subject to inspection by the landlord's architect; if the landlord's architect finds the work is substandard in quality, the tenant must either have the deficiencies in the work corrected at its own expense under the supervision of the landlord's architect, restore the premises to adequate condition before expiration of the lease term, or be subject to arbitration to determine the landlord's right to money damages or restoration of the premises.

The lease term will commence _____ , 199 _____ .

□ The Pegasus Building is under construction. Completion is scheduled for _____ , 199 _____ . The landlord agrees to furnish all work up to building standard, as shown on the plans; the tenant agrees to perform all finish and design work above building standard at its own expense, using architects and workers of its own choice, but subject to inspection by the landlord's architect and remedies as detailed above. If the tenant wishes modifications in the premises, they can be performed at the tenant's expense if the tenant's architect submits plans for the modifications in duplicate, one copy to the landlord and one to the landlord's architect, on or before _____ , 199 _____ .

Commencement of the lease term will not occur before the premises are completed and have been inspected, and the necessary certificates are issued, and until the premises are ready for occupancy (including common areas and elevators), although the term will commence if the premises are ready for use and corridors and elevators are completed and usable but the lobby has not been decorated or the lobby stores have not been completed or tenanted.

However, the landlord is not responsible for delays in construction or approval, and will not be obligated to pay damages to the tenant if the premises are not ready when the tenant wants to use them; except that if commencement has not occurred by _____ , 199 _____ , the tenant will have the option of either accepting further delay or declaring the lease terminated. If the tenant declares the lease terminated, the landlord will return the deposit, plus _____ % interest running from the time the landlord received the deposit until the date of the tenant's notice to terminate.

**5. *Term and Options:*** The term of the lease is five years from commencement. The tenant will have the option to renew the lease once, on the same terms (except that the renewal lease will not contain an option to renew).

The landlord agrees to notify the tenant whenever additional space is available in the Pegasus Building or other comparable buildings owned by the landlord, and all the landlord's tenants will be able to lease this space, on a first-come, first-served basis, before the landlord notifies nontenants of the availability of the space.

**6. *Rent:*** To secure payment of the rent, on signing of this lease, the tenant will make a deposit of $ _____ /a letter of credit in the amount of $ _____ /secure a guarantee from an individual or corporation whose credit is acceptable to the landlord. Any cash deposit, less amounts retained by the landlord for unpaid rent or damages to the premises, will be returned on termination of the lease.

On or before December 15 of each year, the landlord will notify the tenant of the rent to be paid in the following year. Rent increases will be calculated based on the landlord's actual and accrued expenses for the prior year. Rent will be payable in equal monthly installments, due on the _____ of each month. A late charge of _____ % will be imposed if any payment is more than _____ days late. The landlord has the option of deducting the late charge from the next installment of rent as finally paid, deducting it from the deposit, or bringing an arbitration proceeding to collect the late charge.

The base rent will be $ _____ per square foot per year. The base rent will be adjusted (either upward or downward) as follows:

☐ Changes in the Consumer/Producer Price Index for the area of _____ , as computed by
☐ _____ % of the landlord's actual fuel expenses
☐ _____ % of the landlord's actual utility bills
☐ _____ % of the landlord's actual operating expenses, defined as follows:

   ☐ A "porter's wage rate increase" of _____ cents for every dollar of wage increases in the collective bargaining agreement signed by the landlord and covering the year in question
   ☐ _____ % of the real estate taxes/the increase in the real estate taxes over the base year of 199 _____ assessed on the Pegasus Building; if the landlord protests the assessment, any refund will be distributed to the tenants in proportion to their share of the taxes; however, tenants will be proportionately responsible for increases resulting from the landlord's protest of the assessment.

**7. *Tenant's Warranties:*** The tenant agrees to use the premises as office space and for no other purpose, and agrees not to install any equipment weighing more than _____ lbs. or to impose an average load on the floor of more than _____ lbs. The tenant agrees to refrain from creating unnecessary noise or otherwise disturbing the other tenants' use of the premises. The tenant agrees to give the landlord a copy of all keys to all doors within the premises, and to give the landlord's agents reasonable access in emergencies, to make repairs, and to make reasonable inspections of the condition of the premises.

**8. *Landlord's Warranties:*** The landlord agrees to provide heat, hot water, electricity, elevator access, building security guards, ventilation, and air conditioning as required 24 hours a day, seven days a week/during normal business hours/during normal business hours or as requested by the tenant on at least one week's notice. The landlord will maintain the temperature of the building at all times as no cooler than 60 degrees and no warmer than 75 degrees. The landlord will make arrangements with the telephone company to have cabling, etcetera installed suitable for the installation of telephone lines within the premises; however, the tenant will be responsible for securing the actual installation of the telephone lines and paying the bills.

**9. *Change in Tenancy:*** The tenant agrees to give the landlord at least _____ months' notice of its intention to sublease all or part of the premises or assign the lease. The landlord agrees not to withhold its consent unreasonably when the tenant requests the right to sublease or assign. However, if the request is for an assignment, the landlord will have the right to refuse the request and terminate the lease as of the date of requested assignment, releasing the tenant from all further obligations under the lease and returning the security deposit (less any unpaid rent or damage to the premises), whereupon the landlord will enter directly into a lease with the potential assignee.

**10. *Arbitration:*** Landlord and tenant agree to submit all lease disputes (including attempts to collect unpaid rent) to arbitration under American Arbitration Association rules.

# SHOPPING CENTER LEASE

**1. *Parties:*** The landlord is the Vista Verde Mall Development Corporation. The tenant is Alix's Glassware Shoppe, Inc. Both are corporations validly organized and doing business in the state of Roosevelt.

**2. *Lease Term:*** Both parties desire to enter into a three-year lease for a ____ -square-foot shop, #132 on Level B of the plans of the Vista Verde Mall (Exhibit A). The lease term will begin

☐ When this lease is signed.

☐ When at least ____ % of the square footage shown in the plans of the Vista Verde Mall (Exhibit A) has been completed, has been inspected and issued Certificates of Occupancy, and is ready for tenant occupancy, provided that the common areas and parking lots are also ready for occupancy.

☐ When at least two of the three anchor tenants (Fensterheim's Department Store, Shop'n'Snack, and the Bank of Commerce) plus at least ____ other tenants have occupied their premises and opened for business.

**3. *Storage and Common Areas:*** Rental of the premises also entitles the tenant to the use of ____ square feet of storage space in Storage Level C, to use of the common areas for its customers and deliveries of its merchandise, and to the reserved use of ____ parking spaces for its staff and ____ parking spaces for its customers.

**4. *Vista Verde Association:*** The tenant agrees to join, and maintain membership in good standing at all times that it is a tenant, in the Vista Verde Association, the mall's merchants' association. The tenant will have ____ of the total of ____ votes on Vista Verde Association policies. The tenant agrees to pay the dues as set by the organization, to be open for business during all hours prescribed by the organization, and to conform to the restrictions on signage and window displays as set out in the association handbook (as amended).

**5. *Merchandise:*** The Vista Verde Mall is intended to be a first-class mall of quality and luxury merchandise. The tenant agrees to stock and sell only merchandise fitting these definitions, and not to permit the sale of inferior merchandise or merchandise tending to discredit the mall's image by any sublessee or assignee.

The tenant agrees that it will use the premises only for the sale of quality useful and art objects of glass and pottery, and for no other purpose. Furthermore, the Vista Verde Mall has already entered into exclusive agreements with certain merchants, precluding the sale of certain merchandise on the premises by the tenant (describe):

The landlord agrees to grant the tenant an "exclusive" by precluding any merchant entering into a lease with the landlord subsequent to this lease from selling merchandise described as: _____ . However, this exclusivity clause will not prevent the following merchants, who have already entered into leases at the Vista Verde Mall, from selling merchandise as described herein (describe): _____

**6. *Rent:*** Base rent for the premises will be $ _____ per square foot per year. The tenant also agrees to pay common area charges of $ _____ per square foot per year and to pay additional rent equaling _____ % of sales. For this purpose, "sales" means all sales of merchandise made on the premises either by tenant or by any sublessee, or made by the tenant or any of its officers or directors acting as an individual if such sales are made at business premises within a _____ -foot radius of the Vista Verde Mall. "Sales" also includes sales made by catalog or mail order from the Vista Verde Mall and amounts charged for delivery, shipping, packaging, or wrapping of merchandise. However, sales do not include sales tax or any amount returned to customers for returned or unsatisfactory merchandise.

Rent will be paid quarterly, on the first of February, May, August, and November, based on sales for the preceding quarter.

The tenant agrees to make a security deposit of $ _____ and to replace any part of the deposit that is used by the landlord to repair damage caused by the tenant. The landlord agrees to return the unused portion of the deposit within _____ days of the termination of the lease (as extended).

**7. *Subleases and Assignments:*** On _____ months' notice and on consent of the landlord (which consent will not be unreasonably refused), the tenant shall have the right to sublease part or all of the premises. However, it will not be unreasonable for the landlord to refuse consent to a prospective subtenant it deems financially insecure, whose merchandise or merchandise mix is not suitable to the image of Vista Verde Mall, or whose merchandise or merchandise mix infringes on an "exclusive" granted to another tenant.

If the tenant desires to assign its lease, the landlord has the option of either granting the tenant's request or refusing the request and releasing the tenant from all obligations under the lease as of the date of the desired assignment; if the tenant is released, the landlord will promptly return the security deposit, less $ _____ for cleaning and refitting the premises, and less any damage caused by the tenant.

**8. *Extensions, Options:*** The tenant shall have the option to extend this lease three times, on the same terms (except that the third extension will not include an option to renew), by giving the landlord at least _____ months' notice of intention to extend. Moreover, if at any time there is any vacant space within the Vista Verde Mall, or in other malls in the _____ area developed by the landlord, the landlord will give notice to all tenants in the Vista Verde Mall and other mall(s); all tenants will have the right to bid competitively to lease this space before any listings or attempts to lease the space to outsiders are made.

**9. *Choice of Law:*** This lease will be interpreted according to the laws of the state of Roosevelt.

# Chapter 5

# COMMERCIAL FORMS AND THE UNIFORM COMMERCIAL CODE

## INTRODUCTION

Maybe in the "good old days" shopkeepers could conduct an entire business based on their memory and a few notes scratched on a slate. Today, businesses depend on high volume of transactions. In order to stay out of trouble, businesses must maintain at least minimal records for tax and state corporation regulatory purposes. In order to grow and stay profitable, businesses must be able to analyze which of their products or services are most popular, and which are the most profitable (the two answers aren't always the same). Therefore, businesses would want to keep fairly detailed records of sales orders, purchase orders, and invoices merely for their own benefit.

If an order consists of thousands of units, meeting dozens of specifications, and especially if merchandise is custom manufactured for the customer's needs, obviously some kind of written record is a practical necessity. It's also helpful to have a written record of matters such as prices, discounts, pricing terms (must the account be settled at the end of the month, or will the seller finance the purchase? is a discount given for prompt payment—e.g., "2/10, net 30" or a 2% discount for payment within 10 days, with payment expected within 30 days?), and shipping. Agreement is important—otherwise almost every commercial transaction would end up as a lawsuit.

### Uniform Commercial Code

Therefore, there must be established and agreed-upon rules of law. Furthermore, interstate commerce is the lifeblood of American business. It's important for the rules to be uniform, or almost uniform, throughout the country. A committee of legal experts has drafted, and continually revises, the Uniform Commercial Code (UCC). All the states except Louisiana have adopted the UCC—and even Louisiana has adopted most of it. But the name Uniform Commercial Code is something of a misnomer; there are various versions of the UCC, and states are allowed to adapt it, so commercial law is not entirely uniform throughout the 50 states. So check with your lawyer to make sure that the forms you use conform to UCC practice both in your state and in the states of your trading partners.

The UCC sets out the rights of buyers and sellers with respect to important matters such as definition of terms, rejection of merchandise, and cancellation of contracts. The UCC also has rules to cope with the "battle of the forms." Let's face it, in an average transaction both the buyer and the seller want the terms of the transaction to be as favorable to themselves, and as unfavorable to the other party, as possible. (This is highlighted by the Purchase and Sale Orders printed in this chapter—the seller wants to transfer as much risk, as early as possible, to the buyer, and wants to disclaim all warranties without, of course, saying that their merchandise isn't any good. The buyers want the risks to stay with the seller as long as possible, they want to be able to cancel without penalty, and they want maximum warranty protection.)

The simple answer is to think all these issues through, iron them out in negotiations, and express the terms in a contract of sale such as the form given here. But things don't always work that way. For a routine order, it's more common to use purchase orders (issued by the buyer) or sale orders (issued by the seller). Then there's a risk of the "battle of the forms." Suppose the two forms contradict each other, or one form deals with a subject that is not covered by the other? The first question is whether there has been a "meeting of the minds": if the potential buyer and seller agree on enough important terms for there to be any kind of contract at all. If the sales order refers to a minimum quantity of 10,000 units at 15c a unit, packed in cardboard boxes, and the purchase order calls for a 10c unit price on an order of 500 units packed in Tyvek envelopes, the two aren't even within shouting distance of one another!

The UCC's general rule is that a written confirmation or definite acceptance of an offer is enough to create a contract, even if it has extra or different provisions— unless the original offer was explicitly phrased in "take it or leave it" terms excluding alterations. The new terms become part of the original contract if they are minor, nonfundamental matters, or unless the other party objects to them. A direct conflict of forms is considered to constitute a mutual objection. In that case, the contract between buyer and seller consists of anything that the parties expressly agreed to, terms on which the two forms agree, and matters set out for all business transactions by the Uniform Commercial Code. The conflicting terms simply drop out of the contract.

## COMMERCIAL CONTRACT ROADMAP

- Identification of the parties
- Description of the goods to be sold (by quantity and quality and, if an assortment is made, who selects the items)
- Warranties (of title, quality, fitness for the buyer's use; the seller's disclaimer of warranties or limitation on the seller's liability)
- When title to the goods will pass to the buyer
- When risk of loss passes to the buyer
- Who must purchase and pay for insurance
- The time, place, and manner of delivery (e.g., will all goods be delivered at once, or in several lots?)
- Whether the seller has the right to cure an improper delivery by delivering the correct goods
- When the buyer can reject the goods or revoke an acceptance of goods (right or duty to inspect, permitted reasons for rejection, notice that must be given to the seller, what the buyer must do to care for the goods until they are returned)
- Price of the goods, payment terms
- The seller's remedies under the contract (which typically include acceleration, termination of the contract on the buyer's insolvency, and liquidated damages—an amount set in advance if it is too difficult or impossible to determine the actual amount of damages)

---

## REQUEST FOR FIRM OFFER

Please give us your best price for delivery FOB our plant in Robinard, Tyler, payment by certified check 2/10, net 30, with the price remaining firm until _____ , 199 ____

*Description* _____ *# of Units* _____ *Unit Price* _____

subject to the following special instructions for the preparation, packaging, and shipment of goods:

# CONTRACT FOR THE SALE OF GOODS

**Dated** _____ , 199____

1. *Parties:* The buyer is Fleming's Hardware, 309 Centre Avenue, Martino, Madison. The seller is Jasmine Metal Fabricating, Finishing, and Distribution, Inc., Garden Industrial Park, North Cotterville, Roosevelt.

2. *Goods Sold:* Buyer and seller have entered into this agreement so that the seller will sell and deliver goods as described below. The buyer will accept and receive the goods shipped (if they conform to the contract description) and pay for them in accordance with the contract.

| Quantity | Item | Buyer's Invoice# | Seller's Item # | Price* |
|---|---|---|---|---|
| 5,000 | 3-part Burkett clips | 5932 | A1922B | $118.07 |
| 5,000 | 1/4" freeble pins | 5933 | A2816K | $719.53 |
| 2,000 | Cheswick gimlet pickers | 5934 | C2304M | $624.99 |

*All prices after applicable discounts.

Where a brand name is specified, the seller agrees to ship goods of the specified brand; if the specified brand is unavailable, the seller agrees to contact the buyer and determine whether substitute goods will be acceptable at the same or a reduced price. The same procedure will be followed if a specified quality, finish, or dimension is unavailable.

If no brand name, quality, finish, or other designation is specified, the seller will supply goods conforming to the catalog description and sold to customers similar to the buyer within the buyer's territory, which is defined as:

3. *Shipment:* The seller agrees to make a prompt shipment, by UPS, as soon as the entire order has been packed and is ready for shipment. The seller will only ship a partial order on the specific instructions of the buyer. The shipping charge will be $_____ .

4. *Payment Terms:* The buyer agrees to pay:
- ☐ In advance, by check # _____ .
- ☐ By credit card number # _____ , expiring _____ , 199 ____ .
- ☐ By informing the _____ Bank to advance funds to the seller.
- ☐ In _____ installments of $____ each, payable quarterly beginning _____ , 199 ____ and bearing interest at an APR of ____ %.
- ☐ By opening an account with the seller, agreeing to pay at least ____ % of its outstanding account balance each month (and in no event less than $____ in any month in which there is an outstanding balance on the account), and not to incur an outstanding balance of more than $____ in any month. A finance charge of ____ % APR of the oustanding balance will be charged in every month in which there is an outstanding balance remaining from the previous month.

5. *Approval:* This contract is not valid unless it has been assigned by one of the seller's officers or senior managers.

Seller, by: _____
Buyer, by: _____

## SALES ORDER

**(Front)**                                 Bernice B. Wilson Corp.
                                            1432 LaCinda Lane
                                            Martinsville, Roosevelt 90999

Order no:
Sold to:
Sold by (Salesperson's Name):
Date of Order:
Date of Scheduled Delivery:
Shipping Conditions and Instructions:
For each item sold, give:
    Item Number
    Quantity Sold
    Description (include catalog page, if applicable)
    Price Per Unit
    Total Price
    Shipping per Unit
    Total Shipping
Is Item Subject to Sales Tax? If Not, Explain Why Not. ALL ORDERS ARE SUBJECT TO THE TERMS AND CONDITIONS APPEARING ON THIS FORM (INCLUDING THE REVERSE SIDE). BUYERS AGREE TO BE BOUND BY THE TERMS AND CONDITIONS.
Buyer: _____ Bernice B. Wilson Corp., by: _____
Date of approval: _____

## (Back) Terms and Conditions

*1. Home Office Approval:* Orders become valid and binding only after they are accepted by the seller's home office.

*2. Warranties:* Except as otherwise specified, the seller makes no warranties of fitness of the merchandise for specific uses. The seller is not liable for normal variations in the manufacturing process, or for variations from published specifications that fall within the boundary of accepted industrial practice.

*3. Claims:* The seller will treat the buyer as having waived its claims against the seller unless the seller receives written notice of claim within ten days of the date the buyer received the goods. The buyer agrees to give the seller reasonable access to inspect the allegedly defective goods. No claims will be accepted after the buyer has altered the goods in the course of manufacturing or processing the goods. The seller's maximum liability for defective goods is the price of the goods; the seller expressly disclaims any obligation to pay the buyer's lost profits or goodwill, or any other type of consequential damages.

*4. Delivery:* As soon as the seller consigns the goods to a licensed carrier or trucker, the goods are considered delivered to the buyer; at that point, the risk of loss or damage in transit shifts to the buyer. Unless the sales order states to the contrary, the seller will have the right to divide the order into several deliveries, with a separate invoice and payment date for each. If one installment is delayed, the buyer will still have an obligation to accept the other deliveries.

**5. *Cancellation:*** To cancel an order for any reason (including delay in delivery), the buyer must give the seller five days' written notice of intent to cancel; if the seller delivers goods before the five-day period elapses, the buyer has an obligation to accept and pay for the goods. However, the seller disclaims all liability for late delivery or failure to deliver caused by circumstances beyond the seller's control, such as breakdowns, strikes, lockouts, fires, natural disasters, and governmental limitations on delivery.

**6. *Payment Terms:*** Payment per the enclosed invoice is due on each shipment as soon as the shipment is received. Payment must be made by wire transfer, electronic funds transfer, or check drawn on a bank in the state of Roosevelt. No discount will be granted for prompt payment, and interest at an APR of _____ % will be charged on all invoices remaining unpaid ten days after delivery.

**7. *Legal Terms:*** This Sales Order represents the entire contract between buyer and seller and can only be changed or modified by a notice of termination by the buyer or a written modification signed by both buyer and seller. The contract will be governed by the laws of the state of Roosevelt. Any controversy or claim arising out of the sales transaction will be settled by arbitration according to the rules of the American Arbitration Association, not by litigation, although the award can be enforced by a court.

## PURCHASE ORDER

**(Front)**                                       Adler Frammis Polishing Co.
                                                  Dentonville, Roosevelt

Order No: (Please use this order number on all correspondence, invoices, and packages)
Seller's Name: _____
Seller's Address: _____
Date of Order: _____
Delivery Date: _____
Sales Terms: _____
Shipping Terms and Instructions: _____

***# Units*** _____ ***Unit Price*** _____ ***Description*** _____ ***Total Price*** _____
SEE THE TERMS AND CONDITIONS ON THE REVERSE OF THIS FORM.
Adler Frammis Polishing Co., by: _____
Accepted by Seller: _____

## (Back)

THE OFFER TO PURCHASE IS SUBJECT TO THESE TERMS AND CONDITIONS: _____

**1. *Quality:*** The merchandise covered by this Purchase Order is intended for use in precision, high-speed, computer-controlled metal processing and finishing. Every unit must therefore meet precise specifications, or the goods will be useless or even damaging to the buyer's machinery and operations. Therefore, the buyer retains the right to cancel an order and return all or any part of any shipment found to be defective, and further retains the right to claim damages including manufacturing costs, lost profits, lost opportunity, and damage to goodwill.

The order is premised on the goods being warranted as fit for their intended use for this purpose, and on the seller's agreement to indemnify the buyer and hold it harmless against all damage and liability to third parties incurred by the buyer because the goods are defective and this warranty is breached.

**2. *Delivery:*** The risk of loss or damage remains with the seller until delivery, which is defined as the buyer's actual receipt and acceptance of the goods, whether or not the buyer is responsible for separate payment of shipping charges. Time is of the essence in this contract, and the buyer has the right to refuse any shipment that is delayed and to cancel the order if any part of the order is delayed, even if the buyer has already accepted shipments. The buyer has the right to return goods after they have been accepted.

**3. *Legal Terms*** [same as above].

## BUYER'S NOTICE OF BREACH

### NOTICE to Dentelle de Lyons Lace Mfg. Co., Inc.

You are in breach of a contract between your corporation and Nochebuena Lingerie Designs Co., dated _____ , 199 ____ , calling for delivery no later than _____ , 199 ____ (with time of the essence) of 20,000 yards (200 spools) of top-quality nylon lace, ¾" width, of your Pattern No. 2633K, shade no. 144 ("Candleglow").

FIRST, delivery was not made until _____ , 199 ____ ( ____ days late), causing us damages in the form of direct and opportunity costs

SECOND, one carton (10 spools) arrived dented, torn, and water-damaged, causing damage to the lace within the carton

THIRD, analysis performed by the commercial testing laboratory of the textile science department at the University of Adams shows a polyester content of 20%, although the contract called for 100% pure nylon

FOURTH, the pattern of the lace does not conform to Pattern 2633K in your sample book

FIFTH, only 179 of the spools are shade no. 144 ("Candleglow") as ordered; 15 are shade no. 142 ("Romance Ecru") and 6 are shade no. 145 ("Honeymoon Amber").

We intend to pursue all remedies legally available to a purchaser who has not received goods as ordered.

Valencio Diaz, President, Nochebuena Lingerie Designs Co.

## SHIPMENT OF NONCONFORMING GOODS AS AN ACCOMMODATION

Dear _____ :

We are unable to fill your order for 7,500 "Little Bulldog" brand 2-part bushing clamps (¾") because the factory producing the "Little Bulldog" brand has been on strike since _____ , 199 ____ , and all shipments have ceased.

However, in order to prevent delay or cancellation of your order, we have shipped by UPS/parcel post/truck/rail/air freight 7,500 "Tru-tuth" ¹³⁄₁₆" 2-part bushing clamps. We have made this shipment as an accommodation. Because these goods do not conform to your original order, you have the right to return them to us freight collect if you do not wish to accept them. If you do return the "Tru-tuth" clamps, please indicate if you wish to cancel your order (in which case we will return the $297.47 you have paid for the goods) or if you wish us to maintain your order in force until we have received a new shipment of "Little Bulldog" bushing clamps from which your order can be filled.

## PRODUCT LICENSE AGREEMENT

### Introduction

Scotia Regina, Inc., an Adams corporation, has developed and trademarked the Mary Queen of Scots doll and developed a related line of costumes, accessories, books, cartoons, and video games. Dollrags, Inc., also an Adams corporation, wishes to design, manufacture, and market clothing for the Mary Queen of Scots doll. Therefore, the two corporations have entered into a licensing agreement under which Dollrags will be permitted to market its designs using the name, style, trademark, and logo developed as part of the corporate and product identity of the Mary Queen of Scots doll, in return for royalty payments on all units sold.

### Grant of License

Scotia Regina, Inc., hereby grants an exclusive license for a period of five years to Dollrags under which Dollrags will be the sole entity entitled to design, manufacture, and market clothing for the Mary Queen of Scots doll within the United States and Canada. The license is renewable for a further five-year period on the same terms, renewal to be made one year before expiration.

### Maintenance of Quality

All clothing manufactured pursuant, to this license must be made exclusively of natural fibers, with dyes, patterns, fit, and finish of quality comparable to the clothing designed and manufactured by Scotia Regina, Inc., prior to the grant of the license. All designs and colors must be certified for historical accuracy by a person accepted by Scotia Regina, Inc., as an expert in sixteenth-century clothing and textile design. All designs must permit operation of the unique "removable head" feature of the doll. All packaging and advertisements must be submitted for approval of Scotia Regina, Inc. All manufacturing must be done either by Dollrags in its own plant or subcontracted to a facility approved by Scotia Regina, Inc., which contracts to abide by these quality standards.

Any failure on the part of Dollrags to abide by quality standards, to submit designs, and colors for approval, and to abide by the manufacturing and subcontracting requirements will be grounds for immediate termination of the license.

### Royalty

Dollrags agrees to make quarterly payments of 10% of gross receipts (less returns and allowances) from all sources attributable to sales of clothing for the Mary Queen of Scots doll. Payments must be made within 30 days of the end of the calendar quarter. Dollrags agrees to maintain separate accounting records showing sales, returns, and proceeds of sales of clothing for the Mary Queen of Scots doll, and to make the records and supporting documents (e.g., invoices, bank deposit slips) available for inspection by Regina Scotia, Inc.'s delegate at any time during normal business hours. However, each royalty payment is subject to a minimum of $ ____ and a maximum of $ ____ . Failure to make payments promptly, or misrepresentation of the amount due, shall be grounds for immediate termination of the license.

## Inventory

Dollrags agrees at all times to maintain an inventory of reasonable size and reasonably balanced among various styles to meet seasonal demand and avoid back orders and minimize returns due to shipment at inappropriate times.

## Insurance and Indemnification

Dollrags agrees to purchase, pay for, and maintain at all times insurance in commercially reasonable types and amounts covering its plant, raw materials, and products against loss, damage, injury, injury in transit, and business interruption; to purchase, pay for, and maintain products liability insurance in a commercially reasonable amount naming Scotia Regina, Inc., as an additional insured; and to indemnify Scotia Regina, Inc., and hold it harmless against all liability and all claims arising out of Dollrags' performance or default under this agreement.

Scotia Regina, Inc., will indemnify Dollrags and hold it harmless against all claims and liability arising out of Scotia Regina's trademark or grant of trademark license.

## License Only

This agreement governs only the grant of a license by one independent corporation to another, and shall not be deemed to create a partnership or merger, to make one corporation a subsidiary of the other, or to create a controlled group of corporations.

## No Assignment or Transfer

This license is granted only to Dollrags and is not amenable to voluntary assignment, transfer, or sublease. Termination of Dollrags' corporate existence by merger, consolidation, acquisition by another company, or dissolution, or its bankruptcy, receivership, or assignment for the benefit of creditors shall operate to terminate this license.

## Voluntary Termination

Dollrags may terminate this license at any time upon three months' written notice. A final payment of not less than $ ____ and not more than $ ____ shall be due 30 days after the effective date of termination.

Date: _____ , 199____
Signed, Scotia Regina, Inc., by: _____
Dollrags, Inc., by: _____

# Chapter 6

# CREDIT AND COLLECTIONS

## INTRODUCTION

A business can operate for a while on a strict cash-only basis—provided that the business has no ambitions to get much larger than a pushcart. In order to operate and expand in the modern environment, the business must be able to tap various financing sources (as discussed under the Corporate Finance heading) and must develop a series of relationships with other businesses in which credit is used and extended to others. After all, significant time elapses between purchase of raw materials or merchandise for resale and the time your customers pay for the merchandise. Buying on credit (if there is no extra charge for the deferral, or as long as the interest rates are affordable) gives you the opportunity to defer payment until you have cash in hand from sales.

In turn, if you extend credit to your customers, the added convenience may lead them to buy more, and if you charge interest, you have an additional source of income (as long as you don't pay your bank a higher rate to borrow the money than you charge for the use of credit!).

### Laws Governing Consumer Credit Extension

When the credit transaction involves "merchants" (business firms purchasing merchandise for business use), ordinary commercial law applies. However, if you extend credit to consumers (i.e., permit payment in four or more installments, charge any interest or finance charge), you must abide by the federal consumer protection laws. The federal laws do not set maximum interest rates, but they impose extensive "disclosure" burdens (consumers must be given a great deal of information about the credit transaction before they enter into it).

*Practice Tip:* Check with your attorney before you use any new or revised contracts or other forms in a consumer credit transaction, to make sure that they conform to federal and state requirements. States are not allowed to weaken the federal protection of consumers—but they can impose their own, stricter standards.

Although extending credit expands the potential volume of business, it also carries risks. Most buyers are creditworthy and will pay their bills, sooner or later. Some, however, require a certain amount of persuasion to get them to do so, or the creditor requires a certain amount of patience to wait until a basically honest credit purchaser works through a cash flow crisis. In the consumer context, federal laws forbid discrimination in the granting of credit. Limits are placed on the use of credit reports, and, although it is permissible for a creditor or collection agency to contact a debtor to collect the amount due, it is illegal to use threats or to behave in a harassing manner (to telephone a debtor at five-minute intervals, for instance, or to discuss the debt with people who have no right to know about it, in an attempt to embarrass the debtor at work).

## State Laws Governing Creditors

State law gives creditors a number of remedies, such as acceleration (the right to declare the entire remaining balance of the debt due, as soon as default occurs), repossession of collateral, selling the collateral, and pursuing the debtor for the balance if the sale of collateral did not raise the entire amount owed. (If the sale raised more than the amount owed, the difference must be returned to the debtor.) One of the most important tasks in drafting a contract involving credit sales (from the seller's point of view) is to make sure that all legal remedies are made available to the fullest extent. The buyer's point of view is that the seller's remedies must be strictly limited to prevent oppression!

---

## APPLICATION FOR OPEN-END CONSUMER CREDIT

Note: Under federal law, if you are applying for an account for which you will have full legal responsibility for payment, we will consider only your own income, assets, and credit history—not your spouse's or ex-spouse's—*unless* you choose to report your alimony, maintenance, or child support income as a source you will use in paying your bills under this account. (You do not have to report this kind of income to us if you prefer not to, or if it is too small or too uncertain to rely on in paying bills under this account.)

We have a right (and it is our policy to do so) to consider your spouse's income, assets, and credit history if you and your spouse are applying for a joint account. We will consider your spouse's or ex-spouse's income, assets, and credit history if you are relying on alimony, maintenance, or child support as a source of payment.

We only give joint accounts to married couples. However, you can designate another person (such as your spouse, fiance or fiancee, person you live with, brother or sister, child or parent) who can use the account for which you are solely responsible for making the payments.

## Part One   Background Information

Do NOT complete the information about your spouse if it is not applicable.

| | YOU | YOUR SPOUSE OR EX-SPOUSE |
|---|---|---|
| Full name | | |
| Other names used | | |
| Address | | |
| Present employer | | |
| Employer's address | | |
| Job title | | |
| No. of years worked | | |
| Salary | | |
| Previous employer | | |
| Address | | |
| Job title | | |
| Past salary | | |
| Dates of employment | | |
| Number of dependent children | | |
| Type, amount of Nonsalary | | |
| Income per year | | |
| Savings account number | | |
| Bank | | |
| Checking account number | | |
| Bank | | |
| Have you ever had an account with us? If so, when? | | |
| What is your current account balance? | | |
| Names and addresses of two credit references | | |

## Part Two   Your Personal Financial Status

| A. Assets | YOURS | YOUR SPOUSE'S OR EX-SPOUSE'S |
|---|---|---|
| Cash, bank accounts | | |
| Car (make, model, year) | | |
|   Book value less outstanding loan(s) | | |
| Real estate | | |
|   Description | | |
|   Value after mortgage(s) | | |
| Stocks and other securities | | |
| Other (explain) | | |
| Total | | |

| B. Debts (give current balance) | YOURS | JOINT | SPOUSE'S |
| --- | --- | --- | --- |
| Home mortgage | | | |
| Credit card (describe) | | | |
| Student loan (describe) | | | |
| Other loan (describe) | | | |
| Obligation to pay alimony or child support | | | |
| Total | | | |

Have you been declared bankrupt within the past ten years?
    ☐ No              ☐ Yes, Case # _____ in the Bankruptcy Court for the District
of _____ on _____ , 199 ____ .
Has any court issued a judgment against you that you have not paid in full? ☐ No ☐ Yes, a balance,
of $ ____ remains on the judgment in the case of _____ v. _____ Index
No. _____ , issued by the _____ Court of _____ on _____ ,
199 ____ .
Are there any other positive or negative factors that would affect your creditworthiness? If so, explain
    here: _____
Do you want us to issue a card that can be used by someone else (while you remain fully responsible
for paying the account balance)? ☐ No ☐ Yes, issue a card to _____ , who is my
(relationship): _____
[For secured credit, add: The following property is provided as collateral to secure payment of my
obligations under this account: _____
☐ I am the sole owner of the property
☐ All co-owners of the property agree to its use as collateral.]
If you are married and the collateral is your family home, give your spouse's name even if he or she
    is not responsible for account payments: _____

SIGNATURE(S): I am applying for a _____ Account with _____ . To the best of my
knowledge, this application is accurate and complete. I give you my permission to perform a credit
check to determine my creditworthiness.

Date: _____ , 199____
Signed: _____
Spouse: ( joint account only) _____

## SECURITY AGREEMENT (Consumer Credit)

Note: This is a document with significant legal consequences. Read it carefully before you sign it.
You may want to consult a lawyer before you sign it. You have a right to get a copy of this agreement
that is completely filled out; don't sign a copy that has blank spaces left to be completed later.
    This agreement explains the rights and obligations of the Buyer and Seller. The Seller is
Marshalsea Furniture Store Corp. The Buyer is James Brereton. The term "Buyer" also covers both
Buyers (if the purchase is made jointly) and the heirs and assigns of the original Buyer.
    The Buyer has agreed to buy a bedroom set and dining room set from the Seller for a total of

$2,500. The Buyer has given a down payment of $500. The Seller has agreed to finance the balance of $ _____ according to the terms of a retail installment sale contract dated _____ , 199 _____ . The retail installment sale contract should be read together with this security agreement for a full understanding of the legal relationship between Buyer and Seller.

The Seller is willing to extend credit in part because the Buyer agrees to provide security by giving the Seller a Security Interest in the following collateral: _____ That is, if the Buyer fails to meet his or her obligations under the Retail Installment Sale Agreement and Security Agreement, the Seller will have the right to take the collateral, sell it, and apply the sales proceeds to the debt. If this is a Purchase Money Security Interest (if the collateral is the merchandise covered by the Retail Installment Sale Agreement), the Seller has additional legal rights. This Security Interest □ is □ is not a Purchase Money Security Interest.

The collateral is used primarily for □ business □ farming □ personal, family, or household use. The collateral is/is not attached to (or will be attached to) real estate. If it is or will be, or if the collateral consists of farm crops, describe the real estate and give the name and address of the owner of record: _____

By signing this Agreement, the Buyer gives the Seller a [Purchase Money] Security Interest in the collateral and allows the Seller to file a Financing Statement covering the collateral. The Buyer states that he or she owns the collateral free and clear. As long as there is any balance outstanding under the Retail Installment Sale Agreement, the Buyer agrees that he or she:

○ Will not give away the collateral, sell it, lease it, or use it as collateral in any other transaction

○ Will use it carefully and keep it in good repair

○ Will not modify it without advance permission from the Seller

○ Will maintain a reasonable amount of insurance (payable to the Seller to the extent of the Seller's interest under the Retail Installment Sale Agreement) covering the collateral against loss or damage

○ Will make all reasonable efforts to protect the value of the collateral and the Seller's security interest in the collateral.

If the collateral does undergo loss or damage (for instance, in a fire) the Seller has the right to decide whether to use the insurance proceeds to repair the collateral, replace it, or substitute for the collateral by reducing the balance under the Retail Installment Sale Agreement.

The Buyer will be in default when any of these events occurs:

○ The Buyer dies or becomes incompetent.

○ The Buyer becomes insolvent or bankrupt.

○ The Buyer fails to meet any obligation under this Security Agreement, the Retail Installment Sale Agreement, or any other agreement with the Seller—for instance, failure to make all payments according to schedule.

○ The value of the collateral declines more than _____ %.

○ Insurance on the collateral is canceled.

When default occurs, the Seller has all of a creditor's remedies under the Uniform Commercial Code, including the right to demand immediate payment of the entire remaining balance under the Retail Installment Sale Agreement, and/or seize the collateral and sell it. The Buyer is entitled to ten days' notice before the sale. The Seller's expenses of enforcing its rights will be added to the balance under the Retail Installment Sale Agreement and will carry the same rate of interest. It is up to the Seller to decide which of its legal remedies to use in case of default; if it fails to enforce its remedies when one event of default occurs, it has not wavied (given up) the right to use the full range of remedies if another event of default occurs.

The legal relationship between Buyer and Seller is set out completely in this Security Agreement and the Retail Installment Sale Agreement. The relationship can't be modified by oral changes or agreements; all amendments and modifications must be written and signed by both parties.

Date: _____ , 199____
Buyer(s): _____
Seller: _____
By (title): _____

## CONSUMER RETAIL INSTALLMENT SALE AGREEMENT

*1.* The Buyer is/are: _____

*2.* The Seller is: _____

The Seller has the right to assign its rights under the contract at any time, without consent of or notice to the Buyer. The assignee will have all of the rights that the Seller had at the time of the assignment. By the same token, the Buyer will have the same defenses against the assignee that it would have had against the Seller (for instance, that payment has already been made as scheduled, that the merchandise is defective). If the Seller tells the Buyer that this Retail Installment Sale Agreement has been assigned, it will be the Buyer's obligation to make the remaining payments directly to the assignee.

*3.* The property covered by this Retail Installment Sale Agreement is: _____

*4.* The Buyer agrees to pay $ ____ for this property. After the deposit and any trade-in is deducted, the Buyer will owe a balance of $ ____ . The Buyer promises that any trade-in property was owned free and clear before it was traded in.

*5.* The Buyer agrees to make _____ monthly payments of $ ____ each [plus a final balloon payment of $ ____ ] starting on _____ , 199 ____ . Each payment represents a repayment of part of the principal plus interest on the unpaid balance at an annual percentage rate (APR) of ____ %.

### Itemized Disclosures Required by State and Federal Law

| | |
|---|---|
| 1. Cash price | $ |
| 2. Sales tax | $ |
| 3. Total cash price (1+2) | $ |
| 4. Downpayment | |
|    Trade-in | $ |
|    Cash downpayment | $ |
|      Total downpayment | $ |
| 5. Balance of cash price (3 − 4) | $ |
| 6. Charges | |
|    [Joint] credit life insurance | $ |
|    Credit accident/health insurance | $ |

| | |
|---|---|
| Other | $ |
| Total | $ |
| 7. Unpaid balance (amount financed, 5 + 6) | $ |
| 8. Finance charge | $ |
| 9. Total payments (7 + 8) | $ |
| 10. Deferred payment price (3 + 6 + 8) | $ |
| APR% | |

## Credit Insurance

Credit insurance is a special type of insurance that pays the Seller if you die or are injured while you still owe the Seller money. You do not have to have credit insurance unless you want it. You can buy it from your own agent or broker, or pay the Seller to buy it for you. If this Retail Installment Sale Agreement covers the sale of an automobile, the Seller cannot force you to buy your auto insurance from or through the Seller; you have the right to choose your own broker or agent.

☐ I do not want any credit insurance.

☐ I want credit life insurance, which will cost $ ____ for the life of the loan; maximum coverage is $ ____ .

☐ My spouse and I are both Buyers under this Agreement. We both want joint credit life insurance, which will cost $ ____ for the life of the loan; maximum coverage is $ _____ .

☐ I want credit accident and health insurance, which will cost $ ____ for the life of the loan; maximum coverage is $ ____ .

---

**6.** The Buyer agrees to pay a late charge of 5% (but not more than $5) on any installment that is not paid within 10 days of its due date.

**7.** The Buyer has the right to prepay any amount at any time. If the financial calculation known as the "Rule of 78" shows that the Buyer has overpaid the finance charge, the Seller must promptly refund the excess.

**8.** To secure payment under the Retail Installment Sale Agreement, the Buyer agrees to give the Seller a security interest in the collateral described in the Security Agreement, according to the terms of that agreement.

**9.** The risk of loss is on the Buyer: that is, the Buyer still has to pay if the property is lost, destroyed, or stolen (although the Buyer may have claims against the Seller or Seller's assignee if the merchandise is defective).

**10.** The Buyer will be in default if:

○ Any of the statements made in this Retail Installment Sale Agreement or Security Agreement is false

○ The Buyer fails to make any payment on schedule

○ The Buyer dies or becomes bankrupt or insolvent

○ The Seller feels itself insecure (believes that it is unlikely to be paid on schedule throughout the term of the Retail Installment Sale Agreement) for any reasonable cause

**11.** On default, the Seller has the right to demand immediate payment of the entire balance then remaining under the Retail Installment Sale Agreement, plus collection costs (such as attorney's fees and court costs). Furthermore, as explained by the Security Agreement, The Seller has the right to repossess and sell the collateral securing the Retail Installment Sale Agreement. If there is still a balance after the sale, the Buyer remains indebted to the Seller in that amount and can be sued for collection; if the proceeds of the repossession sale are greater than the amount owed, the Seller will refund the difference promptly to the Buyer. If the Seller excuses one instance of default, it retains all its legal rights with respect to other defaults.

*12.* This Retail Installment Sale Agreement will be interpreted under the laws of the state of _____ .

Date: _____ , 199____
Signed, Buyer(s): _____
Seller, by (title): _____

## NOTICE OF MECHANICS' LIEN

No Pane, No Gain Window & Door Service, Inc., hereby gives notice of Mechanics' Lien to James and Esther Fitzallen, record owners of a house located at 193 Mockingbird Lane, Greene City, Roosevelt, as required by Title 15 Section 2203-B of the Revised Statutes of Roosevelt.

No Pane, No Gain provided labor, skill, and materials by installing a set of thermopane windows (wholesale price $800) and a new door (wholesale price $650) at 193 Mockingbird Lane, beginning on December 12, 1990 and completing the job December 23, 1990. The work was done pursuant to a contract dated December 3, 1990 and signed by Mr. and Mrs. Fitzallen calling for a total payment of $2,500. A deposit of $500 and one progress payment of $500 have been made, but the balance of $1,500 remains unpaid and for which amount No Pane, No Gain claims a lien on the Mockingbird Lane property.

Date: _____ , 199____
Signed, _____ President of No Pane, No Gain Window & Door Service, Inc.
Address: 29D Freedonia Turnpike, Evansville, Roosevelt

## NOTICE OF INTENT TO REPOSSESS

Note to readers: If the collateral consists of consumer goods, and 60% or more of the payments have been made, Section 9-505(1) of the Uniform Commercial Code requires the creditor to sell the repossessed collateral, within the period that begins 15 days after the notice and ends 90 days after the notice. Otherwise, the creditor can keep the collateral unless the consumer debtor objects in writing after receiving a notice.

Dear Debtor:

Under the terms of a retail installment sale agreement and security agreement dated _____ , 199 ____ , you have an obligation to make an installment payment of $ ____ on _____ , 199 ____ . We have not received this payment. Therefore, we are exercising our "right of acceleration" to declare that the entire balance under the retail installment sale agreement, $ ____ , is now due and payable.

Under the retail installment sale agreement and security agreement we also have the right to repossess the collateral, which consists of _____ . We will repossess the collateral unless you make payments of at least $ _____ by _____ , 199 _____ to bring your account back to current status, or unless you contact our office by _____ , 199 _____ and arrange a payment schedule.

☐ You have already paid 60% of the price under the retail installment sale agreement. Therefore, after we repossess the collateral, we are legally obligated to sell it during the period that begins 15 days after we notify you that repossession has taken place and ends 90 days after notice.

☐ If you have paid less than 60% of the price, we are entitled to keep the collateral unless you mail us a notice within 30 days of the day you receive this notice, informing us that you insist on a sale of the collateral.

We will notify you before any sale of the collateral. If the sale price is less than the amount you owe, you will continue to owe the difference between the balance on your account and the sale proceeds.

## NOTICE OF REPOSSESSION

Dear Debtor:

You failed to respond to our earlier letter, dated _____ , 199 _____ . Therefore, we have repossessed the collateral, which consists of: _____

At this time, you owe us a total of $ _____ , consisting of your unpaid balance of $ _____ plus our expenses of repossession, $ _____ , and storage charges of $ _____ per day. We will continue to assess storage charges until the collateral is either redeemed or sold.

You can redeem the collateral by paying us $ _____ (plus additional storage charges). Once this is done, you can pick up the collateral at _____ , where it is being stored. You are responsible for collecting the collateral and getting it home.

We are legally obligated to sell the collateral during the period that begins 15 days after the date of this notice, and ends 90 days after the date of this notice, IF you have paid at least 60% of your obligation under the retail installment sale contract. Otherwise, we have the right to either keep the collateral or sell it, but we must sell it if you write to us within 30 days of the date of this notice and instruct us to sell it.

## NOTICE OF SALE

Dear Debtor:

We hereby NOTIFY you that we intend to use the procedures set out in UCC 9-504 to sell the collateral, _____ , which we repossessed on _____ , 199 _____ as a result of your default under the retail installment sale agreement and security agreement, by

☐ Private sale

☐ Public sale

☐ Public auction sale with/without reservation to be held on _____ , 199 _____ at _____ M, at _____ where the goods are located.

If the amount we receive from the sale is less than the amount you owe under the retail installment security agreement ($ _____ ), you will still owe us the difference.

## NOTICE OF DEFICIENCY

TO THE DEBTOR:

The collateral securing your obligations under the retail installment sale agreement and security agreement was sold on _____ , 199 _____ . At that time, the unpaid balance you owed was $ _____ .

The sale of the collateral produced gross proceeds of $ _____ . However, we were required to pay expenses of $ _____ (repossession expenses of $ _____ , legal fees and costs $ _____ , $ _____ to recondition the collateral for resale, $ _____ in storage charges, $ _____ to advertise the sale, and the auctioneer's commission of $ _____ ). Therefore, the net proceeds of the sale were $ _____ , or $ _____ less than the amount you owe. We hereby demand that you pay the deficiency of $ _____ on or before _____ , 199 _____ .

## COLLECTION NOTICES

[Note: If you don't want to send out individual collection letters, business stationers sell various forms for collections, such as stickers that can be attached to overdue bills or multipart forms that can be typed once to yield several increasingly urgent demands for payment. Be sure and set up a "tickler system" that will alert you to accounts that are due and 20, 40, 60, or more days overdue.]

*1.* According to our records, payment under Invoice # _____ , in the amount of $ _____ , was due on _____ , 199 _____ but, as of _____ , 199 _____ , had not been received. Please check your records and inform us how and when payment was made. If payment has not been made, please remit your payment promptly.

*2.* Your account is now overdue. You have received the following merchandise: _____ but have not paid for it/owe us a total of $ _____ . We accepted your offer and supplied merchandise in good faith, and we are entitled to be paid. We will not make further shipments of merchandise until your account has been brought back to current status.

*3.* Your balance of $ _____ under Invoice # _____ is now seriously overdue. In order to preserve your credit rating, you must immediately pay this balance. Unless you contact us and make arrangements for payment/pay your bill in full by _____ , 199 _____ , we will be forced to pursue our further remedies as creditors.

*4.* Unless your [certified/cashier's] check in the amount of $ _____ is received by _____ , 199 _____ , we will submit your account to a collection agency for collection/instruct our attorney to institute a suit for collection of your account.

Be aware that referral of the account for collection is likely to impair your credit rating, and if you are a party to a suit, you are likely to encounter legal fees and may be required to pay our legal fees and court costs as well.

# Chapter 7

# TAXES

## INTRODUCTION

Tax payment and tax planning are definitely not do-it-yourself matters; they call for top-flight legal and accounting advice. However, it's important for all business people to have some insight into some basic tax concepts.

A corporation is an "artificial person"—and, like a natural person, an ordinary corporation is a taxpayer. The federal tax form for an ordinary ("Subchapter C" or "C" Corporation) is the Form 1120. However, small corporations are allowed to file the shorter, less complex Form 1120A. To file a Form 1120A, the corporation must have gross receipts and income for the year and assets all under $250,000. The corporation must not own any non-U.S. corporations; must be a corporation that operates to earn money through business operations, not investments; must be at least 50% owned by U.S. citizens; and if engaged in dissolution or liquidation must use the long-form, not the Form 1120A short-form return.

Corporations, like individual taxpayers, are also required to make quarterly estimated tax payments (Form 1120W)—in the case of a corporation, if the estimated tax for the quarter (the tax liability minus any available credits) is $500 or over.

### "Subchapter S" Corporations

Once a corporation earns money, the earnings are exposed to taxation; then, when they are paid out in the form of dividends, the stockholders have to pay taxes on the dividends paid to them. This "double taxation" is widely criticized. To alleviate the double taxation problem, and to help small or start-up corporations, the federal tax code contains a "Subchapter S." An "S" corporation does not have to pay federal taxes on its earnings; instead, each stockholder is taxed on a proportion of the corporation's earnings, just as a partner is taxed on a share of the partnership's earnings. (In either case, the tax is based on percentage of ownership, not on the amount actually paid out, so if earnings are plowed back into the business instead of paid out to owners, business owners may have to pay taxes on amounts they haven't been given by the corporation.) Also like partnerships, S Corporations must file annual information returns with the IRS.

Status as an S Corporation is not automatic. Not only must the corporation qualify, but all its shareholders must agree to make an S Corporation "election," using IRS Form 2553. In order to qualify, the corporation can have only 35 stockholders. (However, if a married couple both own stock in the corporation, they count as only one stockholder.) Only individuals, estates of individuals, and certain trusts can be stockholders in S Corporations—other corporations and partnerships cannot. Individual stockholders need not be U.S. citizens, but they cannot be nonresident aliens. The corporation is only allowed to have one class of stock (although if it has both voting and nonvoting common stock, that is considered a single class of stock)—so if the corporation has both common and preferred stock, it can't be an S Corporation.

*Practice Tip:* A common ploy of Subchapter S stockholders who are in conflict with corporate management is to threaten to sell stock to an ineligible stockholder, thus destroying the S election—an important power play that can be foiled if the corporation imposes transfer restrictions.

## State Taxation

In addition to federal taxes, the corporation will probably have to pay some kind of state taxes: perhaps a corporate income tax, a franchise tax (for the privilege of doing business within the state), or both. State tax liability may be based on some combination of earned income and assets held within the state. Most of the states recognize S corporations to some degree, either by exempting them from state tax (but requiring them to file information returns) or by reducing their income taxes.

*Practice Tip:* If your corporation is licensed to do business in more than one state, it will also probably have to pay franchise and/or income taxes in all states in which it is qualified. Calculations—which can be quite difficult—must be made to allocate assets and income among states.

*Practice Tip:* Not only are state tax returns based on the federal return (so that the usual practice is to complete the federal return and use the calculations to prepare the state return(s)), it's likely that you will be required to attach copies of part or all of the federal tax return, so have plenty of extra copies made.

| Form **2553** (Rev. October 1989) Department of the Treasury Internal Revenue Service | **Election by a Small Business Corporation** (Under section 1362 of the Internal Revenue Code) ▶ For Paperwork Reduction Act Notice, see page 1 of instructions. ▶ See separate instructions. | OMB No. 1545-0146 Expires 2-28-91 |
|---|---|---|

**Notes:** 1. *This election, to be treated as an "S corporation," can be accepted only if all the tests in General Instruction B are met; all signatures in Parts I and III are originals (no photocopies); and the exact name and address of the corporation and other required form information are provided.*
2. *Do not file Form 1120S until you are notified that your election is accepted. See instruction E.*

**Part I   Election Information**

| | A Employer identification number (see instructions) | B Principal business activity and principal product or service (see instructions) |
|---|---|---|
| Name of corporation (see instructions) | | |
| Number and street | C Name and telephone number of corporate officer or legal representative who may be called for information | |
| City or town, state, and ZIP code | D Election is to be effective for tax year beginning (month, day, year) | |

*(left margin: Please Type or Print)*

E (1) Is the corporation the outgrowth or continuation of any form of predecessor?  ☐ Yes   ☐ No | F Date of incorporation

If "Yes," state name of predecessor, type of organization, and period of its existence ▶ . . . . . . . . . . . . . . . . . . . . . | G State of incorporation

(2) Check here ☐ if the corporation has changed its name or address since applying for the employer identification number shown in item A above.

H   If this election takes effect for the first tax year the corporation exists, enter month, day, and year of the **earliest** of the following: (1) date the corporation first had shareholders, (2) date the corporation first had assets, or (3) date the corporation began doing business. ▶

I   Selected tax year: Annual return will be filed for tax year ending (month and day) ▶ . . . . . . . . . . . . . . . . . . . . . . . . . . . . .
See instructions before entering your tax year. If the tax year ends on any date other than December 31, except for an automatic 52–53-week tax year ending with reference to the month of December, you must complete Part II on the back. If the date you enter in item I is the ending date of an automatic 52–53-week tax year, write "52–53-week year" to the right of the date. See instructions.

| J Name of each shareholder, person having a community property interest in the corporation's stock, and each tenant in common, joint tenant, and tenant by the entirety. (A husband and wife (and their estates) are counted as one shareholder in determining the number of shareholders without regard to the manner in which the stock is owned.) | K Shareholders' Consent Statement. We, the undersigned shareholders, consent to the corporation's election to be treated as an "S corporation" under section 1362(a). (Shareholders sign and date below.)* | L Stock owned | | M Social security number or employer identification number (see instructions) | N Shareholder's tax year ends (month and day) |
|---|---|---|---|---|---|
| | | Number of shares | Dates acquired | | |
| | | | | | |
| | | | | | |
| | | | | | |
| | | | | | |
| | | | | | |
| | | | | | |
| | | | | | |
| | | | | | |
| | | | | | |

*For this election to be valid, the consent of each shareholder, person having a community property interest in the corporation's stock, and each tenant in common, joint tenant, and tenant by the entirety must either appear above or be attached to this form. (See instructions for Column K, if continuation sheet or a separate consent statement is needed.)

Under penalties of perjury, I declare that I have examined this election, including accompanying schedules and statements, and to the best of my knowledge and belief, it is true, correct, and complete.

Signature and Title of Officer ▶                                                      Date ▶

**See Parts II and III on back.**                                                    Form **2553** (Rev. 10-89)

Form 2553 (Rev. 10-89)                                                                                          Page **2**

**Part II** Selection of Fiscal Tax Year (All corporations using this Part must complete Item O and one of Items P, Q, or R.) (See Instructions for Information about a user fee, if applicable, required attachments, and other details.)

**O**  Check the applicable box below to indicate whether the corporation is:

☐ A new corporation adopting the tax year entered in item I, Part I.

☐ An existing corporation retaining the tax year entered in item I, Part I.

☐ An existing corporation changing to the tax year entered in item I, Part I.

**P**  Check the applicable box below to indicate the representation statement the corporation is making as required under section 4 of Rev. Proc. 87-32, 1987-2 C.B. 396.

☐ Under penalties of perjury, I represent that shareholders holding more than half of the shares of the stock (as of the first day of the tax year to which the request relates) of the corporation have the same tax year or are concurrently changing to the tax year that the corporation adopts, retains, or changes to per item I, Part I. I also represent that the corporation is not described in section 3.01(2) of Rev. Proc. 87-32.

☐ Under penalties of perjury, I represent that the corporation is retaining or changing to a tax year that coincides with its natural business year as defined in section 4.01(1) of Rev. Proc. 87-32 and as verified by its satisfaction of the requirements of section 4.02(1) of Rev. Proc. 87-32. In addition, if the corporation is changing to a natural business year as defined in section 4.01(1), I further represent that such tax year results in less deferral of income to the owners than the corporation's present tax year. I also represent that the corporation is not described in section 3.01(2) of Rev. Proc. 87-32. (See instructions for attachments required by section 4.03(3) of Rev. Proc. 87-32.)

**Note:** *If you do not use item P and the corporation wants a fiscal tax year, complete either item Q or R below. Item Q is used to request a fiscal tax year based on business purpose and to make a back-up section 444 election. Item R is used to make a regular section 444 election.*

**Q**  Business Purpose—To request a fiscal tax year based on busines purpose, you must check box Q1. You may also check box Q2 and/or box Q3.

1. Check here ☐ if the fiscal year entered in item I, Part I, is requested under the provisions of section 6.03 of Rev. Proc. 87-32. Attach to Form 2553 a statement and other necessary information pursuant to the ruling request requirements of Rev. Proc. 89-1, 1989-1 I.R.B. 8. The statement must include the business purpose for the desired fiscal year.

2. Check here ☐ to show that the corporation intends to make a back-up section 444 election in the event the corporation's business purpose request is not approved by the IRS.

3. Check here ☐ to show that the corporation agrees to adopt or change to a tax year ending December 31 if necessary for the IRS to accept this election for S corporation status in the event: (1) the corporation's business purpose request is not approved and the corporation makes a back-up section 444 election, but is ultimately not qualified to make a section 444 election, or (2) the corporation's business purpose request is not approved and the corporation did not make a back-up section 444 election.

**R**  Section 444 Election—You must check box R1 and you may also check box R2.

1. Check here ☐ to show the corporation will make, if qualified, a section 444 election to have the fiscal tax year shown in item I, Part I. To make the election, you must complete **Form 8716,** Election To Have a Tax Year Other Than a Required Tax Year, and either attach it to Form 2553 or file it in accordance with the instructions for Form 8716.

2. Check here ☐ to show that the corporation agrees to adopt or change to a tax year ending December 31 if necessary for the IRS to accept this election for S corporation status in the event the corporation is ultimately not qualified to make a section 444 election.

**Part III** Qualified Subchapter S Trust (QSST) Election Under Section 1361(d)(2)**

| Income beneficiary's name and address | Taxpayer identification number |
|---|---|
| | |
| Trust's name and address | Taxpayer identification number |
| | |

Date on which stock of the corporation was transferred to the trust (month, day, year) ▶

In order for the trust named above to be a QSST and thus a qualifying shareholder of the S corporation for which this Form 2553 is filed, I hereby make the election under section 1361(d)(2). Under penalties of perjury, I certify that the trust meets the definition requirements of section 1361(d)(3) and that all other information provided in Part III is true, correct, and complete.

_____        _____
Signature of income beneficiary or signature and title of legal representative or other qualified person making the election        Date

**Use of Part III to make the QSST election may be made only if stock of the corporation has been transferred to the trust on or before the date on which the corporation makes its election to be an S corporation. The QSST election must be made and filed **separately** if stock of the corporation is transferred to the trust after the date on which the corporation makes the S election.

⋆ U.S. Government Printing Office:1989-261-151/00018

| Form **1120S** | **U.S. Income Tax Return for an S Corporation** | OMB No. 1545-0130 |
|---|---|---|
| Department of the Treasury Internal Revenue Service | For the calendar year 1989, or tax year beginning _____, 1989, ending _____, 19 \_\_\_\_ ▶ **For Paperwork Reduction Act Notice, see page 1 of separate instructions.** | 19**89** |

| **A** Date of election as an S corporation | Use IRS label. Other- wise, please print or type. | Name | **C** Employer identification number |
|---|---|---|---|
| **B** Business code no. (see Specific Instructions) | | Number and street (P.O. box number if mail is not delivered to street address) | **D** Date incorporated |
| | | City or town, state, and ZIP code | **E** Total assets (see Specific Instructions) $ |

**F** Check applicable boxes: (1) ☐ Initial return  (2) ☐ Final return  (3) ☐ Change in address  (4) ☐ Amended return

**G** Check this box if this is an S corporation subject to the consolidated audit procedures of sections 6241 through 6245 (see instructions before checking this box) . . . ▶ ☐

**H** Enter number of shareholders in the corporation at end of the tax year . . . . . . . . . . . . . . . . . ▶

**Caution:** Include **only** trade or business income and expenses on lines 1a through 21. See the instructions for more information.

**Income**

| | | |
|---|---|---|
| **1a** Gross receipts or sales |  **b** Less returns and allowances |  **c** Bal ▶ | **1c** |
| **2** Cost of goods sold and/or operations (Schedule A, line 7) . . . . . | **2** |
| **3** Gross profit (subtract line 2 from line 1c) . . . . . . . . . . . | **3** |
| **4** Net gain (or loss) from Form 4797, line 18 (see instructions) . . . . | **4** |
| **5** Other income (see instructions—attach schedule) . . . . . . . . | **5** |
| **6** **Total** income (loss)—Combine lines 3, 4, and 5 and enter here . . . . ▶ | **6** |

**Deductions (See instructions for limitations.)**

| | | |
|---|---|---|
| **7** Compensation of officers . . . . . . . . . . . . . . . . . | **7** |
| **8a** Salaries and wages |  **b** Less jobs credit |  **c** Bal ▶ | **8c** |
| **9** Repairs . . . . . . . . . . . . . . . . . . . . . . . | **9** |
| **10** Bad debts (see instructions) . . . . . . . . . . . . . . . | **10** |
| **11** Rents . . . . . . . . . . . . . . . . . . . . . . . | **11** |
| **12** Taxes . . . . . . . . . . . . . . . . . . . . . . . | **12** |
| **13** Interest (see instructions) . . . . . . . . . . . . . . . . | **13** |
| **14a** Depreciation (attach Form 4562) (see instructions)   **14a** | |
| **b** Depreciation reported on Schedule A and elsewhere on return   **14b** | |
| **c** Subtract line 14b from line 14a . . . . . . . . . . . . . . | **14c** |
| **15** Depletion (**Do not deduct oil and gas depletion. See instructions.**) . . | **15** |
| **16** Advertising . . . . . . . . . . . . . . . . . . . . . | **16** |
| **17** Pension, profit-sharing, etc. plans . . . . . . . . . . . . . | **17** |
| **18** Employee benefit programs . . . . . . . . . . . . . . . . | **18** |
| **19** Other deductions (attach schedule) . . . . . . . . . . . . . | **19** |
| **20** **Total** deductions—Add lines 7 through 19 and enter here . . . . . . ▶ | **20** |
| **21** Ordinary income (loss) from trade or business activities—Subtract line 20 from line 6 . . . . | **21** |

**Tax and Payments**

| | | |
|---|---|---|
| **22** **Tax:** | | |
| **a** Excess net passive income tax (attach schedule) . . . . . **22a** | |
| **b** Tax from Schedule D (Form 1120S) . . . . . . . . . **22b** | |
| **c** Add lines 22a and 22b (see instructions for additional taxes) . . . . . . . . . | **22c** |
| **23** **Payments:** | | |
| **a** Tax deposited with Form 7004 . . . . . . . . . **23a** | |
| **b** Credit for Federal tax on fuels (attach Form 4136) . . . . . **23b** | |
| **c** Add lines 23a and 23b . . . . . . . . . . . . . . | **23c** |
| **24** **Tax due**—If line 22c is larger than line 23c, enter amount owed. See instructions for Paying the Tax . . . . . . . . . . . . . . . . . . . . . . . ▶ | **24** |
| **25** **Overpayment**—If line 23c is larger than line 22c, enter amount overpaid . . . . ▶ | **25** |

**Please Sign Here**

Under penalties of perjury, I declare that I have examined this return, including accompanying schedules and statements, and to the best of my knowledge and belief, it is true, correct, and complete. Declaration of preparer (other than taxpayer) is based on all information of which preparer has any knowledge.

| ▶ Signature of officer | Date | ▶ Title |
|---|---|---|

**Paid Preparer's Use Only**

| Preparer's signature ▶ | Date | Check if self-employed ▶ ☐ | Preparer's social security number |
|---|---|---|---|
| Firm's name (or yours if self-employed) and address ▶ | | E.I. No. ▶ | |
| | | ZIP code ▶ | |

Form **1120S** (1989)

Form 1120S (1989)                                                                                              Page **2**

**Schedule A** **Cost of Goods Sold and/or Operations** (See instructions for Schedule A.)

| | | |
|---|---|---|
| 1 Inventory at beginning of year | **1** | |
| 2 Purchases | **2** | |
| 3 Cost of labor | **3** | |
| 4a Additional section 263A costs (attach schedule) (see instructions) | **4a** | |
| b Other costs (attach schedule) | **4b** | |
| 5 Total—Add lines 1 through 4b | **5** | |
| 6 Inventory at end of year | **6** | |
| 7 Cost of goods sold and/or operations—Subtract line 6 from line 5. Enter here and on line 2, page 1 | **7** | |

8a Check all methods used for valuing closing inventory:
   (i) ☐ Cost
   (ii) ☐ Lower of cost or market as described in Regulations section 1.471-4
   (iii) ☐ Writedown of "subnormal" goods as described in Regulations section 1.471-2(c)
   (iv) ☐ Other (specify method used and attach explanation) ▶ ...........................................................

  b Check this box if the LIFO inventory method was adopted this tax year for any goods (if checked, attach Form 970) . . . ▶☐

  c If the LIFO inventory method was used for this tax year, enter percentage (or amounts) of closing
   inventory computed under LIFO                    **8c** |

  d Do the rules of section 263A (with respect to property produced or acquired for resale) apply to the corporation? . . . ☐ Yes ☐ No

  e Was there any change in determining quantities, cost, or valuations between opening and closing inventory? . . . . . ☐ Yes ☐ No
   If "Yes," attach explanation.

**Additional Information Required** (continued from page 1)

|  | Yes | No |
|---|---|---|
| I Did you at the end of the tax year own, directly or indirectly, 50% or more of the voting stock of a domestic corporation? For rules of attribution, see section 267(c). If "Yes," attach a schedule showing: (1) name, address, and employer identification number; and (2) percentage owned. | | |
| J Refer to the listing of business activity codes at the end of the Instructions for Form 1120S and state your principal:<br>  (1) Business activity ▶................................... (2) Product or service ▶ ............................ | | |
| K Were you a member of a controlled group subject to the provisions of section 1561? . . . . . . . . . . . . . . . | | |
| L At any time during the tax year, did you have an interest in or a signature or other authority over a financial account in a foreign country (such as a bank account, securities account, or other financial account)? (See instructions for exceptions and filing requirements for form TD F 90-22.1.) . . . . . . . . . . . . . . . . . . . . . . . . .<br>  If "Yes," enter the name of the foreign country ▶ ----------------------------------------- | | |
| M Were you the grantor of, or transferor to, a foreign trust which existed during the current tax year, whether or not you have any beneficial interest in it? If "Yes," you may have to file Form 3520, 3520-A, or 926 . . . . . . . . . | | |
| N During this tax year did you maintain any part of your accounting/tax records on a computerized system? . . . . | | |
| O Check method of accounting: (1) ☐ Cash (2) ☐ Accrual (3) ☐ Other (specify) ▶ ----------------------- | | |
| P Check this box if the S corporation has filed or is required to file **Form 8264**, Application for Registration of a Tax Shelter        ▶☐ | | |
| Q Check this box if the corporation issued publicly offered debt instruments with original issue discount . . . . . ▶☐<br>  If so, the corporation may have to file **Form 8281**, Information Return for Publicly Offered Original Issue Discount Instruments. | | |
| R If the corporation: (1) filed its election to be an S corporation after December 31, 1986, (2) was a C corporation prior to making the election, and (3) at the beginning of the tax year had net unrealized built-in gain as defined in section 1374(d)(1), enter the net unrealized built-in gain (see instructions) ▶ | | |

**Designation of Tax Matters Person** (See instructions.)

Enter below the shareholder designated as the tax matters person (TMP) for the tax year of this return:

Name of
designated TMP ▶ _____   Identifying
                                             number of TMP ▶ _____

Address of
designated TMP ▶ _____

| Schedule K | Shareholders' Shares of Income, Credits, Deductions, Etc. (See Instructions.) | | |
|---|---|---|---|
| | (a) Pro rata share items | | **(b) Total amount** |

**Income (Loss) and Deductions**

| | | | |
|---|---|---|---|
| 1 | Ordinary income (loss) from trade or business activities (page 1, line 21) | **1** | |
| 2a | Gross income from rental real estate activities | **2a** | |
| b | Less expenses (attach schedule). | **2b** | |
| c | Net income (loss) from rental real estate activities | **2c** | |
| 3a | Gross income from other rental activities | **3a** | |
| b | Less expenses (attach schedule) | **3b** | |
| c | Net income (loss) from other rental activities | **3c** | |
| 4 | Portfolio income (loss): | | |
| a | Interest income | **4a** | |
| b | Dividend income | **4b** | |
| c | Royalty income | **4c** | |
| d | Net short-term capital gain (loss) (Schedule D (Form 1120S)). | **4d** | |
| e | Net long-term capital gain (loss) (Schedule D (Form 1120S)). | **4e** | |
| f | Other portfolio income (loss) (attach schedule) | **4f** | |
| 5 | Net gain (loss) under section 1231 (other than due to casualty or theft) (see instructions) | **5** | |
| 6 | Other income (loss) (attach schedule) | **6** | |
| 7 | Charitable contributions (attach list) | **7** | |
| 8 | Section 179 expense deduction (attach Form 4562). | **8** | |
| 9 | Expenses related to portfolio income (loss) (attach schedule) (see instructions) | **9** | |
| 10 | Other deductions (attach schedule) | **10** | |

**Credits**

| | | | |
|---|---|---|---|
| 11a | Credit for alcohol used as a fuel (attach Form 6478) . | **11a** | |
| b | Low-income housing credit: **(1)** From partnerships to which section 42(j)(5) applies . | **11b(1)** | |
| | **(2)** Other than on line 11b(1) | **11b(2)** | |
| c | Qualified rehabilitation expenditures related to rental real estate activities (attach schedule) | **11c** | |
| d | Credits (other than credits shown on lines 11b and 11c) related to rental real estate activities (attach schedule) . | **11d** | |
| e | Credits related to other rental activities (see instructions) (attach schedule) | **11e** | |
| 12 | Other credits and expenditures (attach schedule) | **12** | |

**Investment Interest**

| | | | |
|---|---|---|---|
| 13a | Interest expense on investment debts | **13a** | |
| b | **(1)** Investment income included on lines 4a through 4f above | **13b(1)** | |
| | **(2)** Investment expenses included on line 9 above | **13b(2)** | |

**Adjustments and Tax Preference Items**

| | | | |
|---|---|---|---|
| 14a | Accelerated depreciation of real property placed in service before 1987 . | **14a** | |
| b | Accelerated depreciation of leased personal property placed in service before 1987 . | **14b** | |
| c | Depreciation adjustment on property placed in service after 1986 | **14c** | |
| d | Depletion (other than oil and gas) . | **14d** | |
| e | **(1)** Gross income from oil, gas, or geothermal properties | **14e(1)** | |
| | **(2)** Deductions allocable to oil, gas, or geothermal properties . | **14e(2)** | |
| f | Other adjustments and tax preference items (attach schedule) | **14f** | |

**Foreign Taxes**

| | | | |
|---|---|---|---|
| 15a | Type of income ........ | | |
| b | Name of foreign country or U.S. possession ........ | | |
| c | Total gross income from sources outside the U.S. (attach schedule) . | **15c** | |
| d | Total applicable deductions and losses (attach schedule) | **15d** | |
| e | Total foreign taxes (check one): ▶ ☐ Paid  ☐ Accrued | **15e** | |
| f | Reduction in taxes available for credit (attach schedule) | **15f** | |
| g | Other foreign tax information (attach schedule) | **15g** | |

**Other Items**

| | | | |
|---|---|---|---|
| 16 | Total property distributions (including cash) other than dividends reported on line 18 below | **16** | |
| 17 | Other items and amounts not included on lines 1 through 16 above, that are required to be reported separately to shareholders (attach schedule). | | |
| 18 | Total dividend distributions paid from accumulated earnings and profits contained in other retained earnings (line 27, Schedule L) . | **18** | |

Form 1120S (1989) Page **4**

## Schedule L — Balance Sheets

| Assets | Beginning of tax year (a) | (b) | End of tax year (c) | (d) |
|---|---|---|---|---|
| 1 Cash | | | | |
| 2 Trade notes and accounts receivable | | | | |
| a Less allowance for bad debts | | | | |
| 3 Inventories | | | | |
| 4 U.S. government obligations | | | | |
| 5 Tax-exempt securities | | | | |
| 6 Other current assets (attach schedule) | | | | |
| 7 Loans to shareholders | | | | |
| 8 Mortgage and real estate loans | | | | |
| 9 Other investments (attach schedule) | | | | |
| 10 Buildings and other depreciable assets | | | | |
| a Less accumulated depreciation | | | | |
| 11 Depletable assets | | | | |
| a Less accumulated depletion | | | | |
| 12 Land (net of any amortization) | | | | |
| 13 Intangible assets (amortizable only) | | | | |
| a Less accumulated amortization | | | | |
| 14 Other assets (attach schedule) | | | | |
| 15 Total assets | | | | |

| Liabilities and Shareholders' Equity | | | | |
|---|---|---|---|---|
| 16 Accounts payable | | | | |
| 17 Mortgages, notes, bonds payable in less than 1 year | | | | |
| 18 Other current liabilities (attach schedule) | | | | |
| 19 Loans from shareholders | | | | |
| 20 Mortgages, notes, bonds payable in 1 year or more | | | | |
| 21 Other liabilities (attach schedule) | | | | |
| 22 Capital stock | | | | |
| 23 Paid-in or capital surplus | | | | |
| 24 Accumulated adjustments account | | | | |
| 25 Other adjustments account | | | | |
| 26 Shareholders' undistributed taxable income previously taxed | | | | |
| 27 Other retained earnings (see instructions) | | | | |
| Check this box if the corporation has subchapter C earnings and profits at the close of the tax year ▶ ☐ (see instructions) | | | | |
| 28 Total retained earnings per books—Combine amounts on lines 24 through 27, columns (a) and (c) (see instructions) | | | | |
| 29 Less cost of treasury stock | | ( ) | | ( ) |
| 30 Total liabilities and shareholders' equity | | | | |

## Schedule M — Analysis of Accumulated Adjustments Account, Other Adjustments Account, and Shareholders' Undistributed Taxable Income Previously Taxed

(If Schedule L, column (c), amounts for lines 24, 25, or 26 are not the same as corresponding amounts on line 9 of Schedule M, attach a schedule explaining any differences. See instructions.)

| | Accumulated adjustments account | Other adjustments account | Shareholders' undistributed taxable income previously taxed |
|---|---|---|---|
| 1 Balance at beginning of year | | | |
| 2 Ordinary income from page 1, line 21 | | | |
| 3 Other additions | | | |
| 4 Total of lines 1, 2, and 3 | | | |
| 5 Distributions other than dividend distributions | | | |
| 6 Loss from page 1, line 21 | | | |
| 7 Other reductions | | | |
| 8 Add lines 5, 6, and 7 | | | |
| 9 Balance at end of tax year—subtract line 8 from line 4 | | | |

★U.S.GPO:1989-0-245-268

# Form **1120-A**

Department of the Treasury
Internal Revenue Service

## U.S. Corporation Short-Form Income Tax Return

**Instructions are separate. See them to make sure you qualify to file Form 1120-A.**

For calendar year 1989 or tax year beginning .................. , 1989, ending ................ , 19 .....

OMB No. 1545-0890

**1989**

**A** Check this box if corp. is a personal service corp. (as defined in Temp. Regs. sec. 1.441-4T— see instructions) ▶ ☐

| Use IRS label. Other- wise, please print or type. | Name |
| --- | --- |
| | Number and street (or P.O. box number if mail is not delivered to street address) |
| | City or town, state, and ZIP code |

**B** Employer identification number

**C** Date incorporated

**D** Total assets (see Specific Instructions)
$

**E** Check applicable boxes: **(1)** ☐ Initial return  **(2)** ☐ Change in address

**F** Check method of accounting: **(1)** ☐ Cash  **(2)** ☐ Accrual  **(3)** ☐ Other (specify) . . ▶

### Income

| | | | | | |
| --- | --- | --- | --- | --- | --- |
| **1a** | Gross receipts or sales | **b** Less returns and allowances | | **c** Balance ▶ | **1c** |
| **2** | Cost of goods sold and/or operations (see instructions) | | | | **2** |
| **3** | Gross profit (line 1c less line 2) | | | | **3** |
| **4** | Domestic corporation dividends subject to the 70% deduction | | | | **4** |
| **5** | Interest | | | | **5** |
| **6** | Gross rents | | | | **6** |
| **7** | Gross royalties | | | | **7** |
| **8** | Capital gain net income (attach Schedule D (Form 1120)) | | | | **8** |
| **9** | Net gain or (loss) from Form 4797, Part II, line 18 (attach Form 4797) | | | | **9** |
| **10** | Other income (see instructions) | | | | **10** |
| **11** | **Total** income—Add lines 3 through 10 | | | ▶ | **11** |

### Deductions

*(See Instructions for limitations on deductions.)*

| | | | | | |
| --- | --- | --- | --- | --- | --- |
| **12** | Compensation of officers (see instructions) | | | | **12** |
| **13a** | Salaries and wages | **b** Less jobs credit | | **c** Balance ▶ | **13c** |
| **14** | Repairs | | | | **14** |
| **15** | Bad debts | | | | **15** |
| **16** | Rents | | | | **16** |
| **17** | Taxes | | | | **17** |
| **18** | Interest | | | | **18** |
| **19** | Contributions **(see instructions for 10% limitation)** | | | | **19** |
| **20** | Depreciation (attach Form 4562) | | | **20** | |
| **21** | Less depreciation claimed elsewhere on return | | **21a** | | **21b** |
| **22** | Other deductions (attach schedule) | | | | **22** |
| **23** | **Total** deductions—Add lines 12 through 22 | | | ▶ | **23** |
| **24** | Taxable income before net operating loss deduction and special deductions (line 11 less line 23) | | | | **24** |
| **25** | **Less: a** Net operating loss deduction (see instructions) | | **25a** | | |
| | **b** Special deductions (see instructions) | | **25b** | | **25c** |

### Tax and Payments

| | | | | | |
| --- | --- | --- | --- | --- | --- |
| **26** | Taxable income—Line 24 less line 25c | | | | **26** |
| **27** | **Total tax** (Part I, line 7) | | | | **27** |
| **28** | **Payments:** | | | | |
| | **a** 1988 overpayment credited to 1989 | **28a** | | | |
| | **b** 1989 estimated tax payments | **28b** | | | |
| | **c** Less 1989 refund applied for on Form 4466 | **28c** ( ) | **Bal** ▶ | **28d** | |
| | **e** Tax deposited with Form 7004 | | | **28e** | |
| | **f** Credit from regulated investment companies (attach Form 2439) | | | **28f** | |
| | **g** Credit for Federal tax on fuels (attach Form 4136) | | | **28g** | |
| | **h** Total payments—Add lines 28d through 28g | | | | **28h** |
| **29** | Enter any **penalty** for underpayment of estimated tax—Check ▶ ☐ if Form 2220 is attached | | | | **29** |
| **30** | **Tax due**—If the total of lines 27 and 29 is larger than line 28h, enter amount owed | | | | **30** |
| **31** | **Overpayment**—If line 28h is larger than the total of lines 27 and 29, enter amount overpaid | | | | **31** |
| **32** | Enter amount of line 31 you want: **Credited to 1990 estimated tax** ▶ | | **Refunded** ▶ | | **32** |

**Please Sign Here**

Under penalties of perjury, I declare that I have examined this return, including accompanying schedules and statements, and to the best of my knowledge and belief, it is true, correct, and complete. Declaration of preparer (other than taxpayer) is based on all information of which preparer has any knowledge.

▶ _____ Signature of officer   Date _____   ▶ Title _____

**Paid Preparer's Use Only**

| Preparer's signature ▶ | | Date _____ | Check if self-employed ▶ ☐ | Preparer's social security number |
| --- | --- | --- | --- | --- |
| Firm's name (or yours if self-employed) and address | ▶ | | E.I. No. ▶ | |
| | | | ZIP code ▶ | |

For Paperwork Reduction Act Notice, see page 1 of the instructions.

Form **1120-A** (1989)

Form 1120-A (1989)      Page **2**

## Part I   Tax Computation

| | | |
|---|---|---|
| 1 | Income tax (see instructions to figure the tax). Check this box if the corp. is a qualified personal service corp. (see instructions). ▶ ☐ | 1 |
| 2a | General business credit. Check if from: ☐ Form 3800   ☐ Form 3468   ☐ Form 5884 | |
| |                  ☐ Form 6478   ☐ Form 6765   ☐ Form 8586   **2a** | |
| b | Credit for prior year minimum tax (attach Form 8801) . . . . . . . . **2b** | |
| 3 | Total credits—Add lines 2a and 2b . . . . . . . . . . . . . . . | 3 |
| 4 | Line 1 less line 3 . . . . . . . . . . . . . . . . . . . . | 4 |
| 5 | Recapture taxes. Check if from: ☐ Form 4255   ☐ Form 8611 . . . . . . | 5 |
| 6 | Alternative minimum tax (attach Form 4626) . . . . . . . . . . . | 6 |
| 7 | Total tax—Add lines 4 through 6. Enter here and on line 27, page 1 . . . . | 7 |

### Additional Information (See instruction F.)

G   Refer to the list in the instructions and state the principal:

     **(1)** Business activity code no. ▶ --------------------------------------

     **(2)** Business activity ▶ --------------------------------------

     **(3)** Product or service ▶ --------------------------------------

H   Did any individual, partnership, estate, or trust at the end of the tax year own, directly or indirectly, 50% or more of the corporation's voting stock? (For rules of attribution, see section 267(c).)   Yes ☐   No ☐
If "Yes," attach schedule showing name, address, and identifying number.

I   Enter the amount of tax-exempt interest received or accrued during the tax year . . . . . . . . . . . . . . ▶ |$        |

J   **(1)** If an amount for cost of goods sold and/or operations is entered on line 2, page 1, complete (a) through (c):

     **(a)** Purchases (see instructions) . . .

     **(b)** Additional sec. 263A costs (see instructions —attach schedule) . .

     **(c)** Other costs (attach schedule) . .

     **(2)** Do the rules of section 263A (with respect to property produced or acquired for resale) apply to the corporation? . . . Yes ☐ No ☐

K   At any time during the tax year, did you have an interest in or a signature or other authority over a financial account in a foreign country (such as a bank account, securities account, or other financial account)? (See instruction F for filing requirements for form TD F 90-22.1.) . . . . Yes ☐ No ☐
If "Yes," enter the name of the foreign country ▶ --------------------

L   Enter amount of cash distributions and the book value of property (other than cash) distributions made in this tax year ▶ |$     |

## Part II   Balance Sheets

| | | | (a) Beginning of tax year | (b) End of tax year |
|---|---|---|---|---|
| **Assets** | 1 | Cash . . . . . . . . . . . . . | | |
| | 2a | Trade notes and accounts receivable . . . . . . . . | | |
| | b | Less allowance for bad debts . . . . . . . . . | (     ) | (     ) |
| | 3 | Inventories . . . . . . . . . . | | |
| | 4 | U.S. government obligations . . . . . . . . | | |
| | 5 | Tax-exempt securities (see instructions) . . . | | |
| | 6 | Other current assets (attach schedule) . . . . | | |
| | 7 | Loans to stockholders . . . . . . . . . | | |
| | 8 | Mortgage and real estate loans . . . . . . | | |
| | 9a | Depreciable, depletable, and intangible assets . . . | | |
| | b | Less accumulated depreciation, depletion, and amortization . . | (     ) | (     ) |
| | 10 | Land (net of any amortization) . . . . . . | | |
| | 11 | Other assets (attach schedule) . . . . . | | |
| | 12 | Total assets . . . . . . . . . . . . | | |
| **Liabilities and Stockholders' Equity** | 13 | Accounts payable . . . . . . . . . | | |
| | 14 | Other current liabilities (attach schedule) . . . . . . | | |
| | 15 | Loans from stockholders . . . . . . . . | | |
| | 16 | Mortgages, notes, bonds payable . . . . . . | | |
| | 17 | Other liabilities (attach schedule) . . . . . . | | |
| | 18 | Capital stock (preferred and common stock) . . . . | | |
| | 19 | Paid-in or capital surplus . . . . . . . | | |
| | 20 | Retained earnings . . . . . . . . . | | |
| | 21 | Less cost of treasury stock . . . . . . . | (     ) | (     ) |
| | 22 | Total liabilities and stockholders' equity . . . . | | |

## Part III   Reconciliation of Income per Books With Income per Return (Must be completed by all filers)

| | | | | |
|---|---|---|---|---|
| 1 | Net income per books . . . . . . . . . | | 5 | Income recorded on books this year not included on this return (itemize) -------------- |
| 2 | Federal income tax . . . . . . . . . | | | |
| 3 | Income subject to tax not recorded on books this year (itemize) -------------- | | 6 | Deductions on this return not charged against book income this year (itemize) -------------- |
| 4 | Expenses recorded on books this year not deducted on this return (itemize) | | 7 | Income (line 24, page 1). Enter the sum of lines 1 through 4 less the sum of lines 5 and 6 . . . . |

★ U.S.GPO: 1989-0-245-244

| Form **1120** | **U.S. Corporation Income Tax Return** | OMB No. 1545-0123 |
|---|---|---|
| Department of the Treasury Internal Revenue Service | For calendar year 1989 or tax year beginning _____, 1989, ending _____, 19 ____<br>▶ **Instructions are separate. See page 1 for Paperwork Reduction Act Notice.** | **1989** |

| Check if a— | | Use IRS label. Other-wise, please print or type. | Name | | D Employer identification number |
|---|---|---|---|---|---|
| A Consolidated return | ☐ | | | | |
| B Personal holding co. | ☐ | | Number and street (or P.O. box number if mail is not delivered to street address) | | E Date incorporated |
| C Personal service corp.(as defined in Temp. Regs. sec. 1.441-4T—see instructions) | ☐ | | City or town, state, and ZIP code | | F Total assets (see Specific Instructions)<br>$ |

G Check applicable boxes: (1) ☐ Initial return  (2) ☐ Final return  (3) ☐ Change in address

**Income**

| | | |
|---|---|---|
| **1a** Gross receipts or sales [_____]  **b** Less returns and allowances [_____]  **c** Bal ▶ | **1c** | |
| **2** Cost of goods sold and/or operations (Schedule A, line 7) | **2** | |
| **3** Gross profit (line 1c less line 2) | **3** | |
| **4** Dividends (Schedule C, line 19) | **4** | |
| **5** Interest | **5** | |
| **6** Gross rents | **6** | |
| **7** Gross royalties | **7** | |
| **8** Capital gain net income (attach Schedule D (Form 1120)) | **8** | |
| **9** Net gain or (loss) from Form 4797, Part II, line 18 (attach Form 4797) | **9** | |
| **10** Other income (see instructions—attach schedule) | **10** | |
| **11 Total** income—Add lines 3 through 10 ▶ | **11** | |

**Deductions** (See instructions for limitations on deductions.)

| | | |
|---|---|---|
| **12** Compensation of officers (Schedule E, line 4) | **12** | |
| **13a** Salaries and wages [_____]  **b** Less jobs credit [_____]  **c** Balance ▶ | **13c** | |
| **14** Repairs | **14** | |
| **15** Bad debts | **15** | |
| **16** Rents | **16** | |
| **17** Taxes | **17** | |
| **18** Interest | **18** | |
| **19** Contributions (**see instructions for 10% limitation**) | **19** | |
| **20** Depreciation (attach Form 4562)  **20** [____] | | |
| **21** Less depreciation claimed on Schedule A and elsewhere on return  **21a** [____] | **21b** | |
| **22** Depletion | **22** | |
| **23** Advertising | **23** | |
| **24** Pension, profit-sharing, etc., plans | **24** | |
| **25** Employee benefit programs | **25** | |
| **26** Other deductions (attach schedule) | **26** | |
| **27 Total** deductions—Add lines 12 through 26 ▶ | **27** | |
| **28** Taxable income before net operating loss deduction and special deductions (line 11 less line 27) | **28** | |
| **29 Less: a** Net operating loss deduction (see instructions)  **29a** [____] | | |
| **b** Special deductions (Schedule C, line 20)  **29b** [____] | **29c** | |

**Tax and Payments**

| | | |
|---|---|---|
| **30** Taxable income—Line 28 less line 29c | **30** | |
| **31 Total tax** (Schedule J, line 10) | **31** | |
| **32 Payments: a** 1988 overpayment credited to 1989  **32a** [____] | | |
| **b** 1989 estimated tax payments  **32b** [____] | | |
| **c** Less 1989 refund applied for on Form 4466  **32c** ( [____] )  **d** Bal ▶  **32d** [____] | | |
| **e** Tax deposited with Form 7004  **32e** [____] | | |
| **f** Credit from regulated investment companies (attach Form 2439)  **32f** [____] | | |
| **g** Credit for Federal tax on fuels (attach Form 4136)  **32g** [____] | **32h** | |
| **33** Enter any **penalty** for underpayment of estimated tax—Check ▶ ☐ if Form 2220 is attached | **33** | |
| **34 Tax due**—If the total of lines 31 and 33 is larger than line 32h, enter amount owed | **34** | |
| **35 Overpayment**—If line 32h is larger than the total of lines 31 and 33, enter amount overpaid | **35** | |
| **36** Enter amount of line 35 you want: **Credited to 1990 estimated tax** ▶ [____]  Refunded ▶ | **36** | |

| Please Sign Here | Under penalties of perjury, I declare that I have examined this return, including accompanying schedules and statements, and to the best of my knowledge and belief, it is true, correct, and complete. Declaration of preparer (other than taxpayer) is based on all information of which preparer has any knowledge. |
|---|---|
| | ▶ _____  Signature of officer    Date    ▶ _____  Title |

| Paid Preparer's Use Only | Preparer's signature ▶ | Date | Check if self-employed ☐ | Preparer's social security number |
|---|---|---|---|---|
| | Firm's name (or yours if self-employed) and address ▶ | | E.I. No. ▶ | |
| | | | ZIP code ▶ | |

Form 1120 (1989)                                        Page **2**

## Schedule A  Cost of Goods Sold and/or Operations (See instructions for line 2, page 1.)

| | | |
|---|---|---|
| 1 Inventory at beginning of year | 1 | |
| 2 Purchases | 2 | |
| 3 Cost of labor | 3 | |
| 4a Additional section 263A costs (see instructions—attach schedule) | 4a | |
| b Other costs (attach schedule) | 4b | |
| 5 Total—Add lines 1 through 4b | 5 | |
| 6 Inventory at end of year | 6 | |
| 7 Cost of goods sold and/or operations—Line 5 less line 6. Enter here and on line 2, page 1 | 7 | |

8a Check all methods used for valuing closing inventory:
  (i) ☐ Cost  (ii) ☐ Lower of cost or market as described in Regulations section 1.471-4 (see instructions)
  (iii) ☐ Writedown of "subnormal" goods as described in Regulations section 1.471-2(c) (see instructions)
  (iv) ☐ Other (Specify method used and attach explanation.) ▶ _____
  b Check if the LIFO inventory method was adopted this tax year for any goods (if checked, attach Form 970)  ☐
  c If the LIFO inventory method was used for this tax year, enter percentage (or amounts) of closing inventory computed under LIFO   | 8c |
  d Do the rules of section 263A (with respect to property produced or acquired for resale) apply to the corporation?  ☐ Yes  ☐ No
  e Was there any change in determining quantities, cost, or valuations between opening and closing inventory? If "Yes," attach explanation  ☐ Yes  ☐ No

## Schedule C  Dividends and Special Deductions (See instructions.)

| | (a) Dividends received | (b) % | (c) Special deductions: (a) × (b) |
|---|---|---|---|
| 1 Dividends from less-than-20%-owned domestic corporations that are subject to the 70% deduction (other than debt-financed stock) | | 70 | |
| 2 Dividends from 20%-or-more-owned domestic corporations that are subject to the 80% deduction (other than debt-financed stock) | | 80 | |
| 3 Dividends on debt-financed stock of domestic and foreign corporations (section 246A) | | see instructions | |
| 4 Dividends on certain preferred stock of less-than-20%-owned public utilities | | 41.176 | |
| 5 Dividends on certain preferred stock of 20%-or-more-owned public utilities | | 47.059 | |
| 6 Dividends from less-than-20%-owned foreign corporations and certain FSCs that are subject to the 70% deduction | | 70 | |
| 7 Dividends from 20%-or-more-owned foreign corporations and certain FSCs that are subject to the 80% deduction | | 80 | |
| 8 Dividends from wholly owned foreign subsidiaries subject to the 100% deduction (section 245(b)) | | 100 | |
| 9 Total—Add lines 1 through 8. See instructions for limitation | ///// | ///// | |
| 10 Dividends from domestic corporations received by a small business investment company operating under the Small Business Investment Act of 1958 | | 100 | |
| 11 Dividends from certain FSCs that are subject to the 100% deduction (section 245(c)(1)) | | 100 | |
| 12 Dividends from affiliated group members subject to the 100% deduction (section 243(a)(3)) | | 100 | |
| 13 Other dividends from foreign corporations not included on lines 3, 6, 7, 8, or 11 | | | ///// |
| 14 Income from controlled foreign corporations under subpart F (attach Forms 5471) | | | ///// |
| 15 Foreign dividend gross-up (section 78) | | | ///// |
| 16 IC-DISC and former DISC dividends not included on lines 1, 2, or 3 (section 246(d)) | | | ///// |
| 17 Other dividends | | | ///// |
| 18 Deduction for dividends paid on certain preferred stock of public utilities (see instructions) | ///// | | ///// |
| 19 Total dividends—Add lines 1 through 17. Enter here and on line 4, page 1. ▶ | | ///// | ///// |

20 Total deductions—Add lines 9, 10, 11, 12, and 18. Enter here and on line 29b, page 1   ▶

## Schedule E  Compensation of Officers (See instructions for line 12, page 1.)
Complete Schedule E only if total receipts (line 1a, plus lines 4 through 10, of page 1, Form 1120) are $500,000 or more.

| (a) Name of officer | (b) Social security number | (c) Percent of time devoted to business | Percent of corporation stock owned | | (f) Amount of compensation |
|---|---|---|---|---|---|
| | | | (d) Common | (e) Preferred | |
| 1 | | % | % | % | |
| | | % | % | % | |
| | | % | % | % | |
| | | % | % | % | |
| | | % | % | % | |

2 Total compensation of officers
3 Less: Compensation of officers claimed on Schedule A and elsewhere on return   (     )
4 Compensation of officers deducted on line 12, page 1

Form 1120 (1989)

## Schedule J    Tax Computation

1  Check if you are a member of a controlled group (see sections 1561 and 1563) . . . . . ▶ ☐

2  If the box on line 1 is checked:

  a Enter your share of the $50,000 and $25,000 taxable income bracket amounts (in that order):

   *(i)* |$_____|__|    *(ii)* |$_____|__|

  b Enter your share of the additional 5% tax (not to exceed $11,750) ▶ |$_____|__|

3  Income tax (see instructions to figure the tax). Check this box if the corporation is a qualified personal service corporation (see instructions). ▶ ☐ . . . . . . . . . . . . . . . . . . . . . . . . . | 3 |

| | | |
|---|---|---|
| 4a Foreign tax credit (attach Form 1118) . . . . . . . . | 4a | |
| b Possessions tax credit (attach Form 5735) . . . . . . . | 4b | |
| c Orphan drug credit (attach Form 6765) . . . . . . . . | 4c | |
| d Credit for fuel produced from a nonconventional source (see instructions) . . . . . . . . . . . . | 4d | |

  e General business credit. Enter here and check which forms are attached:

   ☐ Form 3800  ☐ Form 3468  ☐ Form 5884
   ☐ Form 6478  ☐ Form 6765  ☐ Form 8586 . . . . . . | 4e | |

  f Credit for prior year minimum tax (attach Form 8801) . . . . . . | 4f | |

5  Total—Add lines 4a through 4f . . . . . . . . . . . . . . . . . . . | 5 |

6  Line 3 less line 5 . . . . . . . . . . . . . . . . . . . . . . . . . | 6 |

7  Personal holding company tax (attach Schedule PH (Form 1120)) . . . . . . . . | 7 |

8  Recapture taxes. Check if from: ☐ Form 4255 ☐ Form 8611 . . . . . . . . | 8 |

9a Alternative minimum tax (attach Form 4626) . . . . . . . . . . . . | 9a |

  b Environmental tax (attach Form 4626) . . . . . . . . . . . . . . . | 9b |

10  Total tax—Add lines 6 through 9b. Enter here and on line 31, page 1 . . . . . . . . . | 10 |

### Additional Information (See instruction F.)

**H** Refer to the list in the instructions and state the principal:

  (1) Business activity code no. ▶ _____

  (2) Business activity ▶ _____

  (3) Product or service ▶ _____

**I** (1) Did the corporation at the end of the tax year own, directly or indirectly, 50% or more of the voting stock of a domestic corporation? (For rules of attribution, see section 267(c).) . .

   If "Yes," attach a schedule showing: (a) name, address, and identifying number; (b) percentage owned; and (c) taxable income or (loss) before NOL and special deductions of such corporation for the tax year ending with or within your tax year.

  (2) Did any individual, partnership, corporation, estate, or trust at the end of the tax year own, directly or indirectly, 50% or more of the corporation's voting stock? (For rules of attribution, see section 267(c).) If "Yes," complete (a) through (c) . . . .

   (a) Attach a schedule showing name, address, and identifying number.

   (b) Enter percentage owned ▶ _____

   (c) Was the owner of such voting stock a person other than a U.S. person? (See instructions.) **Note:** *If "Yes," the corporation may have to file Form 5472.* . . . .

   If "Yes," enter owner's country ▶ _____

**J** Was the corporation a U.S. shareholder of any controlled foreign corporation? (See sections 951 and 957.) . . . . . . . .

   If "Yes," attach Form 5471 for each such corporation.

Yes | No

**K** At any time during the tax year, did the corporation have an interest in or a signature or other authority over a financial account in a foreign country (such as a bank account, securities account, or other financial account)? . . . . . . . . . . . .

   (See instruction F and filing requirements for form TD F 90-22.1.)

   If "Yes," enter name of foreign country ▶ _____

**L** Was the corporation the grantor of, or transferor to, a foreign trust that existed during the current tax year, whether or not the corporation has any beneficial interest in it? . . . . . . . .

   If "Yes," the corporation may have to file Forms 3520, 3520-A, or 926.

**M** During this tax year, did the corporation pay dividends (other than stock dividends and distributions in exchange for stock) in excess of the corporation's current and accumulated earnings and profits? (See sections 301 and 316.) . . . . . . . . . . .

   If "Yes," file Form 5452. If this is a consolidated return, answer here for parent corporation and on **Form 851,** Affiliations Schedule, for each subsidiary.

**N** During this tax year, did the corporation maintain any part of its accounting/tax records on a computerized system? . . . . .

**O** Check method of accounting:

   (1) ☐ Cash

   (2) ☐ Accrual

   (3) ☐ Other (specify) ▶ _____

**P** Check this box if the corporation issued publicly offered debt instruments with original issue discount . . . . . . . ☐

   If so, the corporation may have to file Form 8281.

**Q** Enter the amount of tax-exempt interest received or accrued during the tax year ▶ |$_____|__|

**R** Enter the number of shareholders at the end of the tax year if there were 35 or fewer shareholders ▶

Form 1120 (1989)                                                          Page **4**

## Schedule L   Balance Sheets

| Assets | Beginning of tax year | | End of tax year | |
|---|---|---|---|---|
| | (a) | (b) | (c) | (d) |
| 1   Cash | | | | |
| 2a   Trade notes and accounts receivable | | | | |
|   b   Less allowance for bad debts | | | | |
| 3   Inventories | | | | |
| 4   U.S. government obligations | | | | |
| 5   Tax-exempt securities (see instructions) | | | | |
| 6   Other current assets (attach schedule) | | | | |
| 7   Loans to stockholders | | | | |
| 8   Mortgage and real estate loans | | | | |
| 9   Other investments (attach schedule) | | | | |
| 10a   Buildings and other depreciable assets | | | | |
|   b   Less accumulated depreciation | | | | |
| 11a   Depletable assets | | | | |
|   b   Less accumulated depletion | | | | |
| 12   Land (net of any amortization) | | | | |
| 13a   Intangible assets (amortizable only) | | | | |
|   b   Less accumulated amortization | | | | |
| 14   Other assets (attach schedule) | | | | |
| 15   Total assets | | | | |
| **Liabilities and Stockholders' Equity** | | | | |
| 16   Accounts payable | | | | |
| 17   Mortgages, notes, bonds payable in less than 1 year | | | | |
| 18   Other current liabilities (attach schedule) | | | | |
| 19   Loans from stockholders | | | | |
| 20   Mortgages, notes, bonds payable in 1 year or more | | | | |
| 21   Other liabilities (attach schedule) | | | | |
| 22   Capital stock: **a** Preferred stock | | | | |
|               **b** Common stock | | | | |
| 23   Paid-in or capital surplus | | | | |
| 24   Retained earnings—Appropriated (attach schedule) | | | | |
| 25   Retained earnings—Unappropriated | | | | |
| 26   Less cost of treasury stock | | (     ) | | (     ) |
| 27   Total liabilities and stockholders' equity | | | | |

## Schedule M-1   Reconciliation of Income per Books With Income per Return (You are not required to complete this schedule if the total assets on line 15, column (d), of Schedule L are less than $25,000.)

| | | | |
|---|---|---|---|
| 1   Net income per books | | 7   Income recorded on books this year not included on this return (itemize): | |
| 2   Federal income tax | | | |
| 3   Excess of capital losses over capital gains | |     a   Tax-exempt interest **$** _____ | |
| 4   Income subject to tax not recorded on books this year (itemize): _____ | | _____ | |
| _____ | | 8   Deductions on this return not charged against book income this year (itemize): | |
| 5   Expenses recorded on books this year not deducted on this return (itemize): | |     a   Depreciation     **$** _____ | |
|   a   Depreciation     **$** _____ | |     b   Contributions carryover **$** _____ | |
|   b   Contributions carryover **$** _____ | | _____ | |
|   c   Travel and entertainment   **$** _____ | | _____ | |
| _____ | | 9   Total of lines 7 and 8 | |
| 6   Total of lines 1 through 5 | | 10   Income (line 28, page 1)—line 6 less line 9 | |

## Schedule M-2   Analysis of Unappropriated Retained Earnings per Books (line 25, Schedule L) (You are not required to complete this schedule if the total assets on line 15, column (d), of Schedule L are less than $25,000.)

| | | | |
|---|---|---|---|
| 1   Balance at beginning of year | | 5   Distributions: **a**   Cash | |
| 2   Net income per books | |                     **b**   Stock | |
| 3   Other increases (itemize): _____ | |                     **c**   Property | |
| _____ | | 6   Other decreases (itemize): _____ | |
| _____ | | _____ | |
| _____ | | 7   Total of lines 5 and 6 | |
| 4   Total of lines 1, 2, and 3 | | 8   Balance at end of year (line 4 less line 7) | |

| SCHEDULE D (Form 1120) | Capital Gains and Losses | OMB No. 1545-0123 |
|---|---|---|
| Department of the Treasury Internal Revenue Service | To be filed with Forms 1120, 1120-A, 1120-DF, 1120-IC-DISC, 1120F, 1120-FSC, 1120-H, 1120L, 1120-ND, 1120-PC, 1120-POL, 1120-REIT, 1120-RIC, 990-C, and certain Forms 990-T | 1989 |

| Name | Employer Identification number |
|---|---|

**Part I  Short-Term Capital Gains and Losses—Assets Held One Year or Less**

| (a) Kind of property and description (Example, 100 shares of "Z" Co.) | (b) Date acquired (mo., day, yr.) | (c) Date sold (mo., day, yr.) | (d) Gross sales price | (e) Cost or other basis, plus expense of sale | (f) Gain (or loss) ((d) less (e)) |
|---|---|---|---|---|---|
| 1 | | | | | |
| | | | | | |
| | | | | | |
| | | | | | |
| | | | | | |
| | | | | | |

| | | | |
|---|---|---|---|
| 2 | Short-term capital gain from installment sales from Form 6252, line 22 or 30 . . . . . . . . . | 2 | |
| 3 | Unused capital loss carryover (attach computation) . . . . . . . . . . . . . . . . | 3 ( | ) |
| 4 | Net short-term capital gain or (loss). (Combine lines 1 through 3.) . . . . . . . . . . . | 4 | |

**Part II  Long-Term Capital Gains and Losses—Assets Held More Than One Year**

| | | | | | |
|---|---|---|---|---|---|
| 5 | | | | | |
| | | | | | |
| | | | | | |
| | | | | | |
| | | | | | |

| | | | |
|---|---|---|---|
| 6 | Enter gain from Form 4797, line 7 or 9 . . . . . . . . . . . . . . . . . . . | 6 | |
| 7 | Long-term capital gain from installment sales from Form 6252, line 22 or 30 . . . . . . . . | 7 | |
| 8 | Net long-term capital gain or (loss). (Combine lines 5 through 7.) . . . . . . . . . . | 8 | |

**Part III  Summary of Parts I and II**

| | | | |
|---|---|---|---|
| 9 | Enter excess of net short-term capital gain (line 4) over net long-term capital loss (line 8) . . . . . . | 9 | |
| 10 | Net capital gain. Enter excess of net long-term capital gain (line 8) over net short-term capital loss (line 4) | 10 | |
| 11 | Total of lines 9 and 10. Enter here and on Form 1120, line 8, page 1; or the proper line on other returns | 11 | |

*Note: If losses exceed gains, see instructions on capital losses for explanation of capital loss carrybacks.*

## Instructions

*(Section references are to the Internal Revenue Code unless otherwise noted.)*

### Purpose of Form

This Schedule D should be used by a taxpayer whose tax year begins in 1989 and who files either Forms 1120, 1120-A, 1120-DF, 1120-IC-DISC, 1120F, 1120-FSC, 1120-H, 1120L, 1120-ND, 1120-PC, 1120-POL, 1120-REIT, 1120-RIC, 990-C, or certain Forms 990-T, to report sales or exchanges of capital assets.

Sales or exchanges of property other than capital assets should be reported on **Form 4797**, Sales of Business Property. These include sales or exchanges of property used in a trade or business, involuntary conversions (other than casualties or thefts), gain from the disposition of oil, gas, or geothermal property, and the section 291 adjustment to section 1250 gains. See the instructions for Form 4797 for more information.

If property is involuntarily converted because of a casualty or theft, use **Form 4684**, Casualties and Thefts.

### Parts I and II

Generally, a corporation should report sales and exchanges, including "like-kind" exchanges, even though there is no gain or loss. No loss is allowed for a wash sale of stock or securities (including contracts or options to acquire or sell stock or securities) or from a transaction between related persons. See sections 1091 and 267 for details and exceptions.

In Part I, report the sale or exchange of capital assets held one year or less. In Part II, report the sale or exchange of capital assets held more than one year.

**What Are Capital Assets?**—Each item of property the corporation held (whether or not connected with its trade or business) is a capital asset except:

1. Assets that can be inventoried or property held mainly for sale to customers.
2. Depreciable or real property used in the trade or business.
3. Certain copyrights; literary, musical, or artistic compositions; letters or memorandums; or similar property.

For Paperwork Reduction Act Notice, see page 1 of the Instructions for Forms 1120 and 1120-A.

Schedule D (Form 1120) 1989

| Form **1120-W**<br>**(WORKSHEET)**<br>Department of the Treasury<br>Internal Revenue Service | **Corporation Estimated Tax**<br>(Keep for Your Records—Do *Not* Send to Internal Revenue Service) | OMB No. 1545-0975<br>19**90** |
|---|---|---|

| | | | |
|---|---|---|---|
| 1 | Taxable income expected in the tax year . . . . . . . . . . . . . . . . | **1** | |
| | **Qualified personal service corporations (defined in instructions): Skip lines 2 through 9 and enter 34% of line 1 on line 10.** | | |
| 2 | Enter the smaller of line 1 or $50,000 (members of a controlled group, see instructions) . . . . . | **2** | |
| 3 | Subtract line 2 from line 1 . . . . . . . . . . . . . . . . | **3** | |
| 4 | Enter the smaller of line 3 or $25,000 (members of a controlled group, see instructions) . . . . . | **4** | |
| 5 | Subtract line 4 from line 3 . . . . . . . . . . . . . . . . | **5** | |
| 6 | Enter 15% of line 2 . . . . . . . . . . . . . . . . | **6** | |
| 7 | Enter 25% of line 4 . . . . . . . . . . . . . . . . | **7** | |
| 8 | Enter 34% of line 5 . . . . . . . . . . . . . . . . | **8** | |
| 9 | If line 1 is greater than $100,000, enter the lesser of: 5% of the excess over $100,000; or $11,750 (members of a controlled group, see instructions) . . . . . . . . . . . . . . . | **9** | |
| 10 | Add amounts on lines 6 through 9 . . . . . . . . . . . . . . . . | **10** | |
| 11 | Estimated tax credits . . . . . . . . . . . . . . . . | **11** | |
| 12 | Subtract line 11 from line 10 . . . . . . . . . . . . . . . . | **12** | |
| 13 | Recapture of: **a** Investment credit and **b** Low-income housing credit . . . . . . . . . . . | **13** | |
| 14a | Alternative minimum tax . . . . . . . . . . . . . . . . | **14a** | |
| **b** | Environmental tax . . . . . . . . . . . . . . . . | **14b** | |
| 15 | Total—Add lines 12 through 14b . . . . . . . . . . . . . . . . | **15** | |
| 16 | Credit for Federal tax on fuels . . . . . . . . . . . . . . . . | **16** | |
| 17 | Total—Subtract line 16 from line 15. **Note:** *If the amount on this line is less than $500, the corporation is not required to make estimated tax payments* . . . . . . . . . . . . . | **17** | |

| | | 18a | | | |
|---|---|---|---|---|---|
| 18a | Enter 90% of line 17 . . . . . . . . . . . . . . . . | **18a** | | | |
| **b** | Enter the tax shown on your 1989 return (**Caution:** *See instructions before completing this line.*) . . . . . . . . . . . . . | **18b** | | | |
| **c** | Enter the lesser of line 18a or line 18b . . . . . . . . . . . . . | **18c** | | | |

| | | | (a) | (b) | (c) | (d) |
|---|---|---|---|---|---|---|
| 19 | **Installment due dates** (see instructions) . . . . . . . . | **19** | | | | |
| 20 | **Required installments.** Enter 25% of line 18c in columns (a) through (d) unless **a** or **b** below applies to the corporation: | | | | | |
| **a** | If you use the annualized income installment method and/or the adjusted seasonal installment method, complete Schedule A and enter the amount from line 45 in each column of line 20. | | | | | |
| **b** | If you are a "large corporation," see the instructions for the amount to enter in each column of line 20 . . . . . . . . | **20** | | | | |

**For Paperwork Reduction Act Notice, see instructions.**

Form **1120-W** (1990)

Form 1120-W (WORKSHEET) 1990                                                          Page **2**

| **Schedule A** | Required Installments Using the Annualized Income or Adjusted Seasonal Installment Methods Under Section 6655(e) |
|---|---|

| Part I—Annualized Income Installment Method | | (a) | (b) | (c) | (d) |
|---|---|---|---|---|---|
| | | Period | | | |
| | | | First 3 months | First 6 months | First 9 months |
| (1)  Enter your taxable income for each period. | 1 | | | | |
| (2)  Annualization amounts. | 2 | | 4 | 2 | 1.33333 |
| (3)  Multiply line 1 by line 2. | 3 | | | | |
| | | Period | | | |
| | | First 3 months | First 5 months | First 8 months | First 11 months |
| (4)  Enter your taxable income for each period. | 4 | | | | |
| (5)  Annualization amounts. | 5 | 4 | 2.4 | 1.5 | 1.09091 |
| (6)  Multiply line 4 by line 5. | 6 | | | | |
| (7)  Annualized taxable income. In column (a), enter the amount from line 6, column (a). In columns (b), (c), and (d), enter the **lesser** of the amounts in each column on line 3 or line 6. | 7 | | | | |
| (8)  Figure your tax on the amount in each column on line 7 in the same manner as you figured line 10, Form 1120-W. | 8 | | | | |
| (9)  Enter other taxes for each payment period (see instructions). | 9 | | | | |
| (10)  Total tax. Add lines 8 and 9. | 10 | | | | |
| (11)  For each period, enter the same type of credits as allowed on Form 1120-W, lines 11 and 16 (see instructions). | 11 | | | | |
| (12)  Total tax after credits. Subtract line 11 from line 10. If less than zero, enter zero. | 12 | | | | |
| (13)  Applicable percentage. | 13 | 22.5% | 45% | 67.5% | 90% |
| (14)  Multiply line 12 by line 13. | 14 | | | | |
| (15)  Enter the combined amounts of line 45 from all preceding columns. | 15 | | | | |
| (16)  Subtract line 15 from line 14. If less than zero, enter zero. | 16 | | | | |

**Part II—Adjusted Seasonal Installment Method (Caution:** *You may use this method only if the base period percentage for any 6 consecutive months is at least 70%. See the instructions for more information.***)**

| | | (a) | (b) | (c) | (d) |
|---|---|---|---|---|---|
| | | Period | | | |
| | | First 3 months | First 5 months | First 8 months | First 11 months |
| (17)  Enter your taxable income for the following periods: | | | | | |
| a Tax year beginning in 1987 | 17a | | | | |
| b Tax year beginning in 1988 | 17b | | | | |
| c Tax year beginning in 1989 | 17c | | | | |
| (18)  Enter your taxable income for each period for your tax year beginning in 1990. | 18 | | | | |
| | | Period | | | |
| | | First 4 months | First 6 months | First 9 months | Entire year |
| (19)  Enter your taxable income for the following periods: | | | | | |
| a Tax year beginning in 1987 | 19a | | | | |
| b Tax year beginning in 1988 | 19b | | | | |
| c Tax year beginning in 1989 | 19c | | | | |
| (20)  Divide the amount in each column on line 17a by the amount in column (d) on line 19a. | 20 | | | | |
| (21)  Divide the amount in each column on line 17b by the amount in column (d) on line 19b. | 21 | | | | |
| (22)  Divide the amount in each column on line 17c by the amount in column (d) on line 19c. | 22 | | | | |

Form 1120-W (WORKSHEET) 1990

Page **3**

| | | (a) | (b) | (c) | (d) |
|---|---|---|---|---|---|
| **(23)** | Add lines 20 through 22. | 23 | | | | |
| **(24)** | Base period percentage for months before filing month. Divide line 23 by three (3). | 24 | | | | |
| **(25)** | Divide line 18 by line 24. | 25 | | | | |
| **(26)** | Figure your tax on the amount on line 25 in the same manner as you figured line 10, Form 1120-W. | 26 | | | | |
| **(27)** | Divide the amount in columns (a) through (c) on line 19a by the amount in column (d) on line 19a. | 27 | | | | ▨ |
| **(28)** | Divide the amount in columns (a) through (c) on line 19b by the amount in column (d) on line 19b. | 28 | | | | ▨ |
| **(29)** | Divide the amount in columns (a) through (c) on line 19c by the amount in column (d) on line 19c. | 29 | | | | ▨ |
| **(30)** | Add lines 27 through 29. | 30 | | | | ▨ |
| **(31)** | Base period percentage for months through and including filing month. Divide line 30 by three (3). | 31 | | | | ▨ |
| **(32)** | Multiply the amount in columns (a) through (c) of line 26 by the amount in the corresponding column of line 31. In column (d), enter the amount from line 26, column (d). | 32 | | | | |
| **(33)** | Enter other taxes for each payment period (see instructions). | 33 | | | | |
| **(34)** | Total tax. Add lines 32 and 33. | 34 | | | | |
| **(35)** | For each period, enter the same type of credits as allowed on Form 1120-W, lines 11 and 16 (see instructions). | 35 | | | | |
| **(36)** | Total tax after credits. Subtract line 35 from line 34. If less than zero, enter zero. | 36 | | | | |
| **(37)** | Multiply line 36 by 90%. | 37 | | | | |
| **(38)** | Enter the combined amounts of line 45 from all preceding columns. | 38 | ▨ | | | |
| **(39)** | Subtract line 38 from line 37. If less than zero, enter zero. | 39 | | | | |

**Part III—Computation of Required Installments**

| | | 1st installment | 2nd installment | 3rd installment | 4th installment |
|---|---|---|---|---|---|
| **(40)** | If you completed one of the above parts, enter the amounts in each column from line 16 or line 39. (If you completed both parts, enter the lesser of the amounts in each column from line 16 or line 39.) | 40 | | | | |
| **(41)** | Divide line 18c, Form 1120-W, by four (4) and enter the result in each column. (**Note:** *"Large corporations" see line 20b instructions on page 5 for the amount to enter.*) | 41 | | | | |
| **(42)** | Enter the amount from line 44 of Schedule A for the preceding column. | 42 | ▨ | | | |
| **(43)** | Add lines 41 and 42 and enter the total. | 43 | | | | |
| **(44)** | If line 43 is more than line 40, subtract line 40 from line 43. Otherwise, enter zero. | 44 | | | | ▨ |
| **(45)** | Enter the lesser of line 40 or line 43 here and on Form 1120-W, line 20. | 45 | | | | |

# Chapter 8

# LIABILITY OF CORPORATE DIRECTORS AND OFFICERS

## INTRODUCTION

Over a hundred years ago, a British lord chancellor asked a rhetorical question: How could anyone expect a corporation to have a conscience when it has "no soul to be damned and no body to be kicked"? Corporations act through human agents—and it is to those agents, the corporation's directors and officers, that would-be plaintiffs turn when they are in a damning and kicking mood. The risk is so great that many distinguished members of the business community are hesitant—or refuse outright—to serve on Boards of Directors and may think twice about accepting, or turn down, important corporate jobs.

It cuts both ways: corporations are also held liable for the wrongful acts and torts (types of wrongdoing that can furnish the basis for a civil lawsuit) of its directors, officers, and employees when they act within the "scope of their employment." That is, if employees do something wrong in the course of their jobs (not something contrary to the corporation's interest such as embezzling corporate funds), the corporation may find itself blamed. The individual wrongdoer can seldom use as a defense the fact that he or she was carrying out the corporation's policy; often, both the corporation and the individual are liable.

But the outlook isn't entirely grim. There are steps that a wise director or officer can take to make sure that he or she complies with all applicable laws. The "business judgment" rule insulates a director from liability when he or she acts in good faith and without abusing the powers of the directorship—even if the director made a mistake that caused economic or other harm to the corporation.

### State Statutes

However, mud sticks; and even defending against a completely baseless accusation takes time and money. State statutes indicate the extent to which corporations can indemnify their officers and directors (that is, compensate them for their legal fees and for judgments or settlements they must pay for actions taken when they were acting on behalf of the corporation)—and the extent to which they *must* indemnify them.

## D & O Insurance

This chapter also discusses "D&O" (Directors' and Officers') insurance: liability insurance purchased by the corporation to pay claims against the corporation and its officers. D&O insurance differs from conventional liability insurance in several important ways that the prudent corporate secretary must understand, both as a potential insured and as an officer who helps to set a corporation's policy of self-insurance or buying insurance policies for this and other purposes.

At least theoretically, under our system of corporate democracy, the Board of Directors elected by the stockholders has the ultimate responsibility for managing the corporation. Most of the important actions taken by the corporation call for a resolution by the Board of Directors (even if consent of the shareholders is also needed, and even if the action was initiated by an officer or an executive who is not an officer). But it is the officers who have day-to-day responsibility. In a small corporation, the founders serve both as directors and officers, so there is little or no tension between the two roles, but in larger organizations, there can be serious political tensions and serious problems of transmitting and evaluating information.

A corporate officer or director (whether he or she is an employee or an outside director) has several duties; failure to meet these duties can lead to liability.

## Duties as Rights of Corporate Directors and Officers

The three primary duties are obedience, diligence, and loyalty. In this context, obedience means not exceeding the authority the corporation has given the individual. Diligence means that these duties are carried out in good faith and that the degree of care that a prudent person would use is devoted to objectives that the director or officer reasonably believes to be in the best interests of the corporation.

The duty of loyalty somewhat overlaps the duty of diligence: both refer to working in the corporation's best interests, not against it, and to refraining from using the official position for secret or private profit ("self-dealing"). The duty of loyalty also constrains directors and officers from taking advantage of opportunities that legitimately belong to the corporation. For instance, it is improper for an officer or director to solicit the corporation's customers or potential customers and try to undercut the corporation's prices.

Directors have a fiduciary duty to the corporation (that is, they have an obligation to protect it and further its interests); they are required to uphold a standard of integrity similar to the standard expected of the trustee of a trust. An important part of the fiduciary duty includes becoming well-informed enough to make valid decisions. A director must be familiar with the corporation's internal financial statements and must make at least periodic checks of compliance with the various laws and have frequent contacts with senior executives in order to comprehend the corporation's activities, trends, successes, and actual and potential problems to be faced.

Directors have a right to access all the corporation's books and records and are entitled to copies of the minutes of all meetings of the Board of Directors and its committees—which imposes a corresponding duty to read and understand them. Whenever a reasonably careful director could become aware of activities contrary to the corporation's best interests by studying the reports, it is negligence to fail to uncover the threats to the corporation.

Directors are also required to make sure that the corporation obeys all relevant laws and regulations, and that it avoids all "ultra vires" acts (acts that are legally improper because they are outside the corporation's powers as defined by the state's corporation laws and the corporation's own Articles of Amendment and Bylaws). In fact, if they neglect this duty and the corporation suffers a loss, the errant directors face liability from two sources: they can be sued by the corporation itself, or stockholders, acting individually or as a class, can bring a "derivative suit" to enforce the corporation's rights. In a derivative suit, the stockholders sue on behalf of the corporation; if they win, the damages are paid to the corporation.

The general rule is that declaring or passing dividends is a matter left to the "honest judgment" of the Board of Directors; courts don't like to second-guess the Board of Directors' discretion on these matters. However, if a refusal to declare dividends makes it impossible for a minority shareholder to sell his or her stock, courts may grant some relief—even, in extreme cases, dissolution of the corporation.

A corporation's officers and directors can be held liable to the corporation's creditors for damages caused by the directors' and officers' fraud or deceit, or even corporate mismanagement that results in specific, identifiable losses that can be traced to that particular director or officer. However, if the officer's or director's misconduct damages the corporation and its creditors in general, not just a specific creditor, then the corporation (or its receiver) is the only party entitled to sue for damages for the misconduct.

Directors must be very careful when they vote for corporate loans to officers, directors, and shareholders. For one thing, it's likely that the loans will be treated as dividends for tax purposes (so that the recipient of the loan will have to pay income tax). Some states (such as Ohio) even make the directors who approved the loans jointly and severally liable to the corporation itself, or to its creditors or bankruptcy trustee, for the amount of the loan plus its interest, if the loan had the effect of impairing the corporation's ability to pay its bills.

## Law of Mergers and Acquisitions

The emerging law of mergers and acquisitions is still unclear, but seems to suggest that the Board of Directors has a duty at all times to maximize the value available to shareholders. Sometimes this may even require the Board to put the corporation up for auction instead of keeping it in business as an independent corporation. There are circumstances under which the Board can "just say no" to an unwanted merger—but not if its members want to protect their own jobs instead of the financial health of the stockholders.

Once a corporation becomes insolvent, its officers and directors are held to the same standard of responsibility as trustees: in effect, they must manage the corporation and protect its resources for the benefit of the corporation's creditors rather than its stockholders. If they fail in this duty, they can be held liable to the creditors—for instance, if they distribute the corporation's assets to its shareholders before making arrangements to pay the corporation's debts, or continuing the corporation's business when they are obliged to liquidate the business and pay off its creditors. Once a bankruptcy petition has been filed, the corporation's assets must be managed for the creditors' benefit, so directors and officers can be held personally liable if they engage in transactions that make the corporation insolvent or lessen the repayment available to creditors.

It is good corporate strategy to obtain the shareholder's consent to transactions that are legitimate but might seem questionable. The shareholders can't ratify a transaction that is void, illegal, or contrary to public policy, but if the corporation would have the option of declaring an agreement void, the shareholders can remove this option by ratifying the agreement after full disclosure, as long as there is no fraud. The ratification by the shareholders doesn't exactly validate the transaction: it makes it clear that the transaction was always valid because no one raised or will raise an objection to it.

Another risk to officers and directors is that, when a leveraged buyout of a corporation operates as a fraudulent transfer, the corporation's directors and officers (and its shareholders) can be sued and forced to return any benefits they got from the transactions.

Sometimes, a corporation's directors will have a personal interest in a corporate transaction: say, a director who is an architect may be retained to do architectural work for the corporation, a director who owns a small importing company may sell materials to the corporation, or a director could be a major stockholder in another corporation which is being acquired. These "interested director" transactions are not necessarily improper, and there is not necessarily any risk of liability—if proper safeguards are observed.

An interested director transaction will probably be acceptable under state corporation law if

○ The director discloses the potential conflict of interest to the Board of Directors right away

○ An adequate number of disinterested directors (those with no private interest in the transaction) vote to approve it, OR a majority of the stockholders vote to approve the transaction OR

○ Even if disclosure is not made, the transaction is in fact fair and reasonable to the corporation—for instance, if the interested director sells the corporation high-quality materials at prices lower than it would have to pay elsewhere

But if these tests are not satisfied, and the corporation or a stockholder sues, once the plaintiff proves that the director took a personal interest in a transaction, the accused director then has the burden of proving that the transaction was fair and promoted the best interests of the corporation and its shareholders. The duty of loyalty to the corporation is considered even more important than the duty of care—so a director can't escape liability merely by showing that he or she acted in good faith. The transaction must *also* be beneficial to the corporation.

Where a director is accused of appropriating a business opportunity that legitimately belongs to the corporation, recent court cases indicate that the corporation's financial inability to take advantage of the opportunity itself (for instance, a shortage of funds that makes it impossible to carry out a contract) will only be a defense for the accused director if the corporation is actually financially insolvent—not if it is merely unable to pay its current bills or get credit.

One possibility (especially useful in a small corporation or a start-up corporation which cannot provide a full-time living for its founders) is for the corporation to adopt Articles of Incorporation provisions that authorize interested director transactions and that shift the burden of proof to the stockholder or other person questioning the transactions. However, even these provisions won't protect a director who has defrauded the corporation or acted in bad faith.

### Sharing of Corporate Directors by More than One Corporation

Another potentially explosive situation occurs when several corporations share directors. This might occur when a business is organized in the form of multiple corporations, for tax or liability purposes, and the corporations do business together, or if a family or group of friends have several businesses.

Dealings between these related companies can lead to litigation; if they do, the courts will look closely at the transactions to see if they are fair to both companies, and to make sure that directors serving on two boards haven't penalized one corporation for the advantage of the other. Unfair contracts can be set aside. The directors have the burden of proof of showing that the transaction was fair; if they can't do this, the transaction may be invalidated; or the transaction may be permitted to go through, but the erring director may have to pay damages to whichever corporation suffered damages.

## Duties of Nondirectors

The position of officers who are not directors is less clearly defined, but certainly they have duties toward the corporation, and must exercise due care. Officers are required to stay within the bounds of their job duties—and if they stray outside, they may have to pay damages to someone outside the corporation who is personally or financially harmed by the unauthorized action (unless the corporation ratifies the action and therefore makes it officially the act of the corporation). An important possibility of personal liability comes about when the officer (usually the Treasurer) who is responsible for remitting Social Security (FICA) and other taxes fails to do so. The corporation is liable for failure to pay the taxes, of course—but the IRS has the legal right to proceed against the officer before moving against the corporation or move *only* against the officer.

Officers should also be aware that, if they sign a contract without indicating that they are signing as corporate officers rather than as individuals, they may be personally liable on the contract. (On the other hand, if the facts justify, a court may let the signer "off the hook"—but it's safest to avoid trouble by affixing the proper signature and using the corporate seal where necessary.)

In at least one respect, the standard expected of officers is higher than is that expected of directors: directors are usually justified in relying on reports received from experts such as the corporation's legal counsel and auditors. Officers are expected to have more firsthand personal knowledge of the corporation's day-to-day operations and financial health.

## The Law of Reliance

The legal concept of "reliance" means that people are entitled to rely on others at certain times—and will not be liable for doing so. Sometimes permissible reliance is spelled out in the state's corporation laws; at other times, it is defined by case law.

The influential Revised Model Business Corporations Act states that a director is entitled to rely on financial data that comes from lawyers, CPAs, or anyone else whom the director reasonably believes is competent to furnish the information (such as a consultant or expert). However, directors can't rely on information that they have personal knowledge is wrong—for example, if the director knows that the publicity department has lied to a management consultant or has provided an unrealistically rosy picture by omitting uncomfortable facts.

A director can cite reliance on legal advice provided by the corporation's counsel to prove that the director acted in good faith or with due care—but this is not an absolute defense, and the director must meet certain tests to qualify. The director in trouble must be able to prove that he or she asked the counsel for advice about whether a proposed transaction was legal, that the director didn't hold back any relevant information, and that the director acted based directly on the counsel's advice that the activity was not unlawful.

Courts aren't in business to serve as back-seat drivers telling corporations how to operate. The fundamental principle of corporation law is that corporations must be managed by their directors, for the benefit of shareholders—and courts will interfere and second-guess only if there has been a real abuse.

A corporation's Board of Directors gets significant protection from the "business judgment rule." That is, they will not be held liable, even for mistakes, even if their decisions were damaging to the corporation, as long as their decisions were based on a good-faith use of their best business judgment. There are five conditions that must be met before directors will be entitled to use the business judgment rule to protect themselves:

- ○ A business decision must have been involved.
- ○ They must have acted in a disinterested manner—they can't have had a personal interest in the controversial transaction; they can't have engaged in self-dealing.
- ○ They must have acted with due care: making an informed decision after they made a reasonable effort to find out the available relevant facts.
- ○ They must have acted in good faith.
- ○ They can't have abused their discretion.

## ROADMAP FOR AVOIDING LIABILITY

There are many safeguards an officer or director can observe to avoid trouble and make sure that he or she will prevail if charges of official misconduct are brought:

- ○ Get full information about the corporation and its affairs—including information from knowledgeable outsiders such as the corporation's attorney and auditor.
- ○ Attend meetings.
- ○ Never sign anything without reading it and considering it carefully.
- ○ Don't acquiesce in questionable or improper transactions, or transactions you don't understand, in order to avoid offending other directors.
- ○ Place your dissent on the record if you disapprove of a corporate action.
- ○ Find out what laws and regulations the corporation must comply with—and make sure that it does comply.
- ○ Make sure that formalities such as those dealing with books and records are complied with.
- ○ Make sure that the corporation sets policies for potentially controversial areas such as equal employment opportunity and environmental protection—and sticks to them!
- ○ Examine all proposed transactions involving the corporation's stock for propriety; make sure that inside information is kept secret, and is not exploited for gain by corporate insiders.
- ○ Make sure that dividends are declared and paid only as permitted by corporation law—that is, that they are neither improperly withheld (which also has negative tax

consequences for the corporation) nor paid out at a time when they impair the corporation's capital.

○ Don't approve loans to corporate directors, officers, or shareholders unless the loans are adequately secured and do not impair the corporation's capital or ability to repay its debts.

○ Make sure that compensation paid to officers and key employees is reasonably related to services performed, comparable to rates paid by other corporations, and is not dividend equivalent (i.e., proportionate to stock ownership rather than to work done for the corporation).

○ Make sure that pension and benefit plans conform to tax law and ERISA requirements and that they do not discriminate improperly in favor of highly compensated employees and against the rank and file workers.

○ Conserve corporate assets; don't allow them to be sold for less than their fair market value.

○ Make sure that the corporation does not engage in any acts forbidden by state corporate law or that are not authorized by the corporation's Articles of Incorporation and Bylaws.

○ Check to see that taxes are withheld and remitted on schedule to the appropriate taxing authorities.

○ If you are involved in a potentially questionable transaction with the corporation, make full disclosure of any possible conflict of interest or relationship with other corporations.

○ Don't appropriate business opportunities that belong to the corporation.

○ If the corporation's financial situation is difficult, examine new transactions (especially sales of assets) to make sure that the corporation is not making "preferential transfers" that benefit corporate insiders, or aid certain creditors at the expense of others.

○ If the corporation adopts antitakeover measures, they must be based on a reasonable belief that the corporation risks a hostile takeover; the measures must be adopted in good faith and must be proportionate to the actual risk.

○ In a merger and acquisition situation, the Board of Directors must consider the interests of the stockholders and their desire to obtain a good price for their stock, not just the Board's desire to remain in power.

## Civil Litigation Against Officers and Directors

Civil litigation against officers and directors for alleged official misconduct can take several forms. A person who claims damage from the action often has the right to sue on his or her own behalf. Another risk to officers and directors is the derivative suit; that is, a suit brought by a shareholder not to enforce personal rights, but on behalf of the corporation itself. If the suit is successful, the officer or director will have to pay damages to the corporation; the plaintiff's reward is seeing that justice is done and benefiting along with the other stockholders as a group.

Federal and many state laws set the rules for stockholders who want to bring derivative suits. In most circumstances ("demand-refused cases"), the shareholder must first make a demand to the Board of Directors that the corporation itself bring the suit to defend its rights. This is not required in a "demand-excused case"—one in which the demand would be useless or futile—for instance, if the stockholder claims that the entire Board of Directors is involved in wrongdoing, and therefore most unlikely to authorize a suit to detect their improper activities! If the demand is refused or is not required, the stockholder can then bring a suit *for* the corporation, and *against* the officer or director.

As long as the Board of Directors acted within the confines of the business judgment rule in refusing to bring suit on the stockholder's demand, the Board will not be subject to liability for the refusal. A derivative suit can only be settled if the court hearing the case approves of the settlement and deems it to be fair—but a corporation's Board of Directors has the right to settle a derivative suit with the court's consent, even if the stockholder who demanded the suit objects to the settlement.

## Indemnification of Officers and Directors

It is important to note that when a corporation indemnifies an officer or director who is a defendant in a derivative suit, indemnification is limited to paying the officer's or director's attorneys' fees and court costs; if the officer or director is sued by a third party (such as a creditor or stockholder claiming to have been damaged as an individual), indemnification can extend to settlements, judgments, and fines as well as the expenses of defending against the accusation.

There are many situations in which an officer or director is criticized, or even sued, for taking actions in the corporation's best interest, or even obeying a direct order from the corporation. Today, when courts are more crowded than ever, it seems that just about anything a person can do will lead to lawsuit from one side or another! The risk of suit, even if the suit is groundless and the claim will be dismissed, is enough to frighten some very qualified people away from accepting top corporate roles. One solution is liability insurance, discussed below, but insurers are becoming more and more wary of writing liability insurance policies and are raising premiums and imposing tougher and tougher conditions on payment of claims.

Another possibility is indemnification; that is, the corporation promises its officers, directors, and/or employees and agents that it will indemnify them—repay them any fines, settlements, or legal fees they incur when their official conduct is criticized. Indemnification can be granted in a corporation's Articles of Incorporation or Bylaws or through an agreement with the indemnitee (person entitled to indemnification).

Consult your state corporation law to find out if there are any limitations on indemnification. For instance, Delaware's law lets a corporation draft (or amend) its charter to provide indemnification for its directors (but not its officers) when they are accused of breach of fiduciary duty to the corporation. However, corporations are not allowed to offer indemnification for accusations of breach of loyalty to the corporation; charges of intentional misconduct; transactions that provide an improper personal profit to the director; declaring dividends, purchasing or redeeming the corporation's stock at a time when it is unlawful to do so; securities violations; and charges under the Racketeer Influenced Corrupt Organizations Act (RICO). Furthermore, indemnification is limited to liability to the corporation and its shareholders—not an outsider such as a creditor or person claiming to have been hurt by the corporation's products.

## D&O Liability Insurance

Some prudent corporations deal with risk by getting insurance; that way, a large, unpredictable risk that could have crushing financial impact on the corporation can be reduced to a manageable, predictable, affordable expense. However, because of increases in litigation, the cost of D&O liability insurance has increased, and its availability has decreased, so that self-insurance (for instance, by setting aside a reserve for litigation expenses, settlements, and judgments) is a meaningful alternative for many companies who simply can't afford the insurance or for whom the risk of litigation is low.

In many ways, D&O liability insurance resembles other forms of casualty insurance purchased by the prudent corporation. However, one important difference is that the D&O insurer does not have a "duty to defend." That is, it is not responsible for providing an attorney or controlling the case; the defendant corporation must take care of this, but must also consult the insurer about the choice of legal counsel and about any settlement the defendant plans to make. (After all, the insurer will probably have to pay for the settlement and the legal fees!) However, the D&O policy normally includes a provision that the insurer will not be unreasonable about refusing consent in these matters.

It is important to note that D&O liability policies are not like other liability policies: they don't directly insure the corporation against liability claims made with the corporation as defendant. Instead, the policy covers two separate but related perils. First, it covers directors and officers as individuals, if they are subject to liability because of certain wrongful acts; this is sometimes called "personal" or "direct" coverage, or the D&O part of the policy. Policies are usually written so that the insurer won't have to pay the individuals if they are entitled to indemnification from the corporation. The second, "corporate reimbursement," coverage reimburses the corporation if it provides indemnification to its officers and directors under the terms covered by the policy.

*Practice Tip:* Many D&O policies exclude coverage of liability in environmental claims and merger and acquisition situations—two areas of greatest risk. Watch out for this when shopping for coverage.

A typical definition of "wrongful act" under a D&O policy is a real or alleged error, misstatement, misleading statement, breach of duty, or act or omission committed by a director or officer while acting in that capacity—or any charge made against a person solely by reason of his or her status as a corporate director or officer. It's important to read the policy carefully to find out just who is covered; sometimes high-level managers such as comptrollers are not treated as "officers" and therefore are not covered by the policy; it may be worthwhile to have such people added to the policy as additional insureds by buying endorsements. Not every kind of wrongdoing or alleged wrongdoing can be covered by a D&O policy. Typically, the policies will exclude SEC charges; charges arising out of mergers and acquisitions, tender offers, greenmail, and the like; and, because the potential damages are hard or impossible to predict, many policies exclude punitive damages.

D&O policies are "claims-made" policies. That is, coverage is provided only for claims that are first made during the policy period. This qualification is very important because liability claims can have "long tails": an action taken today can have consequences that are not discovered, or do not even occur, until far in the future. Insurers, not surprisingly, don't want to be on the hook for claims made during the policy period and extending far back into the future, so the policies often deny retroactive coverage or set a "retroactive date" which is the earliest date of occurrence for which claims made during the policy period will be honored. Another possibility is that the policy will not provide retroactive coverage at all during the first policy year; the inception date of the policy then becomes the retroactive date when the policy is renewed.

Like most insurance policies, D&O liability policies have deductibles, sometimes called "retentions." Usually, the policy provides a "retention" for each individual, for each loss, up to a grand total for all individuals who are accused of wrongdoing, and there will also be a specified deductible that the corporation must pay before it can be reimbursed by the insurance company when it indemnifies directors and officers. The corporate deductible is usually higher than the individual deductible. If a loss arises out of a single act, or the interrelated act of several insureds, it will usually be treated as a single loss, so there will only be one deductible before the insurer is required to start paying.

Last but not least, to discourage claims, most D&O policies have a 5% coinsurance requirement: that is, the insurer only has to pay 95% of claims it would otherwise have to pay.

The D&O policy is normally written to cover legal fees, but, since the policy has a limit on what it will pay, the more that is paid for legal fees, the less that is available to pay settlements, judgments, or return amounts that the corporation paid to indemnify its officers and/or directors. But the insurer is responsible only for legal fees that arise out of claims that are covered by the policy; a complex case often involves some claims (and some defendants) that are covered, others that are not, so be sure your attorney keeps careful time records and renders monthly bills and status reports so that his or her fees can be allocated to the appropriate claims. The problem for corporations is that both the insurer and individual director and officer defendants have a common interest in seeing that as much of the defense costs as possible are assigned to the corporation; that way, more money is available to indemnify the individual defendants if they are found responsible for the conduct they are charged with.

Some policies contain what is known as an "option" clause, giving the insurer the option to advance expenses to directors and officers at their request, to pay them back for defense costs they have incurred, even before the case has been settled. This is a valuable provision, because cases often drag on for years, and officers and directors are apt to get impatient (or go broke) paying these costs, and immediate reimbursement is much more helpful than is the potential of reimbursement years in the future. Other policies (issued only to independent outside directors) entitle the insured directors to reimbursement of defense expenses as they are paid, except for expenses that are paid by the corporation itself or some other party.

If your policy does not contain an "option" clause of this type, and you are involved in a liability suit, it may be possible to enter into an interim funding agreement with your insurer, making it explicit which claims are suitable for immediate advances, and which must wait until a final resolution; how the costs of defending a case will be allocated among claims (especially among claims covered by the policy and those that are excluded); how costs will be allocated among several defendants (especially important if the same lawyer represents both insured and uninsured defendants); how bills will be rendered and how they will be sent to the insurer; and what can be done to reduce defense costs (e.g., by using computers productively) without limiting the effectiveness of the defense.

Most of the states (36 of them) have laws that limit the extent to which a corporation's directors can be held liable to the stockholders. Most of these laws, in turn, were a direct result of the "liability crisis" of the mid-1980s in which insurers made coverage difficult to get or prohibitively expensive.

Thirty of the states let corporations draft their Articles of Incorporation to include a provision limiting or eliminating the monetary liability of directors—as long as there is no disloyalty, intentional misconduct, bad faith, or personal exploitation of the corporation. (If the original charter does not include such a provision, it can be added later by amendment.) Louisiana, Maryland, Nevada, and New Jersey provide the same protection for corporate officers. In six other states (Florida, Indiana, Maine, Ohio, Virginia, and Wisconsin), the corporation does not have to take any specific action for liability to be limited; the statute itself limits liability. Consult your legal advisor to see what can be done in your state to limit director and officer liability—then decide how much it is prudent to spend on insurance for this purpose and whether your charter should be amended to provide broader indemnification.

## INDEMNIFICATION PROVISION (Articles of Incorporation)

Unless prohibited by law, this corporation has the right/is obliged to indemnify its directors, officers, employees, or agents against any claims or threatened claims of any type (except derivative suits to benefit the corporation) incurred because of service in that capacity for the corporation. Furthermore, if the corporation directs anyone to serve as director, officer, employee, or agent of another enterprise (including a trust or pension fund), indemnification is available on the same terms for claims arising out of such service.

Indemnification covers settlements, judgments, and fines, plus court costs and attorneys' fees. [At the discretion of the Board of Directors, advances can be made to pay attorneys' fees, subject to an undertaking by the recipient of the advances to repay any amount later determined to have been improperly paid.]

Indemnification is not available for claims arising out of actions that were not taken in good faith, in a manner that the person acting reasonably believed were in the corporation's best interests, or at least were not opposed to its best interests. Indemnification is not available for transactions yielding improper personal benefits to the director, officer, employee, or agent. Indemnification is not available to the extent that a court has determined that the person acting was guilty of negligence or misconduct toward the corporation itself. Indemnification is available only in criminal proceedings where the person acting reasonably believed his or her conduct was lawful.

However, the fact of a conviction, judgment, order, settlement, or plea of nolo contendere will not by itself be conclusive as to the presence or absence of good faith or the availability of indemnification.

[Partial indemnification is available if part of the settlement, judgment, fine, or costs is traceable to conduct permitting indemnification, and part is traceable to conduct precluding indemnification.]

The corporation will also be entitled to buy and maintain liability insurance covering its directors, officers, employees, and agents and those serving in such capacities in other enterprises at the corporation's request; insurance coverage need not be limited to circumstances under which indemnification would be available.

Indemnification is available only for actions undertaken after the effective date of these Articles of Incorporation. If, at any time, state law broadens the scope of indemnification, this corporation's officers, directors, employees, and agents will automatically be entitled to such broader scope of indemnification, with no need for further action by the corporation. If, at any time, these Articles of Incorporation are amended to decrease the availability of indemnification, indemnification will still be available for actions undertaken before the effective date of the amendment.

Indemnification as provided by this section of the Articles of Incorporation shall not be exclusive and will not limit the rights of any person under this corporation's contracts, bylaws, and ratification by shareholder vote. Indemnification for acts undertaken in a person's capacity as officer, director, employee, or agent will continue after he or she ceases to act in that capacity and will inure to the benefit of his or her heirs, executors, and administrators.

## OPTIONAL PROVISION

Any person entitled to indemnification who has notified the corporation in writing of his or her entitlement and the amount claimed, and who has not been paid in full within 30 days of submission of the claim will have the right to sue the corporation to recover the unpaid portion of the claim. If he or she prevails, expenses of bringing the claim for indemnification will also be recoverable.

However, it will be an affirmative defense for the corporation that the conduct for which indemnification is sought is of a type precluding indemnification.

## SHORT-FORM INDEMNIFICATION PROVISION

Officers, directors, employees, and agents of the corporation are entitled to indemnification against reasonable expenses (e.g., attorneys' fees) actually incurred in any action, suit, or proceeding in which he or she has been successful in the merits or has otherwise been able to secure the withdrawal or dismissal of the claims. [Indemnification will be granted after the person seeking indemnification has given the corporation an undertaking to repay any amount later determined to be inappropriate for indemnification.]

## INDEMNIFICATION CHARTER AMENDMENT

To the extent permitted by state law, directors [officers, employees, and agents] will be indemnified and held harmless against claims for money damages for breach of fiduciary duty in their role as directors [officers, employees, or agents], whether the claims are brought by the corporation itself or its stockholders, provided that the actions complained of occur after the effective date of this amendment, _____ , 199_____ . Changes in state law broadening the scope of mandatory or permissible indemnification will inure automatically to the benefit of the corporation's directors [officers, agents, and employees] without need for further corporate action. Partial indemnification will be available to the extent a divisible claim is attributable to activities qualifying for indemnification.

However, indemnification under this provision will not extend to claims arising out of a breach or alleged breach of the director's duty of loyalty to the corporation and its stockholders, to knowing violation of the law, to intentional misconduct or actions taken in bad faith, or to transactions providing unjust or improper financial benefit to the director.

## CERTIFICATE OF AMENDMENT
### [To be filed with state Secretary of State]

Phillip Fiskerman, Secretary of Delancey Coal Products, Inc., a corporation organized and in good standing under the laws of the State of Madison, hereby certifies that

○ At a meeting held _____ , 199 ____ , a quorum of stockholders entitled to vote was present. By a vote of ____ to ____ , the following Amendment to the Corporation's Articles of Incorporation was adopted: [insert text]

○ Adoption of this Amendment will not have the effect of reducing the corporation's capital.

○ This amendment will become effective upon filing of this Certificate of Amendment, as provided by Chapter 229.6 of the General Laws of the State of Madison.

To WITNESS THE ABOVE, I, Phillip Fiskerman, as Secretary of Delancey Coal Products, Inc., have signed this Certificate in my capacity as Secretary and attached the corporate seal.

Date: _____ , 199 ____
Signed: _____
Seal: _____

## NOTICE OF STOCKHOLDER'S MEETING
### [Include this language when describing the purpose for which the meeting is called]:

○ To vote on a proposed amendment to the corporation's Certificate/Articles of Incorporation to limit the financial liability of its directors when claims are brought by the corporation or its stockholders

○ To vote on a proposed amendment to the corporation's Certificate/Articles of Incorporation extending the corporation's policy of indemnifying its directors, officers, employees, and agents

## INDEMNIFICATION BYLAW

In compliance with this Bylaw, the Board of Directors shall, to the greatest extent lawful and feasible (on consideration of the cost and resources available to the corporation), purchase insurance to protect the corporation's officers and directors against liability deriving from their actions as officers and directors of this corporation.

## INDEMNIFICATION AGREEMENT

Agreement dated _____ , 199 ____ between Cantonia Enterprises, Inc., a corporation organized and doing business in the state of Tyler, and Ian Neff, who serves as Vice-President and Director of the corporation.

*1.* Cantonia takes official notice of the fact that recent trends in litigation against corporations and their officers and directors place officers and directors at great risk of being sued for actions taken as part of their official duties. This risk discourages individuals of superior qualifications from accepting corporate appointments which they could fill with great benefit to the corporation.

**2.** Cantonia's continued business success depends on its ability to attract and retain highly qualified individuals such as Mr. Neff.

**3.** The state law of the state of Tyler permits corporations to enter into indemnification agreements with their officers and directors.

**4.** In consideration of Mr. Neff's service as officer and director in Cantonia, or in any other corporation which he serves at the request of Cantonia, Cantonia agrees to indemnify him and hold him harmless for expenses reasonably incurred to defend against claims made against him and based on his service as officer and/or director.

**5.** For purposes of this agreement, claims include those brought in civil, criminal, and administrative forums and claims threatened to be brought, whether or not the claims are brought by or in the right of Cantonia as a corporation. Indemnification will be provided in the case of otherwise eligible claims arising out of the merger, acquisition, change in control of Cantonia, or any attempt by any party to induce Cantonia to enter into a merger, acquisition, or change of control, whether or not the attempt is successful.

**6.** Expenses means the cost of investigations, hearings, attorneys' fees, court costs, damages, judgments, fines, and settlements, plus any costs of establishing a right to indemnification under this agreement.

If at any time a claim is made and Mr. Neff believes that he is entitled to indemnification for that claim, he can submit proof of payment of expenses to the corporation and receive reimbursement before a final disposition has been made of the claim. However, Mr. Neff agrees to reimburse the corporation for any advances received under circumstances which it is finally determined do not give rise to a right of indemnification.

**7.** The right to indemnification is not unlimited. Mr. Neff will not be entitled to, and Cantonia will not be obligated to offer, indemnification under the following circumstances: _____
○ Federal law, or the law of the state of Tyler, forbids indemnification in a particular circumstance.
○ Mr. Neff receives payment from another source, such as an insurance policy, of expenses otherwise subject to indemnification.
○ Mr. Neff engaged in a knowing violation of law or a deliberate misuse of corporate information or opportunities.
○ A claim or case is settled on terms specifying that, or a court decision or determination concludes that, Mr. Neff entered into an action for improper private profit contrary to the best interests of the corporation.

**8.** This agreement does not limit any right to indemnification available to Mr. Neff under any other agreement, insurance policy, or the statutory and case law of the state of Tyler.

**9.** In order to receive indemnification, Mr. Neff shall apply to the Board of Directors of Cantonia by making a written request for indemnification; the Board (or such portion of the Board as does not constitute interested directors involved in the transaction at issue) will consider the request and will promptly rule whether or not indemnification is available; if it is, they will promptly take any action necessary (e.g., resolving to appropriate funds to pay Mr. Neff's attorneys' fees, resolving to reimburse him for sums expended in settlement or judgment of a case).

**10.** If any part of this agreement is found to be improper, invalid, illegal, or unenforceable, the remainder of the agreement will continue in force after severance of the offending portions, and Mr. Neff will be entitled to indemnification to the maximum extent permissible under the revised agreement.

*11.* This agreement binds and benefits the successors and assigns of both Neff and Cantonia, particularly but not limited to corporate successors of Cantonia.

Date: _____ , 199_____
Signatures: _____

# SELF-INSURANCE PLAN

Whereas, the Maxfield Motor Corporation has investigated the availability of D&O liability insurance, the coverage limits, premium charges, and claims records of the various insurers doing business in the state of Adams and has determined that purchase of such a policy of insurance would not be in the corporation's best interests, in light of the probable ratio of costs to benefits, Maxfield Motor Corporation has determined that the most prudent corporate course of action would be to establish a plan of self-insurance.

The plan of self-insurance will provide benefits to the Board of Directors and the corporation's officers (defined as its President, all Executive and Senior Vice-Presidents, Secretary, and Treasurer), enforceable to the same extent as if they were signatories of this plan. If this plan is amended or terminated, officers and directors will retain the right to receive and enforce benefits that accrued during the time the plan was in force, or in force according to its original terms.

The plan of self-insurance commences on _____ , 199_____ for a period of two years; when the period expires, it can be renewed for a further two-year term, or terminated, at the option of the Board of Directors (subject, as stated above, to the right of the officers and directors to receive benefits from the plan with respect to claims arising out of the period during which the plan was in force).

Under the plan, the corporation will pay any loss from all claims made while the plan is in force, subject to the exclusions given below, up to a limit of $_____ per person and a total of $_____ per year.

The following claims against insured officers and directors shall be excluded from coverage under this plan:

○ Sums that an insured person is required to pay to the corporation (whether by judgment, verdict, or settlement) because they were originally received by the insured person as excessive or improper compensation

○ Short-swing profits or insider trading profits for which the insured person is compelled to account

○ Sums that an insured person is required to pay to the corporation (whether by judgment, verdict, or settlement) because of the insured person's exploitation of corporate information or opportunity for improper personal advantage

○ Sums payable because of an intentional act of dishonesty or intentional violation of law or regulation

○ Sums payable to the insured person under an insurance policy or under another arrangement with this corporation or any other entity

In order to obtain indemnification under this plan of self-insurance, the insured person must notify the corporation as soon as possible after a claim has been made against the insured person and must cooperate fully in the corporation's investigation of the circumstances of the claim and whether it is coverable under this arrangement.

The self-insurance plan will advance/reimburse the reasonable expenses of defending against claims covered by this plan/provide legal counsel to insured persons who are subject to claims covered by this plan.

Indemnification under this plan of self-insurance is nonexclusive and will not limit the rights of the insured person to obtain indemnification from other sources, provided that the insured person agrees to reimburse the corporation for sums advanced under the plan that are later found to have been improperly paid. To prevent double recoveries and windfalls, the insured persons will be obligated to repay the corporation any sum paid by the corporation which the insured person also recovers from any other source.

The corporation will fund this plan by establishing a reserve in the amount of $ _____ , with annual additions of $_____/by funding a trust with the capital sum of $ _____ . The reserve/trust will be kept separate and segregated to the needs of this plan as long as this arrangement remains in force, and for a further two years after its termination so that funds will be available for claims arising during the period when the arrangement was in force.

# Chapter 9

# PERSONNEL MATTERS

## INTRODUCTION

In many closely held corporations, the corporate secretary's responsibilities include supervision and policy-making in personnel areas. Therefore, the corporate secretary's job includes setting policies that lead to hiring the best people, motivating them to succeed, and developing the skills and talents of people already inside the organization. On a less hopeful note, the responsibilities often include disciplining or firing employees who have not worked out successfully, as well as implementing layoffs during economic downturns.

Smaller companies usually can't compete with *Fortune* 500–type corporations by offering higher salaries and bigger pension and benefit packages; in fact, smaller companies usually can't even afford to match the bigger companies in these respects. Therefore, small companies must find other incentives. If the company is developing a new technology, it can attract talented scientists and others who are willing to take risks for the chance to make technical advances (or the chance to own thousands of shares of stock in a company that becomes Wall Street's darling!).

But if the company works in a mature industry, perhaps the best chance it has is to promise a better *way* of working: a "Theory Z" company that allows all employees as much responsibility as they can handle, and one where employees' ideas get a fair hearing, instead of a "Theory X" authoritarian company where only the big bosses can make their ideas heard. An important part of this strategy is promoting from within, and finding out what skills and potentials employees have developed, instead of awarding all the good jobs to outsiders. An employee hired for office or factory work may have earned a college degree or MBA in the meantime, or an employee may have talents that, with proper training, could make him or her a productive skilled worker, scientist, or manager.

Sometimes employers feel embattled and defensive, fearing that almost any personnel or management action will lead to a lawsuit. It is true that there is a complex system of federal and state statute and case law forbidding discrimination and wrongful termination. However, very small companies are probably exempt (because most of the laws apply only to companies with more than 15 to 20 employees).

## Avoiding Discrimination Liability in Hiring

Other companies must be aware that it is illegal to discriminate on the basis of race, nationality, sex, age over 40, disability, or religion in hiring, firing, working conditions, or compensation.

It constitutes illegal sex discrimination to discriminate on the basis of pregnancy, as long as the pregnant woman is capable of doing her job. A difficult issue is the question of "fetal protection programs"—programs that exclude pregnant or fertile women from jobs that could cause miscarriage or fetal deformity. If you believe that such a program is necessary in your business, consult your lawyer and the local office of the federal Equal Employment Opportunity Commission or your state Human Rights Agency for guidelines about ways to set up and implement a fetal protection program without violating the law.

Employers should be aware that, in addition to deliberate discrimination by "disparate treatment" (treating one group differently, such as hiring men with a high school diploma, but requiring women to have a college degree to get the same job), "disparate impact" discrimination is also illegal. Disparate impact occurs when a policy that seems to be fair and nondiscriminatory hurts one group more than another. For example, if an employer decides to ignore all experience more than ten years old in hiring decisions, this has a disparate impact on older workers (who lose the benefit of some of their work experience) and on working women (who often have to interrupt their career to raise children).

Also be careful about preemployment tests. Using a professionally developed test is lawful, even if it has a disparate impact on a protected group of applicants or employees—as long as the test is valid and really measures skills and experience that are needed for the job. But passing a calculus exam isn't relevant to working as a truck driver, and requiring military combat experience isn't relevant if you're hiring somebody to repair washing machines or supervise a typing pool!

*Practice Tip:* Small companies sometimes develop a pattern of hiring discrimination quite unintentionally. Let's say that the initial group of workers comes from an Irish-American neighborhood near the factory or office. As time goes by, the initial workers quit, are fired, or retire and are replaced by their friends and relatives from the neighborhood. The company gets enough of these applications to fill its needs, so doesn't bother to look elsewhere. People from other backgrounds don't know about the jobs, or don't apply because they think it would be useless. To avoid this problem, and to have access to the full pool of top talents, be sure to diversify your search for new workers. Try participating in job fairs at high schools and colleges in different neighborhoods (including religious-run institutions); run help-wanted ads in newspapers of ethnic interest. If you're looking for a top manager or a candidate for your Board of Directors, consult women's, religious, and ethnic organizations so you will have a diverse group of candidates to consider. (Businesses often complain that they would like to have more woman managers, or black or Hispanic or Asian managers, but can't find anyone with the relevant experience and qualifications; at the same time, women and minorities protest the lack of opportunities open to them.)

## Liability Possibilities When Firing

Firing, as well as hiring, can be a problem area. Ex-employees often sue—and sometimes win—for wrongful discharge. It *is* illegal to fire someone on the basis of race, sex, nationality, age, pregnancy, or other "suspect classification"; it *is* illegal to fire someone for performing a public duty such as serving on a jury. In many cases, it is illegal to fire a "whistleblower" who informs the public or a government agency about illegal or improper conduct (or threatens to do so). Sometimes employees succeed by proving that the employee manual promised them lifetime employment.

It's still legal for employers to exercise legitimate business judgment; to fire employees for theft, excessive tardiness, or nonperformance of their jobs; or to cut back on the work force to save money in hard times. A common solution to the need for cutbacks is to offer incentives for early retirement, so that employees will leave voluntarily. But this can be an expensive solution (especially if the retirees get lifetime health coverage from the employer) and one that creates legal problems from *both* directions (from employees who claim that they were forced out instead of retiring voluntarily—and from those who say that they wanted the extra benefits, but were not given a chance to get them!).

## Handling Retirement Liability Concerns

In short, early retirement incentives can be useful, but only if they're offered after legal and accounting advice is given, and "reduction in force" plans should be examined carefully to see if they have a discriminatory disparate impact. Sometimes a plan that seems to be neutral is actually motivated by subconscious desires to eliminate older, female, or minority workers, or those workers can be judged much more harshly than white males, and suffer discipline or discharge under circumstances that would not bring the same penalties to other workers.

*Practice Tip:* Make sure you establish a "paper trail" for every disciplinary action and discharge: maintain records of evaluations, complaints, grievances, warnings, and suspensions so that you can show that discharges were the only step you could take after the worker failed to improve after warnings and less serious disciplinary action.

Make sure that your evaluation process really gives workers insights into their job performance and how they can improve. The whole process often degenerates into a heart-warming but meaningless exchange of compliments, because supervisors don't want to be negative or risk the anger of reprimanded workers. (Supervisors may also be afraid that they'll be blamed for workers' poor performance, so they claim that everyone who works for them is a superior achiever.) Not only is this a waste of valuable time, and an even more valuable chance to improve work skills—it backfires if an employee gets fired after several years of high raises, bonuses, and good evaluations. The employer knows that the worker was fired for persistent poor work, attitude problems, lateness, or misuse of company property, but the jury thinks that the firing must have been caused by discrimination, because the company's own records show that the employee was doing a great job.

*Practice Tip: Never* send a letter or memo, or make a permanent entry into an intracompany file or other document without first thinking about how your worst enemy could interpret your words and use them against you. Lawyers who represent angry employees often find documents in the company's file that act as a "smoking gun" to prove discrimination or wrongful termination.

With that in mind, is it worthwhile to have an employee manual at all, or does the manual do more to help employees sue than to orient them to the corporate culture? If it's used *carefully,* the manual can help the employer. Employees can't claim that they're entitled to take leftover or spoiled inventory (or entitle to spoil inventory so they can take it!) if the manual explains the company's policies in this regard. They can't claim that they were promised lifetime employment if the manual not only reserves the employer's right to hire and fire at will, but makes it clear that oral promises by an interviewer will not be allowed to contradict the written terms of the manual. They can't complain about overtime or weekend work, or rotating or split shifts, if these matters were all explained clearly in advance. (Well, they *can* complain—they're human, after all—but they can't say that they're surprised.)

The corporate secretary's personnel role has a negative function (making sure that the company doesn't get into any trouble). It also has a positive function: hiring the best candidates, giving workers the best training, and monitoring their performance to make sure that the company runs as smoothly and efficiently as possible.

# INTERNAL JOB ANALYSIS

[Use this form to analyze the training, skills, and personal qualities needed for the job, so you can recruit and interview effectively.]

Job title: _____

Other titles used for similar jobs: _____

Summary of the job: _____

Employee reports to: _____

Others who report to this employee: _____

List ten tasks normally performed by the holder of this job: _____

   1. _____
   2. _____
   3. _____
   4. _____
   5. _____
   6. _____
   7. _____
   8. _____
   9. _____
10. _____

List any other tasks occasionally performed by the holder of this job: _____

Experience required for this job: _____

Formal education required for this job: _____

Other education or training required for this job (e.g., in-service courses, vocational education, computer tutorials, seminars): _____

Salary range: _____

Promotion potential: _____

Current employees who could be promoted or transferred laterally to this job (list pros and cons for each): _____

Applicants' resumes already on file for this or similar jobs: _____

Candidates recommended for this job (list who recommended them, and the nature of the reference): _____

Media to place help-wanted ads (include general-circulation, ethnic, and professional or trade journals): _____

Other sources of recruitment (e.g., employment agencies, "headhunters"; job fairs): _____

Start date for job: _____

Date to start recruitment: _____

Date(s) to place advertisements: _____

Interview dates: _____

Interview notes: _____

## RECRUITMENT ROADMAP

○ Avoid discriminatory terms in advertising—not just "man wanted" or "girl Friday" instead of "administrative assistant"—but "recent graduate" or "bright beginner," which can discriminate against older people, those who have been in the work force for a long time, and women seeking an entry-level position after years of full-time childrearing.

○ Candidates probably look at display ads before classified ads and pay more attention to them.

○ Consider using a box number so you can screen applications without being disturbed by calls from job-seekers.

○ Help-wanted ads must specify *what* candidates must do to apply (visit the personnel office? telephone for an appointment? send a resume and writing sample? resume and two references?), where to apply (some ads include a lengthy job description, but no employer's name, address, or box number, or give just a box number and no address!) and the close date for applications.

○ State explicitly that you are an equal opportunity employer and that all qualified applicants will be considered for the job in a nondiscriminatory manner.

○ Let your current employees bid for the job.

○ Check the resumes already on file; an earlier applicant, or an applicant for another job, may be perfect for this vacancy.

○ Applying for a job is a frustrating, stressful busines. Respect this by responding to all applications—if necessary, with a form letter or printed postcard.

---

## REJECTION LETTER (No Interview Scheduled)

Dear _____ :

Thank you for responding to our advertisement for a Production Scheduling Coordinator (Box Number A334 in the Sunday, May 19 edition of the *Courier-Advertiser*). We have reviewed your application and have decided not to schedule an interview at this time. However, we will keep your application on file and wish you good luck with your career plans.

## LETTER ASKING FOR INTERVIEW

Dear _____ :

Your application for the job of commercial artist at Wickerwood Domestic Products (Box Number 15K in the March issue of *American Artists' Monthly*) has been reviewed by our commercial art, advertising, and personnel departments, and we are all very impressed by your background and by the tearsheets and slides you submitted.

Please call Emily Naylor in our personnel department ((507)001-1947) to arrange an interview. We would like you to give us an entire morning, so we can look at your book, show you our offices, and discuss the tasks and compensation package involved in this job.

We look forward to hearing from you and discussing your goals and our job needs.

## LETTER ASKING FOR A SECOND INTERVIEW

Dear _____ :

Albert Slocum, who interviewed you for the post of Trainee Financial Analyst, has reported to the Recruitment Committee that your qualifications and personal style are very well suited to this position. After reviewing many applications, and after intensive interviewing, we have prepared a "short list" of four serious candidates for the position.

You are one of these candidates, and we would like you to return to our offices on Tuesday, August 21, for a full-day interview (please arrive at 10 A.M.) at which you and the other "short-list" candidates will meet the Financial Analysts with whom the successful candidate will work, speak with senior management, and see our business methods and style in operation. Please call Eleanor Parloa at (999) 439-1743, extension 202, to confirm your availability for the full-day interview.

Thank you for your interest in our company.

## LETTER TURNING DOWN A PERSON WHO HAS BEEN INTERVIEWED

Dear _____ :

I enjoyed our meeting on March 9, and found many of the points you raised interesting and challenging. Thank you for giving us your time and suggestions. However, one consequence of the current economic situation is that every time we advertise a position, we are approached by a large number of candidates, many of whom are fully qualified for the job and could fill it adequately or even with distinction. That gives us, as interviewers, the luxury of selecting a candidate with truly exceptional qualifications, but also gives us the unhappy task of turning down many fine candidates.

Although we were impressed by your background, work experience, and personal qualities, we are unable to extend a job offer at this time. We will keep your resume on file for future openings and hope that you will be successful in your career goals.

## OFFER TO A JOB APPLICANT

Dear _____ :

We interviewed many candidates for the position of Department Manager for the Grinding, Milling, and Polishing Department. Overall, we found that your resume and interview were the most impressive, and we would like to offer you the job. Please contact Martin O'Leary as soon as possible and let him know if you accept the offer.

As we discussed, you need to give your present employer four weeks' notice. Therefore, the start date for the Department Manager's job is June 9. If you accept the job, the salary will be $48,203 per year, plus participation in our Pension Plan, 401(k) Plan, and Health Care Benefit Plan. It is our policy to make bonuses available based on company profit and employee performance, and we have paid bonuses in each of the last seven years, but there is no guarantee that bonuses will be paid in the future. In addition, we will pay your documented relocation expenses in an amount up to $2,500 and provide you with a midsize car from our company motor pool.

If you accept this job, we ask you to report to the Personnel Office on June 9 to complete forms for your personnel and benefits records. June 10 and 11 will be used for orientation; we will pay for your attendance at the National Metal Fabrication Institute annual conference on June 12–13.

Welcome to our company! We hope you will accept this offer, leading to a long, productive working relationship.

## JOB APPLICATION FORM

NOTICE: Ferminor Corporation is an Equal Opportunity Employer. All hiring, compensation, and personnel decisions are made without discrimination on the basis of age, sex, race, color, nationality, or religion. Ferminor Corporation complies with the Americans with Disabilities Act. Reasonable attempts are made to accommodate employees' physical limitations and religious practices.

Ferminor Corporation is also an at-will employer and retains the right to terminate any employee, at any time, for any lawful reason. Hiring an employee does not constitute an implied contract of continued employment. No employee of Ferminor Corporation is authorized to make spoken statements that constitute an implied contract of continued employment or a promise that employees will be discharged only for good cause after a hearing.

Job Applied for: _____                    Date of Application: _____

Your name: _____

Telephone number: _____

Social Security number: _____

Are you a: □ U.S. citizen    □ legal U.S. resident (give visa category and expiration date):  □ other (explain): _____

Present employer or school: _____

Job currently held/course of study: _____

How long have you held your current job?

What is your job title?

What are your current job duties?

□ Resume (curriculum vitae) is attached

□ Describe the education, training, and experience you have received to qualify you for the job for which you are applying (attach a separate sheet if necessary)

List memberships in professional societies, professional honors, publications in the field, etc. (attach a separate sheet if necessary): _____

References: For each, give name, affiliation, title, and work address; indicate if any of them is related to you by blood or marriage.

Date(s) and time(s) on which you are available for an interview: _____
Date you could start work if hired: _____

## Confidentiality Statement

I hereby agree that any information about the company, its processes, its products, or its financial or securities transactions that I learn in the course of a job application, interview, or if I am hired will remain confidential, and I will not disclose it to anyone except in response to a subpoena or with the consent of the company.

Date: _____ , 199_____
Signed: _____

## Reference Check

I hereby state that all information given on this application is, to the best of my knowledge, complete and accurate. I authorize the company to verify all educational and employment information given here, including using the services of a credit bureau if the company deems it desirable to do so. I understand that, if I am hired, the company's discovery that I have deliberately misrepresented any item of information on this application is grounds for immediate termination.

Date: _____ , 199_____
Signed: _____

## INTERNAL CHECKLIST FOR CONDUCTING INTERVIEWS

[Note: Be sure and take notes on each interview—it's harder than you think to remember the details of an interview, especially if the interviews are spread out over a long period of time, or if you must interview many candidates or do several rounds of interviews.]

Position to be filled: _____
Name of candidate: _____
Date/time of interview: _____
First impression: Rate candidate's appearance, manner, way of speaking: ☐ Exceptional ☐ Excellent ☐ Very good ☐ Good ☐ Average ☐ Below average
Notes: _____
Candidate's current job/school/training: _____
Why does the candidate say he/she wants to leave?
Do you think this is the real reason?
Rate candidate's background and work experience:
☐ Exceptional ☐ Excellent ☐ Very good ☐ Good ☐ Average ☐ Below average
Notes: _____
Why does the candidate feel that he/she should have this job?
Your comments: _____

Candidate's current compensation: _____
Candidate's requirements for compensation: _____
Availability date: _____
Any conditions on availability?
Potential conflict of interest problems: ☐ No   ☐ Yes
How did the candidate find out about this job?
How does the candidate compare to the present holder of the job?
How does the candidate compare to the other candidates?
Recommendation: ☐ Turn down   ☐ Schedule follow-up interview   ☐ Make an offer
Follow-up: if necessary, contact the candidate's references:
    Name: _____
    Address: _____
    Name: _____
    Address: _____
☐ Not necessary
☐ To do on _____ , _____ . Check when done: ☐ Result of reference check: _____
☐ Letter(s) to candidate (check when sent): _____
☐ Turn-down   Keep resume, application on file: ☐ Yes   ☐ No
☐ Request for further interview
☐ Offer   ☐ Accepted   ☐ Rejected

## Outline for Employment Contract

○ Duration
○ Title
○ Duties
○ Full time and effort required
○ Compensation (including deferred and fringe benefits)
○ Authority
○ ○ Acquire and dispose of assets
○ ○ Borrow money, give security
○ ○ Enter into contracts
○ ○ Deposit and withdraw corporate funds
○ ○ Hire and fire employees
○ ○ Determine corporate policy
○ ○ Buy, sell, lease plant and equipment
○ Termination provisions (disability, discontinuance of business, on notice, failure to meet goals)
○ Covenant not to compete
○ Golden parachute
○ Assignability
○ Governing law
○ Arbitration

## Checklist for Joint Venture Agreement

○ ID of parties—clarify who acts in what capacity

○ Whether joint venture will be a one-off, partnership, or corporation

○ Purpose—keep joint venturers from engaging in extraneous activities

○ Respective contributions of the parties: amount of money (and schedule of payments), provision of office space (footage, requirements for electricity, phone service, etc.), bringing in contracts to be performed by the joint venture, technology and know-how, personnel (whose employees are they? who pays them? who's liable if they screw up? who pays their pension? to whom does their work belong?)

○ Patent rights (who applies for the patents? who has rights to the patents post–joint venture? what happens if the joint venture infringes on a patent already owned by a venturer?)

○ Who has the right to borrow on the venture's behalf? who signs the checks?

○ Venture should probably have separate books and records—but who keeps them? where? who can see them? (generally, any venturer during reasonable business hours)

○ What happens if a joint venturer dies or is financially unable to keep up participation?

○ Assignability of contract

○ Arbitration

○ Profit, loss shares (proportionate to initial capital contributions, or contributions of work or contacts to the ongoing venture?)

○ Responsibility for day-to-day management

○ Amount of time that joint venturer can spend on other things; limitations on potential competition with venture, or fiduciary obligation to venture

○ Antitrust problems (chance'd be a fine thing)


## EMPLOYMENT APPLICATION: PROHIBITION ON DISCLOSURE

If I am employed by StarGaze Realty, Inc., I agree that, as long as I work for StarGaze, and after my employment ends, I will not directly or indirectly give or disclose to anyone (whether for my own or another's benefit), any of the following:

○ StarGaze's client and prospect lists

○ Its proprietary computer software

○ Marketing methods it has developed separate and apart from the ordinary techniques of real estate marketing

○ Any other information, know-how, trade secrets, or confidences acquired from any person, in any way, during my employment.

OR

Employee agrees that, during his or her employment by DeeDee's Eco-Di-Dee Co and for a term of five years after termination of employment, he or she will not use or disclose proprietary information, manufacturing and marketing techniques, and/or client and customer lists developed by

DeeDee's for its manufacture and marketing of biodegradable disposable diapers, unless a duly authorized officer of DeeDee's has consented to such use or disclosure.

## EMPLOYMENT CONTRACT CLAUSE

Employee acknowledges that his/her job duties as outlined in this contract give him/her access to trade secrets and confidential information belonging to Bellerophon Industrial Co. (e.g., formulas; manufacturing processes; techniques for packaging, marketing, and shipping products; lists of past, present, and potential customers). As long as s/he is employed by Bellerophon, he or she will devote full time and attention to the affairs of the corporation, and will not engage in any other business activity (whether or not it competes with Bellerophon). The Employee agrees not to become affiliated with any other business as principal, officer, or director without Bellerophon's prior consent (although he or she may invest passively in another corporation's securities).

The responsibilities of the Employee's job include using his or her best efforts and maximum diligence to protect such secret and confidential material and refraining from disclosing it to any person without authorization. On leaving Bellerophon's employment, the Employee agrees not to take any files, computer disks or printouts, address books or files, or other unpublished material belonging to Bellerophon unless he or she has obtained prior written approval for removing such material.

### Confidentiality Warning to Be Stamped on Documents

WARNING: This document is the sole property of McNally Castings, Inc., and contains proprietary information. Access to this document is restricted to authorized persons. It is not permitted to copy this document without authorization, to use its contents without consent of the corporation, or to disclose any part of its contents to persons outside the corporation without authorization by a corporate officer or duly authorized representative of the corporation. Violation of this Warning may result in civil liability for the employee violating it and, in a serious case, will constitute good cause sufficient to result in termination of the employee's employment.

## TECHNOLOGY ASSIGNMENT BY EMPLOYEE

I, Felix Redmond, Ph.D., agree to accept employment in the Research and Development Department of Kappa Gamma Technologies, Inc. In return for my salary and other compensation, I agree to disclose promptly to Kappa Gamma whenever I create an invention, improve an existing invention or process, or make a scientific or technological discovery.

My obligation to disclose extends as long as I am a Kappa Gamma employee and relates in equal force to scientific and technical work done outside working hours and away from Kappa Gamma facilities, as long as I continue to be employed. However, my obligation extends only to scientific and technological discoveries, advances, and applications that can be used in any way in connection with Kappa Gamma's business of designing and manufacturing high-temperature ceramics and glassware.

I also agree to convey to Kappa Gamma all right, title, and interest that I may have in practical domestic or foreign applications of my scientific and technical discoveries, advances, and improvements. I also agree to sign all applications for patents, assignment forms, and other documents needed to carry out such assignments. Kappa Gamma agrees to pay me a one-time bonus of $_____ for each such discovery, advance, or improvement which, in the judgment of Kappa Gamma, justifies a patent application.

## FORM LETTER RE UNSOLICITED SUBMISSION

Dear _____ :

On _____ , 199____ , your unsolicited manuscript/screenplay/material about your invention/material about your business idea was received. In accordance with our company policy, as soon as a mailroom employee discovered that unsolicited materials were enclosed, your envelope was resealed and returned to you with this letter [or, we are holding your materials and will return them on receipt of return postage].

The process of innovation and creation is such that it is common for several people to have and implement the same idea independently. To avoid problems, we do not let any of our creative/marketing/technical/research and development personnel see any unsolicited outside material, at any time, unless the person submitting the material signs a release. That way, it's clear that if, coincidentally, our own personnel develop the same or similar idea, they were not influenced by unsolicited material unless the person submitting the material consented to disclosure of the ideas contained in the material.

If you would like your material considered, please sign the release on the back of this letter and resubmit your material, enclosing return postage. [Note: Placing the release on the back of the letter makes it difficult for the submitter to claim that s/he was not informed of the corporation's policy on unsolicited material.]

## RELEASE FORM FOR UNSOLICITED SUBMISSION

I, _____ , am making an unsolicited submission of _____ pages of material (e.g., notes, drawings, financial statements, and projections), dealing with _____ , to Eastbrook Diversified Manufacturing, Inc.

I hereby agree that Eastbrook and its representatives may examine this material to see if it is suitable for commercial exploitation by Eastbrook. I understand that it is possible that Eastbrook arrived at similar ideas and processes independently, and that I will have no claim against Eastbrook if it commercially exploits ideas and processes developed by its own personnel or by permission of others, if my ideas were not misappropriated by Eastbrook.

I further agree that if my ideas can be embodied in a form entitled to copyright protection, that if Eastbrook hires and pays me to further develop my ideas, the final product will be a "work for hire," and Eastbrook will be entitled to register the copyright; I will not be entitled to register the copyright unless Eastbrook explicitly waives the right to do so on its own behalf and permits me to register the copyright.

## EMPLOYEE POLICY MANUAL

NOTICE TO ALL EMPLOYEES: This Manual sets out the policies that the company uses in hiring, management, compensation, vacations, discharge, and other aspects of the employer-employee relationship. However, it is intended ONLY for the information of employees. The provisions in this Manual do not create a contract and do not constitute a promise of lifetime employment or a guarantee that employees will not be discharged without a hearing. The employer also reserves the power to change the provisions of this Manual at any time, without prior notice to, or consent of, the employees.

### Introduction

The management of this Company wants the Company to be a pleasant, productive, efficient place to work. This Company obeys all relevant local, state, and federal laws, including laws forbidding discrimination and those involving the environment. In order to be fair to all employees, and to prevent arbitrary and inconsistent judgments, it is necessary to set policies about the way the company will be administered and work will be done. Although the Company welcomes suggestions from its employees, setting and enforcing company policy is a legitimate prerogative of management, and, as explained, the Company retains the right to change its policies when it deems it necessary to do so.

*1. Company Organization.* Legal responsibility for managing the Company belongs to its Board of Directors. For the year \_\_\_\_-\_\_\_\_ , the following people serve on the Company's Board of Directors: Thomas Swinton, Martha Swinton, Michael Briggs, Edward O'Harragh, Julian Schauffen, Clara Felton, Rev. Luis Almendario, Todd Dignan, Robert Pawlsin, Richard Jerrome, John P. Choveck, John M. Choveck II, Stanley Gates. The company's officers are responsible for carrying out the policies set by the Board of Directors. The company's officers are President, Thomas Swinton, Corporate Vice President, Michael Briggs, Secretary, Clara Felton, Treasurer, Peter Dignan.

The Company has three Divisions, Plastic Molding, Metal Molding, and Metal Reprocessing. Each Division is headed by a Vice-President. The three Vice-Presidents are Benjamin Braddock, Theodore Hawke, and Lucille Stebbins. Within each Division, there are two Assistant Vice-Presidents (in alphabetical order): Lewis Altige, James Collins, Richard Fillmore, Barney Lacey, David Mittman, and Andrew Pokorny.

Each Division is organized into groups, with a first-line supervisor (foreman or forewoman) in charge of each group. Production employees are supervised directly by their first-line supervisors. Office employees are supervised directly by the three Office Managers, Madolyn Ross, Jennifer Kemball, and B. R. LeMoyne.

*2. Personnel Office.* The Personnel Office, headed by Barbara Krueger, is in charge of processing all applications for employment, notifying employees of changes in employment policy, processing the payroll, administering employee benefits, administering the Employee Assistance Program, and handling grievances from employees and disciplinary action against the employees.

*3. Employee Classifications.* Production employees are hourly workers, classified into Grades 1 through 6. Hourly wages are as follows: Grade 1 [etc.] plus time and a half (in cash or "comp time") for overtime, defined as more than 40 hours a week of work, or weekend or holiday work that is not part of the worker's normal shift. Day shift workers work from 8 A.M. to 4 P.M., Tuesday through

Saturday; interim shift workers work from 4 P.M. to 12 midnight, Tuesday through Sunday; and night shift workers work from 12 midnight Sunday to 8 A.M. Monday. Under normal circumstances, the factory is closed on Mondays after 8 A.M.

Office employees and executives are salaried workers, receiving individually negotiated salaries. Normal office hours are Monday through Friday, 9 A.M. to 5:30 P.M. They do not receive additional pay or comp time for overtime.

**4. *Employee Benefits.*** All employees become participants under the Company's Pension Plan and Health Benefit Plan according to the terms and conditions of those plans. The Pension Plan is □ noncontributory—the employer makes all the payments □ requires mandatory contributions, as described in the Summary Plan Description for the plan □ does not require employee contributions, but accepts voluntary contributions from employees up to ____ % of compensation.

The Health Benefit Plan covers employees, their spouses, and their dependent children under age 18 for hospital, medical, prescription drug, and dental care. □ The employer pays the full premium □ Employees are responsible for paying part of the premium, as described in the Health Plan Brochure; employee premiums are deducted from their paychecks.

**5. *Holidays, Vacations, Comp Time, and Personal Days.*** The factory and office will be closed on national holidays, for example, New Year's Day, Martin Luther King, Jr., Day, President's Day, Easter Monday, Memorial Day, July Fourth, Labor Day, Columbus Day, Election Day, Thanksgiving (Thursday and Friday), and Christmas (two days).

Employees must work for at least six months before taking any vacation days or personal days (unless they have permission to take time off for a personal or family emergency). In their first year, employees will be entitled to one week of paid vacation; in their second year, to seven days of paid vacation; in their third year, to two weeks; in their fourth year, to twelve days; and in their fifth and subsequent years, to three weeks.

Employees who are entitled to overtime pay can (if their first-line supervisor agrees to the time they will be absent) take their overtime pay in the form of "comp time" (1 ½ hours of paid comp time for every hour of overtime worked).

Employees who have a doctor's note can take up to five paid sick days a year. Unused sick days cannot be carried over to the next year. Employees can use sick days only if they themselves are ill; they must use personal days if a family member is ill. If the employee is too sick to come to work but not sick enough to see a doctor (e.g., severe cold, flu, 24-hour virus), the employee can use any unused vacation or personal days. Employees who have a doctor's note and who have used up all vacation and personal days, or who want to save the vacation and personal days, are entitled to up to ten unpaid sick days per year. If an employee or employee's spouse gives birth to or adopts a child, the employee is entitled to up to six months' unpaid parenthood leave for child care in addition to any sick leave taken as maternity leave for the physical events of birth and recovery. (If both parents are Company employees, only one can take the parenthood leave.)

All employees (office or production) can, with the consent of their first-line supervisors or office managers, take their vacation time either in one solid block or in some combination of vacation and individual personal days. Personal days can be used for circumstances such as family events (weddings, funerals, christenings, bar and bas mitzvahs, graduations), personal relaxation, care of family members, children's school events, and so on.

However, employees with direct responsibility for handling money, bank accounts, or checks must take at least half their vacation time in a unit at least once a year.

If two or more employees want to take vacation or personal days when only one can be accommodated, then the more senior employee will be entitled to the time off, unless the employees can come to an agreement between themselves to permit the more junior employee to take the vacation or personal day.

Up to five days of unused vacation, comp time, or personal days can be carried over to the following year; other unused vacation, comp time, and personal days will be forfeited unless the employee is prevented from using desired vacation time because the supervisor cannot schedule the vacation time without disrupting production or office routine.

**6. *Petty Cash and Expense Accounts*.** Employees should use every effort to plan ahead for expenses they will have to incur and supplies and equipment they will need so that, if possible, the Company itself can incur and pay the expenses. Employees are instructed to make arrangements for business travel with the Away We Go Travel Agency, which has a relationship with the Company under which it handles airline, train, and hotel reservations and rental cars for Company employees traveling on business.

However, under certain circumstances, employees will be required to incur business-related expenses that properly belong to the Company. Under these circumstances, employees can draw petty cash of up to $100 by presenting a petty cash voucher, signed by a first-line supervisor or office manager, to the Personnel Office, or can be reimbursed by the Personnel Office for amounts they have advanced if they present copies of receipts countersigned by their first-line supervisor or office manager.

Professional and management employees may be entitled to expense accounts, to be individually negotiated.

**7. *Reasons for Discipline or Dismissal*.** A first-line supervisor or office manager can discipline an employee for any of these reasons: _____
○ Failing to meet work norms that have been explained to the worker
○ Deliberately sabotaging or intentionally damaging inventory, raw materials, or equipment
○ Drinking or using illegal drugs or being under the influence of alcohol or illegal drugs during working hours
○ Taking equipment, inventory, raw materials, or office supplies without permission
○ Misusing company funds, company credit cards, or expense accounts
○ Making personal telephone calls, mailing personal items, using company vehicles, or using office equipment for personal use without permission and/or without paying the posted charges
○ Performing work poorly
○ Fighting or persistent conflict with other employees
○ Exhibiting excessive lateness and/or absenteeism
○ Making intentional misstatements on any application on intracompany on outside document
○ Intentionally disclosing any inside information about the company's securities or financial condition, or any trade secrets or proprietary information belonging to the company.

The usual procedure will be for the first-line supervisor or office manager to begin by discussing the problem with the employee. If the problem is not resolved, the next step will usually be a written warning, which will be placed in the employee's personnel file. If the problem is still not resolved, the employee can be terminated on request of the supervisor, reviewed by the appropriate person at the Assistant Vice-President or Vice-President level. Current policy calls for an informal grievance procedure under which the employee can present his or her side of the story to the Assistant Vice-President or Vice-President. Notice and severance pay are a matter of individual negotiation.

However, the Company specifically reserves the legal right to fire employees even if they have not been guilty of poor performance or misbehavior, if economic conditions require a reduction in force. The Company also specifically reserves the legal right to terminate employees without giving oral or written warnings or a hearing, if in the judgment of the first-line supervisor, Assistant Vice-President, or Vice-President, the welfare of the company justifies the immediate termination of the employee without completion of the full cycle.

The usual procedure for demotion also calls for an oral warning, a written warning, consultation with an executive, and a grievance hearing. However, the Company specifically reserves the legal right to perform an immediate demotion without completion of the full cycle.

*8. Status Changes.* In order to keep the Company informed and to make sure that employees will be granted all benefits to which they are entitled, employees are required to report the following events to the personnel office:

○ Marriage
○ Divorce
○ Entry of a Qualified Domestic Relations Order affecting the payment of pension plan benefits
○ Birth or adoption of a child
○ Child reaching adult age or otherwise becoming emancipated
○ Immigrant employee becoming a U.S. citizen.

The Company agrees to protect the confidentiality of information in employees' personal files within limits (i.e., information can be disclosed in response to a subpoena; in response to an inquiry from a credit reporting agency or prospective employer) and not to disclose it to unauthorized individuals.

*9. Cost Control.* In order to reduce costs, make the Company more profitable, and make more funds available for employee compensation and benefits, the Company adopts a policy of economy. The Company will pay a bonus of $100 to $500 (depending on the nature of the suggestion) for every employee suggestion that is adopted and that results in a significant cost saving. Employees are requested to conserve paper, metal, plastic, and other materials and to use recycled materials wherever this can be done without sacrificing product quality or office efficiency.

All "frequent flyer" miles and other bonuses accruing as a result of business travel will belong to the Company, not to its employees. Employees are instructed to make maximum use of these bonuses to save travel expenses; however, they are also instructed to travel using the least expensive carrier and shortest route. All employees must travel coach class on trips scheduled at six hours and under, and business class (not first class) on trips scheduled at over six hours unless an upgrade is available at no cost to the company, or unless the employee pays for the upgrade him- or herself.

Employees who must rent a car for business purposes are instructed to rent a subcompact or compact unless they are required to travel with a colleague or customer or potential customer, or unless they must transport merchandise or promotional materials. In any case, they must rent an economy or standard, not a luxury model, as long as any nonluxury cars are available for rental.

Employees who travel on business are instructed to rent motel rather than hotel rooms where there is a motel within a reasonable distance of the site of the business trip. (However, employees attending a seminar or conference held at a hotel or convention center can rent rooms within the conference site.) Employees who rent hotel accommodations must rent rooms instead of suites unless the living room is required to display merchandise or entertain customers or potential customers.

*10. Nonwork Use of Premises.* It is our position that the Company's premises can be used *only* to promote the Company's business. Therefore, with the sole exception of organization or union activity protected by the National Labor Relations Act, employees may not use the Company premises, or use their paid work time, mealtime, or breaks, for any of the following:

○ Sale of "party plan" merchandise (e.g., Tupperware, Mary Kay, Avon, Amway)
○ Political or election activities
○ Charitable solicitations
○ Gambling, including raffles and "pools"
○ Religious services or evangelization
○ Watching television or videocassettes, even on the employee's own equipment.

**11. Smoking Policy.** Smoking is not permitted on or near any assembly line, spray-painting room, or chemical store, for safety reasons. There will be a designated smoking room on each floor, and employees will be permitted to smoke in the smoking room during mealtimes or breaks. There will be a separate smoking area within the cafeteria, but at least three quarters of the cafeteria seats will be in no-smoking areas.

Smoking is not permitted in rooms with computers. Otherwise, office workers can smoke in their offices provided that all the employees within the office agree. There will be a designated smoking room on each floor, and employees who are not permitted to smoke in their offices will be permitted to smoke in the smoking room during mealtimes or breaks.

**12. Company Cafeteria and Executive Dining Room.** The Company's location is somewhat isolated, and there are few facilities for meals that are inexpensive and conveniently located. For the convenience of the employer, to reduce the time that employees must spend for meal breaks, and to make sure that employees will be available if emergencies arise during their meal breaks, the Company will maintain a cafeteria which will serve meals between the hours of 7–9 A.M., 12–2 P.M., and 5–7 P.M. Meals will be served at cost. In addition, refrigerators and microwave ovens will be made available for employees who prefer to bring meals from home or to buy meals outside the premises.

The Company will maintain an Executive Dining Room serving lunch and dinner to executives and their guests, and available for catering receptions for suppliers, potential suppliers, customers and potential customers.

**13. Antinepotism Policy.** Many of our best workers are relatives of people who also work for the Company, and we are proud when several generations choose to work for the Company as a family tradition. However, there is a high risk of abuses and conflicts if family members work together within the same unit. Therefore, it is against Company policy for an employee to supervise his or her own spouse, child, parent, brother or sister, brother- or sister-in-law, aunt, uncle, niece, nephew, or first cousin. No employee can be transferred or promoted to a position that would conflict with the antinepotism policy unless the relative is also transferred or promoted in a way that avoids the conflict and is not unduly disruptive of tasks and scheduling.

**14. Suggestions, Inventions, and Discoveries.** The Company strongly encourages employees to submit suggestions for ways in which the Company's marketing, product line, and production and office procedures can be improved. Suggestions must be submitted in writing, to the Personnel Office. All suggestions will be reviewed by the appropriate supervisors and executives. If the suggestion is adopted, a commendation will be placed in the employee's file, the suggestion and the employee proposing it will be featured in the employee newsletter, and a bonus of $100 or more (depending on the effort involved in developing the suggestion, and its benefit to the company) will be paid to the employee. In appropriate cases, the employee will be promoted based wholly or in part on the creativity and initiative shown.

All inventions and discoveries developed by the Company's employees on Company time will become the property of the Company, and any patents so resulting will be taken in the name of the Company. Employees agree not to disclose trade secrets or proprietary information belonging to the Company (even if the secrets or information were developed by the employee him- or herself) to anyone outside the Company without the Company's consent (except in response to a subpoena, or as part of the process of preparing a patent application).

**15. *Employee Assistance Program.*** In order to help employees with their personal problems, and to make them more efficient and productive, the Company agrees to contract with an independent organization to provide an Employee Assistance Program which will provide, in strict confidence, referrals and treatment for problems with substance abuse, smoking, and marital and family relations. The personnel department will administer the Employee Assistance Program, but will not keep records of which employees are referred, or the problems for which they are treated.

**16. *Dependent Care.*** The Company recognizes that many employees lose a great deal of productive work time because of the tasks of caring for minor or disabled children or incapacitated elderly parents—and because of their anxiety about their children and parents. To help them, and to increase their efficiency, one of the functions of the personnel department will be to maintain a complete and accurate file of information and referrals about dependent care programs, especially insofar as they are free or paid for by public benefits such as Medicare, and to consult with employees about this information at no charge.

**17. *Work Environment.*** Every employee is entitled to a work environment free of racial harassment and sexual harassment (in the form of unwanted sexual solicitations and comments from fellow employees as well as direct threats of job disadvantage for refusal to comply with a supervisors' sexual demands). All employees are hereby put on notice that racial or sexual harassment of other employees (whether co-employees or employees under their supervision) is a very serious offense and, if detected, will lead to discipline and, in appropriate cases, to dismissal. All employees are asked to consider that a remark, series of remarks, putting up "pin-ups," use of obscene language, or practical jokes, even if they are not intended as insulting or offensive, may be seen as offensive or even threatening by other employees. We insist that all employees treat one another with respect and cooperate in creating a work environment that is not harsh, insulting, harassing, or threatening.

**18. *Time Cards.*** All production and office employees, other than professional and executive employees, will be required to "punch in" at the time clock when they report for work, and to "punch out" for meal breaks and when they finish work. It is an offense subject to discipline and (in appropriate cases) dismissal to falsify a time card, to punch in or out for another employee if that has the effect of overstating the hours worked by the other employee, or to have another employee punch in or out with the effect of overstating hours worked.

## POSTACQUISITION CONSULTING AGREEMENT

Mark Parloe ("Parloe") is/was President/Vice-President for Research/Secretary/Treasurer of Amethyst Corporation [from _____ , 199 ____ to _____ , 199 ____ ] and was largely responsible for the corporation's efficiency, achievements, and financial success. Amethyst Corporation has entered into an agreement to merge with/consolidate with/sell its assets to/sell its stock to Peacock Acres Ltd.

To motivate Parloe to agree to this transaction, and to ensure continued smooth operation and profitability after the transaction, Peacock Acres Ltd. and Mark Parloe hereby enter into a five-year consulting agreement.

The agreement begins on the effective date of the merger/consolidation/acquisition. For the five years after that date, Parloe agrees to be available to the surviving/reconstituted corporation for up to 20 hours a week, 30 weeks a year, to use his knowledge, experience, and contacts to solve business problems. If elected, Parloe agrees to serve on the Board of Directors (receiving the same compensation and entitled to the same indemnification as the other directors). He will perform these tasks as an independent contractor, not an employee.

Parloe will receive $25,000 a year for his consulting services, plus reimbursement of any expenses of consulting and the use of a company car and driver while he is engaged in consulting.

During the term of the consulting agreement, he agrees not to compete with the surviving/ reorganized corporation by practicing the business/profession of _____ within the city/state of _____ or by soliciting former customers or clients of Amethyst Corporation in order to induce them not to do business with the surviving/reorganized company. However, he is permitted to engage in noncompetitive business activities provided that they do not interfere with his ability to render consulting services pursuant to this agreement when requested.

Parloe agrees not to use, appropriate, or divulge to any person without consent any trade secrets or proprietary information of Amethyst or the surviving/reorganized corporation obtained during his service as an officer of Amethyst or as a consultant.

Peacock Acres Ltd. agrees to indemnify Parloe against claims, loss, and liability arising out of any action as a consultant taken in good faith and with a [reasonable] belief that the activity was lawful and in the best interests of the corporation.

Date: _____ , 199____
Signed, _____

                                                                Mark Parloe
                                                                Peacock Acres Ltd., by:


## AGREEMENT WITH A FOREIGN SALES REPRESENTATIVE

This agreement, dated _____ , 199 ____ , represents the entire agreement and all the terms under which Albrecht von Meisen ("VM") will serve as the exclusive representative selling Daisy Dainty Corporation's ("DDC's") toiletries and hygiene products in East and West Germany and Austria.

*1.* VM agrees to work diligently to promote the sales of DDC products to creditworthy customers throughout the territory.

*2.* DDC agrees not to appoint any other representatives within the territory and not to attempt to make sales directly or to accept direct orders not solicited by VM.

*3.* VM agrees not to represent any competing products defined to include products for washing, complexion care, and hygiene but not perfume, color cosmetics, or hair styling products. He may represent noncompeting products provided that he has time to perform the duties of a full-time sales representative of DDC.

**4.** DDC agrees to provide order forms, catalogs, advertising and promotional materials, updated at least twice a year, written in German, and produced by a local advertising agency to reflect local business patterns and cultural norms.

**5.** DDC agrees to use its best efforts to provide VM with "leads" (potential customers) and to refer all direct inquiries within the territory to VM.

**6.** VM agrees to use his best efforts to obtain orders for wholesale quantities of DDC products from pharmacies, supermarkets, department stores, beauty shops, and other suitable outlets, at the prices and on terms and conditions set out by DDC. No order shall become binding on DDC until and unless it is accepted by the DDC home office in Kansas City. Orders will be payable in either DM or U.S. dollars at the option of the home office, at an exchange rate to be stipulated by the home office.

**7.** On or before the _____ day of every month, VM will submit a report to the home office listing all sales calls and other contacts made during the preceding month; the result of each; all orders; and all complaints of nondelivery, damage, poor quality or nonconformity with the goods ordered, and so on.

**8.** VM will receive a commission of ____ % of all orders submitted by him and accepted by the home office, net of returns and allowances. A commission check, payable in either DM or U.S. dollars at the option of the home office (at the exchange rate quoted in *The New York Times* on the date the check is issued) will be issued to VM, based on the figures stated in the monthly report, within five business days of receipt of the report.

**9.** VM is an independent contractor, not an employee, and is not entitled to pension, payment of social insurance, health benefits, or other employee benefits from DDC.

**10.** This agreement is terminable with or without cause by either party on six months' notice. VM can be terminated immediately for good cause, for example, violation of the noncompete clause, submission of false reports, bribery, acceptance of kickbacks, misappropriation of DDC merchandise, substitution of other for DDC merchandise.

Date: _____ , 199_____
Signed: _____

Albrecht von Meisen
Daisy Dainty Corp., by:

# Chapter 10

# COMPENSATION PLANNING

## INTRODUCTION

There are several elements in the compensation of any employee: the most obvious (and sometimes merely the tip of the iceberg) is the regular wages or salary. Another element, which can range from nonexistent to trivial (a Christmas turkey) to enormous, is the bonus linked to corporate profits or to the employee's own achievements. The advantage of bonuses is that they are flexible and can be cut back or discontinued as economic conditions require. Furthermore, by making a direct connection between results and bonuses, they can inspire employees to work harder and more productively. The disadvantage of bonuses is that even a large bonus can backfire. Other employees, who got less or nothing, may be angry at the employer and jealous of the top producer, and the employee receiving the bonus, generous as it is, can feel that it really isn't enough. Employees may also expect a larger bonus every year—even if productivity or profitability have dropped.

The task of setting salaries is a difficult one. A raise to one employee may have to be matched to motivate others to join the company, or refrain from quitting. But it is almost impossible to get employees to accept salary cuts in bad years (unless they really believe that things will improve, and they will be rewarded for their patience—or unless things are so bad for the economy or the industry that they have no reasonable prospect of getting a better job elsewhere).

### Tax Laws and Compensation

The tax laws impose further levels of complication. Especially since tax rates went down in 1986, employees often want to increase their current compensation, which they can spend right away. They have to pay income tax on their earnings and Social Security tax on a portion of their earnings (a portion that becomes smaller as earnings increase), but they have immediate use of the money. Therefore, employees (especially younger employees, or those who do not expect a large pension) tend to press for more salary, higher bonuses, better health insurance, and the like, instead of better pension plans. But older employees and those in higher tax brackets tend to prefer improved pension plans; they get tax deferral, with the prospect of collecting the pension money in a relatively short time.

## Salary Deductions

A corporation can deduct "reasonable" salaries paid to its employees. Reasonableness is a very subjective matter, of course, but family businesses have to avoid the temptation to put spouses, brothers and sisters, sons and daughters on the payroll with titles reflecting duties that they are not qualified to perform, or that they don't bother to perform because they have "no-show" jobs, then pay them a hefty salary. Another risk is that corporations are entitled to deduct salaries paid to employees, but not dividends paid to stockholders; the IRS is likely to challenge so-called "salary" payments that are proportionate to stock ownership rather than duties performed or results achieved. However, it is well known that entrepreneurs must often devote years of unpaid or underpaid work to building up an enterprise, and the tax laws acknowledge that a dramatic leap in income can still be a reasonable salary if it reflects past contributions.

*Practice Tip:* Make sure that the minutes of your board meetings reflect instances in which salary payments recompense past hard work—and make it clear that the salary payments are in proportion to services performed, not investment in the form of stock holdings.

## ERISA and Other Pension Plans

In addition to this current compensation, most companies provide deferred compensation such as pension plans. The basic form of deferred compensation is the "qualified plan"—so called because it qualifies under the Internal Revenue Code and the Employee Retirement Income Security Act of 1974 (ERISA). If an employer establishes and maintains a qualified plan, it will qualify for a tax deduction for the amounts contributed to the plan. The converse—and a powerful weapon to keep plans in line—is that if a plan violates the numerous and complex tax and labor law rules governing qualified plans, it can be disqualified. If the disqualification is retroactive, the plan may have to repay large amounts that were deducted many years earlier.

Qualified plans also help rank and file employees, because they get to defer taxation on part of their earnings; that is, the amounts earned by employer and employee contributions to the plan on the employee's behalf are not taxed until the employee starts drawing plan benefits. In addition to contributions from the employer, many plans allow employees to make their own contributions to the plan (voluntary contributions) or even require the employee to make contributions (mandatory contributions). However, plans are not permitted to accept voluntary contributions that exceed 10% of the employee's aggregate compensation. (The theory behind this is that highly compensated employees can afford to tuck away a large part of their salaries, but the rank and file need all or most of their compensation to live on, so accepting a higher level of voluntary contributions would be discriminatory.)

The qualified plan is especially important to the owners of small businesses, because the plan can be used to defer taxation on substantial amounts of money, and to provide substantial retirement benefits for the business owners. (In fact, the availability of large retirement benefits is one way that younger-generation executives can induce older-generation business founders from hanging on forever!) The natural tendency is for the business owners to draft a plan that gives them all, or most, of the benefits of the plan. But ERISA and the Internal Revenue Code combine to mandate that all qualified plans be nondiscriminatory, set maximum amounts of employer contributions and employee benefits, and impose a 10% excise tax on excess plan contributions.

One reason that pension plan law is so complex, and changes so often, is that the antidiscrimination tests are constantly being changed. The current rule is that a qualified plan must cover either 50 employees or 40% of all the business' employees (whichever is smaller). The plan must meet one of several coverage tests:

○ It can cover 70% of all employees who are not "highly compensated" (defined shortly).

○ The percentage of nonhighly compensated employees covered by the plan must be at least 70% of the percentage of highly compensated employees covered. For example, if a company has 10 highly compensated employees, 8 of whom are covered, and 50 nonhighly compensated employees, 30 of whom are covered, the plan is qualified. The percentage of highly compensated employees covered is 80%; 70% of that is 56%; and 30/50 nonhighly compensated employees (60%) are covered, so the test is satisfied.

○ The average benefit percentage (the employer-provided benefits for the employee, divided by the employee's compensation) for nonhighly compensated employees is at least 70% of the average benefit percentage for highly compensated employees—*and* the plan must benefit a class of employees that the IRS has specifically found to be nondiscriminatory. For example, if the average benefit percentage for highly compensated employees is 30%, the average benefit percentage for the rank and file must be at least 21%. Note that the highly compensated employees can legitimately get much larger pensions (because they earn more) without violating this test.

Highly compensated employees are defined as

○ Owners of 5% or more of the business

○ Those who earn over a certain amount (the 1989 amount is $81,720; this amount is adjusted for inflation)

○ Those who earn more than another figure ($54,980 for 1989) and are among the company's top 20% of earners

○ Company officers who earn more than $49,032 (1989 figure; will be adjusted for inflation)

It is important to note that "top-heavy" plans—those that provide 60% or more of their benefits to highly paid employees and/or business owners rather than the rank and file—must meet especially stringent antidiscrimination tests to maintain their status as qualified plans. Many small companies' plans are top heavy, simply because they consist of a small number of professional or business staff, and an even smaller number of support staff, say, an office with four architects and two secretaries.

In addition to maintaining one or more qualified plans, some companies find it worthwhile, as a financial planning or motivational device, to maintain one or more nonqualified plans to benefit management, for instance, by providing them with additional retirement benefits or with medical expense reimbursement. However, these plans must never be adopted without a thorough review of their financial, cash flow, and tax consequences.

*Practice Tip:* The entire subject of compensation planning is a difficult, volatile, and technical one. This discussion, and these forms, are intended only as aids to make it easier for you to work with your lawyer, accountant, actuary, and other planning professionals. Do not adopt these forms without professional advice about any modifications that may be legally required for your individual situation or that would make these forms more helpful to you and your employees.

ERISA and the Internal Revenue Code give detailed (if confusing) guidance about every aspect of establishing and administering a qualified plan. Some of the most important areas are *participation* (in general, every full-time permanent employee who is at least 21 years old, and who has worked for the employer for at least one year, must be permitted to participate; employers are allowed to be more generous than this, but not more restrictive) and *vesting*.

Vesting is an employee's right to receive all or part of the pension contributions made on his or her behalf. Before ERISA, employees often worked for many years, only to be told at retirement that they had failed to qualify for pensions (or were fired just before they would qualify). Now, employees must always be fully 100% vested in any voluntary or mandatory contributions they made to the pension plan. There are several different "vesting schedules" that are legal; the employer can select one. If a plan is not top heavy, the permitted vesting schedules are

○ Employee is not eligible for plan participation at all for the first two years of employment, then is 100% vested

○ Employee is eligible for plan participation either immediately or after one year of employment, but is not vested at all for five years—when he or she is 100% vested ("cliff vesting")

○ Employee is 20% vested after three years, 40% vested after four years, 60% vested after five years, 80% vested after six years, and 100% vested after seven years ("seven-year graded vesting").

Top-heavy plans must use a faster vesting schedule: either 100% vesting after two years (instead of three) or two- to six-year graded vesting (instead of three- to seven-year graded vesting). The significance of vesting is that an employee must be entitled to receive all vested amounts whenever he or she leaves employment (whether at retirement, or because he or she quits or is laid off or fired)—although the employer can make the employee wait until normal retirement age before receiving the amount. Frequently, employers allow employees to receive their vested amounts in a lump sum; for tax reasons, the employees often choose to "roll over" these lump sums into an IRA or into the new employer's qualified pension plan.

*Practice Tip:* Starting April 1, 1990, pension benefits must be paid to all employees (whether they're retired or still working) starting on April 1 of the year *after* the calendar year in which they reach age 70½. (Under earlier law, this was only required of 5% owners of the business.) However, rank-and-file employees born before January 1, 1917 are exempt from this rule.

There are two basic types of pension plans: the deferred compensation and the deferred benefit plan. A defined contribution plan (such as a money-purchase plan, profit sharing, stock bonus, 401(k), or ESOP plan) maintains an individual account for each participant. Each year, the employer makes contributions to the account of each participating employee (but not more than 25% of compensation, and not more than the "annual limitation," which is the greater of $30,000 or 25% of the maximum permitted defined benefit described shortly). The size of the employee's pension varies, depending on the amount in the account at retirement and also on the investment success that the plan had in investing the account balance.

## Profit-Sharing Plans

The profit-sharing plan is one of the most popular types of defined contribution plan. Since 1985, the name is something of a misnomer, because the contributions no longer have to be made from profits. Profit-sharing plans generally have a formula, such as 5% of the corporation's profits over and above $100,000. However, there is a limit on the maximum contribution that can be made: 15% of the total compensation of all plan participants or 6% of the corporation's net income, whichever is smaller. Profit-sharing plans can accept voluntary employee contributions (up to 10% of compensation), or even impose a requirement of mandatory contributions, as long as the employer can prove the requirement is nondiscriminatory. One popular type of plan, the "thrift plan," allocates the employer's contribution on the basis of matching part or all of the employee's mandatory contribution.

Corporations don't have to contribute to their profit-sharing plans every year—but the contributions must be made regularly, not on a one-time or intermittent basis, or the plan will lose its qualified status.

## Defined Benefit Plans

A defined benefit plan, in contrast, starts by defining the benefit the employee will be able to receive at retirement. usually expressed as a certain number of dollars per year of preretirement credited service for the employer. Then the employer consults actuaries who make calculations based on the number and age of plan participants and inform the employer how much must be contributed to the plan for each employee. But there is only one plan account, not a separate account for each employee. Therefore, the employees are at risk if the employer does not make the required contributions, or becomes bankrupt and unable to make future pension payments. This is why defined benefit plans—but not defined contribution plans—must participate in a federal insurance program, the Pension Benefit Guaranty Corporation (PBGC). The current PBGC premium that the employer must pay is $16.00 per employee, plus an additional amount based on experience ratings (similar to the experience ratings used in assessing unemployment insurance premiums).

The Internal Revenue Code limits the maximum defined benefit that can be paid under a qualified plan: either $90,000 as adjusted for inflation (the 1989 figure is $98,064) or 100% of the employee's average compensation for the best-paid three years of employment—whichever is smaller. Further calculations are required if the employee retires before the Social Security early-retirement age (currently 62, but it will increase to 65 by the year 2022), in which case the maximum benefit must be reduced actuarially because the benefit will be paid for a longer time, or if the employee retires after age 70, in which case the benefit must be increased because there will be fewer years of benefit payments.

## Social Security Benefits

The employer-paid pension is only one element in the employee's retirement income. (Retirement security is sometimes referred to as the "three-legged stool"—the employee's own savings and investments, the employer-paid pension, and Social Security benefits.) Social Security benefits are financed by FICA taxes paid both by employer and employee. In other words, then, the employer has made substantial contributions to the Social Security benefit. Social Security taxes are only due up to a certain amount ($48,000 for 1989); after that, the employer and employee do not have to pay any further FICA taxes. Therefore, for rank and file employees, the employer pays FICA taxes on the entire salary; for highly paid employees, on only part of the salary. This fact is recognized by the concept called "plan integration," under which employers can use complex formulas to reduce plan benefits or plan contributions for lower-paid employees to take into account the FICA taxes paid by the employer. If you want an integrated plan, get careful guidance from your planning team, because the integration rules are difficult and change frequently.

*Practice Tip:* If your plan documents require the Board of Directors to act in order to make each year's plan contributions, make sure the minutes reflect the board action. If the plan requires contributions to come only from profits, make sure that the minutes reflect this too—or amend the plan to permit contributions to be made in a year in which there is no formal profit.

ERISA and the Internal Revenue Code cover not only the employer's setting up and administration of the plan, but the way that pension benefits are paid out. ERISA requires that all plans be operated for the exclusive benefit of plan participants and their beneficiaries. This means that, although the employer can remove excess assets from plans that are overfunded (have more assets than are reasonably predicted to be needed to pay benefits in the future), the employer can't treat the plan as a sort of piggy bank, to be raided whenever cash is necessary.

It also means that an employee's creditors can't seize his or her pension account and that employees can't assign away their future pension rights. There's one important exception to this rule: present or future pension benefits can be divided as part of the economic settlement involved in a divorce. The plan can make payments to a worker's ex-spouse under a "Qualified Domestic Relations Order" (QRDO).

Usually, a defined contribution plan will make its payouts in the form of a lump sum (although the plan can only force a reluctant worker to "cash out" if he or she is owed less than $3,500; plans are allowed to avoid the hassle of making continuing payments of small sums). The alternatives are payments in installments and purchase of an annuity contract. If the employee is married, the normal way of making payments under a defined benefit plan is the "joint and survivor annuity" (payable for the lives of both the employee and his or her spouse), although if both spouses can consent, the annuity can be paid only for the life of the employee (which will mean larger payments). The plan must also provide a "qualified survivor annuity" if an employee with vested pension benefits dies before retirement age. Note that there is a 15% excise tax on excess distributions from a pension plan, defined as yearly benefits exceeding $150,000 a year. (Certain employees who accrued benefits over approximately $562,000 on or before August 1, 1986 are exempt from this tax.)

Pension plans also have substantial responsibilities to make reports to the Department of Labor (which administers ERISA) and to the IRS: a formal Plan

Description that sets out the terms of the plan and a Summary Plan Description (SPD) given to plan participants.

*Practice Tip:* Make sure the SPD is an accurate, though readable, description of the plan provisions; employees who relied on the SPD and therefore lost rights under the Plan itself have successfully sued their employers.

The reporting obligation also calls for an Annual Report to DOL and IRS and a Summary Annual Report (SAR) to be distributed each year to plan participants, and when employees leave employment, they must be informed of their accrued benefits, and how much of those benefits are vested. If the employer intends to terminate a plan, employees must get at least 60 days' notice; at least 15 days' notice of plan amendments is required. Plans must explain to their participants how joint and survivor annuities work, and if a QDRO is entered, the plan must send a notice of explanation to the employee whose pension will be shared with the ex-spouse.

## Setting Up Plan Trusts

Usually, the formal legal document that sets up a pension plan is a trust, under which certain trustees (e.g., corporation executives, professional fund managers) agree to manage the money in the pension fund for the exclusive benefit of the plan participants and their beneficiaries. ERISA imposes strict duties on these "plan fiduciaries" (in legal parlance, a fiduciary is someone who is responsible for taking care of someone else's money). They must not only manage the plan honestly and with care, skill, prudence, and diligence; they are legally required to diversify the plan's investments—unless it is more prudent *not* to diversify. Certain "prohibited transactions" (such as the plan buying property from a fiduciary, or from an executive of the corporation) are only legal if they get prior approval from IRS and the Department of Labor.

*Practice Tip:* Anyone who chooses plan fiduciaries—a role that often falls to the corporate secretary—will also be considered a fiduciary for some purposes, so you must be careful when you select plan fiduciaries, and you must supervise them carefully.

Although ERISA does not regulate salaries or working conditions, it does cover "employee welfare benefit plans" such as health insurance plans. There is no obligation for employers to provide any health insurance, but once an employer does institute such a plan, the plan must be nondiscriminatory, and the employer is limited in its ability to amend the plan and increase the contributions expected of employees. Because health care is so expensive, and it can be difficult for individuals to get health insurance, employers are required to provide (and inform terminated employees about) "continuation coverage"—the right to continue their coverage under the employer's group policy for a period of time after layoff, quitting, being fired, or retiring. The employee pays the premium that the employer paid; the employer can collect a service charge, which may not exceed 2% of the premium, for administration.

---

## NOTICE OF RIGHT TO CONTINUATION COVERAGE

Note: This notice must be sent to every employee covered under the plan and to his or her spouse. (One notice can be sent to spouses if the last address the plan has shows them living together.) Send the notice by first-class mail to the address the plan has for the employee.

Dear Plan Participant:

A federal law known as COBRA (the Comprehensive Omnibus Budget Reconciliation Act, Public Law 99-272), passed April 7, 1986, gives employees the right to continue coverage under their employer's health plan for a certain amount of time after they leave employment. Employees must pay for this "continuation coverage," but they gain valuable rights by maintaining insurance coverage without having to shop for policies, undergo examinations, pay individual policy rates, or undergo an additional waiting period to collect health insurance benefits. PLEASE READ THIS NOTICE CAREFULLY. IT EXPLAINS YOUR RIGHTS, AND YOUR FAMILY'S RIGHTS, TO CONTINUATION COVERAGE. If your address changes, or if you marry, go through a legal separation or divorce, or your son or daughter is no longer a "dependent child" as defined by the plan, you have an obligation to notify the Plan Administrator, _____ , at _____ promptly so the plan's records can be kept current. Also contact the Plan Administrator if you have any questions about your health plan or about this notice or your rights to continuation coverage. Your employer will notify the Plan Administrator of employees' death, reduction in hours, termination of employment, or Medicare eligibility.

If you work for the Fleming Frammis Finishing Company, and are covered by its Salaried Employees' Group Health Plan, and if you lose your group health coverage because you retire, quit your job, are laid off, or are terminated for any reason except gross misconduct, you have a right to get continuation coverage at your own expense.

If your husband or wife is covered by the Salaried Employees' Group Health Plan, there are four events that qualify you to choose continuation coverage at your own expense in order to avoid loss of your own health benefits:

○ Your spouse dies.

○ Your spouse's working hours are cut, or his or her employment is terminated (for any reason except gross misconduct).

○ You and your spouse go through a legal separation or divorce.

○ Your spouse becomes eligible for Medicare (and therefore no longer eligible under the Salaried Employees' Group Health Plan), but you are not old enough or otherwise eligible for Medicare.

If you are a dependent of a parent who works for Fleming Frammis Finishing, you have the right to continuation coverage if one of these five events would otherwise lead to your loss of health care coverage:

○ Your employee-parent dies.

○  Your parent's working hours are reduced, or his or her employment is terminated for any reason other than gross misconduct.

○  Your parents undergo a legal separation or get a divorce.

○  Your employee-parent becomes eligible for Medicare.

○  You are still a dependent of your employee-parent, but you no longer fit the definition of "dependent child" under the Salaried Employees' Group Health Plan.

If you are entitled to continuation coverage, but do not choose to take it, your coverage under the Salaried Employees' Group Health Plan will end, and you will be uninsured unless you buy health insurance yourself or are hired by another employer who provides coverage. You have 60 days from the last date of coverage under the Salaried Employees' Group Health Plan to make up your mind.

If you do choose to take continuation coverage, you will retain the same coverage you had under the Salaried Employees' Group Health Plan. You do not have to prove insurability to get this coverage. However, you must pay _____ % of the premium the employer pays for this coverage; the employer will bill you quarterly. If you are entitled to continuation coverage because of termination of employment or reduction of hours, you are entitled to 18 months of continuation coverage; if your entitlement comes from one of the other reasons, you are entitled to 3 years (36 months) of continuation coverage. When this period ends, you will be allowed to enroll in an individual conversion health plan provided by the Salaried Employees' Group Health Plan. However, the coverage will not necessarily be as comprehensive as the continuation coverage, and federal law does not impose a limit on the premium you can be charged.

Fleming Frammis Finishing has the right to end your continuation coverage for one of five reasons:

○  The Salaried Employees' Group Health Plan itself is terminated.

○  You fail to pay the bill for your coverage.

○  You get another job and are covered by that employer's group health insurance plan.

○  You become eligible for Medicare.

○  You became eligible for continuation coverage because of your divorce from a Fleming employee; later, you remarry and get coverage under the new spouse's group health plan.

## Summary Plan Description Outline

The SPD is a fairly long document and is very individual, reflecting facts about each corporation. However, it must include certain provisions, and certain required notices, which are summed up here:

○  The formal and common name of the plan

○  The type of plan (e.g., pension or profit sharing, defined contribution or defined benefit)

○  The Employer Identification Number (EIN) and plan number

○  The names, addresses, and telephone numbers of

○  ○  The employer sponsoring the plan

○  ○  The plan's administrator

○  ○  The plan's trustees

○  ○  The agent for service of process (the one who receives notice when the plan is being sued)

○ A description of the relevant provisions of any collective bargaining agreements affected by the plan

○ Requirements for participation

○ Source of financing for the plan

○ The identity of the organization providing benefits (i.e., many plans are funded by the purchase of insurance contracts, so the insurance company would be named here)

○ Date of the end of the plan year

○ Whether the plan's records are kept by calendar year, policy year, or fiscal year

○ Where plan contributions come from (employer and/or employee, employee organization); how the contributions are calculated (a defined benefit plan can simply say that the contributions are actuarially determined)

○ How the plan determines years of service

○ The plan's vesting provisions

○ A description of how the plan can be amended to change participants' rights, including any amendments that can be made under IRS's "cutback" rule

○ A description of the joint and survivor annuity form of payment

○ If the plan is not insured, a statement that it is not and an explanation of why it is not (e.g., the plan is a defined contribution plan), or a statement that it is insured, and a statement of this type:

Benefits under this plan are insured by the Pension Benefit Guaranty Corporation (PBGC) if the plan terminates. Generally the PBGC guarantees most vested normal age retirement benefits, early retirement benefits, and certain disability and survivor's pensions. However, PBGC does not guarantee all types of benefits under covered plans, and the amount of benefit protection is subject to certain limitations.

The PBGC guarantees vested benefits at the level in effect on the date of plan termination. However, if a plan has been in effect less than five years before it terminates, or if benefits have been increased within the five years before plan termination, the whole amount of the plan's vested benefits or the benefit increase may not be guaranteed. In addition, there is a ceiling on the amount of monthly benefit that PBGC guarantees, which is adjusted periodically.

For more information on the PBGC insurance protection and its limitations, ask your Plan Administrator or the PBGC. Inquiries to the PBGC should be addressed to the Office of Communications, PBGC, 2020 K Street NW, Washington, DC 20006. The PBGC Office of Communications may also be reached by calling (202) 254-4817.

○ Circumstances under which benefits can be forfeited

○ Circumstances that will lead to an employee's disqualification from the plan or denial or loss of benefits

○ The procedure for presenting claims under the plan and appealing benefit denials. The notice of denial *must* be in writing and must entitle the participant to a full and fair review of their claims

○ A statement that the employee has rights under ERISA, in a form such as

As a participant in this plan, you are entitled to certain rights and protections under the Employee Retirement Income Security Act of 1974 (ERISA). ERISA provides that all plan participants shall be entitled to:

Examine, without charge, at the plan administrator's office and at other specified locations, such as worksites and union halls, all plan documents, including insurance contracts, collective bargaining agreements and copies of all documents filed by the plan with the U.S. Department of Labor, such as detailed annual reports and plan descriptions.

Obtain copies of all plan documents and other plan information upon written request to the plan administrator. The administrator may make a reasonable charge for the copies.

Receive a summary of the plan's annual financial report. The plan administrator is required by law to furnish each participant with a copy of this summary annual report.

Obtain a statement telling you whether you have a right to receive a pension at normal retirement age (age _____) and if so, what your benefits would be at normal retirement age if you stop working under the plan now. If you do not have a right to a pension, the statement will tell you how many more years you have to work to get a right to a pension. This statement must be requested in writing and is not required to be given more than once a year. The plan must provide the statement free of charge.

## EMPLOYEE REQUEST FOR VESTING INFORMATION

Note to Employee: You have a right to make one request for this information per year. Send your request to the Personnel Department/Employee Representative/Payroll Department/Pension & Benefit Office. There is no charge for receiving this information.

I, _____ , have been an employee of this company since _____ , 19_____ . I have been employed continuously from that date to the present/I had (a) break(s) in service beginning on _____ , 19_____ and lasting until _____ , 19_____ (repeat as necessary). My current job title, grade, and salary are _____ . My date of birth is _____ . Please inform me of

☐ The earliest date on which I could retire, without permission of the employer, and receive a full, unreduced pension

☐ The earliest date on which I could retire with the employer's permission and receive a reduced, early-retirement pension

☐ My current account balance

☐ The percentage of vesting I have in my account balance

☐ If I am now entitled to receive a pension at normal retirement age; if not, an explanation why not

☐ The pension to which I would be entitled at normal retirement age if I left the employer's work force today

☐ The pension to which I would be entitled if I remained employed until normal retirement age, assuming that my salary remains the same. [Note: Your real pension would probably be higher, because you would probably qualify for salary increases.]

## NOTICE TO PARTICIPANTS ABOUT PLAN PAYMENTS
### (Defined Contribution Plan)

Dear Employee:

You are a participant in the employer's qualified retirement plan ("Plan"). Under federal law, all plans must provide information to their participants about the payment of plan benefits and what happens to plan benefits when the employee dies.

### Unmarried Employees

Unless you give the Plan Administrator notice during the 90 days before payments are scheduled to begin, your retirement benefits will be paid to you each month in the form of a "single-life annuity."

The payments will stop when you die. Our records indicate that your monthly benefit at normal retirement age is estimated to be $_____ . THIS FIGURE IS ONLY AN ESTIMATE. It could change based on your own contributions to the plan, the employer's contributions to the plan, and investment conditions when you retire.

If you do not want a single-life annuity for your retirement benefits, you can choose any one of these options:

○ Receiving the entire balance in your account in a lump sum when you retire.

○ Payment of your account in _____ annual installments beginning when you retire. The number of installments you select cannot be greater than your life expectancy. However, if you die before all the payments have been made, the remaining payments will become part of your estate.

○ Having the employer buy an annuity for you from an insurance company. Payment terms will depend on the insurer's business methods.

## Notice of Waiver Instructions

Complete this notice IF you will be retiring within 90 days, AND you do not want a single-life annuity. Send the notice to the Plan Administrator, _____ , at _____ . I, _____ , am a plan participant. My scheduled retirement date is _____ , 199_____ . I am aware of the size of my account balance and the consequences of rejecting a single-life annuity. I have chosen to give up ("waive") payments in single-life annuity form. Instead, I want my retirement benefits to be paid in the form of

□ A lump sum

□ _____ yearly installments

□ purchase of a single-life/joint and survivor annuity with _____ as the other life from the _____ Life Insurance Co.

    I know that if I change my mind, I can withdraw this Waiver at any time before payments begin. Signed: _____ Participant Date:_____
Received, Date: _____ _____ Plan Administrator

## Married Employees

Federal law seeks to protect the rights of plan participants and their spouses. In order to carry out duties under federal law, the Plan Administrator must be notified whenever an employee's marital status changes by marriage, divorce, or widowhood.

    Federal law requires that the normal method of paying benefits to married employees must be the "joint and survivor annuity," under which monthly payments are made as long as either the retiree or his or her spouse is still alive. Under our Plan, annuity payments are level/the payment to the survivor is 50% of the payment that was made while both spouses were alive. It is estimated that your vested account balance of $_____ will entitle you to a monthly joint and survivor annuity of $_____ [for 50% survivor annuity add: while both you and your spouse survive, and of $_____ during the lifetime of the survivor].

    However, if annuity payments were made only for your life, stopping with your death, it is estimated that you would be entitled to annuity payments of $_____ a month. (The payment is higher because the plan has to make payments for a shorter time than if both spouses' lives were covered.)

Unless you and your spouse both agree to waive (give up) the joint and survivor annuity, the plan will pay your benefits in joint and survivor annuity form.

## Waiver

Instructions: File this form during the 90-day period before your retirement date. Your spouse's signature must be witnessed by a plan agent or Notary Public.

This Waiver is signed by _____ , an employee and plan participant, and his/her spouse, _____ . We are aware of the consequences of waiving a joint and survivor annuity. We know that this waiver may have the effect of depriving the employee's spouse of benefits, and therefore both spouses must consent. We know that the employee spouse can revoke this Waiver at any time before benefit payments begin and that the nonemployee spouse can only revoke his or her consent if the employee spouse revokes this Waiver.

Instead of a joint and survivor annuity, we want the account balance as of the employee's planned retirement date of _____ , 199____ to be distributed

☐ In a single lump sum.

☐ In annual/quarterly/monthly installments lasting _____ years, whether or not the retiree is still alive. (Note: The period of years chosen must be equal to or smaller than the employee's life expectancy.)

☐ By purchasing a commercial single-life/joint and survivor annuity contract from the Life Insurance Company.

Signed: _____ Employee Date: _____ , 199____

Spouse: _____ Witness: _____ Date: _____

Received, Date: _____ _____ Plan Administrator

If a married participant dies before the payment of plan benefits begins, the Plan will use the entire vested balance in the Employee's account to buy an annuity providing lifetime benefits to the Employee's spouse *unless* the Employee chooses (and his or her spouse agrees to) a different arrangement.

If you are over 35, and your spouse agrees, you can choose a different beneficiary or have payment of preretirement survivor benefits made to your spouse in a form other than an annuity. If you are under 35, you can still make the waiver, *but* your waiver becomes invalid in the Plan Year in which you reach 35, and would have to be repeated at that time.

## Waiver

We are aware of federal requirements about preretirement survivor annuities, and both wish to waive the preretirement survivor annuity. The Employee's spouse's Date of Birth is _____ , 199____ ; s/he is over/under age 35.

☐ We want survivor benefits to be paid to the spouse, but in the form of

☐☐ A lump sum.

☐☐ _____ annual installments. (Note: The number of installments cannot exceed the spouse's life expectancy.)

☐ We want _____ , and not the spouse, to be the beneficiary if the employee dies before payments begin; and we want _____ to be the alternate beneficiary if _____ dies before the employee does. We want the beneficiary or alternate beneficiary to receive

☐☐  A lump sum.

☐☐ _____ installments (a number lower than his or her life expectancy).

We know that the employee can revoke this waiver throughout his or her lifetime and that the nonemployee spouse can only revoke his or her consent if the employee revokes the waiver.

Signed: _____ Employee Date: _____ , 199_____

Spouse: _____ Witness: _____ Date: _____

Received, Date: _____ _____ Plan Administrator

## PENSION NOTICE TO TERMINATED EMPLOYEE
### (Defined Contribution Plan)

To:_____

As of your scheduled termination date, _____ , 199_____ , the balance of your account will be $_____ . On that date, you will have completed _____ years of service under the Plan.

☐ This length of time is less than the _____ years required for vesting. Therefore, you are entitled to return of the $_____ you have contributed to the plan, but you are NOT entitled to receive a pension from the employer.

☐ You are _____ % vested; that is, you are entitled to a pension based on _____ % of your account balance, or $_____ .

If this amount is less than $3,500, it is the plan's policy to "cash out," that is, to pay the terminated employee his or her vested account balance within _____ days of the date of termination.

If this amount is over $3,500, you have the right to demand payment of your balance in a lump sum at the time of termination. If you are married, your spouse must consent to the demand. The amount you receive is likely to be taxable income. To defer taxation, you have the right to "roll over" part or all of the lump sum by depositing it in an IRA, or another employer's qualified plan, within 60 days of the date you receive the lump sum. (If your receive several such payments, the 60-day period starts when you receive the *last* payment.) If your balance is over $3,500 and you do not demand a lump-sum payment, payment of your pension begins with the *earliest* of these events:

☐ You reach early retirement age *and* have satisfied the plan's service requirement *and* apply for early retirement.

☐ You reach normal retirement age.

☐ You die.

☐ You become permanently and totally disabled as defined by the Social Security Act.

### Demand for Lump-Sum Distribution

I, _____ , who have left/will leave the employment of _____ on _____ ,

199_____ , hereby call for payment of my vested account balance of $_____ in lump-sum form.

☐ I am unmarried.

☐ I am married, and my spouse joins in this demand.

By choosing a lump-sum payment, I/we hereby release the Plan, its Trustee, and its Administrator from all claims with respect to my interest in the plan. I/we understand that this request prevents any nonemployee spouse from receiving survivor benefits under the plan.

Signed: _____ Employee Date: _____
Spouse: _____ Witness: _____ Date: _____
Received, Date: _____ _____ Plan Administrator

## ELECTION TO MAKE VOLUNTARY PLAN CONTRIBUTIONS

I, _____ , am a plan participant. I want to make voluntary plan contributions, and I understand that this designation will remain effective until and unless I revoke it.

☐ I agree to make a monthly/quarterly/annual contribution to the plan, totaling _____ % of my compensation each year.

☐ I agree to have the employer deduct _____ % of my compensation from each paycheck and contribute this amount to the plan on my behalf.

My voluntary contributions will be kept in a separate account. I have the right to make withdrawals from this account at any time, but I know that the plan will not accept additional voluntary contributions until one year after a withdrawal.

Signed: _____ Employee Date: _____ , 199_____
_____ Plan Administrator Date: _____ , 199_____

## ACKNOWLEDGMENT ABOUT MANDATORY CONTRIBUTIONS

I understand that the terms of the _____ Plan require that I must make a mandatory plan contribution in each year, equal to _____ % of compensation/ranging from _____ % to _____ % of compensation in order for the employer to make contributions to the plan on my behalf.

I understand that my mandatory contributions (and the interest or investment income they earn) are kept in a separate account and are always 100% vested.

I hereby agree to make mandatory contributions as required for the employer to make contributions to my account [for payroll deduction plan, add: and agree that the appropriate amount will be deducted from each paycheck].

Date: _____ _____ Employee
Date: _____ _____ Plan Administrator

## TRUSTEED PENSION PLAN

*1. Creation:* _____ , ("Employer") hereby creates and defines the terms and provisions of a defined contribution/defined benefit trusteed pension plan to be known as _____ ("Plan").

[For defined benefit plan add: ☐ The plan is insured by the Pension Benefit Guaranty Corporation ☐ PBGC insurance is not required for the plan because: _____ .]

**2. *Employer's Address:*** The Employer is a [Subchapter S] corporation incorporated in the state of _____ . Its address for the service of process is _____ .

**3. *Plan Administrator:*** _____ , whose address is _____ , will serve as the Plan Administrator.

**4. *Trustee:*** _____ , whose address is _____ , will serve as the Plan Trustee.

**5. *Years:*** The Employer operates on a calendar year/fiscal year ending _____ . The Effective Date of the Plan will be _____ , 199_____ . The Plan Year will be a calendar year/the same as the employer's Fiscal Year/run from _____ to _____ .

**6. *Top-Heavy Plan:*** As of the Effective Date, the Plan is/is not a top-heavy plan.

**7. *Coverage:*** The Plan benefits all employees meeting the Plan's eligibility requirements/all salaried employees meeting eligibility requirements/all employees earning more than the plan's Integration Level/all employees other than highly compensated employees/all nonunionized employees/all employees who are not covered by another plan maintained by the employer.

**8. *Limitations:*** [Omit if all employees are eligible for participation as soon as they are hired.] To be eligible, the employee must be over 18/21 and have completed 6 months/1 year/18 months/2 years of service for the Employer.

**9. *Definition of Compensation:*** "Compensation" is defined as the first $200,000 of compensation paid/paid or accrued, and includes
☐ Overtime
☐ Commissions
☐ Bonuses
☐ 401(k) salary reductions
☐ Internal Revenue Code Section 125 salary reductions
☐ Other: _____
but excludes:
    ☐ Overtime
    ☐ Commissions
    ☐ Bonuses
    ☐ 401(k) salary reductions
    ☐ Code Section 125 salary reductions
    ☐ Other:_____

**10. *Integration:*** The plan is/is not integrated with Social Security. [Defined benefit plan] If integrated, it is integrated with/without final pay using a fixed/unit/offset benefit formula calculated as follows: _____ [Defined contribution plan] If integrated, it is integrated by contribution/allocation as follows: _____

**11. *Vesting:*** Vesting is based on years of service, not years of plan participation. The vesting schedule is
☐ 100% on becoming eligible for participation
☐ Three-year cliff
☐ Five-year cliff
☐ Six-year graded
☐ Seven-year graded.

**12. *Forfeitures***
☐ The plan will not have forfeitures, because all employees are 100% vested
☐ Forfeitures will be
    ☐☐ Used to reduce the employer's contributions
    ☐☐ Allocated to plan participants in the prior year, based on compensation
    ☐☐ Allocated to plan participants in the current year, based on compensation
    ☐☐ Added to employee compensation and allocated with the employee compensation
Terminated participants
☐ Will be cashed out
☐ Will not share in Plan contributions or forfeitures
☐ Will share in all allocations if they have completed a year of service (1,000 or more hours) during the year of termination

**13. *Normal Retirement Age:*** Normal retirement age is defined as
☐ 65
☐ The Social Security retirement age prevailing at the time of retirement
☐ _____ , the retirement age prevailing in the employer's industry
    Employees will become fully vested at normal retirement age [provided that they have completed _____ years of plan participation.] [Note: The number chosen must not exceed ten] [provided that employees hired within five years of normal retirement age can be required to complete five years of service before retiring and becoming fully vested].
    Retiring plan participants will not share in allocations for the year of retirement/will share in allocations whether or not they complete 1,000 hours of service in that year.
    A participant's Normal Retirement Date is his or her
☐ Birthday
☐ The plan anniversary following his or her birthday
☐ Other:_____
    However, distribution of plan benefits will begin no later than April of the year following the year in which any employee reaches age 70½, whether or not the employee has retired. [For defined benefit plan, add: The retirement benefit will be increased actuarially for retirement after age 70].

**14. *Early Retirement:*** The employee can retire early, and be fully vested, at
☐ Age 55
☐ Age_____
☐ Age _____ , provided that s/he has completed _____ years of service
[For defined benefit plan, add: However, for retirement before the Social Security retirement age then prevailing, the plan benefit will be reduced actuarially according to this formula: _____ .]

**15. *Disability Retirement:*** ☐ The plan does not provide disability retirement benefits; a disabled employee, like any other terminated employee, will receive a distribution of vested account balances/vested benefits.

☐ When an employee becomes permanently and totally disabled as defined by the Social Security Act/certified by the physician designated by the Plan Administrator, the employee will be eligible for retirement and full vesting including/not including allocations for the year of disability.

**16. *Mandatory cash-outs:*** The plan will/will not mandatorily cash out amounts under $3,500 payable to terminated employees. The plan will permit employees owed over $3,500 to demand payment in lump-sum form.

**17.  *Rollovers:*** The plan does/does not accept rollovers from other qualified plans. The plan accepts rollovers from "conduit IRAs" (IRAs established solely to receive contributions from one employer's qualified plan in order to roll over the amount to another qualified plan) but not from other types of IRA.

**18.  *Mandatory Contributions:*** [Omit if plan does not require mandatory contributions]: The plan requires mandatory employee contributions of _____ % of compensation.

**19.  *Voluntary Contributions:*** The plan does not accept after-tax voluntary employee contributions/ the plan accepts voluntary contributions up to 10% of contributions. Employees wishing to make voluntary contributions must send the amounts in question to the Plan Trustee.

**20.  *Direction of Accounts:*** [For defined contribution plans only]: Vested plan participants may not make investment decisions about their plan accounts/may direct investment of their accounts as follows:_____

**21.  *Plan Loans:*** □ The plan will not make loans □ The Trustee will have discretion to make loans to participants if the loan is prudent and adequately secured and if loans are made available to all employees on a nondiscriminatory basis. [For an S Corporation's plan, add: No loan will be made to any shareholder-employee unless a Prohibited Transaction exemption has been issued.] All loans will require regular monthly/quarterly payments, at a reasonable rate of interest. All loans other than mortgage loans on the participant's principal residence must be fully amortized within five years, without a balloon payment. No loans can exceed $50,000 (minus the highest outstanding loan balance in the previous 12 months) or half the present value of the participant's vested account balance, whichever is less.

**22.  *Contribution Formula for Defined Contribution Plan:*** In each year, the employer will contribute _____ % of compensation [in excess of the Social Security wage base]/_____ % in the plan's first Fiscal Year, then _____ %/_____ % of compensation up to the Social Security wage base plus _____ % of compensation over and above the Social Security wage base.

The employer will make contributions to the Trustee for each Plan Year no later than date of the last extension for the employer's filing of its federal income tax return for the Fiscal Year in which the Plan Year ended.

The employer contribution, plus forfeitures allocated to the participant's account for each year, must be at least _____ % of the employee's compensation as defined by Section 415 of the Internal Revenue Code, but annual additions to the employee's account in any plan year will not exceed $30,000 or 25% of his or her compensation as defined by Section 415, whichever is smaller.

**23.  *Benefit Formula for Defined Benefit Plan:*** The formula used to provide benefits under the plan, and used by the plan's actuaries to determine the amount the employer must contribute each year, is

□ _____ % of average monthly compensation (AMC)

□ _____ % of AMC times the number of years of credited service

□ $_____ of pension benefits for each month of credited service

□ _____ % of AMC plus _____ % of compensation over the integration level

□ _____ % of AMC offset by _____ % of compensation below the integration level

□ _____ % of AMC times the number of years of service, plus _____ % of compensation over the integration level times the number of years of service.

PROVIDED that the benefit will be actuarially reduced for retirement (other than disability retirement) before age 62 and will be increased actuarially for retirement after age 70, AND

ALSO PROVIDED that the plan will provide a minimum benefit of $_____ per month and a maximum benefit of $_____ per month/_____ % of AMC per month, and no benefit will ever exceed $90,000 a year (as adjusted for inflation) or 100% of the participant's compensation as averaged over his or her three best paid "limitation years" as defined by the Internal Revenue Code. AMC is computed for all years of service/all years of plan participation/the participant's final _____years/highest paid _____years (Note: The number must be at least three)/highest compensation within ten years, excluding the five years immediately preceding retirement.

**24. *Antialienation Clause:*** Because this plan is maintained exclusively for the benefit of participants and their beneficiaries, plan benefits cannot be assigned by participants, and cannot be attached, seized, or garnished except in response to a Qualified Domestic Relations Order issued in connection with the legal separation or divorce of a plan participant.

**25. *Administrator's Duties and Powers:*** The Plan Administrator's task is to administer the Plan on behalf of participants and their beneficiaries, in accordance with the terms of the Plan. The Administrator will have the duty and power to make determinations about interpretation of the Plan; to furnish information as required by the Department of Labor and the Internal Revenue Code, to the Participants about the terms of the Plan and their duties and rights under the Plan; to work with and provide guidance to the Plan Trustee; to inform the Employer of the amount and timing of contributions to the Plan; and to maintain records and file necessary reports and forms with the Internal Revenue Service, Department of Labor, and any other agency entitled to such reports and forms.

The Administrator will devise and implement a procedure for adjudicating the claims of participants who believe that they have been deprived of benefits which they are entitled to under the Plan. The Administrator must provide notices, in plain English, to participants regarding their rights, the claims procedure, and the outcome of any claims procedure.

The Employer agrees to provide all necessary information (e.g., employee hours of service, compensation) required by the Administrator to carry out these functions. The Employer agrees to pay any and all such reasonable expenses incurred by the Administrator in carrying out these duties (including professional fees of attorneys and accountants); if the Employer does not pay, the Administrator is entitled to recover the expenses from the Trust itself.

**26. *Trustee's Powers and Duties:*** The Trustee will have all powers reasonably required to carry out the functions of supervising Plan investments and the payment of benefits, including but not limited to maintaining Plan funds in cash; investing Plan funds in real estate, financial instruments, and securities (whether or not issued by the Employer); maintaining bank, brokerage, and money market accounts; borrowing money; lending money on adequate security and at a reasonable interest rate; retaining and paying professional advisors; and suing and being sued. The Trustee will be required to abide by the fiduciary standards of ERISA and to diversify Plan investments at all times unless it is prudent to avoid diversification.

**27. *Plan Amendment, Termination, or Merger:*** In general, the Employer retains the right to amend this Plan at any time, with the amendment to become effective as provided by its own terms. However, any amendment affecting the rights, duties, or responsibilities of the Plan Administrator and/or Trustee requires the advance written consent of the Administrator and/or Trustee. Furthermore, no Plan amendment can become effective if it would have the effect of diverting any portion of Plan funds for any purpose other than operating to the exclusive benefit of participants and their beneficiaries, of reducing the balance credited to any participant's account, or diverting any Plan funds to the Employer except as permitted by federal law. However, Plan funds can be used to pay taxes and reasonable administrative expenses. Nor may a Plan amendment, transfer, or merger become effective if it has the effect of eliminating or reducing protected Plan benefits in a manner forbidden by the Internal Revenue Code (particularly Section 411).

The Employer retains the right to terminate the Plan at any time by giving written notice of termination to the Administrator or Trustee. On termination, all participants will immediately become 100% vested and will not be at risk of subsequent forfeiture. All unallocated amounts will be allocated to participants' accounts. On termination, the employer will direct distribution of Plan assets in cash, in property, or by purchase of irrevocable contracts (e.g., annuities) from a commercial insurer, in accordance with the respective rights of each Plan participant.

Any merger or consolidation with another Plan must be carried out on terms that would at least maintain (or enhance) the benefits and other rights available to Plan participants.

| Form **5500-C/R**<br>Department of the Treasury<br>Internal Revenue Service<br><br>Department of Labor<br>Pension and Welfare Benefits Administration<br><br>Pension Benefit Guaranty Corporation | **Return/Report of Employee Benefit Plan**<br>**(With fewer than 100 participants)**<br>This form is required to be filed under sections 104 and 4065 of the Employee<br>Retirement Income Security Act of 1974 and sections 6039D, 6057(b), and<br>6058(a) of the Internal Revenue Code, referred to as the Code.<br>See separate instructions. | OMB No. 1210-0016<br><br>**1989**<br><br>**This Form Is Open<br>to Public Inspection.** |
|---|---|---|

**For the calendar plan year 1989 or fiscal plan year beginning** _____ **, 1989, and ending** _____ **, 19** _____ .

**You must check either box (5) or (6), whichever is applicable. See instructions.**

**A**  If *(1)* through *(4)* do not apply to this year's return/report, leave the boxes unmarked. This return/report is:

(1) ☐ the first return/report filed for the plan (complete all information);

(2) ☐ an amended return/report;

(3) ☐ the final return/report filed for the plan; or

(4) ☐ a short plan year return/report (less than 12 months).

**For IRS Use Only**

EP–ID

**(5) Form 5500-C filer check here.** . . . . . . . ☐
(Complete only pages 1 and 3 through 6.)

**(6) Form 5500-R filer check here.** . . . . . . . ☐
(Complete only pages 1 and 2. Detach pages 3
through 6 before filing.)

Information in 1a through 6b is used to identify your employee benefit plan. Check it for accuracy and make any necessary corrections. Also complete any incomplete items in 1a through 6b. This page must accompany your completed return/report.

**B**  IF YOU HAVE MADE ANY CHANGE TO THE PREPRINTED INFORMATION OR FILLED IN ANY INCOMPLETE INFORMATION IN 1a THROUGH 6b BELOW, CHECK HERE ▶ . . . . . . . . . . . ▶ . . . . . . . . . . . ☐

**C**  If your plan year changed since the last return/report, check this box ▶ ☐

| 1a  Name and address of plan sponsor (employer, if for a single-employer plan) | 1b  Employer identification number |
|---|---|
| | 1c  Sponsor's telephone number |
| | 1d  Business code number |
| | 1e  CUSIP issuer number |
| 2a  Name and address of plan administrator (if same as plan sponsor, enter "Same") | 2b  Administrator's employer identification no. |
| | 2c  Administrator's telephone number |

**3**  If you are not filing a page one with the historical plan information preprinted and the name and EIN of the plan sponsor or plan administrator is different than that on the last return/report filed for this plan, enter the information from the last return/report in **a** and/or **b** and complete **c**.

**a**  Sponsor _____ EIN _____ Plan number _____

**b**  Administrator _____ EIN _____

**c**  If **a** indicates a change in the sponsor's name and EIN, is this a change in sponsorship only? (See instruction 3c for definition of sponsorship.)
Enter "Yes" or "No."

**4**  Plan entity code (Enter only one code—see instructions.)

| 5a(i)  Name of plan ▶ _____<br><br>-----------------------------------------------<br><br>(ii)  Does this plan cover self-employed individuals? (Enter "Yes" or "No.") ▶ | 5b  Effective date of plan (mo., day, yr.) |
|---|---|
| | 5c  Enter three-digit<br>plan number ▶ |

6a(i)  Welfare benefit plan (Enter the applicable codes—see instructions.) . . . . . . . .

(ii)  If you entered a code M, N, or O is the plan funded? (Enter "Yes" or "No.") ▶ _____

**6b**  Pension benefit plan (Enter the applicable code—see instructions.) ▶

Be sure to include all required schedules and attachments.

Under penalties of perjury and other penalties set forth in the instructions, I declare that I have examined this return/report, including accompanying schedules and statements, and to the best of my knowledge and belief, it is true, correct, and complete.

Signature of employer/plan sponsor ▶ _____ Date ▶ _____

Signature of plan administrator ▶ _____ Date ▶ _____

**For Paperwork Reduction Act Notice, see page 1 of the instructions.**                          Form **5500-C/R** (1989)

Form 5500-C/R (1989)      **5500-R filers complete this page. 5500-C filers skip this page and complete pages 3 through 6.**      Page **2**

| | | | Yes | No |
|---|---|---|---|---|
| **6c** | Other plan features:  (1) ☐ Master trust    (2) ☐ Common/Collective trust    (3) ☐ Pooled separate account | | | |

**7a** Total participants: *(i)* At the beginning of plan year ..................... *(ii)* At the end of plan year ...................

**b** *(i)* Were any participants in the pension benefit plan separated from service with a deferred vested benefit for which a Schedule SSA (Form 5500) is required to be attached? . . . . . . . . . . . . . . . . . . . . . . . .  **7b(i)**

*(ii)* If "Yes," enter the number of separated participants required to be reported ▶

**8a** Was this plan terminated during this plan year or any prior plan year? If "Yes," enter the year _____  **8a**

**b** Were all the plan assets either distributed to participants or beneficiaries, transferred to another plan, or brought under the control of PBGC? . . . . . . . . . . . . . . . . . . . . . . . . . . . . . .  **8b**

**c** If **a** is "Yes" and the plan is covered by PBGC, is the plan continuing to file PBGC Form 1 and pay premiums until the end of the plan year in which assets are distributed or brought under the control of PBGC?  **8c**

**9** Is this a plan established or maintained pursuant to one or more collective bargaining agreements? . . . . . . .  **9**

**10** If any benefits are provided by an insurance company, insurance service, or similar organization, enter the number of Schedules A (Form 5500), Insurance Information, that are attached. (If none, enter "-0-.") ▶

**11a** Were any plan amendments adopted during the plan year? . . . . . . . . . . .  **11a**

**b** If **a** is "Yes," did any amendment result in a retroactive reduction of accrued benefits for any participant? . . . .  **11b**

**c** If **a** is "Yes," did any amendment change the information contained in the latest summary plan description or summary description of modifications available at the time of the amendment? . . . . . . . . . . . .  **11c**

**d** If **c** is "Yes," has a summary plan description or summary description of modifications that reflects the plan amendments referred to in 11c been both furnished to participants and filed with the Department of Labor? . . .  **11d**

**12a** If this is a pension benefit plan subject to the minimum funding standards, has the plan experienced a funding deficiency for this plan year (defined benefit plans must answer this question and attach Schedule B (Form 5500))? . . . . . . . . . . . . . . . . . . . . . . . . . . . . . . . . . . . . . . .  **12a**

**b** If **a** is "Yes," have you filed Form 5330 to pay the excise tax? . . . . . . . . . . . . . . . . . . .  **12b**

**13a** Total plan assets as of the beginning ..................... and end ..................... of the plan year.

**b** Total liabilities as of the beginning ..................... and end ..................... of the plan year.

**c** Net assets as of the beginning ..................... and end ..................... of the plan year.

**14** For this plan year, enter: **a** Plan income ...............................

**b** Expenses ....................... **c** Net income (loss) ...............................

**d** Plan contributions ....................... **e** Total benefits paid .......................

| | | | Yes | No | Amount |
|---|---|---|---|---|---|
| **15** | The following applies to item 15: (i) you may **NOT** use **N/A** in response to any line item and (ii) if "Yes" is checked you must enter a dollar amount in the amount column. During this plan year: | | | | |
| **a** | Was this plan covered by a fidelity bond? . . . . . . . . . . . | **15a** | | | |
| **b** | Was there any loss to the plan, whether or not reimbursed, caused by fraud or dishonesty?" . . . | **15b** | | | |
| **c** | Was there any sale, exchange, or lease of any property between the plan and the employer, any fiduciary, any of the five most highly paid employees of the employer, any owner of a 10% or more interest in the employer, or relatives of any such persons? . . . . . . . . . . . | **15c** | | | |
| **d** | Was there any loan or extension of credit by the plan to the employer, any fiduciary, any of the five most highly paid employees of the employer, any owner of a 10% or more interest in the employer, or relatives of any such persons? | **15d** | | | |
| **e** | Did the plan acquire or hold any employer security or employer real property? . . . . . . . | **15e** | | | |
| **f** | Has the plan granted an extension on any delinquent loan owed to the plan? . . . . . . . | **15f** | | | |
| **g** | Has the employer owed contributions to the plan which are more than 3 months overdue? . . . | **15g** | | | |
| **h** | Were any loans by the plan or fixed income obligations due the plan classified as uncollectible or in default as of the close of the plan year? . . . . . . . . . . . . . . . . . . | **15h** | | | |
| **I** | Has any plan fiduciary had a financial interest in excess of 10% in any party providing services to the plan or received anything of value from any such party? . . . . . . . | **15I** | | | |
| **J** | Did the plan at any time hold 20% or more of its assets in any single security, debt, mortgage, parcel of real estate, or partnership/joint venture interests? . . . . . . . . . . | **15j** | | | |
| **k** | Did the plan at any time engage in any transaction or series of related transactions involving 20% or more of the current value of plan assets? . . . . . . . . . . . . . . . . | **15k** | | | |
| **l** | Were there any noncash contributions made to the plan the value of which was set without an appraisal by an independent third party? . . . . . . . . . . . . . . . . . . . | **15l** | | | |
| **m** | Were there any purchases of nonpublicly traded securities by the plan the value of which was set without an appraisal by an independent third party? . . . . . . . . . . . . | **15m** | | | |
| **n** | Has the plan failed to provide any benefit when due under the terms of the plan because of insufficient assets? . . . . . . . . . . . . . . . . . . . . . . . . . . . . . | **15n** | | | |

**16a** Is the plan covered under the Pension Benefit Guaranty Corporation termination insurance program?

☐ Yes    ☐ No    ☐ Not determined

**b** If **a** is "Yes" or "Not determined," enter the employer identification number and the plan number used to identify it.

Employer identification number ▶                Plan number ▶

Form 5500-C/R (1989)

| | Yes | No |
|---|---|---|

**6c** Other plan features:  *(1)* ☐ ESOP      *(2)* ☐ Leveraged ESOP      *(3)* ☐ Participant-directed account plan
  *(4)* ☐ Pension plan maintained outside the United States  *(5)* ☐ Master trust (see instructions)
  *(6)* ☐ 103-12 investment entity (see instructions)    *(7)* ☐ Common/collective trust  *(8)* ☐ Pooled separate account

----------------------------------------------------------------------------
----------------------------------------------------------------------------

**d** Single-employer plans enter the tax year end of the employer in which this plan year ends ▶ Month _____ Day ____ Year _____
**e** Is the employer a member of an affiliated service group? . . . . . . . . . . . . .   **6e**
**f** Does this plan contain a cash or deferred arrangement described in Code section 401(k)? . . . . . .   **6f**

**7a** Total participants: *(i)* At the beginning of plan year_____ *(ii)* At the end of plan year_____

  **b** *(i)* Were any participants in the pension benefit plan separated from service with a deferred vested benefit for which a Schedule
      SSA (Form 5500) is required to be attached? . . . . . . . . . . . . . .   **7b(i)**
      If "Yes," enter the number of separated participants required to be reported ▶

**8a** Were any plan amendments adopted during the plan year? . . . . . . . . . . .   **8a**
  **b** Did any amendment result in the retroactive reduction of accrued benefits for any participant? . . . . .   **8b**
  **c** Enter the date the most recent amendment was adopted  . . ▶ Month _____ Day _____ Year _____
  **d** If **a** is "Yes," did any amendment change the information contained in the latest summary plan descriptions or summary
      description of modifications available at the time of the amendment? . . . . . . . . .   **8d**
  **e** If **d** is "Yes," has a summary plan description or summary description of modifications that reflects the plan amendments
      referred to in **d** been both furnished to participants and filed with the Department of Labor? . . . . . .   **8e**

**9a** Was this plan terminated during this plan year or any prior plan year? If "Yes," enter year ▶ _____   **9a**
  **b** Were all plan assets either distributed to participants or beneficiaries, transferred to another plan, or brought under the control of
      PBGC? . . . . . . . . . . . . . . . . . . . .   **9b**
  **c** Was a resolution to terminate this plan adopted during this plan year or any prior plan year? . . . . .   **9c**
  **d** If **a** or **c** is "Yes," have you received a favorable determination letter from IRS for the termination? . . . .   **9d**
  **e** If **d** is "No," has a determination letter been requested from IRS? . . . . . . . . . .   **9e**
  **f** If **a** or **c** is "Yes," have participants and beneficiaries been notified of the termination or the proposed termination? . . .   **9f**
  **g** If **a** is "Yes" and the plan is covered by PBGC, is the plan continuing to file a PBGC Form 1 and pay premiums until the end of the
      plan year in which assets are distributed or brought under the control of PBGC? . . . . . . . .   **9g**
  **h** During this plan year, did any trust assets revert to the employer for which the Code section 4980 excise tax is due? . . . .   **9h**
  **i** If **h** is "Yes," enter the amount of tax paid with your Form 5330 ▶

**10a** Was this plan merged or consolidated into another plan(s), or were assets or liabilities transferred to another plan(s) since the end
  of the plan year covered by the last return/report Form 5500 or 5500-C which was filed for this plan (or during this plan year if
  this is the initial return/report)? . . . . . . . . . . . . . . . .   **10a**

| If "Yes," identify the other plan(s): | **c** Employer identification number(s) | **d** Plan number(s) |
|---|---|---|
| **b** Name of plan(s) ▶ _____ | _____ | _____ |

**e** Has Form 5310 been filed? . . . . . . . . . . . . . . . .   ☐ Yes ☐ No

| **11** Enter the plan funding arrangement code | **12** Enter the plan benefit arrangement code |
|---|---|
| (see instructions) ▶ | (see instructions) ▶ |

| | Yes | No |
|---|---|---|

**13** Is this a plan established or maintained pursuant to one or more collective bargaining agreements? . . . . .   **13**
**14** If any benefits are provided by an insurance company, insurance service, or similar organization, enter the number of Schedules A
  (Form 5500), Insurance Information, that are attached. If none, enter "-0-." ▶

## Welfare Plans Do Not Complete Items 15 Through 28. Skip To Item 29.

**15a** If this is a defined benefit plan subject to the minimum funding standards for this plan year, is Schedule B (Form 5500) required
  to be attached? . . . . . . . . . . . . . . . . . . .   **15a**

  If "Yes," attach Schedule B (Form 5500).

  **b** If this is a defined contribution plan, i.e., money purchase or target benefit, is it subject to the minimum funding standards (if a
    waiver was granted, see instructions)? . . . . . . . . . . . . . . .   **15b**

    If "Yes," complete *(i)*, *(ii)*, and *(iii)* below:
    *(i)* Amount of employer contribution required for the plan year under Code section 412 . . **15b(i)** $
    *(ii)* Amount of contribution paid by the employer for the plan year . . . . . . . **b(ii)** $
      Enter date of last payment by employer ▶ Month _____ Day _____ Year _____
    *(iii)* If *(i)* is greater than *(ii)*, subtract *(ii)* from *(i)* and enter the funding deficiency here.
      Otherwise, enter zero. (If you have a funding deficiency, file Form 5330.) . . . . . **b(iii)** $

**16** Has the plan been top-heavy at any time beginning with the 1984 plan year? . . . . . . . . .   **16**
**17** Has the annual compensation of each participant taken into account under the plan been limited to $200,000? . . . . .   **17**

Form 5500-C/R (1989)                                                                 Page **4**

|  |  | Yes | No |
|---|---|---|---|
| **18a** | If the plan distributed any annuity contracts this year, did these contracts contain a requirement that the spouse consent before any distributions under the contract are made in a form other than a qualified joint and survivor annuity? . . . . . . . . . **18a** | | |
| **b** | Did the plan make distributions to participants or beneficiaries in a form other than a qualified joint and survivor annuity (a life annuity if a single person) or qualified preretirement survivor annuity (exclude deferred annuity contracts)? . . . . . . **18b** | | |
| **c** | Did the plan make distributions or loans to married participants and beneficiaries without the required consent of the participant's spouse? . . . . . . . . . . . . . . . . . . . . . **18c** | | |
| **d** | Upon plan amendment or termination, do the accrued benefits of every participant include the subsidized benefits that the participant may become entitled to receive subsequent to the plan amendment or termination? . . . . . . . . . **18d** | | |
| **19** | Were distributions made in accordance with the requirements of Code sections 411(a)(11) and 417(e)? (see instructions) . . . **19** | | |
| **20** | Have any contributions been made or benefits accrued in excess of the Code section 415 limits, as amended by the Tax Reform Act of 1986? . . . . . . . . . . . . . . . . . . . . . . . . . **20** | | |
| **21** | Has the plan made the required distributions in 1989 under Code section 401(a)(9)? . . . . . . . . . . . . . **21** | | |

|  | Number |
|---|---|
| **22a** *(1)* Number of employees, include all self-employed individuals and employees of entities aggregated with the employer under Code sections 414(b), (c), (m), or (o) . . . . . . . . . . . . . . . . . **22a(1)** | |
| *(2)* Number of leased employees treated as employees of any of the entities described in *(1)* above under Code section 414(n) or (o) (see specific instructions) . . . . . . . . . . . . . . . **22a(2)** | |
| **b** Total number of employees (add lines a(1) and (2)) . . . . . . . . . . **22b** | |
| **c** Number excluded under the plan because of: (i) minimum age or years of service, (ii) employees covered under a collective bargaining agreement, and (iii) nonresident aliens who receive no earned income from United States sources. (If the plan benefits employees covered by a collective bargaining agreement, see specific instructions.) . . . . . . . . . . **22c** | |
| **d** Number of employees not excluded (subtract line c from line b) . . . . . . . . . . . . **22d** | |
| **e** Number of employees included in the number listed for line d who are highly compensated within the meaning of code section 414(q). (If there are none, do NOT complete lines f through l.) . . . . . . . . . **22e** | |
| **f** Number of employees included in the number listed for line d who are not highly compensated employees within the meaning of Code section 414(q). (Subtract line e from line d. If there are none, do NOT complete lines g through m.) . . . . . **22f** | |
| **g** Number of employees benefiting under this plan (see specific instructions). . . . . . . . . . . **22g** | |
| **h** Number of employees included in the number listed for line g who are highly compensated within the meaning of Code section 414(q). (If there are none, do NOT complete lines i through l.) . . . . . . . . . **22h** | |
| **i** Number of employees included in the number listed for line g who are not highly compensated employees within the meaning of Code section 414(q). (Subtract line h from line g.) . . . . . . . . . . **22I** | |

### Ratio Percentage Test

| | Number |
|---|---|
| **j** Divide line i by line f . . . . . . . . . . . . . . . . . . . . . . . **22j** | |
| **k** Divide line h by line e . . . . . . . . . . . . . . . . . . . . . . . **22k** | |
| **l** Divide line j by line k. (If the result is less than .70, complete line m and see specific instructions.) . . . . . . . **22I** | |

### Line of Business

| | Number |
|---|---|
| **m** If the plan satisfies the coverage requirements of Code section 410(b) on the basis of separate lines of business or operating units, enter the total number of separate lines of business and operating units. (see specific instructions) . . . . . . **22m** | |

### Participation Test

**n** Does the plan contain more than one benefit structure? . . . . . . . . . . . . . . . . ☐ Yes ☐ No

**o** If the plan contains more than one benefit structure, does the plan benefit at least the lesser of 50 employees or 40 percent of the employer's employees under each current benefit structure? If "No," see specific instructions . . . . . . ☐ Yes ☐ No

### Concentration Percentage

| | Number |
|---|---|
| **p** Divide line f by line d . . . . . . . . . . . . . . . . . . . . . . . . . **22p** | |

Form 5500-C/R (1989)                                                                                          Page **5**

| | | Yes | No |
|---|---|---|---|

**23a** Is it intended that this plan qualify under Code section 401(a)? . . . . . . . . . . . . . . . . .  **23a**

If "Yes," complete **b** and **c.**

**b** Enter the date of the most recent IRS determination letter— Month _____ Year _____

**c** Is a determination letter request pending with IRS? . . . . . . . . . . . . . . . . . . .  **23c**

**24a** If this is a plan with Employee Stock Ownership features, was a current appraisal of the value of the stock made immediately before any contribution of stock or the purchase of the stock by the trust for the plan year covered by this return/report? . . .  **24a**

**b** If **a** is "Yes," was the appraisal made by an unrelated third party? . . . . . . . . . . . . . .  **24b**

**c** If dividends paid on employer securities held by the ESOP were used to make payments on ESOP loans, enter the amount of the dividends used to make the payments . . . . . . . . . . . . . . . . . . ▶ | **24c** |

**25** Does the plan provide for permitted disparity, see Code sections 401(a)(5) and 401(l)? . . . . . . . . .  **25**

**26** Does the employer/sponsor listed in 1a of this form maintain other qualified pension benefit plans? . . . . . . .  **26**
If "Yes," enter the total number of plans, including this plan ▶

**27** If this plan is an adoption of a master, prototype, or regional prototype plan, indicate which type by checking the appropriate box:

**a** ☐ Master   **b** ☐ Prototype   **c** ☐ Regional prototype

**28a** Is the plan covered under the Pension Benefit Guaranty Corporation termination insurance program? ☐ Yes   ☐ No   ☐ Not determined

**b** If **a** is "Yes" or "Not determined," enter the employer identification number and the plan number used to identify it.
Employer identification number ▶                     Plan number ▶

**29** The following applies to item 29: (i) you may **NOT** use "N/A" in response to any line item and (ii) if "Yes" is checked you must enter a dollar amount in the amount column.

| | | Yes | No | Amount |
|---|---|---|---|---|
| During this plan year: | | | | |
| **a** Was this plan covered by a fidelity bond? . . . . . . . . . . . . . | **29a** | | | |
| **b** Was there any loss to the plan, whether or not reimbursed, caused by fraud or dishonesty? . . . . . . | **29b** | | | |
| **c** Was there any sale, exchange, or lease of any property between the plan and the employer, any fiduciary, any of the five most highly paid employees of the employer, any owner of a 10% or more interest in the employer, or relatives of any such persons? . . . . . . . . . . | **29c** | | | |
| **d** Was there any loan or extension of credit by the plan to the employer, any fiduciary, any of the five most highly paid employees of the employer, any owner of a 10% or more interest in the employer, or relatives of any such persons? . . . . . . . . . . . . . . . | **29d** | | | |
| **e** Did the plan acquire or hold any employer security or employer real property? . . . . . . . . . | **29e** | | | |
| **f** Has the plan granted an extension on any delinquent loan owed to the plan? . . . . . . . . | **29f** | | | |
| **g** Has the employer owed contributions to the plan which are more than 3 months overdue? . . . . . . | **29g** | | | |
| **h** Were any loans by the plan or fixed income obligations due the plan classified as uncollectible or in default as of the close of the plan year? . . . . . . . . . . . . . . . | **29h** | | | |
| **i** Has any plan fiduciary had a financial interest in excess of 10% in any party providing services to the plan or received anything of value from any such party? . . . . . . . . . . . . . | **29i** | | | |
| **j** Did the plan at any time hold 20% or more of its assets in any single security, debt, mortgage, parcel of real estate, or partnership/joint venture interests? . . . . . . . . . . . . . | **29j** | | | |
| **k** Did the plan at any time engage in any transaction or series of related transactions involving 20% or more of the current value of plan assets? . . . . . . . . . . . . . . . . | **29k** | | | |
| **l** Were there any noncash contributions made to the plan whose value was set without an appraisal by an independent third party? . . . . . . . . . . . . . . . . . | **29l** | | | |
| **m** Were there any purchases of nonpublicly traded securities by the plan whose value was set without an appraisal by an independent third party? . . . . . . . . . . . . . . . | **29m** | | | |
| **n** Has the plan failed to provide any benefit when due under the terms of the plan because of insufficient assets? | **29n** | | | |

**30** Current value of plan assets and liabilities at the beginning and end of the plan year. Combine the value of plan assets held in more than one trust. Allocate the value of the plan's interest in a commingled trust containing the assets of more than one plan on a line-by-line basis unless the trust meets one of the specific exceptions described in the instructions. Do not enter the value of the portion of an insurance contract which guarantees during this plan year to pay a specific dollar benefit at a future date. Round off amounts to the nearest dollar.

|  | **Assets** | | (a) Beginning of year | (b) End of year |
|---|---|---|---|---|
| a | Cash | 30a | | |
| b | Receivables | 30b | | |
| c | Investments: | | | |
| | (i) U.S. Government securities | c(i) | | |
| | (ii) Corporate debt and equity instruments | c(ii) | | |
| | (iii) Real estate and mortgages (other than to participants) | c(iii) | | |
| | (iv) Loans to participants: | | | |
| |     A Mortgages | (iv)A | | |
| |     B Other | (iv)B | | |
| | (v) Other | c(v) | | |
| | (vi) Total investments (add (i) through (v)) | c(vi) | | |
| d | Buildings and other property used in plan operations | 30d | | |
| e | Other assets | 30e | | |
| f | Total assets | 30f | | |
|  | **Liabilities** | | | |
| g | Payables | 30g | | |
| h | Acquisition indebtedness | 30h | | |
| i | Other liabilities | 30i | | |
| j | Total liabilities | 30j | | |
| k | Net assets (f minus j) | 30k | | |

**31** Plan income, expenses, and changes in net assets for the plan year. Include all income and expenses of the plan including any trust(s) or separately maintained fund(s) and payments/receipts to/from insurance carriers.

|  | **Income** | | (a) Amount | (b) Total |
|---|---|---|---|---|
| a | Contributions received or receivable in cash from: | | | |
| | (i) Employer(s) (including contributions on behalf of self-employed individuals) | 31a(i) | | |
| | (ii) Employees | a(ii) | | |
| | (iii) Others | a(iii) | | |
| | (iv) Add (i) through (iii) | a(iv) | | |
| b | Noncash contributions (enter total of a(iv) and b in column (b)) | 31b | | |
| c | Earnings from investments (interest, dividends, rents, royalties) | 31c | | |
| d | Net realized gain (loss) on sale or exchange of assets | 31d | | |
| e | Other income (specify) ▶ _____ | 31e | | |
| f | Total income (add b through e) | 31f | | |
|  | **Expenses** | | | |
| g | Distribution of benefits and payments to provide benefits: | | | |
| | (i) Directly to participants or their beneficiaries | 31g(i) | | |
| | (ii) Other | g(ii) | | |
| h | Administrative expenses (salaries, fees, commissions, insurance premiums) | 31h | | |
| i | Other expenses (specify) ▶ _____ | 31i | | |
| j | Total expenses (add g through i) | 31j | | |
| k | Net income (loss) (subtract j from f) | 31k | | |

| SCHEDULE B<br>(Form 5500)<br>Department of the Treasury<br>Internal Revenue Service<br>Department of Labor<br>Pension and Welfare Benefits Administration<br>Pension Benefit Guaranty Corporation | **Actuarial Information**<br>This schedule is required to be filed under section 104 of the Employee Retirement Income Security Act of 1974, referred to as ERISA, and section 6059(a) of the Internal Revenue Code, referred to as the Code.<br>▶ **Attach to Form 5500, 5500-C/R, or 5500EZ if applicable.** | OMB No 1210-0016<br>**1989**<br>**This Form Is Open to Public Inspection** |

For calendar plan year 1989 or fiscal plan year beginning _____ , 1989, and ending _____ , 19 ___

▶ **Please complete every item on this form. If an item does not apply, enter "N/A."** ▶ **Round off amounts to nearest dollar.**

▶ **Caution:** A penalty of $1,000 will be assessed for late filing of this report unless reasonable cause is established.

Name of plan sponsor as shown on line 1a of Form 5500, 5500-C/R, or 5500EZ | **Employer identification number**

Name of plan | Enter three-digit plan number ▶ | **Yes** | **No**

1  Has a waiver of a funding deficiency for this plan been approved by the IRS? . . . . . .
   If "Yes," attach a copy of the IRS approval letter.
2  Is a waived funding deficiency of a prior plan year being amortized in this plan year? . . . . .
3  Have any of the periods of amortization for charges described in Code section 412(b)(2)(B) been extended by IRS? .
   If "Yes," attach a copy of the IRS approval letter.
4a Was the shortfall funding method the basis for this plan year's funding standard account computations? . . . .
 b Is this plan a multiemployer plan which is, for this plan year, in reorganization as described in Code section 418 or ERISA section 4241? . .
   If "Yes," you are required to attach the information described in the instructions.
5  Has a change been made in funding method for this plan year? . . . . . . . . . . . .
   If "Yes," attach either a copy of the letter showing IRS approval or state applicable Revenue Procedure authorizing approval if used.
6  Operational information:
 a Enter most recent actuarial valuation date ▶ _____
 b Enter date(s) and amount of contributions received this plan year for prior plan years and not previously reported:
   Date(s) ▶ _____ Amount ▶ _____
 c Current value of the assets accumulated in the plan as of the beginning of this plan year .
 d Current liability as of beginning of plan year:

| | **(1) No. of Persons** | **(2) Vested Benefits** | **(3) Total Benefits** |
|---|---|---|---|
| (i) For retired participants and beneficiaries receiving payments | | | |
| (ii) For terminated vested participants | | | |
| (iii) For active participants . . . . . . . | | | |
| (iv) Total . . . . . . . . . . . | | | |

 e Expected current liability increase as of mo. ____ day ____ yr. ____ attributable to benefits accruing during the plan year . . . . . . . . . . . . . . . .
 f Expected benefit payments
7  Contributions made to the plan for the plan year by employer(s) and employees:

| (a)<br>Month Day Year | (b)<br>Amount paid by employer | (c)<br>Amount paid by employees | (a)<br>Month Day Year | (b)<br>Amount paid by employer | (c)<br>Amount paid by employees |
|---|---|---|---|---|---|
| | | | | | |
| | | | | | |
| | | | | | |
| | | | | | |
| | | | | | |
| | | Total . . . | | | |

**Statement by Enrolled Actuary (see instructions before signing):**
To the best of my knowledge, the information supplied in this schedule and on the accompanying statements, if any, is complete and accurate, and in my opinion each assumption used in combination, represents my best estimate of anticipated experience under the plan. Furthermore, in the case of a plan other than a multiemployer plan, each assumption used (a) is reasonable (taking into account the experience of the plan and reasonable expectations) or (b) would, in the aggregate, result in a total contribution equivalent to that which would be determined if each such assumption were reasonable. In the case of a multiemployer plan, the assumptions used, in the aggregate, are reasonable (taking into account the experience of the plan and reasonable expectations)

_____ | _____
Signature of actuary | Date

_____ | _____
Print or type name of actuary | Enrollment number

_____ | _____
Name and address | Telephone number (including area code)

For Paperwork Reduction Act Notice, see the instructions for Form 5500 | Schedule B (Form 5500) 1989

Schedule B (Form 5500) 1989                                                                    Page **2**

**8**   Funding standard account and other information:

**a**   Accrued liability as determined for funding standard account as of (enter date) ▶ .......................

**b**   Value of assets as determined for funding standard account as of (enter date) ▶ .......................

**c**   Unfunded liability for spread-gain methods with bases as of (enter date) ▶ .......................

**d**   *(i)* Actuarial gains or (losses) for period ending ▶ ..................................................

    *(ii)* Shortfall gains or (losses) for period ending ▶ ...............................................

**e**   Amount of contribution certified by the actuary as necessary to reduce the funding deficiency to zero, from **9o** or **10h** (or the attachment for **4b** if required) . . . . . . . . . . . . . . . . . . . . .

**9**   Funding standard account statement for this plan year ending ▶ ................................

    **Charges to funding standard account:**

**a**   Prior year funding deficiency, if any . . . . . . . . . . . . . . . . . . . . . . . . . .

**b**   Employer's normal cost for plan year as of mo. ...... day ...... yr. ...... . . . . . . . . .

**c**   Amortization charges:                                                               Balance

    *(i)* Funding waivers (outstanding balance as of mo. ......... day .... yr. ...... ▶ $ ..................)

    *(ii)* Other than waivers (outstanding balance as of mo. ...... day .... yr ...... ▶ $ ..................)

**d**   Interest as applicable on **a, b,** and **c** . . . . . . . . . . . . . . . . . . . . . . .

**e**   Additional funding charge, if applicable (see item 13, page 3) . . . . . . . . . . . . . . .

**f**   Additional interest charge due to late quarterly contributions . . . . . . . . . . . . . .

**g**   Total charges (add **a** through **f**) . . . . . . . . . . . . . . . . . . . . . . . . .

    **Credits to funding standard account:**

**h**   Prior year credit balance, if any. . . . . . . . . . . . . . . . . . . . . . . . . . .

**I**   Employer contributions (total from column (b) of item 7) . . . . . . . . . . . . . . . . .

**j**   Amortization credits (outstanding balance as of mo. ......... day .... yr. ...... ▶ $ ..................)

**k**   Interest as applicable to end of plan year on **h, I,** and **j** . . . . . . . . . . . . . . . . .

**l**   Miscellaneous credits:

    *(i)* FFL credit before reflecting 150% of current liability component . . . . . .

    *(ii)* Additional credit due to 150% of current liability component . . . . . . .

    *(iii)* Waived funding deficiency . . . . . . . . . . . . . . . . . . . . .

    *(iv)* Total . . . . . . . . . . . . . . . . . . . . . . . . . . . . .

**m**  Total credits (add **h** through **I**) . . . . . . . . . . . . . . . . . . . . . . . .

    **Balance:**

**n**   Credit balance: if **m** is greater than **g**, enter the difference . . . . . . . . . . . . . .

**o**   Funding deficiency: if **g** is greater than **m**, enter the difference. . . . . . . . . . . . . .

    **Reconciliation:**

**p**   Current year's accumulated reconciliation account:

    *(i)* Due to additional funding charge as of the beginning of the plan year . . . . .

    *(ii)* Due to additional interest charges as of the beginning of the plan year . . . . .

    *(iii)* Due to waived funding deficiency:

      *(a)* Reconciliation outstanding balance as of mo. ...... day ...... yr. ...... .

      *(b)* Reconciliation amount (**9c(i)** balance minus **9p(iii)(a)**) . . . . . . . . .

    *(iv)* Total as of mo. ...... day ...... yr. ...... . . . . . . . . . . . . . . . . . .

**10**  Alternative minimum funding standard account (omit if not used):

**a**   Was the entry age normal cost method used to determine entries in item 9, above . . . . . . . . .   ☐ Yes   ☐ No

    If "No," do not complete **b** through **h**.

**b**   Prior year alternate funding deficiency, if any . . . . . . . . . . . . . . . . . . . .

**c**   Normal cost . . . . . . . . . . . . . . . . . . . . . . . . . . . . . . .

**d**   Excess, if any, of value of accrued benefits over market value of assets . . . . . . . . . .

**e**   Interest on **b, c,** and **d** . . . . . . . . . . . . . . . . . . . . . . . . . . .

**f**   Employer contributions (total from column (b) of item 7) . . . . . . . . . . . . . . . .

**g**   Interest on **f** . . . . . . . . . . . . . . . . . . . . . . . . . . . . . . .

**h**   Funding deficiency: if the sum of **b** through **e** is greater than the sum of **f** and **g**, enter difference . . . .

Schedule B (Form 5500) 1989 | Page **3**

**11** Actuarial cost method used as the basis for this plan year's funding standard account computation:

- **a** ☐ Attained age normal   **b** ☐ Entry age normal   **c** ☐ Accrued benefit (unit credit)
- **d** ☐ Aggregate   **e** ☐ Frozen initial liability   **f** ☐ Individual level premium
- **g** ☐ Other (specify) ▶

**12** Checklist of certain actuarial assumptions:

| | Pre-retirement | | Post-retirement | |
|---|---|---|---|---|
| | Yes | No | Yes | No |
| **a** Rates specified in insurance or annuity contracts | ☐ | ☐ | ☐ | ☐ |

**b** Mortality table code:
- (i) Males
- (ii) Females

**c** Interest rate:
- (i) Current liability ......... %  %
- (ii) All other calculated values ... %  %

**d** Retirement age ......... %  %

**e** Expense loading

| | Male | Female |
|---|---|---|
| **f** Annual ... rate | | |
| (i) Age 25 | % | % |
| (ii) Age 40 | % | % |
| (iii) Age 55 | % | % |

**g** Ratio of salary at normal retirement to salary at:
| | Male | Female |
|---|---|---|
| (i) Age 25 | % | % |
| (ii) Age 40 | % | % |
| (iii) Age 55 | % | % |

**h** Estimated investment return on actuarial value of plan assets for the year ending on the valuation date ... %

**13** Additional Required Funding Charge—Plans with NO unfunded current liability or plans with 100 or fewer participants check the box at the right and do not complete the rest of this item ... ☐

- **a** Current liability as of valuation date
- **b** Adjusted value of assets as of valuation date (subtract line **9h** from line **8b**)
- **c** Funded current liability percentage (**b** divided by **a**) ... %
- **d** Unfunded current liability as of valuation date (subtract **b** from **a**)
- **e** Outstanding balance of unfunded old liability as of valuation date
- **f** Liability attributable to any unpredictable contingent event benefit
- **g** Unfunded new liability (subtract **e** and **f** from **d**)
- **h** Unfunded new liability amount ( ___ % of **g**)
- **i** Unfunded old liability amount
- **j** Deficit reduction contribution (add **h** and **i**)
- **k** Net amortization charge for certain bases
- **l** Unpredictable contingent event amount:
  - (i) Benefits paid during year attributable to unpredictable contingent event
  - (ii) Unfunded current liability percentage (subtract the percentage on **13c** from 100%) ... %
  - (iii) Transition percentage ... %
  - (iv) Enter the product of lines (i), (ii), and (iii)
  - (v) Amortization of all unpredictable contingent event liabilities
  - (vi) Enter the greater of line iv or line v
- **m** Additional funding charge as of valuation date (excess of **j** over **k** (if any) plus **l**(vi))
- **n** Assets needed to increase current liability percentage to 100%
- **o** Lesser of **m** or **n**
- **p** Interest adjustment
- **q** Additional funding charge (add **o** and **p**)
- **r** Adjustment for plans with more than 100 but less than 150 participants ( ___ % of **q**)

| SCHEDULE SSA (Form 5500) | **Annual Registration Statement Identifying Separated Participants With Deferred Vested Benefits** | OMB No. 1210-0016 |
|---|---|---|

Under Section 6057(a) of the Internal Revenue Code

Department of the Treasury
Internal Revenue Service

▶ File as an attachment to Form 5500 or 5500-C/R.

▶ For Paperwork Reduction Act Notice, see page 1 of the instructions for Form 5500 or 5500-C/R.

**1989**

This Form Is NOT Open to Public Inspection

For the calendar year 1989 or fiscal plan year beginning          , 1989, and ending          , 19

▶ This form must be filed for each plan year in which one or more participants with deferred vested benefit rights separated from the service covered by the plan. See instructions on when to report a separated employee.

▶ Type or print in ink all entries on this schedule. File the originals.

▶ All attachments to this form should have entries only on the front of the page.

**1a** Name of sponsor (employer if for a single employer plan)

Address (number and street)

City or town, state, and ZIP code

**1b** Sponsor's employer identification number

**1c** Is this a plan to which more than one employer contributes? ☐ Yes ☐ No

**2a** Name of plan administrator (if other than sponsor)

Address (number and street)

City or town, state, and ZIP code

**2b** Administrator's employer identification no.

**3a** Name of plan

**3b** Plan number ▶

**4** Have you notified each separated participant of his or her deferred benefit? . . . . . . . . . . . . . . . ☐ Yes ☐ No

**5** Separated participants with deferred vested benefits (if additional space is required, see instruction, "What To File"):

| (a) Social Security Number | (b) Name of participant | Enter code for nature and form of benefit | | Amount of vested benefit | | | (h) Plan year in which participant separated |
|---|---|---|---|---|---|---|---|
| | | (c) Type of annuity | (d) Payment frequency | (e) Defined benefit plan—periodic payment | (f) Units or shares | (g) Total value of account | |
| | | | | | | | |

**The Following Information Is Optional (See Specific Instruction 6)**

**6** Use this item to report (i) separated participants with deferred vested benefits who were previously reported on Schedule SSA (Form 5500) and who have received part or all of their vested benefits or who have forfeited their benefits during the plan year for which this form is being filed, and (ii) to delete participants erroneously reported on a prior Schedule SSA (Form 5500):

**Note:** *Participants listed in this item, because they have received part of their vested benefits, must also be reported in item 5 above listing their remaining vested benefits.*

| (a) Social Security Number | (b) Name of participant | Enter code for nature and form of benefit | | Amount of vested benefit | | | (h) Plan year in which participant separated |
|---|---|---|---|---|---|---|---|
| | | (c) Type of annuity | (d) Payment frequency | (e) Defined benefit plan—periodic payment | (f) Units or shares | (g) Total value of account | |
| | | | | | | | |

Under penalties of perjury, I declare that I have examined this report, and to the best of my knowledge and belief, it is true, correct, and complete.

Date                                    Signature of plan administrator

| Form **5500EZ** | **Annual Return of One-Participant (Owners and Their Spouses) Pension Benefit Plan** | OMB No. 1545-0956 |
|---|---|---|
| Department of the Treasury<br>Internal Revenue Service | For the calendar year 1989 or fiscal plan year beginning ☐ , 19 ☐ ,<br>and ending ☐ , 19 ☐ . | **1989** |
| Please type or<br>machine print | | **This Form Is Open<br>to Public Inspection** |

This return is: *(i)* ☐ the first return filed  *(ii)* ☐ an amended return  *(iii)* ☐ the final return

| Use IRS<br>label.<br>Other-<br>wise,<br>please<br>type or<br>machine<br>print. | **1a** Name of employer | **1b** Employer identification number |
|---|---|---|
| | Address (number and street) | **1c** Telephone number of employer |
| | City or town, state, and ZIP code | **1d** If plan year has changed since last<br>return, check here . . . . . ▶ ☐ |

**2a** *(i)* Name of plan ▶ -----------------------------------------

*(ii)* ☐    Check if name of plan has changed since last return

| **2b** Date plan first became effective | | |
|---|---|---|
| Month | Day | Year |

**2c** Enter three-digit
plan number . . ▶ ☐ ☐ ☐

| | | Month | | Year | | Yes | No |
|---|---|---|---|---|---|---|---|
| **3a** | Enter the date the most recent plan amendment was adopted . . . . . . . | | | | | | |
| **b** | Enter the date of the most recent IRS determination letter · · · · · · · | | | | | | |
| **c** | Is a determination letter request pending with IRS? . . . . . . . . . . | | | | | | |

**4a** Enter the number of other qualified pension benefit plans maintained by the employer . . . ▶ _____

**b** If you have more than one pension plan and the total assets of all plans are more than $100,000, check this box . . ▶ ☐

**5** Type of plan: *a* ☐ Defined benefit pension plan (attach Schedule B (Form 5500))  *b* ☐ Money purchase plan
      *c* ☐ Profit-sharing plan  *d* ☐ Stock bonus or ESOP plan

**6** Were there any noncash contributions made to the plan during the plan year? . . . . . . . .

**7** Enter the number of participants in each category listed below:

| | | Number |
|---|---|---|
| **a** Less than age 59½ at the end of the plan year . . . . . . . . . . . . . . . | **7a** | |
| **b** Age 59½ or more at the end of the plan year, but less than age 70½ at the beginning of the plan year . . . | **b** | |
| **c** Age 70½ or more at the beginning of the plan year. . . . . . . . . . . . . . . | **c** | |

**8a** A fully insured plan with no trust and which is funded entirely by allocated insurance contracts that fully guarantee the amount of
benefit payments should check the box at the right and not complete 8b through 10d . . . . . . . . . ▶ ☐

| | | | |
|---|---|---|---|
| **b** | Contributions received for this plan year . . . . . . . . . . . . . . . . . | **8b** | |
| **c** | Net plan income other than from contributions . . . . . . . . . . . . . . | **c** | |
| **d** | Plan distributions . . . . . . . . . . . . . . . . . . . . . . . | **d** | |
| **e** | Plan expenses other than distributions . . . . . . . . . . . . . . . . | **e** | |
| **9a** | Total plan assets at the end of the year . . . . . . . . . . . . . . . . | **9a** | |
| **b** | Total plan liabilities at the end of the year . . . . . . . . . . . . . . . | **b** | |

**10** During the plan year, if any of the following transactions took place between the plan and a
party-in-interest (see instructions), check "Yes" and enter amount. Otherwise, check "No."

| | | Yes | Amount | No |
|---|---|---|---|---|
| **a** Sale, exchange, or lease of property . . . . . . . . . . . . . . . | **10a** | | | |
| **b** Loan or extension of credit . . . . . . . . . . . . . . . . . | **b** | | | |
| **c** Acquisition or holding of employer securities . . . . . . . . . . . | **c** | | | |
| **d** Payment by the plan for services . . . . . . . . . . . . . . . | **d** | | | |

| | | Yes | No |
|---|---|---|---|
| **11a** | Does your business have any employees other than you and your spouse (and your partners and their spouses)? . . . | | |
| | If "No," do NOT complete the rest of this question; go to question 12. | | |
| **b** | Total number of employees (including you and your spouse and your partners and their spouses) ▶ _____ | | |
| **c** | Does this plan meet the coverage test of Code section 410(b)? . . . . . . . . . . .<br>See the specific instructions for line 11c. | | |
| **12** | Answer this question only if there was a benefit payment, loan, or distribution of an annuity contract made during the<br>plan year and the plan is subject to the spousal consent requirements (see instructions). | | |
| **a** | Was there consent of the participant's spouse to any benefit payment or loan within the 90-day period prior to such payment or loan? | | |
| **b** | If "No," check the reason for no consent: *(i)* ☐ the participant was not married<br>*(ii)* ☐ the benefit payment made was part of a qualified joint and survivor annuity *(iii)* ☐ other | | |
| **c** | Were any annuity contracts purchased by the plan and distributed to the participants? . . . . . . . . . . . | | |

Under penalties of perjury and other penalties set forth in the instructions, I declare that I have examined this return, including accompanying schedules and statements, and to the best of my knowledge
and belief, it is true, correct, and complete

Signature of employer/plan sponsor ▶                        Date ▶

**For Paperwork Reduction Act Notice, see page 1 of the instructions.**     ★U.S.GPO:1989-0-245-348     Form **5500EZ** (1989)

# Chapter 11

## PURCHASE, SALE, OR MERGER OF A CLOSELY HELD CORPORATION

### INTRODUCTION

Although there is a great deal of media attention given to the epic battles for takeover of giant corporations, most business combinations are in fact friendly, not hostile, transactions. What usually happens is that a business owner decides to retire and seeks a buyer; or there is conflict within top management that makes it infeasible to keep operating the business; or additional capital, equipment, or expertise are needed. Another frequent reason for sale or merger of a business is that the business's founders have not made adequate plans for succession, and the founders plan retirement or have died and there are no family members or executives of the business available to take over.

From the buyer's point of view, there are many reasons to buy a business or propose a merger. It is often cheaper and easier to buy a business than to "grow" one—for instance, if a business that has succeeded in one geographic area wants to expand into another area, but lacks local contacts and goodwill, or if a business that has money wants to achieve control of a superior technology developed by another company.

After investigation, advertisement, perhaps the services of a business broker, a buyer or merger partner is found. Then there is a merger or consolidation (combination of two corporations: in a merger, one corporation is merged into, and disappears into, the surviving corporation; in a consolidation, the two former corporations are combined into a new surviving corporation) or other type of reorganization.

### Mergers and Tender Offers

In a sense, there are two major paths to corporate combination or acquisition of one corporation by another: the merger (which must be approved by the corporation's

Board of Directors, who are usually not required to consult the shareholders' opinions) and the tender offer. In a tender offer, a would-be buyer asks shareholders to "tender" (surrender) their shares in exchange for a designated amount per share. Usually, if the tender offer succeeds, the two paths converge. Once the bidder owns enough shares, it can elect its own delegates to the Board of Directors, control the corporation, and order a merger. If the corporation's charter and bylaws permit, the bidder may even be able to call a special meeting to take action or ratify the merger.

When a would-be buyer examines closely held businesses that are for sale, perhaps the most important question is why the business is for sale! The business may be an excellent one, but the owner(s) want to retire or enter another line of business. It could be a business with a lot of potential, but one that is undercapital-ized or badly managed, and can be turned around with more money and skill. Or the business in its present form could be unsalvageable, but there is one or more major assets which can be purchased inexpensively by acquiring the business: for instance, a patent or trade secret; useful machinery; real estate; or a long-term, low-rent lease on a choice store or office location. The acquiring corporation may also want to eliminate actual or potential competition. Certain large corporations have to apply for permission from the federal government to merge, because the merger could violate the antitrust laws. However, under Presidents Reagan and Bush, very few mergers have been forbidden on antitrust grounds, and this would not be a concern in mergers of small, privately held corporations.

## Auctions

An increasing trend is for closely held corporations to be auctioned. That way, a corporation seeking a merger partner or buyer can get the widest range of bids and, it is hoped, increase the price that will be paid for the company. The process usually begins when the company's advisors (investment bankers if the transaction involves a lot of money; perhaps a lawyer, accountant, or business broker for a smaller transaction) create a short summary of the business's history and financial status. (Sometimes the name of the business is kept confidential until a prospective buyer shows interest.) Then the summary is sent to potential buyers, who agree to keep the information confidential if they express an interest in receiving further, more detailed information. Once the possible buyers have a full picture of the corporation's assets, liabilities, and business methods, they can place their bids and increase the bids if they wish to outbid other potential buyers. (The disadvantage of the auction process is that a potential buyer that expected keen competition may discover that it is the only serious contender, and thus bid less than it might have been willing to pay for the company.) Finally, when the winning bidder emerges, the final terms of the deal (such as financing, payment schedules, who will serve on the Board of the surviving company) can be negotiated.

## LBOS & MBOS

Another type of merger/acquisition transaction that has attracted a lot of attention in recent years is the "LBO" (leveraged buyout) or "MBO" (management buyout) in which a small group of shareholders, usually led by a corporation's top management, acquires enough shares to take over the corporation. A deal is "leveraged" if the people acquiring the shares borrow most or all of the money to finance the takeover.

Typically, the buyers in an LBO or MBO agree to transfer restrictions lasting several years after the takeover (except for transfers to members of their own families)—perhaps a right of first refusal given to the corporation or the other investors; the buyers may get a "put" option (the right to sell shares back to the corporation, so they can get cash without opening up sale of the shares to outsiders). The management group in an LBO usually gets employment contracts lasting three to six years so they'll have time to implement their management strategies (and will stay around long enough to be accountable). The LBO buyers typically sign shareholder agreements dealing with the postacquisition capital structure of the company, how their shares will be voted, who will serve on the Board and as officers of the reorganized corporation, and how conflicts will be resolved.

The process of investigating a potential business purchase or combination is called the "due diligence" process: the corporate management of both businesses diligently assess the pros and cons of the deal and negotiate an agreement that is supposed to be fair to the stockholders of both corporations. It is the duty of a corporation's Board of Directors to use their business judgment to protect the interests of the stockholders, and, as explained in the section on directors' and officers' liability (pages 166–167) failure to do so makes them liable to the stockholders.

### Corporate Director's Prevention of Takeovers

One of the most controversial areas in modern corporate and securities law is just how far a Board can go to prevent a merger or takeover that the Board feels is improper. One theory is that the Board's duty as managers is to take steps to keep the corporation independent and to prevent unfair deals. Another theory is that stockholders must be given a fair chance to decide whether to accept or reject a bidder's offer for their shares. Under this theory, the Board's efforts to prevent the takeover are motivated by "entrenchment"—the desire to keep their own jobs even though the takeover would enable the stockholders to get full value for their shares immediately. The paradox is that the Board of Directors and the shareholders are supposed to be on the same side—and the Board is supposed to protect the shareholders' interests; yet often they seem to be in conflict, or even to be enemies.

### Corporate Reorganizations

For tax purposes, there are many kinds of reorganization. The most significant are the "Type A" reorganization (merger or consolidation), "Type B" (a "stock for stock" reorganization in which one corporation uses its stock to buy all or a controlling interest in the stock of the acquired corporation), and "Type C" (in which the acquiring corporation uses its stock to buy the assets of the acquired corporation instead of its stock). If the Type A, B, and C rules are followed strictly, the reorganization itself is not an event that generates federal income taxes. To be tax free, a reorganization must be motivated by a valid business purpose, and there must be a continuity of both "enterprise" and "interest" in the form of people who remain shareholders both before and after the acquisition. There are no limits on the kind of consideration (funds paid) used in a Type A reorganization; the stockholders in the nonsurviving corporation can get any combination of cash, stock in the surviving corporation, stock in the acquiring corporation (if it survives), and property. But in Type B and Type C reorganizations, nearly all the consideration must be in the form of the stock of the acquiring corporation. Stockholders who want cash instead of stock (which can fluctuate in value, and may be worth very little when the stockholders want to sell it) may resist a Type B or C reorganization.

The choice of the form of reorganization depends on practical factors (for instance, whether cash, stock, or assets are most easily available, or most acceptable to the sellers) as well as tax factors. For tax reasons, the buyer often prefers to buy assets instead of stock (because that way, the buyer gets a higher basis, or tax cost, for the assets, and thus has to pay less tax on profit if it later sells assets acquired in the transaction). However, since 1986, there is "double taxation" on an asset sale: the selling corporation pays taxes on its profit on the assets that it sells, and then the selling corporation's stockholders have taxable income when the selling corporation distributes the proceeds of the sale to them. So the question becomes whether the buyer is powerful enough to demand an asset sale (or the buyers are willing to absorb the tax consequences). Another factor is that the buyer of a corporation's assets is also stuck with its liabilities (including its risk of being sued). The buyer of stock becomes a stockholder, of course—and, unless the corporate veil can be pierced, stockholders are not personally liable for corporate liabilities.

## Hostile Takeovers

In addition to negotiated, friendly mergers and acquisitions, a certain number of hostile takeovers and takeover attempts occur each year. (Until recently, there was a clear trend showing an increasing amount of takeover activity each year; however, a number of legal and economic factors have led to a slowdown in the pace of takeover activity). Hostile takeovers create many regulatory and philosophical problems. Protakeover theorists say that the bidders shake up inefficient management and make it possible for stockholders to get the highest possible price for their shares. Antitakeover theorists say that the raiders disrupt profitable businesses, leading to break-ups, loss of jobs, and diversion of money and talent from productive use to investment bankers and lawyers.

What steps can a corporation's management take to protect the corporation against hostile takeovers? The answer depends on the type of corporation, its relationship to its stockholders, the state of incorporation, and, crucially, when the steps are taken. Merger and acquisitions law is a very fast-moving area, and today's brilliant strategy can be tomorrow's catastrophic courtroom defeat.

## Protection Against Takeovers

In a closely held corporation, a great deal of protection can be found by imposing transfer restrictions on the corporation's stock. That way, all transfers will be made to acceptable transferees, to the other stockholders, or back to the corporation. Competitors or raiders won't be allowed to buy shares. The imposition of transfer restrictions can lead to bitter conflict later on, if minority shareholders feel that they are being frozen out and are not allowed to sell their shares to the highest bidder. (Naturally, once a company has gone public, transfer restrictions won't work; the appeal of publicly held companies is that their stock can be freely traded at all times.)

A corporation's charter and bylaws can be drafted (or amended) to limit the ability of stockholders to call meetings, submit resolutions to meetings, remove directors from the Board of Directors (unless there is good cause, such as proven wrongdoing, for the removal), or act without a meeting. From management's point of view, all these actions could be used by raiders as an opening wedge in a takeover campaign. However, such measures can create terrible hostility within the corporation, if some stockholders feel that they are not trusted by others, or who fear that the current management intends to entrench itself for its own good, rather than the benefit of the company (and its stockholders) as a whole.

## State Antitakeover Laws

Many of the states have antitakeover statutes. Under "merger moratorium" statutes, once a stockholder achieves a certain level of stock ownership (e.g., 15% or 20%), it can be barred from merging with the company for a period of time (e.g., three to five years) unless the merger is approved by the company's Board of Directors. "Control share" statutes prevent certain large stockholders from voting their shares at all without the consent of the other, nonmanagement shareholders and give minority shareholders the right to dissent and appraisal (i.e., the right to have their interest in the corporation bought out for cash) if they disapprove of a merger. Some states have "fair price" laws that make sure that takeover transactions cannot be carried out unless the minority shareholders get a fair price for their stock.

## Corporation Recapitalization as a Defense

If a corporation's management is afraid of takeovers, it can recapitalize the corporation—for instance, issue a lot of new stock and bonds; borrow a lot of money; pay a gigantic dividend to its shareholders, thus emptying the treasury; or sell off its "crown jewel" (major asset) to a friendly buyer. The theory behind this strategy is that the recapitalized corporation will have so much debt that it will either have to become dramatically more efficient or go under—and that the company will be much less attractive to raiders because of its high debt levels and/or loss of significant assets. But of course this is a desperate measure; it's been called the "scorched earth" defense.

### Shareholder Rights Plans

A less drastic, but controversial, measure is the adoption of a "shareholder rights plan" (the slang term for which is a "poison pill"). These plans give a corporation's existing shareholders the right to buy stock in the corporation for a very small amount of money after a takeover. That way, the shares that the raiders acquire lose most of their value right after the takeover. Some poison pill plans even give the target company's shareholders the right to buy stock in the acquiring company at a very low price! The controversy arises in a takeover situation when some or all of the shareholders want to sell their stock to the bidder, but would lose the value of the transaction if the poison pill goes into effect. Therefore, they want (and may end up suing the Board of Directors to force) the poison pill to be "redeemed" (inactivated).

To sum up, the Board of Directors of a target company must walk a very fine line. Current law suggests that they can adopt *reasonable* antitakeover measures if there is a real threat, but must think about the interests of the corporation's stockholders, not just their own desire to keep their jobs. (Another antitakeover strategy, the "golden parachute," makes a takeover more expensive because the target company's top executives have employment contracts calling for enormous severance payments if they lose their jobs after a change in corporate control. It is easy to see this as an example of feathering their own nests at the expense of shareholders who are not directors or officers.)

Once a takeover bid begins, the Board of Directors may be able to "just say no" and block the attempt—provided that they consider the best interests of the shareholders. Some state laws let the Board consider other interests as well, such as the needs of the company's employees, bondholders, and business affiliates. But the Board must be careful not to put the company "into play" by trying to sell it or by favoring a "white knight" friendly bidder. Once a company is in play, the Board's duty is to conduct an open, honest auction so that shareholders can get the highest possible price for their shares.

## DUE DILIGENCE ROADMAP

[Note: These are factors to be considered if you are offering your business for sale or merger, or if you are contemplating acquiring another business.]

○ Corporate name and address

○ State in which it was incorporated

○ State(s) in which it has qualified as a foreign corporation and is doing business

○ Copies of its charter and bylaws

○ Capitalization—what kinds and number of shares of stock are outstanding, whether bonds have been issued, who owns the stock and bonds

○ History of its business

○ Current business—what is being manufactured or sold, customer relationships, number of employees, and so on; domestic and foreign sales, broken down by product or product line; figures showing changes in sales, prices, and profitability over time; research and development programs; planned new products

○ Debts and liabilities, including pending and threatened lawsuits; future cost of paying employee benefits (including pension and retiree health benefits)

○ Corporate assets—property owned, cash on hand, and investments in securities; trademarks, patents, and goodwill; inventory; and accounts and notes receivable. What condition are the assets in? Are they fairly valued?

○ Financial history and current statements (the heart of the due diligence process): management reports; documents filed with government agencies; financial statements, profit and loss statements, accounts receivable, inventory, business ratios (such as comparisons of assets to liabilities, current assets to current liabilities, sales to costs, sales to profits); and trends in all the figures reported

○ "Comparables": a comparison of the company to other, similar businesses to see if it is more or less efficient and profitable and to see what can be done to improve the business's operations and prospects for the future.

---

## EMPLOYMENT AGREEMENT FOR A BUSINESS BROKER

*1. Introduction:* This agreement, between Tru-Shu Boutiques, Inc. (Seller), of 73 Caroline Drive and 95B East Avenue K, Lockwood, Roosevelt, and Mitchell Vanderpool (Broker), of 22-19 35th Avenue, West Lockwood, Roosevelt, regulates the terms and conditions under which Broker is employed as sole broker to sell the Seller's business and its assets including its inventory, fixtures, and goodwill.

*2. Description of Business:* Tru-Shu Boutiques, Inc., owns and operates two shoe stores, both in leased premises, one at the Butternut Valley Mall and the other in the Veterans' Field Plaza.

*3. Broker's Authority:* The Broker is hereby authorized to contact the following potential purchasers, and use his best efforts to bring about a sale: Kaufman's Shoe Shoppes, Heel 'n' Toe, Shigemura Commercial Enterprises, and Leather Loft.

If the Broker believes that another firm is a qualified potential buyer, he may approach that firm only on prior written consent of the Seller; Broker may not approach any potential buyer without the Seller's advance consent.

*4. Purchase Price:* The Broker is employed to sell the business for a principal sum of at least $1.3 million, not including any interest payments due on the principal or any installment payment at any time.

**5. *Commission:*** If the Broker procures the sale of the business to an appropriate buyer, and the sale is consummated within 18 months of the date of this agreement, Seller will be obligated to pay the Broker a commission equal to 3% of the sale price of the business. Broker will not be entitled to a commission under any other circumstances (i.e., Broker attempts a sale to an unauthorized buyer, no authorized buyer enters into a contract with Seller, a contract is signed but the transaction is not consummated within the specified period).

If the commission does accrue and become payable, the Broker will indemnify the Seller against all claims by other persons or firms claiming brokerage commissions, finders' fees, or other amounts related to the sale of the business.

**6. *Commission Terms:*** If the sale terms call for a lump-sum payment for the business, the Broker's full commission will become due and payable at the closing of the transaction.

If the sale terms call for payment of the purchase price in installments, the commission will become payable in cash installments, at the same time as installments of the purchase price are due, and in the same proportion of the total commission that the applicable installment bears to the total sale price of the business.

**7. *Entire Agreement:*** This document represents the entire agreement between the Seller and the Broker, superseding any prior agreement between them. Only a writing signed by both parties can be used to amend, extend, terminate, or waive the agreement between the parties. The agreement will be interpreted under the laws of the state of Roosevelt and may not be assigned by either party.

## OPTION TO BUY BUSINESS

**1. *Parties:*** The *optionor* is Ruthven Caustics & Alkalis, Inc., Terra Village Industrial Park, Mancini, Adams. The *optionee* is Millenia Chemical Co., 9519 Denton Street, Hopewood, Adams.

**2. *Grant of Option:*** In return for $15,000 already paid and received, and for other good and valuable consideration, optionor hereby grants optionee a six-month option (measured from the date of this agreement) to buy the chemical manufacture and processing business operated by the optionor at the above address, for a price of $3,450,000 payable in cash and/or Millenia Chemical Co. common stock (valued for this purpose at $16.75 a share).

The contemplated acquisition includes the real property used in the optionor's business; its plant, equipment, inventory, and goodwill; and other tangible and intangible assets belonging to the optionor on the date that the optionee serves notice of exercise of the option.

**3. *Exercise of Option:*** The optionee can exercise the option at any time during the six-month term on written notice to the optionor. The notice must specify how the option price will be paid (proportion of cash to stock) and the schedule of payments, with at least one-third of the option price to be paid no later than the closing date, and the balance in no more than six equal quarterly installments bearing interest at an APR of 9%.

**4. *Closing:*** The notice must also specify a closing date at least 15, but not more than 45, days from the date of the notice of exercise.

At the closing date agreed on by optionor and optionee, the optionee will make any required payment against delivery of documents (e.g., assignments, bills of sale) which, in the opinion of optionee's counsel, transfer good marketable title to the optionee's business free and clear of all liens, encumbrances, security interests, and restrictions.

If the optionee delivers shares of its common stock in payment, the shares must be fully paid and nonassessable and must either be registered in the optionor's name or endorsed for transfer, bearing any necessary tax stamps.

**5. *Business During the Option Period:*** The optionor agrees, during the option and preclosing periods, to carry on its business in its usual fashion and to refrain from unusual transactions outside the ordinary course of business which might be detrimental to the interest potentially to be acquired by the optionee, unless the optionee has consented in advance or ratified the transactions.

**6. *Provisions Regarding the Agreement:*** This document sets out the entire agreement between the parties; modifications, amendments, or cancellations can be made only in writing signed by both optionor and optionee. Oral modifications will have no force or effect. This agreement is assignable, and both binds and benefits the heirs, successors, and assigns of the optionor and optionee. This agreement will be interpreted under the laws of the state of Adams.

## OFFER TO BUY ALL OF A CORPORATION'S STOCK

Date: _____

*1.* Albert Manning-Prior (the offeror) hereby offers to buy all the stock of Perminella, Inc., from Thomas Mitchelson, Barbara Mitchelson, Gary Trout, and Peter Sarrasin (the offerees), who own all of Perminella's stock, consisting of 2,000 shares of fully paid, nonassessable common stock. Copies of this offer have been sent to all offerees.

Perminella, Inc., is a corporation organized under the laws of the state of Lincoln, having its headquarters at the Terrace Building, Shady Lodge, Lincoln.

*2.* This offer is good until _____ , 199_____ .

*3.* If, but only if, all the offerees accept the offer on or before that date, the offeror will pay each offeree $79 per share in return for surrender of all of his or her shares, endorsed for transfer to the offeror with any necessary tax stamps attached.

*4.* If the offer is duly accepted, closing of the transaction will take place at _____ M. on _____ , 19_____ , at the offices of the law firm of Del Giorno, Carter, and Styles, 227 Bainbridge Road, Valley Acres, Lincoln.

At the closing, the offerees will tender their shares and deliver

○ Perminella, Inc.'s corporate records and papers

○ Its corporate seal, minute book, and book of share certificates

○ Tax returns and auditors' reports for the entire corporate existence of Perminella, Inc.

○ A warranty agreement signed by all the offerees to the effect that the financial statements and documents give an accurate account of the corporation's financial condition, including an agreement by the offerees to indemnify the offeror, in proportion to their stockholdings, for any claim against Perminella, Inc., that is not reflected on its balance sheet.

*5.* This offer is conditional on

○ Perminella, Inc.'s having clear title to the real estate used in its business (the corporate headquarters and the plant in the McMurdoe Industrial Park), free and clear of all encumbrances except the assumable first and second mortgages held by the Second National Bank, and to personal

property in and on such real property, free and clear of all liens and encumbrances other than the Amalgamated Silver Bank and Trust's revolving credit line
○ The absence of unsatisfied recorded judgments and/or pending litigation against Perminella
○ Perminella's continuing to carry on business as usual, refraining from transactions out of its ordinary course of business that do or could affect its assets, liabilities, or ownership of assets

Date: _____ , 199_____
Signature: _____
[If the stock is to be sold for a note, add above: Consideration for the selling shareholders' stock will consist of $_____ already paid, $_____ payable at closing; the balance of $_____ will be paid in the form of a note executed by the buyer, calling for payment in _____equal annual/quarterly/monthly amortized installments of principal and interest. The note will bear interest at the rate of _____ % APR and payable as of _____ , 199_____ .

Prepayments may be made in any amount without penalty on any regularly scheduled payment date; the obligation to make payments of reduced principal and interest, on the original schedule, will continue as long as any amount is due under the note.

Payment of the unpaid balance of principal and interest as it accrues will be secured by a first mortgage on the corporation's real estate, executed by the buyer to the sellers, in a form acceptable to counsel for the sellers.

If at any time, buyer is _____days or more in default on the note or mortgage, this agreement ends as of the date of default; sellers are entitled to cease performing under this agreement, to return of any of their shares in the selling corporation continuing to be held in escrow, and to retain any payments made prior to the breach as liquidated damages (not as a penalty).]

## Acceptance of Offer

Dear Mr. Manning-Prior:
We, all the shareholders of Perminella, Inc., hereby accept your offer to buy all 2,000 shares of the corporation's stock, as detailed in your notice of _____ , 199_____ .

## ROADMAP FOR THE SALE OF A PROPRIETORSHIP BUSINESS

○ Identify the parties and the status of each as a proprietor or corporation
○ Recite the nature of business, and the seller's desire to retire or other motivation for the sale
○ Identify the assets subject to agreement and value of each
  ○ ○ Real estate
  ○ ○ Equipment, furniture, fixtures
  ○ ○ Inventory
  ○ ○ Goodwill, customer lists
  ○ ○ Intellectual property
  ○ ○ Cash on hand and in bank accounts
  ○ ○ Accounts receivable, notes receivable, outstanding contracts

- ○ ○ Insurance policy
- ○ ○ Other
- ○ Describe the consideration for the sale: money; stock; note; assumption of debts, liabilities; other
- ○ Allocate the price paid among the assets transferred (so that the gain or loss on the individual assets can be determined)
- ○ Explain the time and manner of payment
    - ○ ○ Some on signing, balance on closing
    - ○ ○ All on closing
    - ○ ○ Deposit in escrow until closing
    - ○ ○ Installment payments—mortgage or other collateral
- ○ Will there be a personal guarantee by the buyer?
    - ○ ○ Must the buyer forfeit the deposit if purchase price not paid on time?
- ○ Settle the date, place, conditions of the closing
    - ○ ○ Delivery of transfer instruments at closing date
    - ○ ○ Payment of purchase price
    - ○ ○ Business as usual until closing
    - ○ ○ Inspection of assets
    - ○ ○ Necessary rulings, approvals
- ○ Inspection of site, books records (including customer and supplier lists)
- ○ Seller's representations
    - ○ ○ Title to property and assets
    - ○ ○ Authority to enter into agreement
    - ○ ○ Books and records accurate, complete
    - ○ ○ All outstanding obligations (liens, contracts, judgments) disclosed
    - ○ ○ No labor disputes
    - ○ ○ Copyrights, trademarks, patents valid
    - ○ ○ Compliance with all relevant business laws
    - ○ ○ Survival of representations
- ○ Buyer indemnified
- ○ Buyer assumes lease (lessor's consent to assignment obtained)
- ○ Buyer assumes outstanding contracts—contracts not listed by seller are disavowed
- ○ Assumption of collective bargaining agreements
- ○ Payment of broker's commission
- ○ Compliance with bulk sales act (e.g., UCC Art. 6)
- ○ Employment contract or "golden parachute" for the seller
- ○ Seller's covenant not to compete with the buyer (must be reasonable in time and geographic scope, must not unreasonably restrain trade or deprive the seller of the opportunity to earn a living)
- ○ Payment of sales, use tax on asset transfer
- ○ Payment of other taxes
- ○ Transfer of tax ID numbers

- ○ Insurance
- ○ Explain whether the transaction is contingent on anything (e.g., buyer accepted as franchisee, buyer gets license)
- ○ Execution of bill of sale transferring personal property
- ○ Transfer of title to cars, trucks
- ○ Warranty deed to transfer real property
- ○ Include clauses explaining who accepts the risk of loss
- ○ Describe buyer's and seller's remedies on default
- ○ Indicate whether rights under the agreement are assignable, and to what extent
- ○ Indicate the proper manner to modify the agreement
- ○ If desired, include a clause calling for arbitration of disputes (instead of litigation)
- ○ Indicate how notices required under the agreement must be given (e.g., by mail; by fax; in person; to whom, at what address; how much notice must be given)
- ○ Describe the rights of the buyer's and seller's successors and assigns
- ○ Say which state's law will be used to interpret the documents

## SALE OF A BUSINESS ROADMAP

- ○ The Seller's counsel wants provision in the documents that the broker's commission is payable only on actual consummation of the deal—preferably in the same proportions and at the same time as installment payments for the business.
- ○ An option to buy should be very specific about the duration and the assets covered.
- ○ Usually, the Buyer's counsel drafts an offer specifying the terms that would be acceptable to the Buyer as the negotiations draw to a close; this offer then serves as a negotiating point for concluding the deal.
- ○ In drawing up documents for a bulk sale, give the list of creditors as a schedule or have the Seller furnish an affidavit that there are no creditors with any right, title, or lien against the scheduled property.

---

## CONTRACT FOR SALE OF A SOLE PROPRIETORSHIP

## I. Introduction

This agreement, dated _____ , 199_____ , is entered into by Sam Richmond (Seller), a sole proprietor carrying out the business of importing, manufacturing, and purchasing textiles under the name of S. Richmond Fabrics (SRF), and Connolly Apparel, Inc. (CA), a corporation incorporated under the laws of the state of Monroe. The parties intend that CA purchase the entire business and assets of SRF, on terms and conditions described in this agreement. Sam Richmond is a sole proprietor and therefore has full power and authority to enter into this transaction; CA is authorized

to enter into this transaction by a unanimous resolution of its Board of Directors passed
_____ , 199_____ .

## II. Sale of Business

In return for consideration of $_____ , paid as described in Section IV, and adjusted on the closing
date to take into account fuel bills, insurance premiums, and other amounts that must be adjusted for
part-year ownership, Seller agrees to sell, and CA to buy, all of the SRF's business and assets, free
from all liabilities and encumbrances. OR
CA agrees to assume all liabilities disclosed on Schedule I, but disavows responsibility for any
undisclosed liabilities.

## III. Assets and Allocation of Purchase Price

The sale includes the following assets, to which the purchase price is allocated as follows, on the
assumption that cash on hand at the time of the sale will remain with the Seller:

| | |
|---|---|
| 1. Warehouse at Taft Highway near Route 23, Freetown, Monroe | $_____ |
| 2. Lease on offices at 1914 Memorial Drive, Chesterfield, Monroe, expiring _____ , 199_____ | $_____ |
| 3. Equipment, furniture, and fixtures as described in the attached Schedule A | $_____ |
| 4. Inventory on premises or to be delivered on or before the closing | $_____ |
| 5. Accounts and notes receivable as described in attached Schedule B | $_____ |
| 6. Outstanding contracts (Schedule C) | $_____ |
| 7. Goodwill | $_____ |
| 8. Bank accounts (Schedule D) | $_____ |

## IV. Payment Schedule

Seller hereby acknowledges receipt of a deposit of $_____ OR CA's deposit of $_____ has been
placed in escrow and will be maintained there until the closing.

The balance of the purchase price will be paid at the closing. If the closing does not take place for
any reason other than Seller's failure to comply, or demonstrated falsity of any of Seller's
representations, CA will forfeit its deposit. OR

The purchase price will be paid in six equal installments: one on signing of this agreement, one at
closing, then quarterly for the next year. Quarterly installments will bear interest at the rate of 10%
APR on the unpaid balance.

To secure the buyer's obligation to pay the unpaid balance, the seller will have a continuing
security interest in the inventory, equipment, furniture, and fixtures covered by this agreement, as
well as those later acquired by the buyer in the course of operating the business, governed by Article
9 of Chapter 308 of the Laws of Madison. On or before the closing date, the buyer agrees to execute

any note or financing statement reasonably requested by the seller, for the perfection and protection of the seller's security interest.

On the buyer's default in paying any required installment, or if the buyer sells, pledges, or disposes of its interest in the business while the note is still outstanding without getting the prior consent of the seller, the seller will be entitled to accelerate the buyer's remaining obligation and to demand payment of the entire balance then outstanding, plus reimbursement of reasonable attorneys' fees that the seller incurs to collect the accelerated amount.

## V. Closing

Closing of this transaction will take place at the offices of the law firm of Saltmarsh, Essex, and Brown, 329 West 4th Avenue, Bonnieville, Madison, on _____ , 199_____ , at 10 A.M., or at any other date, place, and time mutually agreed on. At the closing, CA will pay [by certified/cashier's check] the amount due on closing as per Section IV of this agreement.

Seller will deliver the instruments needed to transfer SRF and its assets to CA, free and clear of all encumbrances [other than encumbrances specifically disclosed to, and assumed by, CA], such as a warranty deed to the warehouse, a lease to the office bearing the lessor's consent to assignment of the balance of the lease term, bills of sale transferring title to personal property, transfer of sales tax number E29-1974-3319, titles and registrations for automobiles and trucks, tax stamps, and documents evidencing compliance with the Bulk Sales Act, Section 191.35 et. seq. of the Annotated Statutes of Madison.

At the closing, the purchase price will be adjusted to take into account allocation of insurance premiums, fuel bills, tax payments, and other items for part-year ownership. The buyer will become liable for real estate taxes and assessments by state and local taxing authorities as of the closing date. The buyer is obligated to notify the authorities of the change in ownership. If the buyer fails to make all required tax payments, the seller has the right to make the payments and, with or without notice to the buyer, to add the amount so paid to the unpaid balance remaining under this contract.

As of and after the closing date, the buyer agrees to maintain fire and casualty insurance coverage representing the full and fair market value of the owned business premises and the contents of leased premises, and at all times at least equal to any balance owed to the seller under this contract. If the buyer fails to do so, the seller has the right to obtain insurance coverage; the premiums for the coverage so obtained, up to the minimum required amount, operate as an obligation of the buyer to the seller, subject to the same security and bearing the same interest rate as the unpaid balance due to the seller under this contract.

## VI. Seller's Representations and Warranties

Seller is duly authorized and qualified to carry on the textile business in the State of Monroe, has obtained all necessary licenses and maintained them in good standing, and has been in full compliance with all applicable statutes and regulations as long as the business has been operated.

Seller is not a party to any collective bargaining agreements involving his work force.

No broker or finder has been involved in this transaction. OR
Seller admits that Jeffrey Rosenshein. a [licensed] business broker has been instrumental in procuring this transaction, and his fee of $_____ will be paid at the closing.

Schedule E attached to this agreement is a complete and accurate balance sheet of SRF, prepared in accordance with GAAP as of _____ , 199_____ , fully and fairly representing SRF's financial position as of that date.

Seller has good marketable title to all assets set out in Schedules A–E, free and clear of all [undisclosed] encumbrances.

All required taxes have been paid up to _____ , 199_____ ; the balance sheet set out in Schedule E accurately reflects the impact of all federal, state, and local taxes (e.g., income, franchise, sales, inventory, excise).

Seller's motive for this sale is providing funds for his impending retirement. To ensure a smooth transition, Seller agrees to serve as First Vice-President of SRF for the term of two years after the closing at a salary of $60,000 per year and to use his best effort to disclose his methods of operation and his business contacts to CA during this time. After the two-year period has expired, he agrees not to compete with CA by serving as officer, director, or employee of, or consultant to, any business manufacturing, converting, or importing textiles, or manufacturing clothing or household items, within the state of Madison for a term of ten years. Nor will he directly or indirectly solicit any SRF employee, supplier or customer in an effort to induce him/her/it to cease working for or doing business with the successor firm.

## VII. The Preclosing Period

In the interim period between signing of this agreement and closing, seller agrees to continue to operate SRF in the ordinary course of its business, to carry out its contracts, and to refrain from disposing of inventory and assets outside the normal course of business.

Risk of loss by fire, flood, wind damage, and explosion, and impact remains on the seller until the closing. However, if the amount of damage or destruction to the Seller's premises, equipment, and inventory exceeds $_____, the buyer has the right to terminate this agreement and demand return of the entire deposit [from the escrow agent]; repayment of the deposit to the buyer discharges the payor from liability. OR

If property covered under this agreement is damaged or destroyed before the closing (except for wear and tear or consumption of raw materials in the ordinary course of business), the buyer has the right to collect the insurance proceeds; the purchase price of insured damaged assets will not be reduced. If the dollar value of the loss or damage exceeds _____ % of the purchase price, the buyer has the right, instead, to terminate the contract and have the deposit returned.

## VIII. Provisions Respecting This Contract

This agreement represents the entire agreement between Seller and CA, superseding any earlier agreements. As such, it can be modified only in a writing signed by both parties. This agreement is assignable by either party and will bind and benefit the heirs, successors, and assignees of both parties. This agreement will be interpreted under the laws of the state of Madison.

## Optional Clauses

For franchised business, add:

Seller agrees to sell the business's goodwill and its exclusive right to use the trade name Polar Mousse and the other appurtenances of the Polar Mousse franchise, and to assign to the buyer the Polar Mousse franchise agreement dated _____ , 199_____ . ☐ The franchise agreement, by its terms, is freely transferrable. □ The franchisor's consent to the transfer has been granted in a letter dated _____ , 199_____ . □ This agreement is conditional upon the seller's obtaining the franchisor's consent to assignment of the franchise agreement not later than _____ , 199_____ ; if consent is not obtained by that time, the buyer has the option of terminating this agreement and receiving back any deposit or other thing of value tendered.

## AGREEMENT FOR TYPE A REORGANIZATION (MERGER)

### Introduction

After extensive negotiations and advice from attorneys, accountants, investment bankers, brokers, and others, two corporations (Marchigiano Corp. and Cinnabasil, Inc.) and their stockholders agree that it is in the best interests of all parties if the two corporations enter into an agreement and plan of merger, under which Marchigiano Corp. will be the surviving corporation and Cinnabasil, Inc., will be merged into it and will not survive the merger. Marchigiano Corp. will issue shares of its stock to the stockholders of Cinnabasil, Inc., as consideration for their interest in the nonsurviving corporation. The parties agree that, subject to the representations, warranties, and covenants contained in this agreement, the merger will occur on _____ , 199 ____ ("effective date"), and a Plan of Merger will be filed with the appropriate corporate activities.

### Representations by Cinnabasil, Inc.

Cinnabasil, Inc., and its stockholders jointly and severally represent and warrant that the following statements are true as of the effective date:

*1. Organization and Standing:* Cinnabasil, Inc., was duly organized under the laws of the state of Roosevelt on _____ , 19 ____ , and since that date, it has been doing business in Roosevelt and is duly authorized and licensed to do so, and is also qualified as a foreign corporation to do business in the states of Madison and Adams. Cinnabasil, Inc., has never done business in any state in which it was not authorized to do so.

*2. Capitalization:* The authorized capitalization of Cinnabasil, Inc., consists of 25,000 shares of common stock, of which 15,000 shares have been issued and are fully paid and nonassessable, plus 5,000 shares of 5% cumulative preferred stock, all of which have been issued, are fully paid and nonassessable, and all dividends on which are up to date and paid. No stock has ever been issued in violation of any stockholder's preemptive rights. Cinnabasil, Inc., is not subject to any obligation to issue securities under any option, right, or warrant arrangement.

*3. Stock Ownership:* The names, addresses, and shares owned by each of the Cinnabasil stockholders are set out in Appendix A attached to this agreement.

*4. Financial Statements:* The stockholders of Cinnabasil have furnished Marchigiano, Inc., with financial statements and documents that have been [audited and] prepared in accordance with GAAP, consistently applied throughout the relevant period, giving a complete and accurate picture of Cinnabasil's financial condition for the relevant period, such financial statements consisting of

○ A balance sheet as of _____ , 199 ____ ("balance sheet date")

○ An income statement for the _____ -month period ending on the balance sheet date

○ Balance sheets, income statements, and statements of the source and application of funds for the five fiscal years ending immediately prior to the balance sheet date
○ A statement of liabilities as of the balance sheet date (Appendix B)
○ A list of accounts and notes receivable, discounted for bad-debt reserves (Appendix C)
○ A statement of fixed assets (Appendix D), all of which have been appropriately serviced and maintained in good condition. Copies of leases covering such fixed assets are maintained in Cinnabasil, Inc.'s offices available for inspection by Marchigiano, Inc.
5. *Title and Disposition of Assets:* As far as any Cinnabasil stockholder is aware, Cinnabasil has good marketable title to all real and personal property that it owns and uses in its business and has never bought, sold, or disposed of any business asset other than in the ordinary course of business. All assets disclosed to Marchigiano, Inc., as assets of Cinnabasil are owned free and clear and are not subject to any lien, lease, mortgage, or other encumbrance or charge other than those disclosed as part of Appendix D.

## Covenants of Cinnabasil Stockholders

Cinnabasil, Inc., and its stockholders jointly and severally covenant that they will maintain the status quo between the date of this Agreement and the effective date of the merger, that is

1. Cinnabasil's stockholders will not permit Cinnabasil to do any of these unless Marchigiano, Inc., has first given its consent in writing to
○ Enter into a merger or consolidation (or agreement for merger or consolidation) with any other corporation
○ Amend its Articles of Incorporation
○ Issue any securities
○ Redeem or repurchase any of its outstanding securities
○ Declare or pay a dividend
○ Make or agree to make any payment or expenditure outside the ordinary course of business (including salary increases or bonuses to the corporation's employees)
○ Sell or dispose of any property outside the ordinary course of business
Furthermore, the Cinnabasil stockholders agree to use their best efforts to induce Cinnabasil to do the following:
○ Continue to carry out its business as before, continuing to use the same methods of production and marketing
○ Continue to perform under all its contracts and maintain business relationships with sales representatives, customers, and suppliers
○ Keep its business property and assets in good working condition, maintaining insurance coverage in commercially reasonable types and amounts

## Representations Made by Marchigiano, Inc., and Its Stockholders

Marchigiano, Inc., and its stockholders jointly and severally warrant and represent that all the following are true as of the effective date:

1. *Organization and Standing:* Marchigiano is a Roosevelt corporation, duly organized on _____ , 199____ and in good standing ever since. It does not do business in any other state.
2. *Capitalization:* Marchigiano's entire capitalization consists of 10,000 shares of no-par common

stock, 5,000 of which are issued, fully paid, and nonassessable. Marchigiano's Articles of Incorporation specifically deny the existence of preemptive rights in the corporation's shares and do not give the corporation the power to issue rights, warrants, or options that would call for the issuance of further securities.

John Levasseur, Adeline Conti, Peter Dawlish, the Gary Family Trust, and Sarah Porterfield as guardian for Theodore Porterfield (a minor) each own 1,000 shares of Marchigiano's stock. Their holdings are free and clear of all liens and encumbrances.

**3. *Consideration:*** Marchigiano is managed directly by its shareholders, without a Board of Directors. The shareholders have unanimously resolved, by a resolution dated _____ , 199 ____ (a copy of which is attached to this agreement) to issue the 5,000 shares of common stock which are authorized but remain unissued, and to distribute them to the Cinnabasil shareholders in proportion to their premerger ownership of Cinnabasil shares.

## Conditions on the Merger

The Cinnabasil shareholders will not be obligated to go through with the merger transaction unless all of the following conditions are met on or before the effective date:

**1. *Truth:*** All representations made by Marchigiano and its shareholders are true, and Marchigiano delivers to Cinnabasil a certificate signed by each shareholder attesting to the truth of the representations.

**2. *No Material Adverse Change:*** Marchigiano's business and assets, operations, and financial conditions continue normally (including the normal effects of the business cycle) and have not undergone any material adverse change that is atypical of its seasonal operations and that would materially impair Marchigiano's ability to consummate the merger or the value of the stock issued to Cinnabasil stockholders.

**3. *Opinion of Counsel:*** Cinnabasil receives an opinion from Marchigiano's attorney stating that
○ Marchigiano is a corporation validly organized and in good standing, carrying out business in a lawful manner pursuant to any required licenses
○ All of Marchigiano's issued securities are valid, fully paid, nonassessable, were properly issued and do not represent a violation of the preemptive rights of any person; that there are no rights, warrants, or options outstanding that would affect the rights of Cinnabasil stockholders who receive Marchigiano stock
○ Entering into this merger agreement is a proper corporate activity, which has been approved by Marchigiano's Board of Directors and stockholders.

## Other Provisions

**1. *Assignment:*** The Cinnabasil stockholders will not have the right to assign their rights under this agreement; the agreement is equally binding upon the Cinnabasil stockholders and their heirs or legal representatives. Marchigiano will have the right at any time after the effective date to transfer the Cinnabasil stock to a wholly owned subsidiary of Marchigiano.

**2. *Notices:*** Notices may be sent to each corporation at its registered address, and to stockholders at their address as listed on the corporation's stock transfer books.

Date: _____ , 199____
Signed, Marchigiano, by: _____
Cinnabasil, by: _____

# PLAN OF MERGER

This Plan of Merger, dated _____ , 199 ____ , sets out the terms and conditions of a merger scheduled to take place with an effective date of _____ , 199 ____ between the "constituent corporations," Mavor Corp. and Binstead Enterprises, Inc., both of which are Madison corporations. The Boards of Directors of both corporations, upon consideration and skilled professional advice, have determined that the best interests of both corporations mandate the adoption of a plan of merger under which Mavor Corp. will be merged into Binstead Enterprises, which will remain as the surviving corporation, with all shares of Mavor Corp. stock being converted into shares of Binstead Enterprises stock. Pursuant to this plan, the shareholders have entered into a merger agreement containing various representations, covenants, and warranties.

*1. Surviving Corporation:* As of the effective date, the two corporations will be merged into Binstead Enterprises, which will continue to do business as a Madison corporation, with a registered office in Madison. The Board of Directors of the surviving corporation shall consist of 11 directors, 7 drawn from the premerger Binstead Enterprises Board of Directors, 4 from the premerger Mavor Corp. Board.

When the merger becomes effective, the Certificate of Incorporation and Bylaws of Binstead Enterprises will constitute the Certificate of Incorporation and Bylaws of the surviving corporation until and unless they are amended. Binstead Enterprises, as surviving corporation, will succeed to and possess all rights, privileges, powers, franchises, and other attributes of both constituent corporations. Actions approved by Mavor Corp.'s officers, directors, and/or stockholders before the effective date will continue to be effective corporate actions that bind the surviving corporation.

However, to prevent impairment of the rights of creditors, all debts and liens of the constituent corporations also accrue to the surviving corporation as if it had originally been obligated under them. Any legal action or proceeding pending against either constituent corporation on the effective date can be maintained against the constituent corporation as if the merger had not occurred, or Binstead Enterprises can be substituted as a party.

The surviving corporation will maintain books of account and records on which the assets, liabilities, accounts, and reserves of each constituent corporation will either be carried at their values for the records of the constituent corporations or will be adjusted as required by generally accepted accounting principles.

The corporate existence of Mavor Corp. will be terminated as of the effective date of the merger.

*2. Consummation of Merger:* To carry out this merger, every share of Mavor Corp. stock outstanding on the effective date will be automatically converted into one-half share of Binstead Enterprises stock, and the former Mavor Corp. shareholders will be directed to surrender their Mavor shares in return for a certificate for the appropriate number of Binstead Enterprises shares. However, a cash payment of $ ____ per share will be made in lieu of fractional shares.

3. The plan of merger may be terminated at any time before the effective date on consent of the Board of Directors of both constituent corporations.

4. If the Boards of Directors do not choose to terminate the plan, the plan will be submitted to the stockholders of each constituent corporation for ratification. If ratification is obtained, the constituent corporations will then execute, file, and record all documents, and perform all other necessary acts, required to effectuate a merger from the corporate, regulatory, and tax viewpoints.

5. The merger becomes effective upon approval of the plan of merger by each constituent

corporation and the filing of verified Articles of Merger and a copy of the Plan of Merger, as required by the laws of the state of Madison, with the Secretary of State for the state of Madison. THE CONSTITUENT CORPORATIONS HAVE SIGNED AND SEALED THIS PLAN OF MERGER AS EVIDENCE OF THE TERMS OF THE PLAN.

Date: _____ , 199____
Mavor Corp., by: _____
Binstead Enterprises, by: _____
Witnesses and Notary Affidavit: _____

## ARTICLES OF MERGER (for Filing with Secretary of State)

### Articles of Merger of Domestic Corporations

To the Secretary of State:

Please be advised that, in compliance with Chapter 19B of the Corporate Code of the state of Tyler, Rolling-Kitchn, Inc., and Red Tablecloth Trucks, Inc., have adopted a plan of merger under which Red Tablecloth Trucks, Inc., will be the surviving corporation.

Each constituent corporation is a Tyler corporation in good standing. Prior to the merger, Rolling-Kitchn, Inc., had 5,000 authorized and issued common shares and 1,000 authorized and issued preferred shares, all entitled to vote on merger transactions. At a meeting held on, _____ , 199 ____ , the holders of 4,000 shares of the common and all 1,000 shares of the preferred voted to approve the merger (thus satisfying the 75% supermajority requirement for merger transactions imposed by the corporation's Articles of Incorporation).

Prior to the merger, Red Tablecloth Trucks, Inc.'s capitalization consisted of 10,000 shares of Class A voting common stock and 2,000 shares of Class B nonvoting common stock, of which only the former were entitled to vote on merger transactions. At a meeting held _____ , 199 ____ , the holders of 8,712 of the Class A common shares voted to approve the merger. Thus, the attached Plan of Merger was adopted by both corporations.

Date: _____ , 199____
Rolling-Kitchn, Inc., by its President and Secretary
Red Tablecloth Trucks, by its President and Secretary

## CERTIFICATE OF MERGER (Issued by Secretary of State)

### Office of Secretary of State for the State of Roosevelt
### Certificate of Merger of Domestic Corporations

I, Walter Benton, Secretary of State, hereby certify that the appropriate documents, properly signed and in proper form, consisting of Articles of Merger and Plan of Merger between two domestic corporations have been deposited in my office on _____ , 199 ____ . These documents evidence a merger between Franny's Finery, Inc. (the nonsurviving corporation), and Chatfield Hall Apparel, Inc. (the surviving corporation).

By the authority vested in me by the laws of the state of Roosevelt, I hereby issue this certificate of the merger of Franny's Finery, Inc., into Chatfield Hall Apparel, Inc.

Date: _____ , 199____
Walter Benton, Secretary of State

# CONSOLIDATION AGREEMENT

[Note: Mergers and consolidations are both "Type A" reorganizations for tax purposes. The difference between the two is that, in a merger, Corporation A merges into Corporation B, and Corporation A's legal existence is terminated; in a consolidation, Corporation A and Corporation B are both terminated to create a new Corporation C. Therefore, a consolidation involves an extra step: incorporating a new Corporation C and issuing its stock.]

*1. Parties:* In order to create by consolidation a new corporation to be known as Entwhistle & Co., Inc. ("ECI"), the Herbert Entwhistle Corp. ("HE"), the Participle Group, Inc. ("PGI"), and their stockholders enter into this Consolidation Agreement, dated _____ , 199 ____ .

*2. Consolidation:* Subject to the terms and conditions set out in this Agreement, on the effective date (scheduled as _____ , 199 ____ or as adjourned), HE and PGI will enter into Articles of Consolidation (to be filed with the Secretary of State) expressing a Plan of Consolidation under which the HE and PGI stockholders will surrender their shares in exchange for newly issued shares of ECI stock. HE stockholders will receive one share of ECI stock for each share surrendered; PGI stockholders will receive two-thirds of a share of ECI stock for each share surrendered. However, to avoid odd lots and fractional shares, a cash payment of $ ____ per HE and $ ____ per PGI share will be made to anyone who otherwise would receive fractional shares or shares that are not a multiple of 100.

*3. Surrender of Shares:* The HE and PGI stockholders agree to endorse their stock certificates in blank or execute stock powers in blank (with signature guarantees provided by a national bank) and to obtain and pay for all necessary stock transfer tax stamps.

*4. ECI Stock:* The authorized capitalization of ECI will consist of 25,000 shares of common stock, $5 par, of which 15,000 will be issued in connection with the consolidation, and 5,000 shares of 7% cumulative preferred stock, of which 2,500 shares will be issued in connection with the consolidation.

*5. Representations and Warranties:* HE and PGI and their stockholders each jointly and severally represent and warrant to their counterparts that the following are true:

○ The corporation is duly organized, in good standing, and is qualified as a foreign corporation in all states in which it is doing business.

○ Its authorized capitalization, issued and outstanding shares, and the names, addresses, and holdings of its stockholders are as set forth on Schedule A (by HE) and Schedule I (by PGI). All issued stock is validly issued, fully paid, and nonassessable, and was not issued in contravention of preemptive rights. Neither corporation can be compelled to issue any stock pursuant to any right, option, or warrant.

○ The balance sheet as of the balance sheet date, _____ , 199 ____ , the income statement for the ____ months ending on the balance sheet date, and the financial statements for the five-year period ending on the balance sheet dates furnished to their counterparts are complete, current as of their stated dates, accurate, and prepared in accordance with GAAP.

○ The corporation has good marketable title to all real and personal property used in its business, except for liens and encumbrances as disclosed on Schedule B (by HE) and Schedule II (by PGI).

○ The corporation is not in default on any tax payment, or under any contract, agreement, or loan [except as disclosed/except for legitimate disputes].

**6. *Covenants by Stockholders:*** The HE and PGI stockholders each covenant that, in the interim period between the signing of this agreement and the effective date of the merger, they will permit their counterparts reasonable access to their business operations, books, and records during normal business hours and will furnish any financial or operating data or other information reasonably requested as part of the consolidation process.

The stockholders agree that they will induce their corporations, during the interim period,

○ To maintain normal business operations, including employment and customer and supplier relationships

○ To maintain all raw materials, inventory, business equipment, and business premises, in good usable condition, including routine maintenance and maintenance of insurance coverage in commercially reasonable types and amounts

○ To continue to perform under all material contracts and agreements (except insofar as there are legitimate disputes that the corporation, on advice of counsel, believes will excuse performance).

The stockholders agree that they will not give their consent to the corporation, during the interim period,

○ To amend its charter or bylaws

○ To issue any securities

○ To declare or pay any dividend in cash or property

○ To pay a bonus to any officer or director, or increasing the compensation of any officer or director

○ To make, or enter into an agreement to make, any expenditure outside the ordinary course of business

○ To encumber or agree to encumber corporate assets

○ To sell, exchange, dispose of, or agree to do any of those with respect to any corporate asset other than in the ordinary course of business

○ To merge or consolidate with any corporation other than in pursuance of this agreement *unless* the other corporation gives its advance written consent

**7. *Conditions to the Closing:*** The obligations of each corporation and its stockholders to consummate the consolidation are dependent on

○ Each corporation and its stockholders having received a copy of Board and stockholder resolutions authorizing the other corporation to enter into the consolidation

○ The representations and warranties of the other corporation being true

○ The delivery of a certificate signed by each of the other corporation's stockholders to the effect that all representations and warranties are true, and all of the corporation's and stockholders' obligations have been performed.

**8. *Reaffirmation:*** Stockholders of both corporations agree, once they have become stockholders of the new corporation ECI, to use their best efforts to induce ECI to reaffirm and ratify the covenants contained in this Agreement.

**9. *Survivorship:*** All warranties, covenants, representations, and guarantees survive the consolidation transaction.

## SECRETARY'S CERTIFICATE

Loretta Gamson, Secretary of Ensigns Right, Inc., a Madison corporation, hereby certifies that, in her role as Secretary of the Corporation, she served as Secretary of a regular/special meeting of Ensigns Right, Inc., held on _____ , 199 ____ . On the agenda for that meeting was consideration of a Plan of Merger and Articles of Merger between that corporation and Rippling Colours Ltd., under which Ensigns Right, Inc., is the surviving/nonsurviving corporation.

At the meeting, held on due notice to all shareholders, the holders of 17,265 shares voted in person or by proxy. Of those votes, 13,906 were cast in favor of adoption of the merger. Ensigns Right, Inc.'s charter permits a merger on the vote of a majority of the corporation's Board of Directors (which voted unanimously to approve the merger on _____ , 199 ____ ) and the ratification by a simple majority of its shareholders. Thus, the necessary corporate approval has been obtained for the merger transaction.

Date: _____ , 199____
Signed, Loretta Gamson, Secretary
Date: _____ Today, a person who identified herself as Loretta Gamson and as the Secretary of Ensigns Right, Inc., appeared before me and swore that all statements made above were accurate and truthful.
Signed: _____ Notary Public Commission
Number: ____ Commission Expires: _____


## AGREEMENT FOR TYPE B REORGANIZATION
### (Stock for Stock)

The purpose of this agreement, between Bomoxa Corp. ("Bomoxa"), a corporation incorporated in the state of Fillmore, and James Towson, Marjorie Fischer, and Albert Pontormo ("Stockholders") is to govern the stock for stock ("Type B") reorganization of Grafton Lumber & Timber, Inc. ("Grafton").

## A. Exchange of Shares

*1.* On the closing date, each stockholder agrees to transfer 1,500 shares of Grafton stock (par value $25 per share) to Bomoxa, receiving in return a certificate in negotiable form representing shares of Bomoxa common stock (par value $10 per share) with a value of $75,000 per stockholder. The number of Bomoxa shares to be transferred will be based on the closing bid price of Bomoxa stock on the Chicago over-the-counter market on the day before the closing.

*2.* If the value so determined would result in the delivery of a fractional number of shares to a stockholder, the stockholder in question will receive the next highest whole number of shares.

*3.* Bomoxa acquires the Grafton shares, and Grafton stockholders acquire the Bomoxa shares, for investment, not for distribution or resale, and no resales will be made except in compliance with Rule 145(d) promulgated under the Securities Act of 1933.

## B. Closing

*1.* Subject to the conditions described below, the closing will be held on _____ , 199 ____ , at _____ , at the Bomoxa Corp. headquarters, 3904 Acacia Lane, Stillwater, Fillmore (or on any other date or at any other place agreed to by Bomoxa and all stockholders).

*2.* On or before the closing date, the stockholders must, individually or collectively,

○ Deliver their Grafton stock certificates, endorsed in blank and with signatures guaranteed by a bank or trust company, to Bomoxa.

○ Transfer complete and correct copies of Grafton's Articles of Incorporation, bylaws, minute books, and stock transfer books.

○ Provide general releases (in a form acceptable to Bomoxa's counsel) of any claims the stockholders have against Grafton or its officers, directors, agents, and employees, accruing on or before the date of the closing—except for claims for accrued salaries earned in the ordinary course of business.

○ Provide Bomoxa with an opinion of Grafton's counsel (in a form acceptable to Bomoxa's counsel) to the effect that

○ ○ Grafton is validly incorporated and in good standing under the laws of Fillmore and that it has validly qualified and is in good standing as a foreign corporation in each other state in which it is doing business.

○ ○ Grafton's stock is validly issued, fully paid and nonassessable.

○ ○ The certificates for a total of 4,500 shares of common stock delivered by the Grafton shareholders to Bomoxa represent all the issued and outstanding shares of Grafton stock.

○ ○ Grafton's Articles of Incorporation, bylaws, resolutions and share certificates are free from any provisions forbidding or limiting this Type B reorganization.

○ ○ The Type B reorganization does not violate any state or federal laws.

○ ○ Grafton has complied with all federal, state, and local laws and taken all required corporate actions and filed all required returns and reports.

○ ○ Each stockholder has good and marketable title to his or her Grafton shares and has full power and authority to dispose of the stock as he or she wishes; after the exchange, Bomoxa will have good marketable title to the Grafton shares free and clear of all liens, charges, and encumbrances.

○ ○ This agreement has been duly and validly signed and delivered by each stockholder and is valid and binding on them, according to the terms of the agreement.

○ ○ Counsel has no knowledge of any pending or prospective litigation or claim against Grafton or relating to the Grafton shares to be transferred at the closing; counsel has no knowledge of any facts adversely affecting Grafton's title to any of its property, or any stockholder's title to his or her Grafton shares.

## C. Representations, Warranties, and Agreements of Each Grafton Stockholder

*1.* That the shares to be transferred are held free and clear of any and all liens, claims, encumbrances, voting trusts, and/or voting agreements.

*2.* That he or she can and does convey clear and unencumbered title in Grafton shares to Bomoxa.

*3.* That, to the best of his or her knowledge, no person, business, or corporation owns any interest in any intellectual property (patent, patent application, invention, copyright, trademark, trade secret, trade name) used by Grafton in its business or products.

*4.* That he or she is not a party to, and is not aware of, any agreements restricting Grafton's business.

*5.* That he or she will not compete with Bomoxa in the line of business formerly carried out by Grafton, within a 35-mile radius of the city of Stillwater, for a period of five years after the signing of this agreement. Because remedies at law are inadequate when covenants not to compete are breached, Bomoxa will be entitled to injunctive relief in case of breach.

*6.* That he or she has not dealt with a broker or finder in connection with this reorganization transaction.

## D. Representations with Regard to Grafton Made by All Stockholders Jointly and Severally

*1.* Grafton is a corporation validly organized and in good standing under the laws of Fillmore and validly qualified as a foreign corporation in all other states in which it is doing business. It has the corporate power to carry on its business as now conducted. Its authorized capitalization consists of 4,500 shares of common stock (par value $25/share), all of which is validly issued, fully paid, nonassessable, outstanding, and held by the signing shareholders, and all of which will be transferred to Bomoxa pursuant to this agreement.

*2.* Grafton has no subsidiaries and does not own any interest in any other business.

*3.* Grafton has no authorized but unissued stock.

*4.* The documents submitted in connection with this transaction and described as Articles of Incorporation as amended, bylaws as amended, and minutes of meetings are complete, true, and correct copies of the originals.

*5.* All financial statements submitted to Bomoxa (covering the past five years) and all Grafton books and records are complete, correct, prepared in accordance with GAAP, and represent a true and correct statement of Grafton's financial condition as of their respective dates. All assets described in the books and records actually exist and are in Grafton's possession at its headquarters, factories, warehouses, or at _____ .

*6.* Grafton has no liabilities or obligations other than those incurred in the ordinary course of its business or disclosed in the financial statements provided in connection with this transaction.

*7.* There has been no material adverse change in Grafton's condition since _____ , 199_____ , the date of the balance sheet provided in connection with this transaction; there have been no changes in financial condition other than those occurring in the ordinary course of business. Stockholders have no knowledge of any developments or threatened developments materially adverse to Grafton's business.

*8.* There are no suits or administrative proceedings in process or pending against Grafton or in connection with the stock to be transferred in this reorganization.

*9.* The stockholders have no knowledge of any pending or contemplated action to condemn real property owned or used by Grafton, or to change the zoning or building ordinances affecting such property.

*10.* Grafton's title to intellectual property used in its business (patents, patent applications, copyrights, trademarkets, trade names, trade secrets) is good; all applications have been filed, and all registrations and grants are current and in good standing in all relevant jurisdictions. Grafton has not sold or licensed any interest in any such intellectual property in any way that conflicts with the proprietary rights of other owners of intellectual property.

*11.* All statements made, and information provided to, Bomoxa concerning Grafton are complete, true, and accurate. No material fact has been withheld from Bomoxa.

## E. Representations Made by Bomoxa to Grafton Shareholders, Effective as If Made on the Closing Date

*1.* Bomoxa's authorized capitalization consists of 10,000 issued and outstanding shares of no-par common stock.

*2.* When Bomoxa stock is issued to Grafton's shareholders, the stock will be duly and validly issued, fully paid, and nonassessable.

*3.* Bomoxa has the corporate power to enter into this reorganization. The reorganization transaction does not violate its Articles of Incorporation, bylaws, or any other agreement entered into with any party. Bomoxa's participation in this transaction is duly authorized by a validly adopted resolution of its Board of Directors (dated _____ , 199____ ), ratified by its stockholders on _____ , 199____ .

*4.* Bomoxa has provided the stockholders with true, complete, and accurate copies of Bomoxa's Articles of Incorporation and bylaws as amended, and of its Annual Report to Stockholders for its 19____–19____ fiscal years, certified by William McMurdoe, CPA. Since _____ , 199____ there has been no material adverse change in Bomoxa's financial or other condition.

## F. Further Assurances and Indemnification by Grafton Stockholders

*1.* The stockholders agree that they will sign and deliver documents, take lawful oaths, give depositions or testify in court, or take any other action reasonably requested by Bomoxa, its successors, or their legal counsel in order to perfect title to the Grafton shares transferred under this agreement, or to Grafton's property. If the actions are made necessary by the default of the stockholders, the stockholders will pay the expenses of the actions; otherwise, Bomoxa will pay the expenses, but will not otherwise compensate the shareholders for undertaking the necessary actions.

*2.* Stockholders will indemnify Grafton and Bomoxa and hold them harmless for all claims at all times after the closing date, and will pay all costs, expenses, and legal fees in respect of

o o Damages or deficiencies suffered by Bomoxa due to any misrepresentation contained in this agreement, or due to breach of any warranty or noncompliance by the stockholders.

o o Any loss or deficiency sustained by Grafton, over and above the reserves set aside for the purpose in Grafton's balance sheet, resulting from failure of any accounts receivable to be paid before the closing date.

o o Tax and other accrued absolute or contingent liabilities and claims against Grafton existing at the time of the closing, or arising out of preclosing transactions or events. However, stockholders will not be liable for claims against Grafton to the extent that the liability or claim was deducted in calculating Grafton's balance sheet, or for obligations that Grafton is required to perform after the closing date in the ordinary course of its business, or under agreements mentioned in or consistent with this plan of reorganization.

## G. Other Provisions

*1.* If any provision of this agreement is later found to be invalid, it will be severed, and the valid portions of the agreement will continue in full force and effect.

**2.** All of this agreement's terms, conditions, warranties, representations, and guarantees will survive the transfer of Grafton's shares at the closing.

**3.** This agreement binds and benefits Bomoxa's successors and assignees, and the next of kin, legatees, successors, assignees, and legal representatives of the stockholders.

**4.** This document (with attachments) constitutes the entire agreement between Bomoxa and the stockholders and supersedes all earlier and contemporaneous agreements dealing with the same subject matter. If separate counterparts of this agreement are signed, together they will constitute a single agreement.

**5.** Notices may be faxed, delivered in person, or sent by registered mail to any party at the address disclosed during the negotiation period, or other address later specified in writing to the other parties.

**6.** This contract will be interpreted under the laws of the state of Fillmore.

IN WITNESS TO ALL OF THE ABOVE, THE PARTIES HAVE SIGNED THIS AGREEMENT ON _____ , 199_____ .

Stockholders: _____                                                  BOMOXA

By _____ , President

[Seal]


## NONCOMPETE: NONUSE OF NAME

Gregory Salmon and Todd Brinker, sellers of the business, agree not to use or cause to be used the names "Salker," "Brinmon," "Salmon," "Brinker," or any name deceptively similar to the transferred names of "Salker" and "Brinmon" in connection with any landscape architecture business in the United States for a term of ten years. The names "Salker" and "Brinmon" are hereby transferred and assigned to the purchaser of the business in return for the sum of $25,000, to be paid as part of the consideration for the sale of the business.


## LIQUIDATED DAMAGES FOR NONCOMPETE

Stockholders and the Corporation agree that it is difficult to measure damages caused by breach of a covenant not to compete; to deal with this difficulty, they agree that, as liquidated damages and not as a penalty, for each violation of this covenant, the stockholder will pay damages equal to _____ % of the previous calendar year's fees/sales to the client/customer improperly approached or solicited. Each calendar year in which an improper approach or solicitation is made to a client/customer counts as a separate violation. However, in no case will liquidated damages exceed 150% of the sales/fees for the 12 months before the first violation.


## AGREEMENT FOR TYPE C REORGANIZATION PLAN
### (Stock for Assets)

### A. Introduction

**1.** This agreement, dated _____ , 199_____ , contains the terms of a plan of "Type C" reorganization under which Green Lake Ventures, Inc. ("Green Lake"), acquires the assets of

Timmy's Software City, Inc. ("Software"), from Timmy Coughlan, Beatrice Coughlan, Catherine Coughlan Lindsay, Jerome Lindsay, and Jerome Lindsay, Jr. ("Stockholders").

*2.* The agreement is made in consideration of certain representations, warranties, and covenants spelled out in the agreement itself. It is a condition to the obligations of each corporation and its stockholders that the representations and warranties of the other corporation's stockholders be true on and as of the effective date of this agreement as if they had been made on that date. This agreement is also conditioned on each corporation's stockholders delivering to the other corporation a certificate, signed by all stockholders and dated on the closing date, to the effect that all agreements required to be performed by the closing date have been performed.

*3.* At the closing, Software will assign the name "Timmy's Software City, Inc.," to Green Lake.

## B. Assets-for-Stock Exchange

*1.* At the closing, to be held _____ , 199____ at ____M. (or other date and time mutually agreed on by Green Lake and Software), the assets of Software described in Schedule A (a sworn statement, showing facts as of _____ , 199____ , also known as the Balance Sheet Date, in detail sufficient to identify the property to be transferred) will be exchanged for 10,000 shares of Green Lake common stock. Green Lake will assume Software's liabilities as disclosed in Schedule B and will assume, as of the closing date, the executory agreements listed in Schedule B-1 (e.g., leases, long-term supplier agreements). Green Lake hereby warrants that it will perform fully under all such agreements.

*2.* As soon as possible after the closing, Software will cease doing business and enter liquidation. It will distribute the proceeds of this sale transaction to its shareholders; its corporate existence will be terminated; and its Certificate of Incorporation will be surrendered. Software and its stockholders warrant that they will take all legal steps required to this end, and will notify Green Lake as each step is carried out.

## C. Bulk Sale

*1.* The exchange constitutes a bulk sale as governed by Chapter 421 of the Code of the State of Buchanan, and therefore the consideration paid by Green Lake will be held by Martin Sacks, Esq., as escrow agent until all the following requirements have been fulfilled:
○ Sacks receives a certified copy of a tax clearance letter from the Treasury Department of the State of Buchanan, releasing Software from all state sales and license tax liability as of the closing date.
○ Sacks receives notice that, as of a date on or after the closing date, Software's property, premises, equipment, and fixtures are free from federal and state tax liens, private liens, financing statements, or other claims recorded or noticed.
○ Green Lake gives Sacks a signed, sworn list of the names and addresses of its creditors (including those asserting disputed claims) and the amount of each claim or indebtedness.
○ Sacks receives certified return receipts from Green Lake showing that all creditors on the list, and all relevant tax and local authorities, received at least ten days' notice of the bulk transfer.
○ Sacks receives Software's affidavit of compliance with Buchanan's Bulk Sales Act.

## D. Covenants, Representations, and Warranties of Software and Its Stockholders

*1.* All representations and warranties in this section are made jointly and severally and both as of the date of this agreement and as of the closing date.

*2.* Software is a corporation duly organized and doing business and in good standing in the state of Buchanan. □ It does not do business in any other state. □ It is validly qualified and in good standing as a foreign corporation in every other state in which it does business.

Software has no subsidiaries and is not part of a controlled group of corporations.

*3.* Software's entire capitalization consists of 5,000 shares of issued and outstanding common stock with a par value of $5 per share, all of which is held by the Stockholders.

*4.* The Stockholders have provided Green Lake with copies of Software's balance sheet, profit and loss statements, and statements of the source and application of funds for the five most recent fiscal years prior to the current year, and with a balance sheet as of the Balance Sheet Date and a profit and loss statement for the _____month period ending on that date. Except as disclosed in a sworn statement signed by all the Stockholders, these statements have been prepared in accordance with GAAP, consistently applied throughout the periods covered by the Statement, and are a fair representation of Software's financial condition.

*5.*

*a.* The Stockholders have provided Green Lake a Schedule A, an accurate and substantially correct schedule of assets as of the balance sheet date, further divided into subschedules of fixed assets and other assets.

*b.* All fixed assets used by Software are either owned by Software or leased under an agreement reflected on a schedule submitted to Green Lake. Copies of leases for any leased real property used by Software in its operations are attached to Schedule A.

*c.* As far as Software's stockholders know and believe, all of Software's machinery and equipment (including automobiles and trucks) is in usable working condition.

*d.* Except as indicated on the subschedule of fixed assets, Software has neither acquired nor disposed of any fixed assets, except in the ordinary course of business, since the Balance Sheet Date.

*e.* With respect to assets other than fixed assets, Software has neither acquired nor disposed of any such assets, except in the ordinary course of business, since the Balance Sheet Date.

*6.* Software's Stockholders have given Green Lake a Schedule C, a list of Software's accounts and notes receivable, accurate as of the Balance Sheet Date. To the knowledge and belief of Software and its Stockholders, all such accounts and notes are collectable except to the extent of the reserve for bad debts noted in Schedule C.

*7.* Software's Stockholders have given Green Lake a Schedule D, a list of all material contracts (e.g., union contracts, loan agreements, mortgages, security agreements, joint venture and partnership agreements) involving a sum over $5,000, to which Software was a party as of the Balance Sheet Date. Except as disclosed in Schedule D, Software was in material compliance with all its obligations under these contracts as of the Balance Sheet Date.

*8.* Software's Stockholders have also provided Green Lake with a Schedule E accurately listing and describing (as of the Balance Sheet Date) all material permits, licenses, franchises, copyrights, patents and patent applications, and trademarks that Software owns or holds. To the knowledge and belief of the Stockholders, all such intangibles are valid and in good standing.

*9.* To the knowledge and belief of the Stockholders, Software has good and marketable title to all tangible and intangible property transferred under this plan of reorganization and listed on Schedules A, C, D, and E, except for any property disposed of in the ordinary course of business between the Balance Sheet Date and the closing. Such title is free from all mortgage, pledge, lien, sales agreement, encumbrance, or charge except for disclosed liens securing specified liabilities (and on which Software has not defaulted), liens for current taxes and assessments which are not in default, and liens arising by operation of law but without the knowledge of Stockholders.

*10.* During the period between the signing of this agreement and the closing date, Software's Stockholders will give Green Lake's officers and authorized representatives access to Software's business premises, books, and records and will comply with any reasonable request made by Green Lake for additional information (e.g., financial and operating data).

*11.* During the preclosing period, the Stockholders covenant that they will use their best efforts to preserve and maintain Software's business and business methods, for example, by retaining employees, suppliers, and customers; keeping the same methods of management, operations, and accounting; maintaining insurance coverage; keeping property, facilities, and equipment in good working order; continuing to perform under all agreements.

*12.* The Software Stockholders covenant that, during the preclosing period, they will not permit Software to take any potentially detrimental financial actions without Green Lake's prior written consent. Potentially detrimental financial actions include, for example, declaring or paying a dividend; entering into a sale, lease, contract, or commitment outside the ordinary course of business; increasing the compensation of any officer or employee; paying a bonus to any officer or employee.

## E. Representations and Warranties of Green Lake and Its Stockholders

*1.* Green Lake is a corporation in good standing under the laws of the state of Buchanan, having corporate power to carry out the business of high-tech venture capital development (including acquisitions of other companies). It has two subsidiaries: Kirwell Hard Disk, Inc., and Manciple Biotech Corporation, both of which are Buchanan corporations in good standing.

*2.* Green Lake's authorized capital stock consists solely of 35,000 shares of no-par common stock, of which 30,000 shares are authorized and outstanding. All issued shares are validly authorized, fully paid and nonassessable, and validly issued without violating any preemptive rights. Green Lake is not subject to any commitment (e.g., warrant or call) obligating it to issue its stock.

Schedule F is a list of all Green Lake Stockholders and their holdings.

*3.* The Green Lake Stockholders have given Software and its Stockholders the following financial statements of Green Lake and its subsidiaries:

○ Balance sheet as of _____ , 199____ ("Green Lake Balance Sheet Date")
○ Profit and loss statement for the _____ month period ending on the Green Lake Balance Sheet Date
○ Balance sheets, profit and loss statements, and statements of source and application of funds for its five most recent fiscal years.

Unless the Green Lake Stockholders expressly make a signed statement to the contrary, all financial statements were prepared in accordance with GAAP, consistently applied throughout the relevant period, and fairly reflect the financial condition of Green Lake and its subsidiaries at the relevant times.

*4.* To the knowledge and belief of Green Lake's stockholders, Green Lake and its subsidiaries have good and marketable title to all tangible and intangible property used in their business (except for property leased under a valid agreement). Schedule G is a listing of all such property. Property listed on Schedule G (except listed property disposed of in the ordinary course of business after the schedule was compiled and before the closing) is free from all mortgages, liens, encumbrances, charges, pledges, or conditional sales agreement, except for liens disclosed on Schedule G as securing specified liabilities which are not in default, liens for current taxes and assessments which are not in default, and liens arising by operation of law. However, except as disclosed in Schedule G, Green Lake's stockholders have no knowledge of the existence of any such liens.

**5.** Between the date of this agreement and the closing. Green Lake's stockholders will allow Software's officers and authorized representatives access to its plants, properties, books, and records and will accede to any reasonable request for additional information (e.g., financial and operating data).

**6.** Between the date of this agreement and the closing. Green Lake's stockholders will use their best efforts to maintain stability in the business operations of Green Lake and its subsidiaries, for example, in business methods, maintenance of insurance, physical maintenance of property, retention of the work force, and relationships with suppliers and customers.

**7.** Between the date of this agreement and the closing, Green Lake's stockholders will not allow Green Lake or its subsidiaries to amend their Articles of Incorporation; issue securities; declare or pay a dividend; buy, redeem, or retire any shares of stock; enter into any contract or commitment to make any capital expenditure outside the ordinary course of business; or give a raise or pay a bonus to any officer or employee; encumber or mortgage any assets; sell, lease, or otherwise transfer property outside the normal course of business; or enter into a merger or acquisition transactions involving any other corporation, unless Software gives its prior written consent to any of these.

## F. General Provisions

**1.** This agreement will be interpreted under the laws of the state of Buchanan.

**2.** All parties to this agreement agree to provide and deliver any additional agreements reasonably required to carry out the objectives of this plan of Type C reorganization. Software and Green Lake will cooperate and use their best efforts to make their officers and directors cooperate by providing information and evidence as required in any actions, proceedings, or disputes arising out of matters before the closing.

**3.** This agreement (including Schedules A–G) and the documents delivered as required by this agreement constitute the entire agreement between the parties. The agreement can be modified only by a signed written agreement that has received any necessary corporate approval. If this agreement is simultaneously executed in two or more counterparts, each one will be considered an original; all of the counterparts, taken together, will constitute a single original. As long as at least one counterpart is executed by each party, it will not be required that all parties execute any particular counterpart.

**4.** This agreement and the rights of the Software Stockholders may not be assigned (except by operation of law); they both bind and benefit the parties to this agreement and their successors and heirs and legal representatives. On or after the closing date, Green Lake has the right to cause Software's assets to be transferred to a wholly owned subsidiary of Green Lake.

**5.** All warranties, covenants, representations, and guarantees made in this agreement survive the closing date. All parties rely solely on the representations, warranties, and agreements contained in this agreement and in schedules and other related documents; their decision to execute and carry out this agreement does not depend on any other representation, warranty, agreement, promise, or information made outside this agreement by any person at any time.

**6.** Notice can be provided by fax, in person, or by first-class mail to a corporation at its headquarters, and to a stockholder at the address given in the listing of stockholders, or at any changed address of which the party sending the notice has received at least ten days' written notice.

IN WITNESS TO WHICH, THE PARTIES HAVE EXECUTED THIS AGREEMENT ON _____ , 199_____ .

Green Lake, by _____ , President

Attested by _____ , Secretary

Software, by _____ , President

Attested by _____ , Secretary

_____ Timmy Coughlan

_____ Beatrice Coughlan

_____ Catherine Coughlan Lindsay

_____ Jerome Lindsay

_____ Jerome Lindsay, Jr.

State of Buchanan

City of Tyler          ss

Today, _____ , 199_____ , two persons whom I know as Timmy Coughlan and Edward Farouchi appeared before me personally and deposed and said that they are the Presidents of Timmy's Software City, Inc., and Green Lake Ventures, Inc., respectively, signatories to this agreement, and that each signed this agreement by order of his corporation's Board of Directors.

_____ Notary Public, Tuscabamba County, Buchanan; my commission expires _____ , 199_____

# Chapter 12

# BANKRUPTCY

## INTRODUCTION

The essence of business is risk. Business planners must make projections, even outright guesses, about the future. Furthermore, in order to be ready for future orders, the business must encounter expenses in advance (sometimes far in advance) to provide raw materials, fabricate them into finished products, and market the products. Therefore, it is difficult to match expenses and income; an essentially sound business may have such poor cash flow that it is unable to continue. Or, the market may change, so that the finished products are unsalable, or salable only at a dramatically cut price. Products can be spoiled in the manufacturing process, or before they can be sold. Interest rates can rise, so that the debt encountered to do research and development, buy raw materials, or improve the factory or marketing can become a heavy, even a crippling, burden. Tax law changes can eliminate anticipated deductions or increase a business' effective tax rate.

Sometimes the troubled business can weather the storm and come back, stronger than ever. Sometimes new sources of capital are available, by finding venture capital investors, additional entrepreneurs, making an offering of stock to the public, or borrowing. But sometimes the business becomes simply untenable, and drastic measures must be taken. Often, the measures are informal: the business owners pay their debts and disband the business, perhaps using the intervention of the court system to appraise the value of stock held by dissenting stockholders.

When informal measures aren't sufficient, a likely outcome is that the business owners will choose to go through a voluntary bankruptcy (either a liquidation or a reorganization that gives the business some breathing space and a chance to start fresh) or will be forced into involuntary bankruptcy by creditors who would rather get a percentage of their debts instead of taking the risk of getting less or nothing.

At one time, bankruptcy was considered a disgrace, and business owners would do almost anything to avoid it. Today, bankruptcy can be a tactic employed even by profitable companies (e.g., those that fear large judgments for products liability), and today's bankrupt businesses are in good company (or anyway, large company) when giant corporations such as Eastern Airlines and Federated Department Stores file for bankruptcy protection.

## Voluntary Petitions

Bankruptcy law is almost wholly a matter of federal law (although the states do have some role to play in deciding what funds and property a debtor can retain). There are three chapters in the federal Bankruptcy Code that might affect business owners: Chapters 7, 11, and 13. Chapter 7, or "straight bankruptcy," calls for liquidation of the bankrupt company and payment of a portion of its debts to the creditors. Chapter 11 is bankruptcy reorganization: the company can continue in business, with certain limitations; the purpose of the bankruptcy plan is to find a way for the business to settle its debts eventually and emerge from bankruptcy.

Chapter 13 sets out the details of the "wage-earner" plan, under which a person who has heavy debts but a regular income can stretch out payments. Strictly speaking, this is a personal rather than a business bankruptcy provision—but owners of closely held businesses often are personally liable if the business is operated in proprietorship or partnership rather than corporate form, if the "corporate veil" is pierced, or if they gave their personal guarantees of corporate obligations. (Another problem is that business owners often invest heavily in their corporation's stock and base their life-style on the stock's peak value, or even their most optimistic estimate of the stock's future value. If the stock declines in value, becomes hard to sell, or becomes completely valueless, they have few other assets to fall back on.)

Any business or individual contemplating bankruptcy should first schedule a planning session with attorneys and accountants, to find out what the assets are, what the debts and other liabilities are, and whether all the liabilities are legally enforceable. (For instance, they may arise out of disputed circumstances, such as merchandise that the company claims was defective, or the legal statute of limitations for enforcing the debt may have expired.)

It's especially important to get legal advice about paying bills, scheduling bonuses, and selling property. As discussed shortly, the bankruptcy court can disregard "preferences": transactions that benefit a corporate insider or a favored creditor at the expense of the other creditors (for instance, selling a valuable asset to a family member for a low price, making sure that a friend receives 100% of his debt, while other creditors end up with only a few cents on the dollar).

*Practice Tip:* This is a quick general outline of the basic rules of bankruptcy practice. However, bankruptcy is a very complex subject, and the various federal districts do have somewhat different rules, so get expert professional advice to make sure that your plan is lawful and conforms to the latest local bankruptcy rules.

Once the decision to file for bankruptcy protection has been made, the official first step is to file Form 1, the Bankruptcy Court petition. (Bankruptcy forms are often referred to as Official Form 1, Form 2, and so on, but in fact there is no form issued by the federal government, the way tax forms are issued. Any document that satisfies the local bankruptcy rules can be accepted for filing.)

*Practice Tip:* Filing a Chapter 7 (liquidating bankruptcy) petition requires the consent of the corporation's Board of Directors; the President can't take this step alone. The debtor must then prove to the court that it is entitled to bankruptcy protection (in abusive cases, the court can suspend or even dismiss the case, after a hearing at which the creditors have a right to be present, if the court believes that bankruptcy is not in the best interests of both debtor and creditors).

When a voluntary Chapter 7 petition is filed, or when a Chapter 11 or 13 filing is converted to Chapter 7, a First Meeting of Creditors (also called a Section 341 meeting, after the relevant section of the Bankruptcy Code) is held about a month after the filing. All the creditors are notified and can appear to state their point of view.

The U.S. Trustee's Office (part of the Bankruptcy Court) reviews the schedules of assets and liabilities submitted by the debtor and makes a tentative determination whether there are any assets to distribute to the creditors. If it appears that there are no assets, the creditors are notified of this and informed that they need not file a Proof of Claim (see the following discussion). They are also told that they will be notified if additional assets are found.

However, if there are assets, the creditors are notified that they have 90 days from the date of the First Meeting to file Proof of Claim; the form is on the back of the notice sent to creditors.

Next, the U.S. Trustee appoints an interim trustee from a panel of trustees who are designated to preside at the First Meetings. The debtor must collect all its assets and turn them over to the trustee for distribution to the creditors. If the debtor fails to perform its duties under the Bankruptcy Code, it can be punished for contempt of court; in really serious cases criminal penalties can be imposed.

The duties of a Chapter 7 debtor are

- To file documents (the bankruptcy forms)
  - List of creditors
  - Form 6, the schedule of assets and liabilities
  - Form 6A, the schedule of current income and expenditures
  - Form 7 or 8, the statement of financial affairs
- File a statement of whether it intends to keep, surrender, or otherwise dispose of consumer debts

○ Cooperate with the trustee including turning over information and all the business property

○ Attend the Section 341 meeting and the discharge hearing (if the federal court district in which the petition is filed holds discharge hearings)

In a Chapter 11 case, the U.S. Trustee generally appoints a committee of unsecured creditors (this step is sometimes omitted in small cases). A committee of equity security holders can be appointed. The committee consists of the seven creditors or security holders with the largest interests who are willing to serve. A typical disclosure statement filed by a Chapter 11 debtor includes

○ A description of the debtor's business and the relevant market in which it operates

○ The debtor's history in business

○ Its reasons for filing a bankruptcy petition

○ Its management and their compensation and transactions with the debtor (e.g., have corporate officers bought property from the corporation, or sold property to it? Were the terms of the deal reasonable compared to arm's-length transactions?)

○ Business projections

○ Disclosure of existing and pending suits by and against the debtor

○ A description of the plan

○ How the plan will be carried out

○ An analysis of what would happen if the business were liquidated instead of reorganized (including tax consequences)

The reorganization plan is the centerpiece of the Chapter 11 filing. It divides the creditors into classes and explains how much each class will receive (for instance, four classes, one receiving 100% of their claims, one 75%, one 60%, and one 15%). The classes within the plan must be substantially similar (although similar claims can be placed in different classes).

The Chapter 11 debtor always has a right to file a reorganization plan; for the first 120 days after the Bankruptcy Court issues its initial order for relief, the debtor is the only party who can file a plan. After that, other parties with an interest in the case (the trustee, the committee) can file a plan if the debtor fails to, or if the debtor's proposed plan is unacceptable. Not all Chapter 11 cases feature the appointment of a trustee. If the debtor qualifies as a "debtor in possession," it will be permitted to continue normal business operations, and even to administer the Chapter 11 plan itself. However, the court can appoint a Chapter 11 trustee on proof of waste, fraud, or gross mismanagement of the debtor's affairs, or in the best interests of creditors and stockholders. In the discussion that follows, substitute "debtor in possession" for "trusteee" with respect to plans that do not have a trustee.

Perhaps the most valuable feature of a Chapter 7 or Chapter 11 bankruptcy (whether voluntary or involuntary) is the "automatic stay." Starting on the date of filing (not the date that creditors find out about a voluntary filing), creditors are not legally permitted to take *any* action to collect their debts. They can't even continue collection cases that were begun before bankruptcy. The IRS can't drag the debtor into Tax Court, and creditors who have court judgments dating from before bankruptcy can't enforce them. The automatic stay is a breathing space, during which the trustee and the debtor can assess how far the company's obligations exceed its assets and figure out a plan for parceling out the available assets fairly.

The Bankruptcy Court can reject the plan or order that it be carried out either by "confirmation" or by "cramdown." To confirm the plan, the court must find that

- ○ It was proposed in good faith
- ○ The plan conforms to the Chapter 11 statute
- ○ Either all the payments scheduled under the plan are reasonable, or the plan requires the court to approve all payments in advance
- ○ The plan discloses who will act as officers and directors of the reorganized company
- ○ Either each creditor with a claim must approve the plan, or the plan must give each creditor as much as it would receive in a Chapter 7 liquidation
- ○ The plan must be feasible—that is, there must be no likelihood that the plan will wind up in a liquidation or a further reorganization unless the plan calls for one

A "cramdown" occurs when a reasonable plan is proposed (whether or not by the debtor) and meets all the tests for confirmation except approval by all creditors. The court will grant an application for a "cramdown" if the plan does not discriminate unfairly and treats the protesting class equitably.

Unless the court orders to the contrary, the debtor is authorized to continue operating its business even during the automatic stay. However, the debtor has an obligation to keep "cash collateral" (such as bank accounts) separately. Cash collateral can be spent on business needs only if there is a court order authorizing its use or if the creditors who have a lien on the cash collateral allow its use. The debtor can also sell noncash collateral (e.g., inventory), but only "in the ordinary course of business" (following normal business practices) or with specific court approval. The collateral can't be given away or sold in an unbusinesslike manner.

The trustee (supervised by the court) has the right to either keep or reject any unexpired lease or any "executory contract" of the debtor's. An executory contract is one to be performed in the future. This is a powerful tool for simplifying the debtor's business and reducing its future obligations—but can also be dangerous, if it deprives the debtor of useful business relationships. The trustee also has a power that is far more welcome to the creditors than to the debtor. The trustee can "avoid" (treat as if it had no legal effect) any transfer of the debtor's property made within one year before the bankruptcy filing, if the transfer was a "fraudulent conveyance." A fraudulent conveyance is a transfer actually made with the intention to "delay, hinder, or defraud" creditors, or one that was made for less than the true value of the property. A transfer can only be a fraudulent conveyance if it was made at a time when the debtor was insolvent (had liabilities exceeding its assets), had an unreasonably small amount of capital, or was likely to incur debts that it could not pay.

## Involuntary Bankruptcy

Creditors who fear that all of the corporation's assets may be wasted before their claims are paid can file an involuntary Chapter 7 or 11 petition on Form 11. Three or more creditors who have claims totaling over $5,000 that are not contingent (dependent on some event) and that exceed the liens they have on property securing the claims are required for an involuntary petition. (If the debtor has fewer than 12 creditors altogether, a single creditor—but not an insider or employee of the corporation—can file an involuntary petition.)

The debtor has the right to contest the filing of the involuntary petition, by presenting defenses and objections to the filing within 20 days of receiving the summons.

*Practice Tip:* The debtor has the right to get a judgment against the creditors, or even collect damages from them, if the involuntary petition is dismissed. The debtor also has an absolute right to get an involuntary Chapter 7 petition converted to Chapter 11, but not vice versa. This requirement is imposed to keep debtors from forcing creditors to accept less in a liquidation than they would receive if the business were maintained as a going concern.

The period between the commencement of an involuntary bankruptcy case and the court's order for relief is called the "gap" period. During the gap period, the debtor has full control of business operations, without restriction (and can incur—and pay—new bills), unless the creditors get a court order placing conditions on the business operations, or unless a trustee is appointed. "Gap creditors" (those who extend credit during the gap period) are treated as having claims that arose before the petition; they get second priority. First priority is given to the secured creditors, the trustee's administrative expenses (including professional fees) and creditors who were entitled to "adequate" protection under the Bankruptcy Code but turned out to have inadequate protection.

When an "involuntary" is tried, the court enters an order for relief if, in general, the debtor is not paying its debts (other than disputed or contingent debts) as they become due, or if the debtor carries out an out-of-court liquidation by transferring substantially all its assets to a custodian in the 120-day period before the filing. The petition can be dismissed if all the petitioners and the debtor agree to dismissal (for instance, if they have worked out a mutually acceptable reorganization plan), if there is a hearing, and all the creditors are notified so they can present their claims, or if the petitioner fails to appear and prosecute the claim.

A trustee can be appointed in an involuntary Chapter 11 case "for cause" (if the debtor's current management has been guilty of fraud, dishonesty, incompetence, or gross mismanagement) or if the court deems this to be in the best interests of creditors, holders of the debtor's securities, and others interested in the estate (such as the debtor's employees).

*Practice Tips:* If you are considering bankruptcy filing, or fear that an involuntary petition can be brought, be sure to get professional advice promptly! In the meantime, these suggestions can make the process somewhat less painful:

○ Of course, you have to cut costs—but keep at least enough accounting staff to provide the figures and prepare the reports you'll need for the Bankruptcy Court.

○ Talk to your banks and other lenders. Maybe they'd rather renegotiate your loans to give you more time to pay than get embroiled in a bankruptcy case. (Make sure that you involve your lawyer in the negotiation process; you don't want to make a preferential transfer.) Investigate to see if it's legal and feasible to move your bank deposits to banks where you do not have loans outstanding: if the bank has a right of setoff, it may deduct the amount you owe from your bank account, leading to bounced checks and bad relations with other creditors.

○ Maintain your insurance coverage—in fact, if you drop your coverage, creditors might feel that your assets are at risk, and they could succeed in getting the court to lift the automatic stay so they can start collection cases against you.

○ Pay your utility bills—it's a normal business expense, not a preference, and if you were fully paid up before the filing, the utilities will probably not be allowed to demand a large security deposit (which could be hard for you to pay) after the filing.

Needless to say, bankruptcy is not a light-hearted, enjoyable process. Many people involved in bankruptcies have deep feelings of personal failure and inadequacy. In practical terms, there are limitations on further bankruptcy filings, and many businesses either refuse to deal with bankrupt companies or insist on their paying cash for everything. But the bankruptcy system often works the way it's intended to: the bankrupt company forms a new plan, eventually satisfies its obligations, and emerges leaner, trimmer, and more efficient.

---

## RETAINER AGREEMENT FOR BANKRUPTCY LAWYER

Date:

This agreement sets out the terms under which the law firm of Seiden, Edwards & Copiague will represent Antique Hay Furniture, Inc., in connection with the filing of its voluntary Chapter 7/Chapter 11 bankruptcy petition.

The firm agrees to provide legal advice and assistance about the business' rights as a debtor and the remedies available to its creditors, to prepare and file all documents necessary to file for bankruptcy relief, and to represent the business at meetings and hearings incident to the bankruptcy petition.

The business agrees to pay the firm at the rate of $ ____ per hours for noncourt time, $ ____ per hour for court time (including all hearings), subject to an agreed minimum of $ ____ . The firm's nonbinding estimate of the time required to file the bankruptcy petition and obtain a judgment of relief is ____ hours. The business also agrees to pay all out-of-pocket expenses involved in preparing and filing the petition, such as court costs, telephone and fax expenses, and photocopying. The firm's nonbinding estimate of these expenses is $ _____ .

The firm retains the right to withdraw from this matter if the minimum fee or any other bill from the firm remains unpaid after 30 days.


## LETTER FROM BUSINESS' ATTORNEY TO A CREDITOR

Re: Antique Hay Furniture, Inc.

My client, Antique Hay Furniture, Inc., has a number of creditors. I am aware that my client owes you a principal sum of $ _____ under a loan agreement/contract/mortgage/other: _____ dated _____ , 199 _____ and calling for regular monthly/quarterly payments, and that _____ payments, totaling $ _____ , are already in arrears. My client's indebtedness is secured by _____ and under normal circumstances you would be entitled to enforce your remedies in case of default.

However, please be advised that Bankruptcy Case No. _____ under Chapter 7/Chapter 11 has been filed on behalf of my client in the U.S. Bankruptcy Court for the District of _____ . Therefore, the Automatic Stay (11 U.S. Code Section 362) has been invoked, and no creditor is permitted to sue, foreclose, or seize collateral. WARNING: Violating the Automatic Stay constitutes contempt of court.

Nevertheless, my client wishes to treat all creditors fairly, and therefore has proposed to pay the entire amount in arrears, by certified/cashier's check on or before _____ , 199 _____ and to resume making the regular scheduled payments as of that date. Please inform me in writing if this arrangement is acceptable to you. If it is not acceptable, you will have to seek remedies in Bankruptcy Court, which will entail delays, may expose you to expense, and creates a risk that you will not be able to collect the entire amount owed to you.


## LETTER FROM A BUSINESS TO A CREDITOR, SUGGESTING A COMPOSITION

To Amalienborg Chemical Works, Inc.:

For a variety of reasons, our company has undergone financial reverses. We are heavily leveraged and are unable to keep up with payments on our current obligations. However, we are confident that this situation is a curable one and that eventually our company will become profitable. But in the meantime, we need relief. If all our creditors agree to a "composition" (to accept a percentage of their debt in full satisfaction of the amount owed), we will get a breathing space and a chance to start again. We believe that a composition is better for everyone than receivership, forced sale of assets, or bankruptcy, because creditors get paid faster, and we can expend more of our available funds on paying our creditors instead of legal fees.

Our records indicate that we own you $ _____ under a contract dated _____ , 19 _____ / invoice number _____ / for your performance of services as follows: _____ / because you have supplied goods as follows: _____ for which you have not been paid.

We offer you _____ % of this debt, to be paid on or before _____ , 199 _____ .

This offer remains open until _____ , 199 _____ during which time we will contact our other creditors and attempt to work out a mutually satisfactory solution to our debt problem.

# ASSIGNMENT FOR THE BENEFIT OF CREDITORS

## Preamble

Despite the best efforts of its management, including efforts to secure additional capital, Dentchenko Film Processing, Inc., is now insolvent and unable to meet its obligations as they mature. The corporation's Board of Directors, after hearing reports from the corporation's financial staff and its independent auditor, has determined that the best way for the corporation to satisfy its creditors is to enter into a general assignment for benefit of its creditors, as described in Chapter 219, Section 5-113 ("Rights and Remedies of Debtors and Creditors") of the Revised Code of the State of Adams. THEREFORE, Dentchenko Film Process, Inc., as Assignor hereby assigns all of its real and personal property that is not legally exempt from levy and execution sale to Laurence P. Corrigan as Assignee and Trustee. Corrigan has agreed to accept the responsibilities of Trustee-Assignee.

*1. Schedule of Assets:* The following assets are hereby conveyed to the Assignee:

*Description* _____ *Location* _____ *Estimated Value* _____ *Encumbrances* _____



*2. Exempt Assets:* The following assets are not being conveyed, because it is the Assignor's contention that they are exempt:

*Description* _____ *Location* _____ *Reason for Exemption* _____



*3. Trustee's Role:* The property being conveyed is conveyed to the Assignee in trust, so that he can use his best efforts to sell the property (by public or private sale, at his discretion) at the best obtainable prices. The Assignee is also charged with collecting amounts owed to the Assignor.

*4. Use of Proceeds:* First priority in the application of the proceeds of collection and sale will go to the reasonable costs and expenses of collection and sale (including the Assignee's commission as provided by Chapter 219, Section 5-113(k) of the Revised Code of Adams). The balance of the proceeds is to be used to satisfy the Assignor's debts and obligations, including interest. If the balance exceeds the debts, the Assignee will pay the surplus to the Assignor (or its successors or assigns). If the balance is equal to the debts and obligations, it will be devoted to the purpose of paying the debts and obligations. If the balance is insufficient, it will be divided among all creditors uniformly in proportion to their debts (i.e., a debt equaling 10% of the overall debts and obligations will receive 10% of the balance).

*5. Designation:* The Assignor hereby appoints the Assignee as its attorney in fact, with full authority to undertake any lawful act in furtherance of the trust objective, such as enforcing claims on behalf of the Assignor against its own debtors, and instituting and defending litigation and executing and delivering deeds, instruments, and releases.

Date: _____ , 199____
Assignor, by: _____Laurence Corrigan

# VERIFIED CLAIM OF CREDITOR

State of Adams
County of Vernon ss: _____
ESSANEFF CELLULOID, INC., by its president, Rosalind Silverberg Fein, has been duly sworn and deposes the following:

*1.* On _____ , 199 ____ , Dentchenko Film Processing, Inc., entered into a contract obligating Essaneff Celluloid, Inc., to deliver 1,000 reels of 35 millimeter film, Extra Grade, to Dentchenko on or before _____ , 199 ____ . Delivery was duly and timely made and was accepted without protest. The merchandise has not been returned, and no complaints have been asserted about its quality. A copy of the contract of sale is attached.

*2.* The contract of sale did not call for security or collateral.

*3.* The contract price was $ ____ . No payments have been made/payments totaling $ ____ have been made, leaving a balance of $ ____ .

*4.* On information and belief, the subject merchandise has been used by the debtor in its business operations and therefore cannot be returned to Essaneff for resale to other customers.

*5.* Therefore, Essaneff Celluloid, Inc., is a creditor of Dentchenko Film Processing, which has made an assignment for benefit of its creditors. Essaneff is entitled to receive a proportionate share of its claim.

# DEED OF ASSIGNMENT

The Assignor corporation, Moose & Velma's Diner, Inc., a Madison corporation, has encountered financial difficulties and is unable to continue normal operations and to pay bills as they come due. In order to deal justly with all creditors, and to grant equal treatment to all creditors free of preferences, the Assignor hereby makes an assignment for the benefit of its creditors. In exchange for $1 and other valuable consideration, the Assignor hereby grants, assigns, transfers, and conveys all of its real and personal property and accounts used in business or held by the Assignor as investments, whether inside or outside Madison, to _____ , the Assignee-Trustee. The Assignee-Trustee will take this property in trust, marshall the assets belonging to the Assignor, then sell or otherwise dispose of the property in order to distribute the proceeds to the creditors proportionate to their claims.

This assignment is a corporate act, as evidenced by the attachment of the corporate seal.

Date: _____ , 199 ____
Moose & Velma's Diner, Inc., by: _____ [Seal]
I, Jeremy Platt, President of the Assignor corporation, hereby acknowledge that this assignment is a valid corporate act, and that the statements made in the acknowledgment and in the attached schedules are, to the best of my knowledge, accurate and complete.

Date: _____ , 199 ____                                    Jeremy Platt, President

| | *Description* | *Location* | *Value* | *Net Unencumbered Value* |
|---|---|---|---|---|
| Real Estate | _____ | _____ | _____ | _____ |
| Cash on hand | _____ | _____ | _____ | _____ |
| Bank accounts | _____ | _____ | _____ | _____ |
| Accounts receivable | _____ | _____ | _____ | _____ |
| Investments | _____ | _____ | _____ | _____ |
| Equipment | _____ | _____ | _____ | _____ |
| Inventory | _____ | _____ | _____ | _____ |
| Raw materials | _____ | _____ | _____ | _____ |
| Other | _____ | _____ | _____ | _____ |
| Total Assets | _____ | _____ | _____ | _____ |

## Schedule II Creditors

| | *Name* | *Address* | *Balance of Claim* |
|---|---|---|---|
| Secured | _____ | _____ | _____ |
| Unsecured | _____ | _____ | _____ |
| Total liabilities | _____ | _____ | _____ |

## BOND OF ASSIGNEE

BE ADVISED THAT Totaltrust Bonding & Surety, a Madison corporation duly chartered and in good standing, is in the business of furnishing fidelity and surety bonds.

On _____ , 199 ____ , Max Kaempfer entered into a transaction under which he will serve as assignee and trustee in order to sell the assets of Moose & Velma's Diner, Inc., and distribute the proceeds to its creditors. This is a fiduciary position calling for the very highest standards of veracity, fidelity, and probity. Should he fail to meet these standards, Totaltrust Bonding & Surety, Inc., as surety, stands bound in the amount of $500,000 and will pay any required portion of such sum to any party adjudicated to have suffered damage because of Kaempfer's failure to comply with his duties as a fiduciary.

Totaltrust Bonding & Surety, Inc., submits itself to the jurisdiction of the Courts of Kettledrum County, Madison, and hereby and irrevocably appoints the clerk of the Intermediate Civil Court of Kettledrum County as its agent for the service of process with respect to all matters that might obligate Totaltrust to perform under this bond, on condition that the Clerk promptly mail copies of all such process to Totaltrust.

Signed, Totaltrust, by: _____ [Seal]

I have examined the bond provided by Totaltrust Bonding & Security on behalf of Max Kaempfer, Assignee/Trustee for Moose & Velma's Diner, Inc., and find it sufficient and appropriate in form and amount. _____ Judge

# ASSIGNEE'S LETTER TO ACCOMPANY COURT ORDER
## IN ASSIGNMENT

## Notice to the Creditors of Moose & Velma's Diner Inc.:

Moose & Velma's Diner, Inc., has named me as assignee and has made an assignment for benefit of its creditors. I have taken possession of the debtor's assets and am in the process of collecting its accounts receivable and selling its assets.

Once the marshalling and sale process has been completed—which will probably take about a year—the proceeds will be distributed to creditors who have filed notarized Proof of Claim forms with the Court Auditor of Kettledrum County on or before _____ , 199 ____ . A copy of the official form is attached for your convenience. IT MUST BE SUBMITTED TO THE COURT AUDITOR, NOT THE ASSIGNEE-TRUSTEE.

The Court Auditor will notify you of the date on which creditors can appear and examine the assignor, and will distribute your share of the proceeds of the assignment for the benefit of creditors.

## Court Order

Intermediate Civil Court of Kettledrum County
-----------------------------------------------------

In re Moose & Velma's Diner, Inc.,          Civ. No. 92K/193
-----------------------------------------------------

## Order for Notice and Proof of Claims

The Intermediate Civil Court of Kettledrum County hereby ORDERS on _____ , 199 ____ that all creditors and other persons claiming to have an interest in the funds or assets of the above named debtor submit their claims to the Court Auditor of Kettledrum County, 3 State Government Tower, Room 1792, on or before _____ , 199 ____ ; AND, to facilitate this process, the Assignee-Trustee, Max Kaempfer, is ORDERED to mail a copy of this Order to all persons known to be creditors or claimants of the debtor, with notice to be mailed to their last-known address, on or before _____ , 199 ____ (60 days before the examination of the debtor). Max Kaempfer is also ORDERED to file an Affidavit of Mailing with the Clerk of this Court once the mailing has been completed as ordered.

Signed, _____                          JUDGE, Intermediate Civil Court

## Affidavit

Max Kaempfer, being duly sworn, deposes and says that he is the Assignee for the benefit of the creditors of Moose & Velma's Diner, Inc.; that, to the best of his knowledge and after due inquiry, he has determined that the identity and last known address of all creditors and claimants against the debtor are as follows:

| *Name* | *Amount of Debt or Claim* | *Address* |
|---|---|---|

and that, on _____ , 199 ____ , he mailed a copy of the court order, a cover letter, and a claim form to each person or entity on that list.

_____ Max Kaempfer, Assignee-Trustee Sworn to and signed in my presence _____ , 199 _____ Notary Public, Commission No. _____ , Expires _____

## CREDITOR'S CLAIM FORM

State of Madison
County of Kettledrum ss: _____
_____ , who has sworn to tell the truth, deposes and says that he/she/it is a creditor of Moose & Velma's Diner, Inc., in the amount of $ _____ / has a $ ____ claim against Moose & Velma's Diner, Inc., in that: _____
and, to the best of his/her/its knowledge upon due investigation the debt/claim is valid, enforceable, and not subject to any setoff or counterclaim.
Signed, _____                                                      [by: _____ ]
Sworn to before me on this _____ day of _____ , 199 ____
_____ Notary Public Commission No. ____ Expires: _____

## ASSIGNEE'S FINAL REPORT AND ACCOUNT

Recorder's Court of Vernon County
In re Dentchenko Film Processing Inc.
Index No. 90-CIV/ADM-1323
 PLEASE BE ADVISED that Laurence Corrigan, whose business address is 219 Kennedy Towers East, has completed service as Assignee/Trustee of Dentchenko Film Processing, Inc.'s assignment for benefit of its creditors. This is his final report and account.

*1.* The assignment for the benefit of creditors was executed by the debtor on _____ , 199 ____ and accepted by the Assignee as trustee on _____ , 199 ____ .

*2.* The debtor engaged in the business of processing film and videotape for photography, and private and theatrical exhibition and distribution, at the business address of 8 ½ Amarcord Drive, Lake Como, Adams.

*3.* Insofar as I was able to ascertain. Dentchenko Film Processing was itself a creditor to the extent of $ ____ of which I was able to marshall and collect $ ____ .

*4.* By order of Hon. Raymond Pfeiffer, dated _____ , 199 ____ , I advertised for creditors to file their claims against the debtor. Time to file expired on _____ , 199 ____ . On the basis of these claims, and on the basis of records submitted to me, I determined that Dentchenko owed a total of $ ____ to _____ creditors.

*5.* Acting under authority given me by the same order, I had the assets of Dentchenko Film Processing sold at public auction by Phillip Mirsky, Licensed Auctioneer, on _____ , 199 ____ . The auction was held at Dentchenko's place of business. The property listed in Schedule A was sold, yielding a total of $ ____ net of the expense of the auction.

**6.** Schedule B lists the costs, fees, and expenses I incurred in administering the assignment for the benefit of creditors, including my own fee of $ _____ as provided by statute.

**7.** The net proceeds of the auction sale, and the debts collected on behalf of Dentchenko, totaling $ _____ , were distributed to the creditors in a process ending _____ , 199 _____ . Each creditor listed on Schedule C received _____ % of its claim. This process of distribution did not prejudice the rights of any creditor. The assignor is not the subject of any voluntary or involuntary bankruptcy proceedings.

**8.** To the best of my knowledge, this document (including the attached schedules) is a complete, honest, and accurate account of the assignment for the benefit of creditors transaction. All expenses listed herein were actually incurred and paid and were reasonable in nature and amount.

Date: _____ , 199_____

Signed: Laurence Corrigan

On _____ , 199 _____ , Laurence Corrigan appeared before me and swore that the signature that appears on this document is his signature and that none of the statements appearing in this document contains any falsehoods.

_____ , Notary Public Commission # _____ Expires: _____

Date: _____ , 199_____

# VOLUNTARY PETITION (Chs. 7, 11) (Form 1)

Diaz, Bailey & Torico, Attorneys for the Petitioner

3265 Elm Avenue

Brookstone Park, Adams, 99999-021

U.S. BANKRUPTCY COURT FOR THE _____ DISTRICT OF_____

In re McKeaney's Olde Public House, aka Ye Publicke House Tavern, EIN 72-7777, Debtor Case No: _____

**1.** McHeaney's Olde Public House, whose mailing address is 8739 East 9th Avenue, Goldwood, Adams, in the County of Nephtha, makes a voluntary petition praying for relief under Chapter 7/Chapter 11 of the Bankruptcy Code.

**2.** Petitioner is a corporation and has attached Exhibit A, which is made a part of the petition.

**3.** The petitioner is qualified to file for bankruptcy and is entitled to the benefits of Chapter 7/Chapter 11.

**4.** The principal assets of the petitioner have been within this district for the past 180 days; hence, this is the appropriate district for filing.

**5.** A copy of the petitioner's proposed plan of reorganization, dated _____ , 199_____ , is attached/the petitioner intends to file a Chapter 7/Chapter 11 plan.

Signed: _____ Attorney for the Petitioner

## APPLICATION TO PAY FILING FEES IN INSTALLMENTS
### (Form 2)

U.S. BANKRUPTCY COURT FOR THE _____ DISTRICT OF_____

In re FasTimes Party Supplies, Inc., Debtor Case No.: _____

The Debtor hereby requests, as permitted by Bankruptcy Rule 1006, permission to pay the filing fee for the bankruptcy case in installments, as follows: _____

An initial $_____ to accompany filing of the petition, and the balance of $_____ on the following schedule: $_____ on _____ , 199_____ ; $_____ on _____ , 199_____ ; $_____ on _____ , 199_____ ; and $_____ on _____ , 199 .

I certify that I have not yet paid an attorney (or any other person) any money or property in connection with any pending bankruptcy case and that I will not make any such payments until the filing fee has been paid in full.

Date: _____ , 199_____

Applicant's Name:_____

Applicant's Address:_____

### Court Order

IT IS HEREBY ORDERED that the debtor be permitted to make installment payments of the filing fee in conformity with the schedule given above, provided that the debtor shall not pay any money or property to any person in connection with services rendered in connection with the bankruptcy case until the filing fee is paid in full.

Date: _____ , 199_____

Judge of the Bankruptcy Court

## UNSWORN DECLARATION UNDER PENALTY OF PERJURY
### (to Be Used in Corporate Petitions) (Form 4)

I, John McHeaney, am president of the corporation petitioning for bankruptcy relief. I hereby certify under penalty of perjury that proper corporate authorization has been obtained for the bankruptcy filing and that all statements in the petition (including Exhibit A) are true and correct.

Date: _____ , 199_____

Signature:_____

## U.S. BANKRUPTCY COURT FOR THE _____ DISTRICT
## OF _____

### Exhibit A

*1.* Petitioner is an Adams corporation, validly qualified to do business in the state of Adams since its incorporation on _____ , 199_____ .

2. The Petitioner's business consists of operating a tavern (liquor license no. _____ , issued
_____ , 199\_\_\_\_\_ ) serving food and alcoholic beverages.

3. John McHeaney and Elizabeth Duplessix each directly control 20% or more of the voting
securities of the corporation. No other individual or corporation directly or indirectly owns, controls,
or holds 20% or more of the corporation's voting securities.

4. The corporation has not issued any securities registered or subject to registration under Section 12
of the Exchange Act.

5. The corporation's authorized capitalization consists of 10,000 shares of common stock, all of
which have been issued, and which are held by a total of 17 individuals. There are no corporate
stockholders. No debt securities have been issued.

6. The latest available corporate financial information, accurate as of _____ ,
199\_\_\_\_\_ , discloses total assets of $619,217 and total liabilities of $1,472,654. Of this amount,
$175,800 is secured debt held by six creditors. The remaining liabilities are unsecured claims of
approximately 75 trade creditors whose claims are liquidated and are not contingent.

I, Robert T. Salem, attorney for the petitioner, McHeaney's Olde Public House, declare that I have
explained the relief available under the various titles of the Bankruptcy Code to the petitioner, and
have informed the petitioner that it is entitled to relief under Chapter 7/Chapter 11.

Date: _____ , 199\_\_\_\_\_
Signed: _____Robert T. Salem

## CERTIFICATE OF COMMENCEMENT OF CASE (Form 5)

U.S. BANKRUPTCY COURT FOR THE _____ DISTRICT OF_____
In re TeeanCee Hardware, Inc., Debtor
Also known as T&C Hardware, Inc.                         Case No.: _____
Employer Identification Number 34-9897
I, Jerome Monaghan, Clerk of the Bankruptcy Court for the _____ District of
_____ , hereby certify that on _____ , 199\_\_\_\_\_ , a Chapter 7/Chapter 11
bankruptcy petition was filed with respect to the above-named debtor voluntarily, by the debtor/
involuntarily, against the debtor.
As of _____ , 199\_\_\_\_\_ , said case had not been dismissed.
Jerome Monaghan, Clerk:_____
By, Sarah Kent Moore, Assistant Clerk:_____

## VOLUNTARY PETITION—SCHEDULE OF ASSETS AND LIABILITIES (Form 6)

U.S. BANKRUPTCY COURT FOR THE _____ DISTRICT OF_____

## Schedule A: Statement of Debtor's Liabilities

Instructions: For Schedules A-1, A-2, and A-3, disclose all claims against the debtor or the debtor's
property as of the date the petition was filed.

## Schedule A-1: Priority Creditors

Instructions: for each claim, state in column (1) the nature of the claim; in column (2) the creditor's name and mailing address (including zip code); in column (3), the date the claim was incurred and the consideration supporting the claim. Indicate if the claim is subject to a setoff, evidenced in writing (e.g., by a judgment or negotiable instrument); whether it was incurred as a partner or joint contractor; and if so, with whom. State in column (4) whether the claim is contingent, disputed, or unliquidated. Give the amount of the claim in column (5). Indicate if any item is not applicable (N/A).

*a.* Wages, salary, and commissions owed to employees (up to $2,000 each) and earned within 90 days before the filing of the petition or the date business ceased. (Include vacation, severance, and sick pay.) Date business ceased:

| 1 | 2 | 3 | 4 | 5 |
|---|---|---|---|---|

*b.* Contributions to employee benefit plans attributable to services rendered within 180 days before the filing of the petition or the date business ceased. Date business ceased:

| 1 | 2 | 3 | 4 | 5 |
|---|---|---|---|---|

*c.* Up to $2,000 per farmer for claims of farmers under 11 U.S.C. Section 507(a)(5)(A)

| 1 | 2 | 3 | 4 | 5 |
|---|---|---|---|---|

*d.* Up to $2,000 per fisherman for claims of United States fishermen under 22 U.S.C. Section 507(a)(5)(B)

| 1 | 2 | 3 | 4 | 5 |
|---|---|---|---|---|

*e.* Up to $900 per depositor, for deposits by individuals for property purchases, rentals, or leases of property or services for personal, family, or household use that the debtor failed to deliver or provide

| 1 | 2 | 3 | 4 | 5 |
|---|---|---|---|---|

*f.* Taxes itemized by type of tax and taxing authority:
Federal taxes: $ _____
State taxes: $ _____
Other taxing authorities: $ _____
Total for Schedule A-1: $_____

**************************************************************************

## Schedule A-2: Secured Creditors

Instructions: For each creditor, give the name and address (including zip code) (column 1); describe the security and the date it was granted to the creditor (column 2); specify the date the claim was incurred and for what consideration, whether it was evidenced in writing; and whether and with whom the debt was incurred as a partner or joint contractor (column 3). Indicate in column (4) if the claim is contingent, unliquidated, or disputed, and the market value of the claim in column (5). In column (6), give the amount of the claim. Do not deduct the value of the security.

| 1 | 2 | 3 | 4 | 5 | 6 |
|---|---|---|---|---|---|

Total for Schedule A-2: $_____

**************************************************************************

## Schedule A-3: Unsecured Creditors Who Do Not Have Priority

Instructions: In column (1), for each claim, give the name and address of each creditor (including zip code). If a negotiable instrument is involved, give the last known holder. In column (2), state when and for what consideration each claim was incurrent; if it is subject to setoff or contingent, unliquidated or disputed; if it is evidenced by a writing; if and with whom incurred as a partnership or joint contractor debt. In column (3), indicate if the claim is contingent, unliquidated, or disputed. Give the amount of the claim in column (4).

| 1 | 2 | 3 | 4 |

Total for Schedule A-3: $_____

\*\*\*\*\*\*\*\*\*\*\*\*\*\*\*\*\*\*\*\*\*\*\*\*\*\*\*\*\*\*\*\*\*\*\*\*\*\*\*\*\*\*\*\*\*\*\*\*\*\*\*\*\*\*\*\*\*\*\*\*\*\*\*\*\*\*\*\*\*\*\*\*\*\*\*\*\*\*\*\*\*\*\*\*

## Schedule B: The Debtor's Property

In Schedules B-1, B-2, B-3, and B-4, include all property belonging to the debtor as of the date of filing of the petition.

## Schedule B-1: Real Property

1. Give the location and description of all real property in which the debtor has any type of interest (e.g., ownership; equitable and future interests; property held by the entireties; community property life estates; leaseholds; rights and powers that can be exercised for benefit of the debtor).

2. Disclose the nature of the debtor's interest in each property, specifying the deeds and written instruments relating to each.

3. State the market value of the debtor's interest in the property. Do not deduct the secured claims of Schedule A-2 or the Schedule B-4 exemptions.

Total for Schedule B-1: _____

## Schedule B-2: Personal Property

For each type of property, itemize the description and location of each item or category and disclose the market value of the debtor's interest. Do not deduct the secured claims of Schedule A-2 or the Schedule B-4 exemptions.

*a.* Cash on hand $_____
*b.* Accounts with banking institutions, savings and loan institutions, brokerage houses, credit unions, etc. $_____
*c.* Household goods, supplies, furnishings $_____
*d.* Books, pictures, objets d'art, collectibles $_____
*e.* Personal possessions such as wearing apparel, jewelry, sporting equipment $_____
*f.* Vehicles (automobiles, trucks, trailers etc.) $_____
*g.* Boats and accessories $_____

*h.* Livestock, animals, poultry                                          $_____
*i.* Farm equipment, supplies, etc.                                       $_____
*j.* Office equipment, supplies, furnishings                              $_____
*k.* Business machinery, equipment, supplies not otherwise disclosed      $_____
*l.* Inventory                                                            $_____
*m.* Other tangible personal property                                     $_____
*n.* General intangibles and their supporting documents (patents, copy-   $_____
rights, licenses, franchises)
*o.* Negotiable and non-negotiable instruments (e.g., bonds)              $_____
*p.* Other liquidated debts owed to the debtor                            $_____
*q.* Estimated value of each contingent and unliquidated claim; disclose  $_____
any counterclaims that the debtor has
*r.* Itemize the issuer and surrender value of each insurance contract in $_____
which the debtor has an interest
*s.* Itemize the name and issuer of annuities in which the debtor has an  $_____
interest
*t.* Itemize the debtor's interests in companies (whether incorporated or $_____
unincorporated)
*u.* Debtors' partnership interests                                       $_____
*v.* Itemize equitable and future interests, life estates, rights and powers $_____
exercisable for the debtor's behalf, and their evidencing instruments, to
the extent the interests are not otherwise disclosed
Total for Schedule B-2                                                    $_____

\*\*\*\*\*\*\*\*\*\*\*\*\*\*\*\*\*\*\*\*\*\*\*\*\*\*\*\*\*\*\*\*\*\*\*\*\*\*\*\*\*\*\*\*\*\*\*\*\*\*\*\*\*\*\*\*\*\*\*\*\*\*\*\*\*\*\*\*\*\*\*\*\*\*\*\*\*\*\*\*\*\*\*

## Schedule B-3: Property Not Disclosed on Other Schedules

Instructions: For each type of property, disclose the type of property; its description and location; and the market value of the debtor's interest. Do not deduct the Schedule A-2 secured claims or the Schedule B-4 exemptions.

*a.* Property that was transferred subject to an assignment for the benefit of
creditors during the 120 days before the petition was filed. Give the date
of the assignment; to whom assigned; amount the assignee realized; and,
insofar as the debtor is aware, the disposition of the proceeds              $_____

*b.* All other property not disclosed on any other schedule                  $_____

Total for Schedule B-3:                                                      $_____

\*\*\*\*\*\*\*\*\*\*\*\*\*\*\*\*\*\*\*\*\*\*\*\*\*\*\*\*\*\*\*\*\*\*\*\*\*\*\*\*\*\*\*\*\*\*\*\*\*\*\*\*\*\*\*\*\*\*\*\*\*\*\*\*\*\*\*\*\*\*\*\*\*\*\*\*\*\*\*\*\*\*\*

## Schedule B-4: Debtors' Claims of Exempt Property

The Debtor claims that the following property is exempt under 11 U.S.C. Section 522(d)/state laws of the state of _____ .

Instructions: For each item or type of property, describe the property (column 1), its location and description (column 2), its use (if that is relevant to the exempt status of the property) ( column 3), the statutory justification for the exemption (column 4), and the claimed exempt value (column 5).

1        2        3        4        5

Total for Schedule B-4: $_____

\*\*\*\*\*\*\*\*\*\*\*\*\*\*\*\*\*\*\*\*\*\*\*\*\*\*\*\*\*\*\*\*\*\*\*\*\*\*\*\*\*\*\*\*\*\*\*\*\*\*\*\*\*\*\*\*\*\*\*\*\*\*\*\*\*\*\*\*\*\*\*\*\*\*\*\*\*\*\*\*

## Summary of Debts and Property

### Debts
| | |
|---|---|
| Wages, etc. with priority (from Schedule A-1) | $_____ |
| Bank accounts and other deposits (A-1) | $_____ |
| Federal taxes owed (A-1) | $_____ |
| State taxes owed (A-1) | $_____ |
| Other taxes owed (A-1) | $_____ |
| Secured claims (A-2) | $_____ |
| Unsecured claims without priority (A-3) | $_____ |
| Schedule A grand total | $_____ |
| | $_____ |

### Property
| | |
|---|---|
| Total value of real property (Schedule B-1) | $_____ |
| Cash on hand (B-2) | $_____ |
| Deposits paid by customers (B-2) | $_____ |
| Household goods (B-2) | $_____ |
| Books, pictures, collections (B-2) | $_____ |
| Personal possessions (B-2) | $_____ |
| Vehicles (B-2) | $_____ |
| Boats (B-2) | $_____ |
| Livestock and animals (B-2) | $_____ |
| Farm supplies and equipment (B-2) | $_____ |
| Office supplies and equipment (B-2) | $_____ |
| Business machinery, equipment, supplies (B-2) | $_____ |
| Inventory (B-2) | $_____ |
| Other tangible personal property (B-2) | $_____ |
| General intangibles (B-2) | $_____ |
| Bonds and other instruments (B-2) | $_____ |
| Other liquidated debts (B-2) | $_____ |
| Contingent and unliquidated claims (B-2) | $_____ |
| Interests in insurance policies (B-2) | $_____ |
| Annuities (B-2) | $_____ |
| Interests in companies (B-2) | $_____ |
| Partnership interests (B-2) | $_____ |
| Equitable and future interests, etc. (B-2) | $_____ |
| Property assigned for benefit of creditors (B-3) | $_____ |
| Miscellaneous property not scheduled (B-3) | $_____ |
| Schedule B grand total | $_____ |

[Add Unsworn Declaration, Form 4]

## VOLUNTARY PETITION—(Statement of Business Debtor's Financial Affairs) (Form 8)

Teleman, Panzram & Stossel, Attorneys for the Debtors
980 Bantam Lane, Suite 209
Roselands, Adams, 99999-324

U.S. Bankruptcy Court for the
Western District of Adams

Instructions: For partnership or corporate debtors, answer the questions on behalf of the partnership or corporation and have the form certified by a partner or duly authorized corporate officer. Answer every question or explain the failure to answer; indicate if a question is not applicable ("N/A") or if the answer is "none." Attach a labelled extra sheet if the space on the form is not large enough to answer the question.

### 1. Business' Name, Location, and Type
*a.* What is the name and location of the business?
    Cornfields Country Products, Inc.
    Oriole Mall, East Jacksonville, Adams, 99999
*b.* When was the business started?
    Date of incorporation: 3/19/87
*c.* What is the nature of the business? (Give the last date of operations for terminated businesses.)
    Manufacture, sale, and distribution of home and housewares products with a country kitchen theme
*d.* If you have carried on business during the six years immediately preceding the filing of the petition under any other names, or in any other location, give the addresses, names of partners or other associates, nature of the business, and date of commencement and termination of the business.
    N/A

### 2. Business Books and Records
*a.* Give the names, addresses, and dates of engagement for everyone who has kept your business' books and records, or has supervised the record keeping, during the six years before filing of the bankruptcy petition (start with the most recent, and work back).
    Landon and Rodriques, CPAs, 2393 Park Road, Columbus,
    Adams, 99998 4/88–present
    Jeremy Liversedge, Accountant, 145 Blair Avenue,
    Columbus, Adams, 99998 3/87–4/88
*b.* Give the names, addresses, and dates of engagement for everyone who has audited your books and records during the six years before the filing of the bankruptcy petition.
    N/A
*c.* Where are the books and records kept, and who has control over them?
    The books and records are kept in the corporation's business offices, under the control of Pat Gagliardi, Treasurer.

*d.* Are all the books and records available? If not, why not?

   All books and records are available except payroll records for the period 11/87–3/88 (damaged by sprinkler leak, 5/89).

*e.* Have any of your books or records been lost, destroyed, or disposed of during the two years before the filing of the bankruptcy petition? If so, explain.

   See above. Also, on advice of CPAs, paper records pertaining to pre-1989 operations were destroyed when the contents of the records were computerized in February 1989.

### 3. Financial Statements

Have you issued any written financial statements (including statements to mercantile, trade, and credit agencies) during the two-year period before the filing of the bankruptcy petition? If so, give the names and addresses of the persons and organizations to whom the statements were issued.

   N/A

### 4. Inventories

*a.* Date your last inventory was taken

   8/19/90

*b.* Who performed or supervised this inventory?

   Store employees, under the supervision of the Treasurer

*c.* Was the inventory taken at ☑ cost ☐ market ☐ other

   [explain].      Total: $179,413.12

*d.* Date of the inventory before the last inventory?

   8/30/89

*e.* Who performed or supervised this inventory?

   See (b), above.

*f.* Was the inventory taken at ☑ cost ☐ market ☐ other

   [explain].      Total: $122,896.45

*g.* Where are your inventory records kept, and under whose control?

   At the business office, under control of the Treasurer

### 5. Nonbusiness Income

For each of the two years preceding the filing of the petition, explain in detail all income received (other than from operation of your business).

   1989: Interest on business savings account, First Federal Bank: $2,417

   Income earned by investing business funds in the stock market: $3,238

   1990: Interest on business savings account, First Federal Bank: $946

### 6. Tax Returns, Tax Refunds

*a.* Where are the copies of your tax returns for the three years before the filing of the petition kept? Who controls them?

   In the office of our CPA firm—see above.

*b.* State in detail all tax refunds received during the two years preceding the filing of the bankruptcy petition

   1989: Federal income tax refund: $950

   State franchise tax refund: $378

   1990: N/A (all taxes underpaid and penalties assessed)

*c.* State in detail all tax refunds which you can reasonably expect to receive this year.

   N/A (all taxes either paid at appropriate level, or underpaid)

### 7. Bank Accounts and Related Financial Devices

*a.* Disclose the institutions, account numbers, and persons authorized to withdraw from the account for each account you have maintained with a bank or related institution (e.g., credit union, brokerage house) during the two years before the filing of the petition.

All: Qualified to withdraw are Michael Hess, President, and the Treasurer

Savings Account, First Federal Bank, #9K-3248-71B

Checking Account, First Federal Bank, #AR3-5264-003

Payroll Account, Fidelity Trust Bank, #89845/435/22B

Certificate of Deposit, Commercial Bank, #87-435,91,04

*b.* For every safe deposit box or depository used for cash and valuables during the two years before the filing of the petition, disclose the name and address of the bank or other depository, the name in which the box, etc. was kept, and the name and address of every person having access to the box. If the box or depository has been transferred, give the name and address of the transferee; if it has been surrendered, give the date of surrender.

N/A

### 8. Property Held for Others

Describe all property held for any other person or organization, and give the name and address of the owner. Disclose all legal documents or instruments relating to your custody of this property.

N/A

### 9. Property Held by Others

Disclose the description and location of any property in which you have an interest that is held by others; disclose who is holding the property, and why.

$8,000 worth of assorted merchandise held by the VFW to be displayed for sale at the Fall Fashion Fair

### 10. Prior Bankruptcy Proceedings

If you have previously filed for bankruptcy, or been the subject of an involuntary bankruptcy petition, give the court in which the petition was filed; the number of the case; the type of case; whether the case was dismissed; whether a discharge was granted or denied; and whether a composition, arrangement, or plan was confirmed.

N/A

### 11. Liquidations (Receiverships, General Assignments)

*a.* Disclose the extent to which, at the time this bankruptcy petition was filed, your property was in the hands of a liquidating agent such as a receiver or trustee. Describe the property and give the name and address of the agent. For court-appointed agents, disclose the name and site of the court, the caption and docket number of the case, and the type of case.

N/A

*b.* Disclose all assignments of property for the benefit of creditors and general settlements with creditors made during the two-year period before the filing of the bankruptcy petition. Give the date of each assignment, the name and address of the recipient, and summarize the terms of the assignment or settlement.

N/A

### 12. Suits, Executions, Attachments

*a.* As of the date of filing of the bankruptcy petition, were you a party to any suit? If so, give the caption and docket number of the case and the court in which it is pending.

No

*b.* If you were a party to any suit terminated during the year before the filing of the petition, disclose the caption and docket number of the case, the court in which it was pending, the type of proceeding, and its outcome.

Civ. No. 87-12, 342-PI/B415, *Ameling* v. *Cornfields Country Products, Inc.,* Country Court of St. Helen's County; personal injury suit brought by shopper who claimed to have suffered a broken ankle after slipping on negligently maintained staircase on our business premises; settled after payment of medical expenses by our premises liability insurance carrier, Farm & Home Assurances, Inc.

*c.* Disclose all property attached, garnished, or seized under legal or equitable process during the year before the filing of the bankruptcy petition (property seized, person garnished, and for whose benefit).

N/A

### 13. Payment of Debts

*a.* Disclose all debt payments you have made during the year before the filing of the petition with respect to loans; installment purchases of merchandise, other goods, and services; and other debts. Disclose the name and address of the creditor, the date the debt was incurred, the original amount of the debt, the dates of all payments during the year; relationship of any payee who is an "insider" or partner (e.g., corporate officer, director, or stockholder, or immediate family member of such).

1. Monthly payments of $650 each to the Independence National Bank, months of August, September, October, and November, in repayment of a $10,000 installment note dated February 3, 1989.

2. Repayment of $2,000 demand loan, made April 3, 1990, to Edward Martino (20% stockholder).

3. Monthly payments of $400 each to StorShow Services, Inc., months of July–March, under a contract for remodeling of store and for showcases and other display equipment (date of contract July 1989; principal amount $15,000).

*a.* Disclose any debts owed to any creditor that were set off by the creditor against a debt or deposit that the creditor owed to you during the year before the filing of the bankruptcy petition. Disclose the names and addresses of parties performing a setoff, the amount of the debts owed by and to you, the dates of the setoffs, and the relationship of any creditor who is a relative or insider.

N/A

### 14. Property Transfers

*a.* Disclose all gifts (other than ordinary and usual family presents and charitable contributions) made during the year before the filing of the bankruptcy petition; give the names and addresses of the donees, the date of each gift, and its description including value).

12/11/89: Steuben glass bowl ($350) to Barry Bowman, Editor, Mall World

12/14/89: Case of champagne ($500) to Carla Davidson Huegli, consumer correspondent, WBTB Radio

*b.* Disclose all other transfers and dispositions made outside the ordinary course of business during the year before the filing of the bankruptcy petition. Disclose the date of the transfer/disposition, nature of the transaction, what was transferred, who received the property, if the transferee was an insider, if any consideration was received, what was done with the consideration.

1/24/90: Transfer of folk art objects appraised at $17,000 to President's ex-wife as part of a divorce settlement, in return for her surrender of all actual or potential, present or future claims against the business

### 15. *Receivables*
Disclose all assignments (absolute or as security) of accounts receivable or other receivables during the year before the filing of the petition. Give the name and address of each assignee.

   N/A

### 16. *Repossession; Returns*
Disclose all property returned to or repossessed by the seller, lessor, or secured party during the year before the filing of the bankruptcy petition giving the name and address of the recipient of the property and the description and value of the property.

   Repossessions: None. Returns: Approximately $3,500 worth of placemats, pot holders, and other soft furnishings returned as defective on November 3, 1989 to the Appalachian Crafts Workshop Center, Pine Holler, Kentucky

### 17. *Business Leases*
Disclose, for each business lease, the name and address of the landlord; the amount of rent you pay; amount of any security deposit held by the landlord; and the date as of which rent was paid when the petition was filed.

   Our landlord is Ace Development & Management, Tower 2, Cody Center, Plainview, Adams. Our rent is $2,000 per month plus 1½% of covered sales, and the land-lord has a $4,000 security deposit in an interest-bearing account. Rent is paid until August, 1990.

### 18. *Losses*
Disclose all losses from fire, theft, or gambling during the year before the filing of the bankruptcy petition, including dates, names, and places of the loss; the amount or value of the loss; what was lost; and the extent to which the loss was insured.

   Shoplifting and other inventory shrinkage of approximately $5,000; uninsured

### 19. *Withdrawals*
Sole proprietors: Disclose all personal withdrawals made from the business during the year before filing of the bankruptcy petition

Partnerships, corporations: Disclose all withdrawals (bonuses, loans, as well as normal compensation) made by or payable to partners, officers, directors, insiders, managers, and shareholders during the year before the filing of the petition. Disclose the name of each recipient, the dates of withdrawals, amounts received, and nature and purpose of each.

   Salaries of President and Treasurer: $45,000 each.
   Christmas bonus paid to President 12/20/89: $4,000
   Christmas bonus paid to Treasurer 12/20/89: $2,000
   Loan to President: $4,000 December 1, 1989 (to pay expenses related to divorce)
   Salary of First and Second Vice-Presidents, Millicent Lakington and Arthur Aalborg, $40,000 each
   Salary of Store Manager, Esther Perlstine, $35,000
   Loan to Store Manager, 8/30/89: $10,000 (used to make down payment on cooperative apartment)

### 20. *Payments to Attorneys, Etc.*
*a.* If you have consulted an attorney during the year before filing of the bankruptcy petition, or after the petition, give date, name, and address: _____

   Many times since October, 1989: Teleman, Panzram & Stossel, address as above
   Summer of 1989, in connection with personal injury suit disclosed above: Dennis DuBow, Esq., 24 East 39th Avenue, Chamfortsville, Adams

*b.* Disclose all fees paid and property transferred to any attorney or other person rendering services to you in connection with this case, including description of property and date of transfers.

Various payments to Teleman, Panzram firm totaling $10,614.93

*c.* Disclose all agreements since the year before the filing of the petition to pay an attorney or other service provider in connection with this case.

Under retainer agreement with Teleman, Panzram firm (dated September 3, 1989) an hourly fee of $100 is payable for services after the initial retainer of $7,500 is exhausted

### 21. Partners or Officers, Directors, Managers

*a.* Disclose the name and address of each partner, or the name, address, and title of each corporate officer, insider, managing executive, and 20% stockholder.

President: Michael Hess, Rosewood Condominium Residences, Rosewood, Adams

First Vice-President/Secretary: Mildred Lakington, 8312 Sandberg Place, Pineview, Adams

Second Vice-President: Arthur Aalborg, Rosewood Condominium Residences, Rosewood, Adams

Treasurer: Pat Gagliardi: "Dunroamin", Sandberg Estates, Adams

20% Stockholder: Edward Martino, "Little Paddocks," Sandberg Estates, Adams

*b.* Disclose the name, address, reason for the withdrawal or termination (if known) and disposition if any partner has withdrawn, or any corporate officer, director, insider, or managing executive has terminated the business relationship, or any 20% stockholder has disposed of more than 50% of the stockholding.

N/A

*c.* Disclose the details of any transaction in which any person has acquired or disposed of 20% or more of the corporation's stock during the year before the filing of the bankruptcy petition (give person's name and address).

N/A

I, Michael Hess, President, declare under penalty of perjury that I have read the preceding statement of affairs and that the information contained therein is true and correct to the best of my knowledge, information, and belief.

Date: _____ , 199____
Signed: _____

## LIST OF CREDITORS HOLDING 20 LARGEST UNSECURED CLAIMS (Form 9)

U.S. Bankruptcy Court for the _____ District of_____

Instructions: Under Rule 1007(d), the Chapter 11 debtor is required to prepare a list of the creditors holding the 20 largest unsecured claims. The creditors to be included in the list do not include (1) anyone who is defined as an "insider" in 11 U.S.C. Section 101(25); (2) secured creditors, unless the unsecured deficiency makes the creditor's claim one of the 20 largest unsecured claims; and (3) governmental units that are not defined as "persons" under 11 U.S.C. Section 101(35).

In Column (1), give the creditor's name and mailing address (including zip code).

In Column (2), give the name, telephone number, and mailing address (including zip code) of an employee or agent of the creditor who is familiar with the claim and who can discuss the claim.

In Column (3), disclose the nature of the claim (e.g., bank loan, judgment, trade debt).

In Column (4), indicate if the claim is contingent, unliquidated, disputed, or subject to setoff.

In Column (5), give the amount of the claim. If it is a secured claim, also state the value of the security.

| *1* | *2* | *3* | *4* | *5* |
|---|---|---|---|---|
| Creditor: | | | | |
| 1. | | | | |
| 2. | | | | |
| 3. | | | | |
| 4. | | | | |
| 5. | | | | |
| 6. | | | | |
| 7. | | | | |
| 8. | | | | |
| 9. | | | | |
| 10. | | | | |
| 11. | | | | |
| 12. | | | | |
| 13. | | | | |
| 14. | | | | |
| 15. | | | | |
| 16. | | | | |
| 17. | | | | |
| 18. | | | | |
| 19. | | | | |
| 20. | | | | |

Date: _____ , 199_____

Debtor's Signature: _____

## INVOLUNTARY CASE:
## CREDITOR'S PETITION (Form 11)

Jamieson & Knapp, Attorneys for the Petitioners
348 Martin Luther King Drive
Paul's Ferry, Tyler, 33333

### U.S. BANKRUPTCY COURT FOR THE
### DISTRICT OF TYLER

*1.* The petitioners in this case are TuffSteel Tools, Inc., 467 March Avenue, North Stratton, Tyler; The Pigment Workshop PAINT Co., 97B Industrial Park, Stratton Township, Tyler; and Prince Albert Victorian Reproduction Wallpapers, Inc., 73 Damaris Lane, Paul's Ferry, Tyler.

*2.* The petitioners are creditors of Colonial Hardware & Decorating, Inc., located in the Shipstead Mall, Stratton Township, Tyler, in the county of Augsburg.

*3.* The claims of the petitioners are as follows:

TuffSteel Tools, Inc., $26,783
The Pigment Workshop, $10,000
Prince Albert Wallpapers, $8,749.

These claims are not subject to bona fide dispute. The debtor's liability as to these claims is not contingent. None of the petitioners has any lien on the debtor's property to secure the claims, hence the aggregate of the claims is significantly greater than $5,000.

*4.* This district is the appropriate district for filing of this petition, in that the debtor's principal place of business is located within this district, and has been so located continuously since its incorporation in 1983.

*5.* An order for relief may be entered against the debtor pursuant to Title 11 of the United States Code.

*6.* The petitioners have made many attempts to telephone or personally contact officers and managers of the debtor, but all these attempts have been unavailing. The petitioners have sent repeated invoices, bills, and collection letters but have not received any payments within the last six months, except for a check for $1,000 to Prince Albert Wallpapers that was dishonored by the bank. The debtor is the subject of 14 collection actions now pending in the courts of the state of Tyler. These facts indicate that the debtor is generally not paying bona fide, nondisputed debts as they become due.

WHEREFORE, Petitioners pray that this court grant them an order of relief against the debtor under Chapter 7/Chapter 11 of the United States Code.

Signed: _____                                   Attorneys for the Petitioners

I, Gilbert Eatonton, President of the Pigment Workshop, am one of the petitioners named in this petition and I declare under penalty of perjury that, to the best of my knowledge, information, and belief, all material contained in the petition is true and correct.

Date: _____ , 199____
Signature: _____

## ORDER FOR MEETING WITH CREDITORS (Form 16)

U.S. Bankruptcy Court for the Southern District of Roosevelt

In re Fiedorek & Sandys Imported Motorcars Inc., aka Fiedorek/Sandys Autodome Showroom Inc., Debtor
EIN 55-55555
Bankruptcy Case No. 91-23, 945TBM
TO ALL PARTIES IN INTEREST:

An order for relief pursuant to a voluntary Chapter 11 petition under Title 11 of the United States Code having been entered on March 3, 1991, and certain acts and proceedings against the debtor and its property having been stayed under 11 U.S.C. Section 362(a), it is ORDERED and notice hereby given that

## Creditors' Meeting

*1.* A creditors' meeting pursuant to 11 U.S.C. Section 341(a) has been set down for August 9, 1991, 10:30 am, at the offices of Hellman & DuParc, Attorneys at Law, 45 Themis Tower, Greenapple, Roosevelt. The meeting may be continued or adjourned if notice to that effect is given at the meeting; no further written notice to creditors is required.

*2.* It is mandatory that the debtor's president or other executive officer appear at the meeting to be examined. Attendance by the creditors is welcomed but is not mandatory.

*3.* At the meeting, creditors will be given an opportunity to file their claims, examine the debtor, and, in appropriate cases, elect a committee of creditors, a trustee, and someone to supervise the meeting. As of yet, no trustee has been appointed for the estate of the debtor.

## Filing of Claims

*4.* The debtor or trustee has filed or will file a list of creditors and equity security holders as required by Bankruptcy Rule 1007. It is permitted, but not required, for creditors whose listed claim is not identified as disputed, contingent, or unliquidated in amount, to file a proof of claim. Filing of a proof of claim, on or before a date to be set later, and of which you will be notified, is required if unlisted creditors or those whose claims are identified as disputed, contingent, or unliquidated in amount want to participate in the case or share in the distribution. Creditors are responsible for determining that their claims are accurately listed.

*5.* Unless the time is extended by this court, all objections to the debtor's Schedule B-4 claim that certain property is exempt must be filed within 30 days after the meeting of creditors is held.

SO ORDERED,

Date: _____ , 199____                                                     BY THE COURT
Bankruptcy Judge: _____


## MOTION FOR APPOINTMENT OF CHAPTER 11 TRUSTEE

Gamsen & Pond, Attorneys for the Movant
192 Courthouse Tower
Brookstone, Adams, 99999-001
U.S. Bankruptcy Court
_____ Dist. of_____
In re McHeaney's Olde Public House, Debtor _____ Case No.: ____ Dilwyn's Fine Ales,
Inc., moves that the Bankruptcy Court of the _____ District of _____appoint a
trustee in the Chapter 11 Bankruptcy case captioned above.

*1.* The Debtor filed a Chapter 11 bankruptcy petition with the Bankruptcy Court of the _____ District of _____on _____ , 199____ .

*2.* Since that time, Debtor has been acting as a Debtor in Possession.

*3.* Dilwyn's Fine Ales, Inc., is an unsecured creditor of the debtor in the amount of $38,629.15.

*4.* The Debtor is a business of a type involving cash payments and few records (and those records are easily subject to manipulation). Unless a trustee is appointed, there is a significant risk that the debtor will understate its income, conceal assets, overstate expenses, refrain from conducting efficient and profitable business operations, and otherwise jeopardize the ability of creditors (especially unsecured creditors) to collect their debts. Appointment of a trustee will lessen or eliminate the risk of such negative consequences.

Date: _____ , 199____
Attorney for the Movant
To _____ , Attorney for the Debtor in Possession PLEASE BE NOTIFIED THAT, ON _____ , 199____ , AT ____M. (or as soon as the matter can be heard), this motion will be brought before the court in Room ____of the courthouse located at _____ .

## Notice to Trustee

U.S. Bankruptcy Court _____ Dist. of_____
   In re Filiato Search Enterprises, Inc., Debtor Case No.: Notice to Henry Falchetti, Esq. of Dimock, Falchetti & Stroeck:
   PLEASE TAKE NOTICE that, pursuant to Bankruptcy Rule 2008, you have been appointed as Trustee of the estate of the debtor named in the caption, and are hereby so notified. You must notify Hon. Helena Lockyear of the Bankruptcy Court of your decision to accept or reject this appointment, within five business days of the day you receive this notice.
   If you accept the appointment, you must post bond in the amount of $_____ with the court on or before _____ , 199 ____ .
   ALSO TAKE NOTICE that the last date for filing a complaint to block the debtor's discharge is _____ , 199 ____ (whether filed by the trustee or any other party in interest).

Date: _____ , 199____
_____Clerk of Bankruptcy Court

## MOTION FOR ENTRY OF CONSENT ORDER CONDITIONING RIGHTS OF DEBTOR IN POSSESSION

Speaight, Landau & Kimpel, Attorneys for the Debtor
693 Elmhurst Drive
Daley City, Tyler, 22222
U.S. Bankruptcy Court for the District of Tyler
In re Bernardine's Hair Fashions, Inc., Case No. K90-346/406
EIN: 44-44444

### Motion for Entry of Consent Order Placing Conditions on the Rights of the Debtor in Possession

Peter T. Rannald, U.S. Trustee for the District of Tyler, and Jeremy Speaight, counsel for the Debtor in Possession, Bernardine's Hair Fashions, Inc., move that this court enter the attached Consent Order Placing Conditions on the Rights of the Debtor in Possession in order to assist the administration of the case commenced by the debtor's filing of a voluntary Chapter 11 petition on January 4, 1991.

---

U.S. Trustee

---

Attorney for the Debtor in Possession

U.S. Bankruptcy Court for the District of Tyler
In re Bernardine's Hair Fashions, Inc., Debtor
EIN 44-4444
Bankruptcy Case No.
K90-346/406

## Consent Order Placing Conditions on the Rights of the Debtor in Possession

Under the agreement reached between the debtor (by its counsel Jeremy Speaight) and the U.S. Trustee for this District, it is hereby ORDERED that, pending further orders of this Court, the debtor shall be permitted to have the status of debtor in possession and continue to operate its business under these conditions:

*1.* The current books of account must be closed. New books of account must be opened and maintained starting with the date of filing of the petition, and showing all earnings, expenses, payments, receipts, and disbursements of the debtor.

*2.* All bank accounts must be closed, and the account proceeds transferred to two Debtor in Possession Accounts to be opened in the authorized federal depository or depositories of the debtor's choice. The first account is the Debtor in Possession Account, to be used for non-tax disbursements in the ordinary course of business, with disbursements to be made only on checks signed by the following individuals who are authorized officers of the debtor: Bernardine Sinclair, President, and Arthur Wickes Sinclair, Jr., Treasurer.

*3.* The second account will be the Debtor in Possession Tax Account, into which the debtor must deposit all funds required to be escrowed by state law, such as payroll taxes, sales taxes, and real estate taxes. The debtor must pay all taxes as they come due, and must file all necessary returns and information statements. As long as the bankruptcy proceeding remains pending, funds can be disbursed from the Tax Account only for the purpose of paying taxes, and only by check signed by debtor's counsel and by its President and/or Treasurer.

For each payroll period, the debtor must deposit all federal payroll taxes in the Tax Account and submit a copy of IRS Form 6123 (Verification of Fiduciary's Federal Tax Deposit), signed by an authorized bank employee, to the office of the U.S. Trustee within two days of each payment.

*4.* The debtor must not use the money or assets of its estate to pay any debt incurred before the petition was filed, or which could come under or be affected by the debtor's plan of reorganization, unless the Court so orders.

*5.* The debtor must notify the creditor's committee and the U.S. Trustee before it hires any additional employees, increases the compensation of any employee, or enters into any new contract under which any type of services will be provided to it.

**6.** The debtor must file a verified monthly report with the Court, the U.S. Trustee, and each member of the creditors' committee, on or before the 10th day of each month (beginning with the month of September 1991). The U.S. Trustee will provide the forms for the report, which must disclose monthly cash flow and profit and loss.

**7.** Until a Plan of Reorganization is filed, the debtor must make regular reports on the status of the case (including progress toward drafting and implementing a Plan of Reorganization). The first report must be filed with the Court, the U.S. Trustee, and with each member of the creditors' committee within 120 days of commencement of this case. An updated report must be filed with the same parties every 90 days after the initial report is filed.

**8.** The U.S. Trustee has the right to demand information about the debtors' business affairs, and the debtor must furnish the information.

The debtor is hereby granted the status of debtor in possession, and may conduct its business affairs without stay or hindrance, subject to the terms and conditions of this order.

Date: _____ , 199____

                                                        _____
U.S. Bankruptcy Judge

We consent to entry of this order

                                                        _____
U.S. Trustee

                                                        _____
Attorney for the Debtor

## ORDER DESIGNATING PERSON RESPONSIBLE FOR PERFORMING DUTIES IMPOSED BY BANKRUPTCY CODE AND RULES

U.S. Bankruptcy Court for the Northern District of Adams
In re Osculla Perfumes & Essences, Inc., Debtor
EIN 22-2222
Bankruptcy Case No. 39,279/90/T

Sherman Henderson, Bankruptcy Judge for the Northern District of Adams, now ORDERS on May 8, 1991, at the Bankruptcy Court for the Northern District of Adams, that Heather Jolliffe, who signed the schedules in the voluntary bankruptcy petition of the debtor, be designated as the person responsible for performing all of the debtor's duties under the Bankruptcy Code (title 11 of the United States Code) and the Bankruptcy Rules promulgated thereunder, until further order of this court.
Signed,                                         _____

                                                         Sherman Henderson, Judge

## REAFFIRMATION AGREEMENT BY DEBTOR IN BANKRUPTCY

United States Bankruptcy Court for the Western District of Adams

------------------------------------------------------------------

In re Carlaparlato, Inc., Debtor _____ Case No.: _____

------------------------------------------------------------------

### Reaffirmation Agreement

Today, _____ , 199 _____ , the Debtor, Carlaparlato, Inc, and Barlow Office Equipment, Inc., its unsecured creditor/creditor, secured by a purchase money security interest on certain machinery and equipment in the amount of $ _____ enter into a reaffirmation agreement subject to the provisions of 11 U.S.C. Section 524(c). The debtor has not yet received a discharge under the Bankruptcy Code.

Despite the prospect of a discharge in the future, Carlaparlato reaffirms its debt and agrees to pay the balance of $ _____ still due and owing to Barlow Office Equipment, Inc., under an agreement dated _____ , 199 _____ . Payments will be made according to the terms and conditions of that agreement [except that there will be 36 monthly payments of $100 each rather than 20 monthly payments of $150 each].

Under federal bankruptcy law, the debtor has the right to rescind the reaffirmation until a discharge in bankruptcy is granted, or until 60 days after this reaffirmation agreement is filed with the Bankruptcy Court—whichever is later.

Debtor, by: _____

Creditor, by: _____

### Declaration by Debtor's Attorney

I, Allan Ziegler, attorney for the debtor, hereby declare under penalty of perjury that I gave the debtor legal advice and counsel while this reaffirmation agreement was being negotiated. It is my professional judgment that the debtor made an informed, voluntary decision to enter into this agreement and that the agreement does not represent an undue burden on the debtor.

Date: _____ , 199_____

Alan Ziegler, Esq.: _____

# Chapter 13

# DEADLOCK, DISSENT, LIQUIDATION, OR APPRAISAL

Closely held corporations are vulnerable to serious political problems. It often happens that the directors and stockholders divide up into two or more factions, with different and irreconcilable ideas about what the corporation should do, especially with regard to the dividends that should be paid! Stockholders of a public corporation who don't trust the management can simply telephone their stock-brokers and sell the shares. But the stock of close corporations, even if it does not have transfer restrictions, can be very hard to sell. If the stockholder does find a buyer and is pleased by the outcome, the corporation's management is likely to be very angry at the result. Yet, because of the nature of the closely held corporation, these struggles tend to be like a fistfight in a rowboat: not only do both combatants get hurt, but the boat tends to get swamped and sink.

## Handling Deadlock

Therefore, several legal mechanisms have evolved for coping with deadlock (the situation in which a corporation cannot get a voting majority on an issue) and with the rights of dissenting stockholders, especially those who object to mergers in which the corporation is engaged. In the most serious cases, many states have a mechanism for "judicial dissolution," in which angry shareholders petition a court to dissolve the corporation and distribute its assets because the Board is too divided to take any action; the shareholders are so hopelessly fragmented that it is impossible to get enough votes to elect any of the candidates to the Board of Directors; or the squabbling has made it impossible to operate the corporation as a productive, profitable business. (The statutes usually set a minimum, such as holders of 20% of the stock, who can petition.)

Many state statutes also protect the rights of shareholders by permitting them to petition a court to dissolve the corporation if the corporation's directors (or other individuals controlling the corporation) are guilty of illegal, fraudulent, or other oppressive action against the shareholders, or of looting the corporate treasury. In order to grant the petition, the court must decide that dissolution is reasonably necessary to protect a substantial number of shareholders—and if it is the *only* way that the dissenting shareholders can be treated fairly. Another possibility is that the court can supervise the purchase of the dissenting shareholders' shares, at fair market value, by the other shareholders.

## Dissolution Situations

In addition to judicial dissolutions, some corporate charters also contain dissolution provisions that do not require court action. That's pretty drastic, and a lesson to all corporate management: if you can't stay on good terms with your stockholders, you're likely to end up without a corporation to manage.

Dissolution of a corporation leads to its liquidation. The corporation is no longer permitted to engage in business. Instead, it must wind up its business, finish performing or settle its contracts, collect its assets and sell them off, and pay all its liabilities. The liquidating corporation notifies its creditors to present their claims within six months. Individual notices must be sent to those that the corporation knows are creditors; public notices must also be published in newspapers.

Once a corporation is liquidated, its assets are distributed in this order:

○ The IRS and state tax authorities (don't forget to file a final franchise tax return)
○ Unpaid wages and unfunded pension liabilities
○ Claims of secured creditors, in order of the priorities their liens have under the law of secured transactions
○ Claims of unsecured creditors, in proportion to the amount they advanced to the corporation
○ If anything is left over—and it's easy to believe that there won't be—to the stockholders, according to the priority schedule for liquidation given in the corporation's charter

Under federal law, IRS Form 966 must be filed within 30 days of the date a corporation adopts a resolution to liquidate or dissolve the corporation. An additional Form 966 must be filed for each amendment to such resolutions. The corporation's final income tax return must include a certified copy of the minutes of the shareholders' meeting that adopted the plan of liquidation, as well as a statement itemizing the corporate assets that were sold, stating when they were sold, whether the corporation had a gain or loss on each, and whether the gain or loss was taxable.

There are other, less drastic, ways to cope with the threat of deadlock. Buy-sell agreements serve many purposes for the closely held corporation. One of them is providing a mechanism for the corporation itself, or for the other stockholders, to buy out an unhappy stockholder and thus eliminate a source of severe conflict. One approach is for the buy-sell agreement to set the price, or provide a mechanism for setting a price, or the agreement can call for an auction of shares among the other shareholders, so market forces will determine the price. Another possibility is to include provisions in the charter, or to make a separate agreement, calling for arbitration of differences before they lead to deadlock.

Dissenting stockholders have rights in another context: if they object to a corporation's merger, exchange of its shares, or sale of all or substantially all of its assets, they have a right to be bought out and receive the fair value of their shares in cash. (In contrast, shareholders who agree to participate in a merger are likely to receive shares of the other corporation's stock instead of cash.)

*Practice Tip:* Shareholders must be notified of their right to dissent in the notice of the meeting contemplating the merger or similar action. Before the vote is taken, the dissenting shareholders must give written notice of their intent to demand payment for their shares. Of course, they must not vote for the action from which they are dissenting.

If the dissenters prove to be in the minority, and the meeting adopts a plan of merger, share exchange, or sale of assets, the corporation must then promptly deliver a written notice to the dissenting shareholders, giving

- A form for demanding cash payment for their shares
- The date on which an announcement about the transaction will be made to the news media
- A demand that the shareholder certify that he or she owned the stock before the date
- Instructions for depositing and being paid for shares (including a deadline not less than 30 or more than 60 days after the date of corporation's notice to the dissenters)

The corporation's duty to the dissenting shareholders is to pay the fair value of their shares, plus accrued interest.

*Practice Tip:* The corporation can't just send a check: the payment must be accompanied by information about the state of the corporation's balance sheet, the corporation's estimate of the fair value of the shares, an explanation of the calculations used to compute the interest, and any information about shareholder rights required by the corporation statutes of the state.

The next move in the game is for the dissenter either to accept the corporation's valuation (and accept the check) or to serve the corporation with a written notice of a demand for a higher payment. The corporation must then either pay the higher amount demanded or petition the appropriate court to set the value of the shares. The court can force the corporation to pay both sides' costs and attorneys' fees if the corporation failed to comply with the requirements of state law—and can do the same to a shareholder who failed to act in good faith.

>        *Practice Tip:* Because this "appraisal" process is so lengthy and expensive, agreements for mergers sometimes contain an "escape clause" calling off the deal if more than a certain number of shareholders dissent.

---

## STAND-BY TRUST OPERATIVE ONLY IN CASE OF DEADLOCK

### Introduction

This agreement, dated _____ , 199_____ , is made between John Sanderson, Michael Gale, Edward Linden, and Paul Dioguardi ("Beneficiaries"), who own all the stock of Sangalen Corporation, and Geoffrey Parker-Tompkins, Esq. ("Trustee"), or his successor as trustee. The purpose of this agreement is to cope with the situation in which the corporation is deadlocked because the stockholders are incapable of reaching an agreement, yet no stockholder or faction can secure enough votes to compel the desired corporate action, by providing a simple and efficient remedy for deadlock.

*1.* The Beneficiaries agree to endorse their stock certificates for Sangalen Corporation's stock in blank; then assign and deliver them to the Trustee, taking any other necessary steps to transfer their shares to the Trustee and have the transfer reflected on the corporation's books.

*2.* This trust continues for a term of ten years from the date of this agreement, unless it is earlier terminated by a written instrument signed by Beneficiaries who together own at least a majority of the Sangalen shares.

*3.* While the trust is in force, Sangalen Corporation will not have the power to issue any further shares of stock. The Trustee agrees not to vote for or approve any amendment to Sangalen's Articles of Incorporation, or to any merger or consolidation of Sangalen with any other corporation, nor to dispose of any Sangalen shares, unless all the Beneficiaries have given their prior written consent.

*4.* The Trustee holds the shares transferred to him for the benefit of the shareholder/Beneficiaries under these terms and conditions:

○ The trustee will collect any dividends and pay the dividends to the Beneficiaries proportionate to their shareholdings before this agreement was created.

○ On request, the Trustee will give any Beneficiary a trust certificate representing the number of shares deposited by the Beneficiary; trust certificates are assignable and transferrable, subject to any transfer restrictions unanimously agreed on by the Beneficiaries.

○ Until and unless a deadlock occurs, the Trustee will vote the shares according to the instructions of the Beneficiaries who hold the majority of the shares.

○ If and when deadlock occurs at any stockholders' or directors' meeting, and when the deadlock continues to exist for 30 days after the meeting, the Trustee will call a special meeting of the Beneficiaries, execute a written consent to dissolution of Sangalen as provided by Title 22, Section 302 of the Consolidated Laws of the State of Roosevelt, and elect himself as sole Director of Sangalen, removing the existing Board of Directors from office. Then, the Trustee will take all steps necessary to wind up the business affairs of Sangalen and to file Articles of Dissolution as required by the laws of Roosevelt. However, on written instructions from holders of a majority of Sangalen's stock, the Trustee will sign a written consent to revocation of voluntary dissolution proceedings as long as the instructions are given before the Secretary of State issues a certificate of dissolution.

**5.** Deadlock exists when the Beneficiaries are unable to agree on instructions to the Trustee to elect a Board of Directors; or, at a Board of Directors' meeting, the Directors are unable to act because there is no quorum or the Directors are evenly divided in their votes. Deadlock is deemed broken if Beneficiaries who own a majority of the shares held by the trustees sign written instructions to the Trustee that will eliminate the deadlock—for example, by electing a new Board of Directors which is able to take action.

**6.** Jane Tomerman, Vice-President of the Corn Chandler's Bank, is hereby designated as successor Trustee if the original Trustee fails to qualify or ever ceases to perform his duties as Trustee; if Jane Tomerman is unable or unwilling to act as Trustee when required, the person then serving as Vice-President of the Corn Chandler's Bank will become successor Trustee; if he or she is unable or unwilling to serve, then the unanimous choice of the Beneficiaries will serve as successor Trustee.

**7.** This trust becomes effective when a counterpart of this agreement is deposited with Sangalen Corporation and the shares are transferred as described in this agreement.

Date: _____ , 199____
Signed: _____
(Stockholders and Trustee)

## NOTICE OF ELECTION

To [stockholder]:
   This is a notice of exercise of my right to demand dissolution of Lutetia Enterprises, Inc., as provided by Section 4.2 of its Articles of Incorporation and Section 625.9 of the laws of the state of Lincoln. As provided, my exercise of this right will lead to dissolution of the corporation 30 days after the date of this notice.

## STOCKHOLDER'S NOTICE OF INTENTION TO DISSENT

I, Elizabeth Laurencin, am a stockholder of Green Meadows, Inc. I own 500 shares of common/preferred stock, represented by Certificate # 1004.

   I object to Green Mountain's announced intention to merge with Purple Cow Dairy Farms/dispose of substantially all its assets/amend its Articles of Incorporation, as evidenced by the action taken at the regular/special meeting of its Board of directors, held on December 14, 1991 at the Green Meadows headquarters.

   As required by state law, I filed a Notice of Objection with the corporation on January 3, 1991; on January 20, 1991, I received Green Meadows' Notice of Authorization (which was dated January 17, 1991).

   As permitted by Section _____ of the laws of the state of _____ , I dissent from Green Meadows' proposed action and demand that I receive a fair payment for my shares.

Date: _____ , 199____
Signed: _____
Address: _____

## PREMEETING NOTICE FROM STOCKHOLDER

### Notice to Ed & Sandy Auto Parts, Inc.

I object to Ed & Sandy Auto Parts, Inc.'s announced intention to dispose of substantially all its assets outside the ordinary course of business. I hereby announce that, if such action is taken as proposed, I will exercise the right of dissent and appraisal as granted by Section 229 of the laws of the state of Jefferson.

Send any required notices to me at 2925 Acacia Avenue, Blake Village, Jefferson, 99999.

Date: _____ , 199____
Signed: _____

## CORPORATE NOTICE OF ACTION

Dear Dissenting Stockholder:

This is an offical notice of the fact that the transaction you objected to, the short-form merger into our parent corporation, Neville's Novelties, Inc., was entered into and became effective on March 2, 1990.

Date of Notice: March 6, 1990          Funtime Toys & Miniatures by Edwin Rawlins, Secretary

## CORPORATION'S CONSENT TO WITHDRAWAL OF A
## NOTICE OF DISSENT

Dear Stockholder:

Shayne Furniture, Inc., has received your notice, dated April 19, 1991, informing Shayne Furniture that you have changed your mind and wish to revoke the Notice of Election to Dissent received by Shayne Furniture on March 3, 1991. As state law requires, Shayne Furniture offered to pay you for your shares of its stock.

However, Shayne Furniture, Inc., is willing to consent to withdrawal of your Notice of Election to Dissent. If you withdraw your Election, all your rights as a shareholder of Shayne Furniture, Inc., will be restored, with an effective date of April 29, 1991. That is, you will be entitled to any dividends or preemptive rights accruing on or after that date. However, you will *not* have the right to receive payment for your shares from Shayne Furniture, Inc.

Date: _____ , 199____
Shayne Furniture, Inc. by Louise Shayne Peterson, President

## NOTICE OF LOSS OF RIGHTS

Dear Stockholder:

On June 2, 1990, Camissco, Inc., received your Notice of Intention to Dissent. However, the laws of the state of Adams require dissenting shareholders to submit the certificates representing all their shares in the corporation's stock to the corporation (or its transfer agent) within 15 days of the filing of the Notice of Intention to Dissent. You did not do this, and therefore you have lost the rights that state law grants to dissenting shareholders.

Date: June 15, 1990                                                        Camissco, Inc.


## CORPORATE NOTICE OF APPRAISAL RIGHTS

Dear Shareholder:

At a regular/special meeting held on September 2, 1991, at its headquarters/at the Petroleum Industry Club, 1904 York Avenue, Carlton, the holders of a majority/over 2/3/over 75% of the oustanding shares of Eternal Flame Oil Co. voted to approve the reorganization of the corporation. [Note: The notice must reflect observation of any "supermajority" provisions in the corporation's charter or bylaws.] Public announcement has been/will be made on ____ , 199 ____ .

However, your shares either were not voted or were voted against the reorganization plan. That entitles you to the rights of a "dissenting stockholder" as defined by Sections 1104–1182 of the laws of the state of Roosevelt. (A copy of the relevant state statutes is attached for your reference.) Eternal Flame Oil Co. has determined that the fair market value of your stock is $103.75 per share.

In order to be paid in cash for your shares, you must send us a written demand within 30 days of the date this notice was mailed, certifying ownership; within this time period, you must also send back all your share certificate(s) to Eternal Flame Oil Co./to its transfer agent, Wilkins Securities Service, 322-79 West 204th Street, Denton.

In your demand, you must indicate whether you accept Eternal Flame's offer or whether you assert that a higher price is the true fair market value of your shares. If you disagree with Eternal Flame's valuation, you have the right to sue the company and have a court set the price that Eternal Flame will pay for your shares. In some cases, you will have a right to be reimbursed by Eternal Flame for lawyers' and appraisers' fees you incur by bringing the suit. YOU ARE REQUIRED TO START ANY SUCH SUIT ON OR BEFORE [date statute of limitations expires].

Date: _____ , 199____
Eternal Flame Oil Co.


## NOTICE OF APPRAISAL RIGHTS (SHORT-FORM MERGER)

Dear Shareholder of Finney's Metal Finishing, Inc.:

Finney's Metal Finishing, Inc. (FMF), is a subsidiary of Globewide Metal Fabrications, Inc. (GMF), which owns 79% of the outstanding shares of FMF. Please be advised that on January 22,

1991, the Board of Directors of Globewide Metal Fabrications, Inc., adopted a resolution to combine the two companies: on or after March 1, 1991, a short-form merger will occur, and FMF will be merged into GMF.

The resolution of the GMF Board of Directors (a copy is attached for your reference; so is a copy of the relevant sections of the state Code of Laws) states that $83 is the fair market value of each of the FMF shares it does not already own. The resolution also describes the cash, stock, or other consideration that is offered to acquire the remaining FMF shares. FMF's Board of Directors has adopted a resolution (dated January 24, 1991) stating that this consideration is fair. A copy of this resolution is attached.

The laws of the state of Adams give you two options. You can either accept GMF's offer, surrender your share certificates, and be paid as described above—or, if you believe the price per share offered is unfairly low, you can become a "dissenting shareholder." [As above.]

## PETITION FOR JUDICIAL DISSOLUTION
### (Where Two Voting Blocks Each Hold 50%)

Recorders' Court of the State of Adams
County of Chacanoggi
-----------------------------------------------------------------

In re the Dissolution of Harbinger                                      Index # C22-1992-3029
Radio-Electronic Components, Inc.
-----------------------------------------------------------------

In and by this petition, William Stahl and Lisa Bankey, Petitioners, hereby allege and respectfully request as follows:

*1.* Harbinger Radio-Electronic Components, Inc., is a corporation duly incorporated in the state of Adams on July 19, 1987, and doing business in good standing. The corporation is not registered as an investment company under the Investment Company Act of 1940, and its shares are neither listed on a national securities exchange nor regularly quoted on an over-the-counter market.

*2.* Harbinger's authorized capitalization consists of 5,000 shares of common stock and 2,000 shares of preferred stock, held as follows:

|                   | *Common* | *Preferred* |
|-------------------|----------|-------------|
| Thomas Marchetti  | 1,500    | 1,000       |
| Gregory Bogan     | 1,000    | 500         |
| William Stahl     | 1,500    | 500         |
| Lisa Bankey       | 1,000    | --          |

Therefore, the Petitioners in this case hold 50% of the corporation's common stock.

*3.* The effect of this capital structure is to make it possible for there to be two voting blocs, each holding 50% of the common stock: one consisting of Petitioners, the other of Marchetti and Bogan. This has in fact happened, leading to a persistent deadlock, and an inability to elect a Board of Directors at the corporation's last regularly scheduled annual meeting, _____ ,199 ____ .

*4.* The stockholders and their counsel have engaged in intensive negotiations, and there is no real likelihood that they will be able to resolve the deadlock, elect a Board of Directors, or make and authorize the decisions that are a necessary part of corporate life.

**5.** Article II, Section 3 of the corporation's Articles of Incorporation and its Bylaw 6B permit any holder of 20% or more of the corporation's common stock to petition the court of appropriate jurisdiction for dissolution of the corporation.

**6.** The corporation is solvent and has assets sufficient to pay all its debts in full.

**7.** If granted, dissolution of the corporation would permit the stockholders to receive fair value for their investment, and to form new organizations to undertake business activities, and would not defraud or disadvantage the corporation's creditors.

**8.** Efficient implementation of the dissolution process would be furthered by appointment of a receiver to supervise the process and carry it out in a manner that is fair to everyone affected by the process.

**9.** No previous application for this relief has been made in any court.

WHEREFORE, the Petitioners request that this court grant an Order to Show Cause directing the Corporation, its officers, directors, and stockholders to show cause why the corporation should not be liquidated and dissolved pursuant to its Articles of Incorporation and Bylaws, and under Section 449.09 of the Consolidated Laws of the State of Adams.

Date: _____ , 199_____
Signed: _____
State of Adams
County of Chacanoggi
William Stahl, who has been duly sworn, deposes and says that he is a Petitioner in this action; that he has read the Petition, and knows its contents; and that the contents of the petition are true to his own knowledge.
_____William Stahl
Sworn to before me this _____ day of _____ , 199 ____ :
_____ , Notary Public Commission # ____ , expires [repeat for each petitioner]

## PETITION FOR JUDICIAL DISSOLUTION
### (Where Wrongdoing Is Claimed)

Intermediate Civil Court of the State of Tyler
County of Lakahawi
-------------------------------------------------

Application of Kevin and Maria                                    Index No. C2291-75
Fleming, Petitioners   for
Judicial Dissolution of
Lewis & Williams Pesticides, Inc.

-------------------------------------------------

Kevin and Maria Fleming, Petitioners, state that, on information and belief, the statements made in this Petition are true, and entitle them to judicial dissolution of Lewis & Williams Pesticides, Inc., pursuant to Section 429.3B et. seq. of the Consolidated Statutes Annotated of the State of Tyler.

**1.** Lewis & Williams Pesticides, Inc., is a duly incorporated Tyler corporation, incorporated in 1983, whose place of business and registered office for service of process is 923 Lackland Lane, Donohue City, Tyler.

*2.* The capitalization of Lewis & Williams Pesticides, Inc., calls for the issuance of 10,000 shares of common stock and 1,000 shares of preferred stock, all of which are issued and outstanding. The corporation has not "gone public," its shares are not listed on any national exchange and are not regularly quoted in over-the-counter markets, and the corporation is not an "investment company" as defined by federal law.

*3.* Section 429.3B of the Consolidated Statutes Annotated of the state of Tyler permits a petition for liquidation to be brought by the holders of 20% or more of a corporation's outstanding shares. Kevin and Maria Fleming each own 15% of the issued and oustanding common and preferred shares. The remaining 85% of the shares are divided among eight other shareholders, five of whom serve as the corporation's officers and directors.

*4.* As a result of this division of shares, it has been impossible to hold the election for Board of Directors scheduled for the annual meeting held on _____ , 199 ____ , because it was not possible to achieve a majority for any director or slate of directors.

*5.* Furthermore, there is significant difference of opinion about whether the corporation should continue in its present form or should merge or consolidate with another enterprise. However, the corporation's charter requires a super majority vote for any such transaction, and an informal poll of the stockholders shows that less than a simple majority would be prepared to vote for a merger or consolidation.

*6.* Five of the corporation's ten shareholders serve as officers and directors of the corporation. They are in complete control of the corporation's finances and policies. They have not declared or paid a dividend on preferred or common shares for the past six years. During this period, however, they have diverted corporate assets to themselves by paying salaries and directors' fees that are excessive and not proportionate either to the compensation of directors and officers in comparable corporations or to the actual services they have performed for the corporation.

Furthermore, certain officers and directors (Mark McElroy and James Dakres) have engaged in self-dealing, the former by selling a piece of real property to the corporation for an inflated price, the latter by purchasing barely used typewriters and other electronic equipment from the corporation at less than scrap prices.

*7.* In that the corporation's officers and directors have engaged in self-dealing and looting of corporate assets; they have denied the five stockholders who are not officers or directors any return on their investment for a period of six years; and in that there is no reasonable prospect of the corporation being able to reach a consensus on its normal operation and future plans, we hereby petition that the court liquidate the Lewis & Williams Pesticides, Inc., corporation and direct the winding-up of its business and distribution of its assets. We further petition the court to appoint a receiver to supervise the process and prevent further misappropriation of corporate assets.

Date: _____ , 199____
Signed: _____
Verification (by each petitioner): I have been duly sworn, and say that I have read the petition and state that, to the best of my knowledge, every statement made within the petition is true and accurate.

## PLAN OF DISSOLUTION AND LIQUIDATION

Exotic East Corp., duly incorporated on _____ , 199 ____ under the laws of the state of Monroe, is capitalized at 20,000 shares of no-par common stock.

By resolution dated _____ , 199 _____ , its Board of Directors has voted that the corporation enter voluntary dissolution and be liquidated; the stockholders resolved to ratify the Board of Directors resolution at a special meeting held _____ , 199 _____ .

*1.* The Exotic East Corporation will be dissolved, pursuant to Chapter 99 of the Revised Statutes Annotated of the State of Monroe, within one year of the effective date of this plan as adopted; the effective date is _____ , 199 _____ .

*2.* As of the effective date, Exotic East Corporation will cease all business activities other than those required to wind up the business, satisfy its liabilities, and distribute any remaining cash and property to the stockholders. The Board of Directors in office on the effective date will remain in office until the corporation is liquidated and will carry out the liquidation process.

The Board of Directors will have the power to do all corporate acts necessary to carry out the plan of liquidation. The death, resignation, or removal of a director will not limit the powers of the remaining directors to carry out the liquidation process.

*3.* The corporation's stock transfer books will be closed as of the effective date, and except if the laws of the state of Monroe require a different result, shareholders will be precluded from selling or otherwise transferring their stock. Distributions of assets remaining after satisfaction of corporate liabilities will be made based on stockholdings on the effective date.

*4.* As soon as possible after the effective date, the Board of Directors will list the liabilities of the corporation and determine if they can be satisfied out of the corporation's cash and liquid assets. If so, the Board of Directors will satisfy all liabilities as soon as commercially feasible. However, no payments may be made if the Board of Directors determines that the corporation will be unable to satisfy all its obligations, and cash payments to certain creditors would operate as a preference; the corporation must, in this case, petition for voluntary bankruptcy and make payments and distribute assets pursuant to a plan of bankruptcy reorganization.

If the corporation can satisfy all its liabilities, but only upon sale of corporate assets, the Board of Directors shall have discretion as to which creditors will be paid out of liquid assets immediately and which must wait for the sale, or whether all creditors will be paid in installments, provided that payment of debts must be completed as soon as commercially feasible after the sale of corporate assets.

*5.* One of the duties of the Board of Directors after the effective date is to determine the size of the reserve required to meet the expenses of carrying out the plan of liquidation, including payment of any required taxes on the liquidation transaction itself, and taxes on business operations that were due but unpaid on the effective date.

When the amount of the reserve has been determined, the Board of Directors will transfer the reserve fund to the trustee(s) elected by the shareholders at the Special Meeting, and after the transfer the trustees (and not the corporation) will have full possession and control of the reserve fund. The trustees will pay the expenses of liquidation from the reserve fund and will distribute any surplus to the stockholders, proportionate to their stockholdings, once all expenses have been paid.

*6.* After all corporate debts have been paid, and after the reserve fund has been transferred to the trustee(s), the Board of Directors will distribute the remaining assets to the stockholders proportionate to the stock certificates surrendered during a period of time not to exceed 12 months from the effective date.

The Board of Directors shall have discretion to determine whether distributions will be made in the form of cash or property, what property will be distributed to which stockholder, and the schedule on which distributions will be made, provided that the process is completed within 12 months.

Unclaimed distributions, and distributions otherwise payable to stockholders who do not surrender their stock certificates for cancellation, will be transferred to the trustees for distribution to the remaining shareholders proportionate to their holdings.

## ARTICLES OF DISSOLUTION

The Captain's Nest, Inc., a [statutory close] corporation organized and doing business in the state of Adams, hereby adopts Articles of Dissolution for the purpose of terminating its corporate existence.

*1.* The names and addresses of the corporation's officers are
President, Robert Barker, 1704 Blenheim Avenue, Trafalgar
Vice-President, Gregory Barker, 2230 Laburnam Terrace, Trafalgar
Secretary, William Bozniak, 19-22 Kennedy Avenue, Trafalgar Estates
Treasurer, Colin McKenna, 203 Franklin Place, Ardleigh

*2.* The names and addresses of the corporation's directors are
Robert Barker; Gregory Barker; Rev. Thomas Mainwaring, St. Cecelia's Rectory, Trafalgar Estates; Janet Parker, 43-19 Kennedy Avenue, Trafalgar Estates; Gary Todd, 229B 17th Street, Ardleigh.

*3.* Lawrence Ellison, a stockholder, has exercised his right under Section 19 of the corporation's Articles of Incorporation and Title 9, chapter 6B of the Laws of the State of Lincoln, to demand dissolution of the corporation. He has sent notice, by certified mail, to all stockholders of The Captain's Nest, Inc. A copy of the notice is attached to these Articles of Dissolution.

*4.* The corporation's liabilities and obligations are greater than its property and assets. However, corporate property and assets have been applied in a just and equitable manner to reduce outstanding liabilities and obligations, leaving nothing for distribution to the corporation's shareholders. OR
The corporation has either paid and satisfied all its debts, obligations, and liabilities (including making adequate provision for satisfying any settlement, judgment, order, or decree that may be entered against the corporation in any litigation pending against the corporation as of the date of these Articles of Dissolution). Any remaining property and assets [including the litigation reserve established by a resolution of the Board of Directors dated _____ , 199____] has been distributed to the stockholders proportionate to their rights and interests in the corporation.

# Chapter 14

# NOT-FOR-PROFIT ORGANIZATIONS

## INTRODUCTION

Not-for-profit organizations are a major part of the American economic landscape: in 1985, for instance, there were nearly 900,000 active organizations that were exempt from federal tax because they were not operated for profit. Nearly one-third of all corporations are organized as not-for-profits. (The term "not-for-profit" is more accurate than "nonprofit," because an organization can be "nonprofit" for reasons other than its charitable purpose. Profits can be absent because of negative economic conditions or bad management, or as a result of a calculated decision to save taxes or fend off an unwanted acquisition.)

### Kinds of Not-For-Profits

Not-for-profit organizations range from the local club or block association, started by a few people with little business experience, to a multibillion-dollar hospital or religious organization managing a staff of thousands and a huge portfolio of prime real estate. Yet all not-for-profit organizations face certain challenges which set them apart from corporations operated to make a profit.

### Tax Advantages

Many (but not all) not-for-profit organizations are exempt from paying federal income tax. (As a bonus, the federal exemption may entitle the organization to exemption from state and local income and real estate taxes.) Even these organizations may be subject to a complex set of rules about when not-for-profit organizations will be subject to federal tax on their "UBTI" (Unrelated Business Taxable Income).

Just because an organization is free from federal tax, it doesn't necessarily follow that contributors will be allowed a tax deduction for their contributions to the organization. Section 170(c) of the Internal Revenue Code ("Code") determines which organizations are "donor deductible": social welfare organizations and business leagues do *not* fall into this category. In fact, Code Section 6113 requires organizations to put a conspicuous disclaimer in their solicitation materials if contributions are not tax deductible; there is a penalty of $1,000 per day for violating this rule. (However, religious organizations and organizations whose gross receipts are less than $100,000 a year are not subject to this rule.) Even a "501(c)(3) organization" (see below)—one which qualifies under that section of the Internal Revenue Code as a charitable organization able to receive deductible contributions—has a further hurdle to face. Unless it can prove it is a "public charity" by meeting both "organizational" and "operational" tests, it will be treated as a "private foundation" and subjected to extra IRS scrutiny in order to keep its exemption.

## Governing IRS Regulations

For federal tax purposes, the Internal Revenue Code sets up a complex hierarchy of organizations. First of all, an organization must qualify for tax exemption by demonstrating that it fits into at least one of the categories set out in the Code (references are to sections of the Code):

○ Probably the best known type of not-for-profit organization is the 501(c)(3) organization, which includes "corporations, community chests, funds, or foundations having religious, charitable, scientific, testing for public safety, literary, or educational purposes or organized for prevention of cruelty to children or animals, or to foster national or international amateur sports competition." (However, these organizations are not allowed to provide any athletic facilities or equipment—a good example of the kind of nit-picking rules these organizations have to follow.) To qualify, the organization
○○ Must be organized and operated EXCLUSIVELY for a charitable, literary, and so on purposes
○○ The organization's net earnings can't benefit private shareholders or individuals to any extent (although, of course, reasonable salaries can be paid to employees)
○○ Can't participate or intervene in any political campaign
○○ Can't carry on propaganda or try to influence legislation as "any substantial part of its activities"—but these organizations are allowed to educate the public, in an objective, nonpartisan way, about controversial subjects of public interest
○○ Can't provide "commercial-type" insurance as "any substantial part of its activities"

The IRS regulations use the term "charitable" in the ordinary sense of the word—helping the poor or underprivileged; advancing religion, education, or science; lessening the burdens of government (e.g., by maintaining public buildings and monuments); promoting social welfare; lessening neighborhood tensions; fighting prejudice; defending civil rights; fighting community deterioration and juvenile delinquency. These organizations can publish newspapers and magazines, but the publications don't qualify for exemption if they are operated "in accordance with ordinary commercial publishing practices"—remember, tax-exempt organizations are not supposed to compete on the same terms with taxable businesses.

There are many other classifications of tax-exempt organizations:

o "Instrumentalities of the United States" (e.g., federal credit unions and other organizations set up under an Act of Congress (501(c)(1))

o Corporations that hold title to property owned by exempt organizations (501(c)(2))

o Civic leagues, social welfare organizations, local associations of employees (501(c)(4)); of course, some of these objectives overlap with some objectives permitted to 501(c)(3) organizations

o Labor/agricultural/horticultural organizations whose object is the betterment of the condition of workers, farmers, and so on; improving their products; and developing more efficient ways of working (501(c)(5))

o Business leagues, chambers of commerce, real estate boards, and boards of trade (501(c)(6))

o Social and recreational clubs (501(c)(7))

o Fraternal beneficiary societies, orders and associations, and domestic fraternal societies that are operated as lodges, or for the exclusive benefit of members of a fraternity that operates through the lodge system; these organizations must also provide death, sickness, accident, or other benefits to members and their dependents (501(c)(8))

o Voluntary employees' beneficiary associations that pay death, sickness, accident, or related benefits to members (501(c)(9))

o "Domestic fraternal societies" in lodge form can qualify for this exemption even if they don't provide death or sickness benefits, as long as their net earnings are devoted exclusively to religious, charitable, scientific, literary, educational, and fraternal purposes (501(c)(10))

o Teachers' retirement fund associations (501(c)(11))

o Benevolent life insurance associations, mutual and cooperative telephone companies, and related organizations (501(c)(12))

o Nonprofit cemetery companies and associations for the administration of perpetual care funds (501(c)(13))

o Credit unions (operated on a nonstock, nonprofit basis); mutual organizations that provide reserves and deposit insurance for building and loan associations; national farm loan associations (501(c)(14))

o Mutual insurance associations that provide insurance to members approximately at cost (501(c)(15))

o Cooperatives that finance crop operations (501(c)(16))

○ Supplemental unemployment benefit trusts (501(c)(17))
○ Employee-funded pension trusts that were created before 1959 (501(c)(18))
○ Veterans' organizations or posts (501(c)(19)); veterans' organizations created before 1880 are exempt under 501(c)(23)
○ Trusts that pay black lung benefits (501(c)(21))
○ Funds that are ready to meet employers' obligations when they withdraw from multiemployer pension plans (501(c)(22))
○ Religious and apostolic organizations (501(d))
○ Organizations that perform cooperative services for hospitals (501(e))
○ Cooperative organizations that undertake collective investment activities for educational organizations (501(f))
○ Child care organizations (501(k))
○ Associations that handle cooperative purchasing and marketing for farmers (521(a)).

The most favorable tax status is for the organization to qualify as a "public charity," one that meets the "organizational" and "operational" tests.

Under the "organizational" test, the organization's Articles of Incorporation must be written in a way that limits the organization's purposes to one or more exempt purposes and that doesn't empower the organization (except in a very minimal way) to do anything that does not further its exempt purposes.

These limitations must be put in the organization's Articles—it isn't good enough to put the limitations in the bylaws, to have the organization's officers state that they intend to operate only for exempt purposes—or even to be able to prove that the organization really did operate exclusively for exempt purposes. (On the state law level, failure to state explicitly which nonprofit purposes the organization was formed for, or inclusion of powers to carry out purposes that are inappropriate for a nonprofit organization, may result in the state Secretary of State refusing to accept the Articles of Incorporation for filing.)

The "operational" test requires the organization to engage primarily in activities accomplishing the exempt purposes, to avoid distributing net earnings to private individuals, and to avoid becoming an "action organization." An action organization is one that devotes a substantial part of its activities to trying to lobby or otherwise influence Congress and state and local legislatures, including measures as mild as urging the public to contact their representatives.

A 501(c)(3) organization that engages in forbidden lobbying activity can lose its tax-exempt status—and even be forced to pay penalty excise taxes: 5% of the lobbying expenditures.

There are two basic structures that can be used by not-for-profit organizations: the corporation and the trust. Although, as described below, there are certain modifications in the Articles of Incorporation and bylaws for not-for-profit organizations, and although not-for-profit corporations are frequently organized to have members but no stockholders, organizing and managing a not-for-profit corporation are quite similar to the same tasks for a profit-making corporation. A trust, on the other hand, is a mechanism for managing a sum of money—for example, a bequest from a wealthy individual. Tax treatment of trusts and not-for-profit corporations is somewhat different; the choice is a matter to be decided by the founders of the organization after consulting legal, tax, and business advisors.

The Articles of Incorporation of a not-for-profit corporation must include three important provisions. First, the Articles must limit the organization's powers to those that are required for its tax-exempt purpose. Second, the Articles must make it clear that the organization will not be run for the personal benefit of stockholders or other individuals. Of course, the organization can pay reasonable salaries to its employees—but it cannot pay dividends or distribute "bonuses" to its members if contributions are unexpectedly generous. Finally, the Articles must provide that, if and when the organization is dissolved or liquidated, its assets will be distributed appropriately (e.g., to other charitable organizations) and, once again, will not be used for private benefit.

Check with your legal advisor about the requirements that the Code imposes on specific types of organizations. For example, organizations claiming exemption as "schools" must prove that they can provide regular faculty and curriculum and a regularly enrolled student body; they must not only avoid racial discrimination, they must provide notice to students and potential students that racial discrimination is not practiced, and they must set out their nondiscrimination policy in the Articles, or in a resolution of the school's governing body. A "medical research" organization is required to maintain a continuous research program in conjunction with a hospital. Organizations that claim to be "publicly supported" must have an identifiable program for soliciting public contributions, which must provide at least one-third of the organization's revenues; not more than one-third of such an organization's revenues can be derived from investment income.

If the organization is a private foundation, it is a good idea for its Articles of Incorporation to obligate the organization to perform any necessary actions, or refrain from any forbidden actions, that would result in imposition of a penalty tax under Sections 4941–4945 of the Code. It's prudent for a charitable trust's governing instrument to include a provision that any gifts that it receives from private corporations will be applied within the United States, because private corporations are not entitled to deduct contributions to trusts if the contributions can be used abroad.

## CHARITABLE ORGANIZATION CHARTER ROADMAP

In addition to these IRS requirements, the Articles of Incorporation should include

- The corporation's name
- Its duration (most state laws allow a perpetual duration)
- The corporation's purposes (drafted, of course, to meet IRS and state criteria)

○ Provisions about the corporation's internal affairs—whether it will have members or stockholders; who is entitled to vote, and how decisions will be reached; number of directors on the initial Board of directors; the names and addresses of those appointed as initial directors; regular and special meetings

○ Initial registered office and agent for service of process

○ The names and addresses of the incorporators

The organization's bylaws will address matters such as the organization's officers; how they are elected and removed; if the organization will have committees and, if so, what their powers will be; who qualifies for membership; who can sign checks; and how resignation and expulsion of members will be handled.

Check with your legal advisor as to whether a state or local license or annual report is required; it may be necessary to get a license if you intend to solicit contributions from the public.

Applications for tax-exempt status are made on IRS Form 1023. Some organizations do not have to file the 1023 to be tax exempt:

○ Churches, integrated auxiliaries of churches, conventions and associations of churches

○ Organizations that are not private foundations (see below) and whose gross receipts are normally under $5,000 a year

*Practice Tip:* Even if receipts are below $5,000 now, it probably pays to file the Form 1023 to be ready for years of expanded activity. However, it is not necessary to make the decision before the organization is formed: an organization can be granted retroactive tax exemption as long as Form 1023 is filed within 15 months from the end of the month in which it was organized. The 15-month period can be extended, if the organization applies to the local IRS district director and shows that more time is needed. [Hint: Even if all the necessary information is not available within the 15-month time frame, it's good policy to file the form with the information that is available at the time, requesting additional time to submit a complete application. That way, if the organization eventually gets an exemption, it will be retroactive to the original filing of the Form 1023, not the later date when all the information is supplied.]

If the organization seeks to be classed as a 501(c)(3) organization (what most people think of as a "charity"), the organization must include a detailed statement of its proposed activities—and including the correct legal names and addresses of organizations to which the organization will donate money. (For example, an organization founded to sponsor the arts may give money to a school or not-for-profit art gallery.)

Once the organization proves to the IRS's satisfaction that it qualifies, the IRS will issue a determination letter or ruling that the organization is in fact tax exempt.

An advance determination can be issued before the organization starts up, if the organization can make a clear, detailed statement about its proposed activities (just rephrasing the language of the Code is not good enough). The organization must disclose, in detail,

○ Its future activities—including its criteria for planning projects
○ Expected sources of funds, such as contributions, grants, ticket sales, fund-raising events such as fashion shows, trade expositions, theater parties
○ Expected use of funds and criteria for spending money on the organization's exempt purpose (for instance, how it will be determined which scientists get research grants; which new composers' works should be performed; which college students get scholarships)

For example, an organization set up to support education must show how it supports education (contributing to schools and colleges, creating special programs of instruction or remediation to be presented in schools, endowing a chair, making research grants to universities). An organization that awards scholarships must disclose how the recipients are chosen and how the program is monitored (to see if students are still in school); it must be clear that there is no favoritism (such as a corporation establishing a "charity" that awards scholarships to the children of top executives).

Legitimate charitable organizations are given special tax treatment as an incentive for such organizations to cope with social problems and improve society; contributions to many such organizations are deductible to encourage people to give generously. However, the advantages of tax-exemption also appeal to those who are operating ordinary retail businesses and want to avoid minor nuisances like tax-paying, or to legitimate charities that compete with ordinary businesses. Therefore, the Internal Revenue Code imposes a tax on Unrelated Business Taxable Income (including Alternative Minimum Tax if an organization has a lot of tax preference items), and generally forbids a not-for-profit organization to use its administrative expenses (such as running an office and paying employees who carry out the organization's exempt function) to offset its UBTI.

UBTI is income from trades or businesses which are carried on on a regular basis, and are not related to the organization's exempt purpose except by producing income that can be used for the exempt purpose. There are no hard-and-fast rules about what constitutes an activity that is "regularly carried on," but clearly an annual dinner dance or bake sale does not qualify. The frequency and continuity of the income-producing activities, the way in which they are conducted, and their similarity to ordinary commercial activities must be assessed. Similarly, it's hard to draw the line between related and unrelated activities; the Internal Revenue Service's regulations say that the test is to compare the size and extent of the trade or business with the nature and extent of the exempt mission. In general, income is not UBTI if it comes from products that results from the performance of the exempt activity, sold in substantially the state they were in when the exempt function was completed—for instance, an organization that benefits the handicapped may have a training program for handicapped workers, and sell the products they make, without generating UBTI. Another important exception to the definition of UBTI is that operations in which substantially all the work is performed by volunteers do not generate UBTI; neither do thrift shops, where substantially all the merchandise is contributed to the organization, and where the proceeds are used for the organization's exempt purpose.

"Feeder" organizations (business corporations set up to earn income and channel it to the not-for-profit) are also taxed on their income. Some not-for-profit organizations are also taxable on their investment income: social clubs and employees' beneficiary organizations fall into this category.

# ARTICLES OF INCORPORATION FOR NONPROFIT ORGANIZATION

*1.* These Articles of Incorporation are drafted to bring into existence an organization to be known as:

_____

*2.* The duration of the corporation's existence will be perpetual/ _____ years/until its objective of (describe) has been achieved.

*3.* The corporation will be a membership corporation/will not have members.

*4.* The corporation is formed for lawful nonprofit purposes and objectives. No stock or securities will be issued. All corporate assets will be dedicated to exempt purposes; although the corporation will be authorized to pay reasonable compensation for services rendered, and to enter into business transactions in furtherance of its exempt purpose, the corporation will not pay dividends, and its assets will not inure to the private profit of any person. If and when the corporation is dissolved, its assets will be distributed for exempt purposes, or will devolve to a government agency for a public purpose. None of the assets will be distributed to private individuals.

*5.* The corporation's objective(s) will be

☐ Religious, in that it will: _____

☐ Educational, in that it will: _____ The organization will not practice racial discrimination in the course of its educational activities.

☐ Charitable, in that it will: _____

☐ Scientific or literary, in that it will: _____

☐ Testing for the public safety, to be performed as follows: _____ with test results disseminated as follows: _____

☐ Civic or social welfare, dedicated to promotion of community welfare

☐ Labor or agricultural education and instruction designed to improve products, efficiency, and working conditions

☐ A private social and/or recreational club whose facilities will be available only to members and their guests, not to the general public at large

☐ Fraternal organization. The organization ☐ will/ ☐ will not provide life, sickness, accident, and/or similar benefits to members.

☐ Veterans' organization
☐ Cooperative hospital service organization
☐ Child care organization

The organization ☐ will ☐ will not seek a federal tax exemption for its own income and ☐ will ☐ will not seek a ruling that contributions to the organization are federally tax deductible. If the organization becomes tax exempt in either category, it will perform any act required to retain tax-exempt status and will refrain from any activities forbidden by Internal Revenue Code Section 501(c)(3).

If the organization is a private foundation as defined by the Internal Revenue Code, it will at all times act in the manner required by Code Sections 4941–5 (as amended) and will refrain from any action that would result in penalty taxes being imposed under those sections.

**6.** At all times, the organization's investments and investment policy will be consistent with its nonprofit purpose, and income and assets will be generated only to carry out the nonprofit purpose, not to generate a profit for any person or organization.

**7.** The corporation will be governed and directed by its officers and directors. The officers will be a President, two Vice-Presidents, a Secretary, and a Treasurer. Officers will be appointed by the Board of Directors and will serve at the pleasure of the Board. The corporation will have a seven-person Board of Directors, who will serve three-year terms. The directors will be elected/appointed as follows: _____ . The officers and directors will not be personally liable for the corporation's debts and liabilities, and their personal property is exempt from seizure or levy to pay obligations of the corporation.

**8.** The powers of the corporation will include all powers granted by the state to nonprofit corporations of the same type. In addition, the corporation's powers will include the following, to the extent not prohibited by state or federal law:

○ To solicit, collect, receive, hold, invest, distribute, and disburse funds in the forms of donations, gifts, bequests, and subscriptions
○ The power to accept gifts from individuals, corporations, and foundations in furtherance of the corporation's nonprofit purpose
○ To borrow funds with or without security, on terms at least as favorable as those offered on the open market, to carry out the corporation's nonprofit purpose, in an amount not to exceed $_____ /as authorized by at least five of the corporation's directors and approved by the state's regulators of charitable organizations
○ The power to engage in fund-raising events, for example, benefits and sales of donated merchandise, provided that these events are infrequent and irregular, not tantamount to maintenance of a profit-making business, and provided that the income derived from these events, net of reasonable expenses, will be entirely devoted to the organization's nonprofit purpose

**9.** The corporation's Board of Directors will meet at least quarterly, with additional meetings as called by three or more Directors. The corporation will hold a general membership meeting at least annually, and meetings can be called by demand of three Directors [or at least ____ members acting by notifying the Board of Directors, which will then notify the membership of the date, time, place, and reason for the special meeting]. [Note: Omit this provision if the organization is not a membership organization.]

**10.** Power to amend the organization's Articles of Incorporation and Bylaws will rest with the Board of Directors [and the membership]; an amendment can be had by vote of _____ % of the Directors/members, at a regular or special meeting [or in writing in lieu of a meeting].

*11.* The organization's incorporators are _____ , _____ , and _____ , all of whom are natural persons over the age of 18 and citizens of this state.

*12.* The organization's initial Board of Directors, which will serve until the election of Directors at the first annual meeting, to be held on _____ , 19____ , will consist of (give names and addresses): _____

*13.* The corporation's initial registered office will be the corporation's headquarters, at _____ . Its initial registered agent for the service of process will be _____ .

## THIRTEEN SAMPLE PURPOSE CLAUSES FOR VARIOUS TYPES OF NONPROFIT ORGANIZATIONS

*1. Charitable Organization:* To be organized and operate for lawful nonbusiness, nonpecuniary purposes to advance the welfare of the community and assist the needy by developing programs of direct financial aid, provision of services, and education.

*2. Charitable Organization (501(c)(3)):* To be organized and operated exclusively for a religious purpose/charitable purpose/scientific purpose/for the purpose of testing to promote the public safety/literary purpose/educational purpose/to prevent cruelty to children/to prevent cruelty to animals/to foster amateur athletic competition, but not to provide athletic facilities or equipment. The net earnings of the organization will never be permitted to benefit a shareholder or private individual to any extent. No substantial part of the organization's activities will ever consist of providing insurance of a type similar to that provided commercially or of carrying on propaganda or attempting to influence legislation or other aspects of the political process. The organization will not take part or intervene in any political campaign.

*3. Fraternal Beneficiary Society; Fraternal Association; Fraternal Order; or Domestic Fraternal Society:* To operate in the form of a lodge or for the exclusive benefit of members of an organization operated in lodge form; to provide benefits (e.g., life, sickness, or accident benefits) to lodge members and their families OR to devote all net earnings exclusively to religious, charitable, scientific, literary, educational, and fraternal purposes (or any combination of such permissible purposes).

*4. Educational Organization:* To operate for the purpose of instructing children/youths/college students/the elderly/the general public in the subject(s) of: _____ and/or to train them in skills such as: _____ , with or without incidental entertainment or recreational aspects. [For a school, add:] It is the policy of the school to avoid racial discrimination in admissions, programs, and the granting of scholarships.

*5. Agricultural Organization:* To advance the agricultural and mechanical interests of farmers and ranchers in the _____ area; to hold agricultural fairs and exhibitions and shows of farm products such as livestock and crops; to educate farmers about improved agricultural methods and to inform the general public about the achievements of farmers and the problems they face.

*6. Environmental Defense Organization:* To preserve, protect, and defend natural resources, wildlife, and ecosystems against pollution, misuse, and damage; to protest misuse of dangerous chemicals; to advocate safe and appropriate use of pesticides; to promote clean air and water; to enforce federal and state environmental protection laws; to preserve endangered species against extinction; to maintain genetic variety of plants and animals; and to conduct research and educate the public about natural resources, living things, and the environment.

*7. Chamber of Commerce:* To promote cooperation among the business community of _____ , to enhance the image of business and businesspeople, to create and maintain a code of ethics in business dealings, to investigate and punish abusive trade practices, to permit businesspeople within the community greater knowledge of the commercial needs of other businesspeople, and to distribute information about the business community.

*8. Cancer Society:* To sponsor statistical and epidemiological studies of the causation and treatment of cancer; to sponsor basic and clinical medical research; to educate and inform the public about the symptoms, diagnosis, and treatment of various types of cancer; to disseminate information about health practices that lessen the risk of cancer; to sponsor or assist self-help groups for cancer patients and their families; to operate a hot-line information service about cancer therapies.

*9. Summer Camps:* To organize, conduct, and maintain summer camps for the recreation and instruction of [retarded/handicapped/artistic/gifted] children/children and teenagers/teenagers/the elderly, and to own or lease, manage and operate camp sites, buildings, and equipment for this purpose.

*10. [Residential] Co-op Corporation:* To purchase, own, operate, and maintain the land and _____ -unit building located at _____ , _____ in the city of _____ , county of _____ , and state of _____ , in the form of a cooperative apartment building; to transfer, lease, sell, convey, or dispose of the building or units within the building; to receive rental income for residential, commercial, or professional space within the building but not in excess of the limit on rental income of cooperative corporations as set by the Internal Revenue Code.

*11. Garden Club:* To help members improve their skills and techniques for gardening; to teach them about plant varieties, organic and chemical pest management methods, and equipment suitable for use in this geographic area; to promote plant genetic diversity and prevent the extinction of endangered species; to exchange seeds, slips, and mature plants; to promote friendly and rewarding associations among members; to hold garden shows; to award prizes for the horticultural achievements of members.

*12. Historical Society:* To study the history of the _____ area/ _____ family/ _____ ethnic group; to preserve relevant documents and objects; to make these research sources accessible to scholars; to assist literary, historical, anthropological, sociological, and scientific scholarship in this area; to educate the public about _____ , notable related personages, and the role of _____ in American and world history.

*13. Nonprofit Home for the Aged:* To establish, maintain, operate, and manage a home for the aged in _____ , by contracting for and either leasing or purchasing real property; making any necessary repairs or alterations to the property to render it suitable; and to lease or purchase the personal property, fixtures, and equipment needed to operate the home for up to _____ elderly and/or disabled individuals. To participate in the screening program for nursing home admissions and to perform periodic recertification of each resident's need for a nursing home level of care. To contract with the state and federal government as a provider of Medicare and Medicaid services. To receive gifts, grants, and bequests subject, however, to the state and federal prohibitions on certain gifts in connection with the admission of Medicaid applicants or recipients to the home and on bequests made to nursing homes.

## ARTICLES OF INCORPORATION FOR HOMEOWNER'S ASSOCIATION FOR CONDOMINIUM CORPORATION

*1.* These Articles signify the terms and conditions on which a Homeowner's Association is created for the Breeze Bay Apartments, which will be owned and operated in condominium form.

*2.* The Association shall have perpetual duration unless dissolved as described below.

*3.* The Breeze Bay Apartments are located at block number 44, lot number 215, in the county of Dickinson, state of Tyler. The street address of the Breeze Bay Apartments is 4922 Lafayette Avenue, Marcatta, Tyler. There are 67 apartment units, 4 commercial units, and 6 professional offices in the Breeze Bay Apartments.

*4.* The principal office and initial registered office of the Breeze Bay Apartments Homeowner's Association ("Association") will be c/o Janine Despres, Esq., 13-22 Acacia Lane, Marcatta, Tyler; Ms. Despres will be the Association's initial registered agent for service of process.

*5.* The Association will be operated to preserve and protect the Breeze Bay Apartments, see that it is managed properly, and defend the rights of owners of units in the Breeze Bay Apartments. A declaration of ownership and operation in condominium form has been drafted and will be filed in the appropriate offices in the County of Dickinson; the Association will have all the rights and obligations of the homeowner's association as stated in the declaration.

*6.* The Association will be entitled to exercise all the lawful powers of a nonprofit organization under the laws of the State of Tyler, including:

○ Setting and collecting common area charges and special assessments for the Breeze Bay Apartments.

○ Buying, receiving by donation, owning, holding, improving, maintaining, transferring, and conveying real or personal property as required for the benefit of the Breeze Bay Apartments and its unit owners.

○ Mortgaging, pledging, creating deeds of trust, and otherwise borrowing with or without security, as necessary and appropriate for the purposes of management of the condominium, provided that any mortgage of common areas will require the affirmative vote of two-thirds of the unit owners and the vote of two-thirds of any voting power retained by the developer. The Association shall not have the right to subject itself to a total indebtedness exceeding 75% of its income for the preceding fiscal year unless two-thirds of the unit owners, and two-thirds of any voting power remaining in the developer, consent to the higher debt level.

○ Engaging in mergers and consolidations with other nonprofit organizations, as permitted by the laws of the state of Tyler, and on affirmative vote of two-thirds of the unit owners, and the vote of two-thirds of any voting power retained by the developer.

○ Dedicating, selling, or transferring any part of the common areas to public agencies and public utilities, on terms and conditions to be agreed on by the membership; a two-thirds affirmative vote (by both unit owners and voting power retained by the developer) shall be required for any such transaction.

○ Retaining and paying professionals such as attorneys and accountants to render services to the Association

○ Entering into transactions with the Directors in their capacity as professionals or business owners, provided that such transactions will be on terms at least as favorable as those entered into at arm's length on the open market, and also provided that no Director vote on any transaction in which he or she has a pecuniary interest.

**7.** The membership of the Association will consist of everyone who owns a unit in the Breeze Bay Apartments, other than those who hold an interest solely as security for performance of an obligation by the actual owner. Each owner will have one membership and one vote, regardless of how many units he or she owns, or the size or price of the units. If a unit is jointly owned or owned in common by several people, the unit will have a single membership and a single vote; it is up to the owners to decide how voting power will be allocated among themselves. Membership and voting rights go along with unit ownership and cannot be transferred independently of unit ownership.

**8.** Every unit owner other than the declarant will have one vote. The developer (as defined in the declaration) will be entitled to three votes for each unit which it owns; however, on _____ , 19 ____ , or when the total number of votes held by unit owners equal the voting power of the developer (whichever comes first), the developer's voting power will be reduced to only one vote per unit owned by the developer.

As long as the developer retains voting power in excess of one vote per unit owned, prior approval from the Federal Housing Authority (FHA) will be required to annex additional properties, merge or consolidate with another nonprofit organization, mortgage the common areas, dedicate or sell the common areas to a public agency or public utility, amend these Articles of Incorporation, or dissolve the Association.

**9.** The Association will be managed by a nine-member Board of Directors. The Association's initial Directors, who will serve until _____ , 19 ____ (or as adjourned) when the initial Association meeting is held, will be [names and addresses]: _____ . Part of the agenda of the initial meeting will be to elect a Board of Directors, who will serve staggered terms; that is, three directors will be elected for a one-year term, three for a two-year term, three for a three-year term. In each later year, three directors will be elected for a three-year term. Directors need not be unit owners or residents of the Breeze Bay Apartments.

The following three members of the initial Board of Directors, each of whom is a natural person over 18 and a citizen of the state of Tyler, serve as the incorporators of the Association:

**10.** At least one annual meeting of the Association will be held on March 13 of each year (or the next business day, if that day is a Saturday, Sunday, or legal holiday). Each member will be given at least 20 days' written notice of the annual meeting. The quorum for transaction of business will be 60% of each class of voters present in person or by duly authorized proxy; if there is no quorum, the meeting will be adjourned; further notice will be sent for another meeting to be held within two weeks; and the quorum at the adjourned meeting will be reduced to 30% of each class of voting power.

**11.** On consent of two-thirds of each class of voting power, the Association can annex additional properties (e.g., additional condominium units and common areas). The developer can procure the annexation of any land within the following metes and bounds: _____ that it develops within ____ years following the incorporation of this Association without taking a vote of the unit-owner membership by recording a certificate of annexation. However, any such annexation must be part of a general plan submitted to and approved by the FHA; if the FHA withholds its approval, the two-thirds vote of the unit-holder members will be required to authorize the annexation.

**12.** Amendment of these Articles of Incorporation will require the affirmative vote of 75% of each class of voting power.

**13.** Dissolution of this Association will require the affirmative vote of two-thirds of each class of voting power. Because this Association is a nonprofit organization and none of its assets can inure to the benefit of any private individual, if and when the Association is dissolved, all its assets will be dedicated to an appropriate public agency selected by the Board because its purposes are as close as possible to those of the Association. If the public agency refuses the dedication, the Board will select another nonprofit organization whose aims are compatible with those of the Association and will convey the assets to such organization.

## ARTICLES OF AMENDMENT (See Model Not-for-Profit Corporations Act Section 35)

*1.* On _____ , 19_____ , a not-for-profit corporation known as _____ held a regular/special meeting at its headquarters located at _____ [or: specify place of meeting].
□ This was a regular membership meeting, and a quorum was present.
□ The corporation has no members, and therefore the power to amend the Articles of Incorporation lies with the majority of the directors.
2. By a vote of _____ to _____ , the following amendment to the corporation's Articles of Incorporation was adopted: _____

Date: _____ , 199_____
Signed: _____President/Vice President
_____Secretary/Assistant Secretary

## NOTICE OF REGULAR MEETING

[Note: MNCA Section 14 requires 10–50 days notice of a meeting]
DEAR MEMBERS OF _____ CORPORATION: _____
    This is a notice informing you that the Corporation's regular annual meeting will be held on _____ , 19_____ at _____ M., at _____

Date: _____ , 199_____
Signed: _____President

## NOTICE OF SPECIAL MEETING

DEAR MEMBERS OF _____ CORPORATION:
    Section _____ of the Articles of Incorporation/Bylaws allows the Board of Directors/any _____ members to call a special meeting of the corporation, on _____ days' notice to the membership.
    This is a notice informing you that the Board of Directors/members _____ ,
_____ , and _____ have called a special meeting, to be held at _____M. on _____ , 19_____ at the corporation's registered office (located at _____) on _____ , 19_____ at _____M. The purpose of this meeting is to discuss the following

issues/vote to approve or disapprove the following corporation action/vote to amend the bylaws to provide/other [describe]: _____
Signed: [members calling meeting; if called by Board, signature of Secretary]

## Proxy

I, _____ , am a member of _____ Corp. Because I am sometimes unable or unwilling to attend regular and special meetings of the corporation as they are called, but wish to remain a voting member of the corporation, I hereby appoint _____ as my proxy for all meetings of the members of _____ Corp. S/he can vote in my place if I am not present at a meeting, and can take any action that I would be entitled to take as a voting member if I attended the meeting.

## MINUTES OF INITIAL MEETING OF THE BOARD OF DIRECTORS

*1.* On _____ , 19_____ , at _____ M, an initial meeting was held at the call of the incorporators of the not-for-profit organization known as _____ . _____ , _____ , and _____ are the incorporators of this organization.

*2.* Under the Articles of Incorporation, _____ , _____ and _____ serve as initial directors of the organization. They were all present [except _____ , who gave his/her proxy to _____ ]. A quorum for this meeting requires _____ directors; therefore, a quorum was present. All directors received at least three days' notice of the meeting.

*3.* On motion proposed by _____ , seconded by _____ and passed unanimously/ by a vote of _____to _____ , the following individuals were elected as officers of the corporation: . All individuals elected accept their offices.

*4.* On motion proposed by _____ , seconded by _____ and passed unanimously/ by a vote of _____ to _____ , the Board of Directors adopted Bylaws consisting of _____ pages. On motion proposed by _____ , seconded by _____ , and passed unanimously/by a vote of _____to _____ , the Board of Directors adopted a corporate seal, which can be described as follows: _____ .

*5.* In addition to the business described above, the following business was transacted at the initial meeting: [describe]

*6.* On consideration of all items on the agenda and all business proposed by attendees, the meeting was adjourned at _____ M. on motion of _____ .

## MOTIONS AND RESOLUTIONS

*1.* RESOLVED that the corporation open a checking/savings/checking and savings account(s) at _____ Bank and that the following officers and individuals be permitted to sign checks on the corporate account: _____ It is further resolved that the Treasurer be permitted to use funds from this account to pay the expenses of organization and incorporation and to reimburse corporation members/directors/officers who have advanced funds for these purposes.

## PLAN OF MERGER OR CONSOLIDATION OF NONPROFIT ORGANIZATIONS

*1.* This is a plan of merger/consolidation between two nonprofit organizations both chartered and operating under the laws of the state of _____ .

*2.* The two corporations participating in the merger/consolidation are _____ and _____ .

*3.* The surviving corporation will be known as _____ and will be chartered and will operate under the laws of the state of _____ .

*4.* The two organizations are undergoing this process because they have discovered that their objectives and methods of operation are so similar that they have the effect of dividing contributions and energy that could be more efficiently deployed if the two organizations were to combine.

*5.* The new organization will adopt terms of the Articles of Incorporation and Bylaws of _____ , with the following modifications: _____

*6.* The Boards of Directors, and at least a majority of at least a quorum of the members of each organization, have approved the plan of merger/consolidation at a special meeting held for the purpose on appropriate notice, and each organization has passed a resolution adopting the plan.

*7.* The new organization's initial Board of Directors will consist of five Directors, two from the Board of _____ , two from the Board of _____ , and a fifth Director chosen by the other four Directors.

*8.* The new organization's registered address will be _____ , and its initial registered agent for the service of process will be _____ OR the new organization hereby designates the Secretary of State of the state of _____ as its agent for the service of process.

## LETTER DEALING WITH DERIVATIVE SUIT

Date: _____
To _____ Corp./The Board of Directors of _____ Corp.

    I, _____ , have been a member of _____ Corp. since _____ , 19_____ , and was a member at the time of all the conduct and transactions which underlie my complaint against _____ .

    Specifically, I allege that _____ Corp. has been the victim of improper activities on the part of _____ , including the following: [give details]

☐ Misappropriation of the corporation's property

☐ Improper distribution of the corporation's property

☐ Breach of the charitable trust created by _____ on _____ , 19_____ through a document entitled _____

☐ Violation of the corporation's Articles of Incorporation/Bylaws

☐ Self-dealing between the corporation and director(s)

☐ Engaging in profit-making transactions endangering the corporation's tax-exempt status

☐ Engaging in partisan political activity endangering the corporation's tax-exempt status

☐ Other: _____

I hereby demand that the corporation/Board of Directors take action immediately to terminate the improper conduct and ensure that the corporation is made whole—if necessary by bringing suit against the offender(s). If the situation has not been remedied before _____ , 19_____ , I intend to bring a derivative suit on behalf of the corporation [add, if state statute provides] and to seek reimbursement of the costs and attorneys' fees I have encountered in connection with the improprieties committed against the corporation.

Date: _____ , 199_____
Signed: _____


# ARTICLES OF DISSOLUTION OF A NONPROFIT
# CORPORATION

## Articles of Dissolution of the Monroe Hemophilia Research Association, Inc., Under Chapter 322 of the Consolidated Statutes of the State of Monroe.

*1.* The Monroe Hemophilia Research Association, Inc., adopts the following Articles of Dissolution in order to dissolve the corporation.

*2.* A regular/special meeting of the membership of the organization was held on _____ , 19 _____ . Adequate notice of the meeting had been given, and a quorum of members was present either in person or by duly authorized proxy. At this meeting, a resolution to dissolve the corporation was proposed and was adopted unanimously/by a vote of _____ to _____ , constituting two-thirds or more of the votes entitled to be cast. OR _____

The organization has no membership, and a resolution of dissolution was proposed at a regular/special Board meeting on _____ , 19 _____ . A quorum of the Board was present at this meeting; the resolution was duly seconded and adopted by a vote of _____ to _____ /unanimously.

*3.* The corporation's debts and liabilities have been paid, or provision has been made for their payment.

*4.* As far as is known by the Board of the organization, there is no litigation against the corporation either in progress or pending OR The corporation is the defendant in a suit captioned _____ v. _____ , File No. _____ , pending in the _____ Court of _____ . However, provision has been made for payment of any settlement or judgment to be rendered in this action, in the form of:_____

*5.* No surplus remains after payment of debts/it is estimated that a surplus of $ _____ will remain after settlement of debts. The resolution of dissolution specifies that this surplus be paid to the North American Hemophilia Research Foundation, whose headquarters are in Minneapolis. The North American Hemophilia Research Foundation has been contacted and agrees to accept the surplus assets for use in its charitable, educational, and research work. No portion of the surplus will redound to the private benefit of any individual or for-profit corporation.

Date: _____ , 199_____
Signed: (President) _____
(Secretary) _____

| Form **990** | **Return of Organization Exempt From Income Tax** | OMB No. 1545-0047 |
|---|---|---|

Under section 501(c) (except black lung benefit trust or private foundation)
of the Internal Revenue Code or section 4947(a)(1) trust
(See separate instructions.)

Department of the Treasury
Internal Revenue Service

**19**8**9**

**Note**: You may be required to use a copy of this return to satisfy state reporting requirements. See instruction E.

For the calendar year 1989, or fiscal year beginning _____, 1989, and ending _____, 19____

| Use IRS label. Other-wise, please print or type. | Name of organization | **A** Employer identification number (see instruction S) |
|---|---|---|
| | Address (number and street) or P.O. box number | **B** State registration number (see instruction E) |
| | City or town, state, and ZIP code | **C** If application for exemption is pending, check here ▶ . . . . . . . . . . □ |

**D** Check type of organization—Exempt under section ▶ □ 501(c) ( ) (insert number),
OR ▶ □ section 4947(a)(1) trust (see instruction C7 and question 92.)

**E** Accounting method: □ Cash □ Accrual
□ Other (specify) ▶

**F** Is this a group return (see instruction Q) filed for affiliates?. . . . . □ Yes □ No
If "Yes," enter the number of affiliates for which this return is filed _____
Is this a separate return filed by a group affiliate? . . . . . □ Yes □ No

**G** If either answer in F is "Yes," enter four-digit group exemption number (GEN) ▶

**H** Check here □ if your gross receipts are normally not more than $25,000 (see instruction B11). You do not have to file a completed return with IRS; but if you received a Form 990 Package in the mail, you should file a return without financial data (see instruction A). **Some states require a completed return.**

**Note:** Form 990EZ is available for organizations with gross receipts less than $100,000 **and** total assets less than $250,000 at end of year.

**501(c)(3) organizations and 4947(a)(1) trusts must also complete and attach Schedule A (Form 990). (See Instructions.)**

| **Part I** | Statement of Revenue, Expenses and Changes in Net Assets or Fund Balances |
|---|---|

| | | | | | | |
|---|---|---|---|---|---|---|
| Revenue | **1** | Contributions, gifts, grants, and similar amounts received: | | | | |
| | **a** | Direct public support . . . . . . . . . | **1a** | | | |
| | **b** | Indirect public support . . . . . . . . . | **1b** | | | |
| | **c** | Government grants . . . . . . . . . . . | **1c** | | | |
| | **d** | **Total** (add lines 1a through 1c) (attach schedule—see instructions) . . . . | | | **1d** | |
| | **2** | Program service revenue (from Part VII, line 93) . . . . . . . . . | | | **2** | |
| | **3** | Membership dues and assessments . . . . . . . . . | | | **3** | |
| | **4** | Interest on savings and temporary cash investments . . . . . . | | | **4** | |
| | **5** | Dividends and interest from securities. . . . . . . . . | | | **5** | |
| | **6a** | Gross rents . . . . . . . . . . . . . | **6a** | | | |
| | **b** | Less: rental expenses . . . . . . . . . | **6b** | | | |
| | **c** | Net rental income (loss) . . . . . . . . . | | | **6c** | |
| | **7** | Other investment income (describe ▶ ) | | | **7** | |
| | **8a** | Gross amount from sale of assets other than inventory . . . . . | (A) Securities **8a** | (B) Other **8a** | | |
| | **b** | Less: cost or other basis and sales expenses | **8b** | **8b** | | |
| | **c** | Gain (loss) (attach schedule) . . . . | **8c** | **8c** | **8d** | |
| | **9** | Special fundraising events and activities (attach schedule—see instructions): | | | | |
| | **a** | Gross revenue (not including $_____ of contributions reported on line 1a) . . . . . | **9a** | | | |
| | **b** | Less: direct expenses . . . . . . . . . | **9b** | | | |
| | **c** | Net income (line 9a less line 9b) . . . . . . . | | | **9c** | |
| | **10a** | Gross sales less returns and allowances . . . . . | **10a** | | | |
| | **b** | Less: cost of goods sold . . . . . . . | **10b** | | | |
| | **c** | Gross profit (loss) (attach schedule) . . . . . . | | | **10c** | |
| | **11** | Other revenue (from Part VII, line 103) . . . . . . . | | | **11** | |
| | **12** | **Total revenue** (add lines 1d, 2, 3, 4, 5, 6c, 7, 8d, 9c, 10c, and 11) . . . | | | **12** | |
| Expenses | **13** | Program services (from line 44, column (B)) (see instructions) . . . . | | | **13** | |
| | **14** | Management and general (from line 44, column (C)) (see instructions) . . . . | | | **14** | |
| | **15** | Fundraising (from line 44, column (D)) (see instructions) . . . . | | | **15** | |
| | **16** | Payments to affiliates (attach schedule—see instructions) . . . . | | | **16** | |
| | **17** | **Total expenses** (add lines 16 and 44, column (A)) . . . . | | | **17** | |
| Net Assets | **18** | Excess (deficit) for the year (subtract line 17 from line 12) . . . . | | | **18** | |
| | **19** | Net assets or fund balances at beginning of year (from line 74, column (A)) . . | | | **19** | |
| | **20** | Other changes in net assets or fund balances (attach explanation) . . | | | **20** | |
| | **21** | Net assets or fund balances at end of year (add lines 18, 19, and 20). . . . | | | **21** | |

For Paperwork Reduction Act Notice, see page 1 of the instructions.                                    Form **990** (1989)

Form 990 (1989)                                                                                                           Page **2**

| **Part II** | Statement of Functional Expenses | | | | |
|---|---|---|---|---|---|

All organizations must complete column (A). Columns (B), (C), and (D) are required for section 501(c)(3) and (c)(4) organizations and 4947(a)(1) trusts but optional for others. (See instructions.)

| *Do not include amounts reported on line 6b, 8b, 9b, 10b, or 16 of Part I.* | **(A) Total** | **(B)** Program services | **(C)** Management and general | **(D)** Fundraising |
|---|---|---|---|---|
| **22** Grants and allocations (attach schedule) . . . . | | | ////// | ////// |
| **23** Specific assistance to individuals . . . . . | | | ////// | ////// |
| **24** Benefits paid to or for members. . . . . . | | | ////// | ////// |
| **25** Compensation of officers, directors, etc. . . . | | | | |
| **26** Other salaries and wages . . . . . . . | | | | |
| **27** Pension plan contributions . . . . . . . | | | | |
| **28** Other employee benefits . . . . . . . | | | | |
| **29** Payroll taxes . . . . . . . . . . | | | | |
| **30** Professional fundraising fees . . . . . . | | ////// | ////// | |
| **31** Accounting fees . . . . . . . . . . | | | | |
| **32** Legal fees . . . . . . . . . . . | | | | |
| **33** Supplies . . . . . . . . . . . . | | | | |
| **34** Telephone . . . . . . . . . . . | | | | |
| **35** Postage and shipping . . . . . . . . | | | | |
| **36** Occupancy . . . . . . . . . . . | | | | |
| **37** Equipment rental and maintenance . . . . | | | | |
| **38** Printing and publications . . . . . . . | | | | |
| **39** Travel . . . . . . . . . . . . . | | | | |
| **40** Conferences, conventions, and meetings . . . | | | | |
| **41** Interest . . . . . . . . . . . . | | | | |
| **42** Depreciation, depletion, etc. (attach schedule) . . | | | | |
| **43** Other expenses (itemize): **a** _____ | | | | |
| **b** _____ | | | | |
| **c** _____ | | | | |
| **d** _____ | | | | |
| **e** _____ | | | | |
| **f** _____ | | | | |
| **44** **Total functional expenses** (add lines 22 through 43) Organizations completing columns B-D, carry these totals to lines 13-15. | | | | |

| **Part III** | Statement of Program Service Accomplishments (See instructions.) | |
|---|---|---|

Describe what was achieved in carrying out your exempt purposes. Fully describe the services provided; the number of persons benefited; or other relevant information for each program title. Section 501(c)(3) and (4) organizations must also enter the amount of grants to others.

**Expenses**
Required for section 501(c)(3) and (4) organizations; optional for others

**a** --------------------------------------------------------------
--------------------------------------------------------------
--------------------------------------------------------------
--------------------------------------------------------------
(Grants and allocations $                    )

**b** --------------------------------------------------------------
--------------------------------------------------------------
--------------------------------------------------------------
--------------------------------------------------------------
(Grants and allocations $                    )

**c** --------------------------------------------------------------
--------------------------------------------------------------
--------------------------------------------------------------
--------------------------------------------------------------
(Grants and allocations $                    )

**d** --------------------------------------------------------------
--------------------------------------------------------------
--------------------------------------------------------------
--------------------------------------------------------------
(Grants and allocations $                    )

**e** Other program services (attach schedule) . . . . . . . . (Grants and allocations $                    )
**f** **Total** (add lines **a** through **e**) (should equal line 44, column (B)). . . . . . . . . . . . . . ▶

Form 990 (1989)

## Part IV    Balance Sheets

Note: *Where required, attached schedules and amounts in the description column should be for end-of-year amounts only.*

| | | | (A) Beginning of year | | (B) End of year |
|---|---|---|---|---|---|
| | **Assets** | | | 45 | |
| 45 | Cash—noninterest-bearing | | | 46 | |
| 46 | Savings and temporary cash investments | | | | |
| 47a | Accounts receivable | 47a | | 47c | |
| b | Less: allowance for doubtful accounts | 47b | | | |
| 48a | Pledges receivable | 48a | | 48c | |
| b | Less: allowance for doubtful accounts | 48b | | 49 | |
| 49 | Grants receivable | | | | |
| 50 | Receivables due from officers, directors, trustees, and key employees (attach schedule) | | | 50 | |
| 51a | Other notes and loans receivable (attach schedule) | 51a | | 51c | |
| b | Less: allowance for doubtful accounts | 51b | | 52 | |
| 52 | Inventories for sale or use | | | 53 | |
| 53 | Prepaid expenses and deferred charges | | | 54 | |
| 54 | Investments—securities (attach schedule) | | | | |
| 55a | Investments—land, buildings, and equipment: basis | 55a | | | |
| b | Less: accumulated depreciation (attach schedule) | 55b | | 55c | |
| 56 | Investments—other (attach schedule) | | | 56 | |
| 57a | Land, buildings, and equipment: basis | 57a | | 57c | |
| b | Less: accumulated depreciation (attach schedule) | 57b | | 58 | |
| 58 | Other assets (describe ▶ _____ ) | | | 59 | |
| 59 | **Total assets** (add lines 45 through 58) | | | | |
| | **Liabilities** | | | 60 | |
| 60 | Accounts payable and accrued expenses | | | 61 | |
| 61 | Grants payable | | | 62 | |
| 62 | Support and revenue designated for future periods (attach schedule) | | | 63 | |
| 63 | Loans from officers, directors, trustees, and key employees (attach schedule) | | | 64 | |
| 64 | Mortgages and other notes payable (attach schedule) | | | 65 | |
| 65 | Other liabilities (describe ▶ _____ ) | | | 66 | |
| 66 | **Total liabilities** (add lines 60 through 65) | | | | |

**Fund Balances or Net Assets**

Organizations that use fund accounting, check here ▶ ☐ and complete lines 67 through 70 and lines 74 and 75.

| | | | | | |
|---|---|---|---|---|---|
| 67a | Current unrestricted fund | | | 67a | |
| b | Current restricted fund | | | 67b | |
| 68 | Land, buildings, and equipment fund | | | 68 | |
| 69 | Endowment fund | | | 69 | |
| 70 | Other funds (describe ▶ _____ ) | | | 70 | |

Organizations that do not use fund accounting, check here ▶ ☐ and complete lines 71 through 75.

| | | | | | |
|---|---|---|---|---|---|
| 71 | Capital stock or trust principal | | | 71 | |
| 72 | Paid-in or capital surplus | | | 72 | |
| 73 | Retained earnings or accumulated income | | | 73 | |
| 74 | Total fund balances or net assets (see instructions) | | | 74 | |
| 75 | **Total liabilities and fund balances/net assets** (see instructions) | | | 75 | |

Form 990 (1989)                                                                                          Page **4**

**Part V**    **List of Officers, Directors, and Trustees** (List each one even if not compensated. See instructions.)

| **(A)** Name and address | **(B)** Title and average hours per week devoted to position | **(C)** Compensation (if not paid, enter zero) | **(D)** Contributions to employee benefit plans | **(E)** Expense account and other allowances |
|---|---|---|---|---|
| - - - - - - - - - - - - - - - - - - - - - - - - - - - - - - - - - - | | | | |
| - - - - - - - - - - - - - - - - - - - - - - - - - - - - - - - - - - | | | | |
| - - - - - - - - - - - - - - - - - - - - - - - - - - - - - - - - - - | | | | |
| - - - - - - - - - - - - - - - - - - - - - - - - - - - - - - - - - - | | | | |
| - - - - - - - - - - - - - - - - - - - - - - - - - - - - - - - - - - | | | | |

**Part VI**    **Other Information**

|  | | Yes | No |
|---|---|---|---|

**76**  Did you engage in any activity not previously reported to the Internal Revenue Service?   . . . . . . . .   **76**

    If "Yes," attach a detailed description of each activity.

**77**  Were any changes made in the organizing or governing documents, but not reported to IRS? . . . . . . . .   **77**

    If "Yes," attach a conformed copy of the changes.

**78a**  Did your organization have unrelated business gross income of $1,000 or more during the year covered by this return?   **78a**

   **b**  If "Yes," have you filed a tax return on **Form 990-T,** Exempt Organization Business Income Tax Return, for this year?   **78b**

   **c**  At any time during the year, did you own a 50% or greater interest in a taxable corporation or partnership? . . . . .   **78c**

    If "Yes," complete Part IX.

**79**  Was there a liquidation, dissolution, termination, or substantial contraction during the year? (See instructions.) .   **79**

    If "Yes," attach a statement as described in the instructions.

**80a**  Are you related (other than by association with a statewide or nationwide organization) through common membership, governing bodies, trustees, officers, etc., to any other exempt or nonexempt organization? (See instructions.) . . . .   **80a**

   **b**  If "Yes," enter the name of the organization ▶ - - - - - - - - - - - - - - - - - - - - - - - - - - - - - - - - - - - - - - - - - - - - - - - - - - and check whether it is ☐ exempt **OR** ☐ nonexempt.

**81a**  Enter amount of political expenditures, direct or indirect, as described in the instructions.    |**81a**|

   **b**  Did you file **Form 1120-POL,** U.S. Income Tax Return for Certain Political Organizations, for this year? . . . . .   **81b**

**82a**  Did you receive donated services or the use of materials, equipment, or facilities at no charge or at substantially less than fair rental value? . . . . . . . . . . . . . . . . . . . . . . . . . . . . . . . . . . . .   **82a**

   **b**  If "Yes," you may indicate the value of these items here. Do not include this amount as revenue in Part I or as an expense in Part II. See instructions for reporting in Part III . . . .    |**82b**|

**83a**  Did anyone request to see either your annual return or exemption application (or both)? . . . . . . . .   **83a**

   **b**  If "Yes," did you comply as described in the instructions? (See General Instruction L.) . . . . . . . .   **83b**

**84a**  Did you solicit any contributions or gifts that were not tax deductible? . . . . . . . . . . . . . . . .   **84a**

   **b**  If "Yes," did you include with every solicitation an express statement that such contributions or gifts were not tax deductible? (See General Instruction N.) . . . . . . . . . . . . . . . . . . . . . . . . .   **84b**

**85a**  *Section 501(c)(5) or (6) organizations.*—Did you spend any amounts in attempts to influence public opinion about legislative matters or referendums? (See instructions and Regulations section 1.162-20(c).) . . . . . . .   **85a**

   **b**  If "Yes," enter the total amount spent for this purpose. . . . . . . . . . . . . . .    |**85b**|

**86**  *Section 501(c)(7) organizations.*—Enter:

   **a**  Initiation fees and capital contributions included on line 12. . . . . . . . . .    |**86a**|

   **b**  Gross receipts, included on line 12, for public use of club facilities (See instructions.) . . .    |**86b**|

   **c**  Does the club's governing instrument or any written policy statement provide for discrimination against any person because of race, color, or religion? (See instructions.) . . . . . . . . . . . . . .   **86c**

**87**  *Section 501(c)(12) organizations.*—Enter amount of:

   **a**  Gross income received from members or shareholders . . . . . . . . . . .    |**87a**|

   **b**  Gross income received from other sources (Do not net amounts due or paid to other sources against amounts due or received from them.) . . . . . . . . . . . . .    |**87b**|

**88**  *Public interest law firms.*—Attach information described in the instructions.

**89**  List the states with which a copy of this return is filed ▶ - - - - - - - - - - - - - - - - - - - - - - - - - - - - - - - - - - -

**90**  During this tax year did you maintain any part of your accounting/tax records on a computerized system? . . . . .   **90**

**91**  The books are in care of ▶ - - - - - - - - - - - - - - - - - - - - - - - - Telephone no. ▶ - - - - - - - - - - - - - - - - - - - - - -

    Located at ▶ - - - - - - - - - - - - - - - - - - - - - - - - - - - - - - - - - - - - - - - - - - - - - - - - - - - - - - - - - - - - - -

**92**  *Section 4947(a)(1) trusts filing Form 990 in lieu of* **Form 1041,** U.S. Fiduciary Income Tax Return.— . . . . . Check here ▶ ☐

    and enter the amount of tax-exempt interest received or accrued during the tax year. . . ▶ |**92**|

Form 990 (1989)                                                                                              Page **5**

## Part VII   Analysis of Income-Producing Activities

Enter gross amounts unless otherwise indicated.

| 93 Program service revenue: | Unrelated business income | | Excluded by section 512, 513, or 514 | | (e) Related or exempt function income |
|---|---|---|---|---|---|
| | **(a)** Business code | **(b)** Amount | **(c)** Exclusion code | **(d)** Amount | |
| (a) _____ | | | | | |
| (b) _____ | | | | | |
| (c) _____ | | | | | |
| (d) _____ | | | | | |
| (e) _____ | | | | | |
| (f) _____ | | | | | |
| (g) Fees from government agencies | | | | | |
| 94 Membership dues and assessments | | | | | |
| 95 Interest on savings and temporary cash investments | | | | | |
| 96 Dividends and interest on securities | | | | | |
| 97 Net rental income (loss) from real estate: | | | | | |
| (a) debt-financed property | | | | | |
| (b) not debt-financed property | | | | | |
| 98 Net rental income (loss) from personal property | | | | | |
| 99 Other investment income | | | | | |
| 100 Gain (loss) from sales of assets other than inventory | | | | | |
| 101 Net income from special fundraising events | | | | | |
| 102 Gross profit (loss) from sales of inventory | | | | | |
| 103 Other revenue: (a) _____ | | | | | |
| (b) _____ | | | | | |
| (c) _____ | | | | | |
| (d) _____ | | | | | |
| (e) _____ | | | | | |
| 104 Subtotal (add columns (b), (d), and (e)) | | | | | |

105 **TOTAL** (add line 104, columns (b), (d), and (e)) . . . . . . . . . . . . ▶ _____

(Line 105 plus line 1d, Part I, should equal the amount on line 12, Part I.)

## Part VIII   Relationship of Activities to the Accomplishment of Exempt Purposes

| Line No. ▼ | Explain below how each activity for which income is reported in column (e) of Part VII contributed importantly to the accomplishment of your exempt purposes (other than by providing funds for such purposes). |
|---|---|
| | |
| | |
| | |
| | |
| | |
| | |
| | |

## Part IX   Information Regarding Taxable Subsidiaries (Complete this Part if you answered "Yes" to question 78c)

| Name, address, and employer identification number of corporation or partnership | Percentage of ownership interest | Nature of business activities | Total income | End-of-year assets |
|---|---|---|---|---|
| | | | | |
| | | | | |
| | | | | |
| | | | | |
| | | | | |
| | | | | |

**Please Sign Here** — Under penalties of perjury, I declare that I have examined this return, including accompanying schedules and statements, and to the best of my knowledge and belief, it is true, correct, and complete. Declaration of preparer (other than officer) is based on all information of which preparer has any knowledge.

| ▶ Signature of officer | Date | ▶ Title |
|---|---|---|

| **Paid Preparer's Use Only** | Preparer's signature ▶ | Date | Check if self-employed ▶ ☐ |
|---|---|---|---|
| | Firm's name (or yours if self-employed) and address ▶ | ZIP code | |

✿U.S. Government Printing Office: 1990-262-151/00066

| SCHEDULE A<br>(Form 990)<br>Department of the Treasury<br>Internal Revenue Service | **Organization Exempt Under 501(c)(3)**<br>(Except Private Foundation), 501(e), 501(f), 501(k), or Section 4947(a)(1) Trust<br>**Supplementary Information**<br>► Attach to Form 990 (or Form 990EZ). | OMB No. 1545-0047<br>**1989** |
|---|---|---|

| Name | Employer identification number |
|---|---|

**Part I  Compensation of the Five Highest Paid Employees Other Than Officers, Directors, and Trustees**
(See specific instructions.)  (List each one. If there are none, enter "None.")

| (a) Name and address of employees paid more than $30,000 | (b) Title and average hours per week devoted to position | (c) Compensation | (d) Contributions to employee benefit plans | (e) Expense account and other allowances |
|---|---|---|---|---|
| | | | | |
| | | | | |
| | | | | |
| | | | | |
| | | | | |

Total number of other employees paid over $30,000 . . . . . . . . . . . . . . ►

**Part II  Compensation of the Five Highest Paid Persons for Professional Services**
(See specific instructions.)  (List each one. If there are none, enter "None.")

| (a) Name and address of persons paid more than $30,000 | (b) Type of service | (c) Compensation |
|---|---|---|
| | | |
| | | |
| | | |
| | | |
| | | |

Total number of others receiving over $30,000 for professional services . . . . . . . . . . ►

**Part III  Statements About Activities**

|  | Yes (1) | No (2) |
|---|---|---|
| 1 During the year, have you attempted to influence national, state, or local legislation, including any attempt to influence public opinion on a legislative matter or referendum? . . . . . . . . . . . . . . . . **1** | | |

If "Yes," enter the total expenses paid or incurred in connection with the legislative activities.  $ _____

Complete Part VI of this form for organizations that made an election under section 501(h) on Form 5768 or other statement. For other organizations checking "Yes," attach a statement giving a detailed description of the legislative activities and a classified schedule of the expenses paid or incurred.

2 During the year, have you, either directly or indirectly, engaged in any of the following acts with a trustee, director, principal officer, or creator of your organization, or any taxable organization or corporation with which such person is affiliated as an officer, director, trustee, majority owner, or principal beneficiary:

| | | |
|---|---|---|
| a Sale, exchange, or leasing of property? . . . . . . . . . . . . . . . . . . . . . . **2a** | | |
| b Lending of money or other extension of credit? . . . . . . . . . . . . . . . . . **2b** | | |
| c Furnishing of goods, services, or facilities? . . . . . . . . . . . . . . . . . . **2c** | | |
| d Payment of compensation (or payment or reimbursement of expenses if more than $1,000)? . . . . . . **2d** | | |
| e Transfer of any part of your income or assets? . . . . . . . . . . . . . . . . . **2e** | | |

If the answer to any question is "Yes," attach a detailed statement explaining the transactions.

| 3 Do you make grants for scholarships, fellowships, student loans, etc.? . . . . . . . . . . . . **3** | | |

4 Attach a statement explaining how you determine that individuals or organizations receiving disbursements from you in furtherance of your charitable programs qualify to receive payments. (See specific instructions.)

For Paperwork Reduction Act Notice, see page 1 of the instructions to Form 990 (or Form 990EZ).          **Schedule A (Form 990) 1989**

Schedule A (Form 990) 1989

Page **2**

## Part IV   Reason for Non-Private Foundation Status (See instructions for definitions.)

The organization is not a private foundation because it is (please check only **ONE** applicable box):

5 ☐ [1] A church, convention of churches, or association of churches. Section 170(b)(1)(A)(i).

6 ☐ [2] A school. Section 170(b)(1)(A)(ii). (Also complete Part V, page 3.)

7 ☐ [3] A hospital or a cooperative hospital service organization. Section 170(b)(1)(A)(iii).

8 ☐ [4] A Federal, state, or local government or governmental unit. Section 170(b)(1)(A)(v).

9 ☐ [5] A medical research organization operated in conjunction with a hospital. Section 170(b)(1)(A)(iii). **Enter name, city, and state**
of hospital ▶ . . . . . . . . . . . . . . . . . . . . . . . . . . . . . . . . . . . . . . . . . . . . . . . . . . . . . . . . . . . . . . . . . . . . . . . . .

10 ☐ [6] An organization operated for the benefit of a college or university owned or operated by a governmental unit. Section 170(b)(1)(A)(iv). (Also complete Support Schedule.)

11 ☐ [7] An organization that normally receives a substantial part of its support from a governmental unit or from the general public. Section 170(b)(1)(A)(vi). (Also complete Support Schedule.)

12 ☐ [8] An organization that normally receives: (a) no more than $1/3$ of its support from gross investment income and unrelated business taxable income (less section 511 tax) from businesses acquired by the organization after June 30, 1975, and (b) more than $1/3$ of its support from contributions, membership fees, and gross receipts from activities related to its charitable, etc., functions—subject to certain exceptions. See section 509(a)(2). ( Also complete Support Schedule.)

13 ☐ [9] An organization that is not controlled by any disqualified persons (other than foundation managers) and supports organizations described in: (1) boxes 5 through 12 above; or (2) section 501(c)(4), (5), or (6), if they meet the test of section 509(a)(2). See section 509(a)(3).

Provide the following information about the supported organizations. (See instructions for Part IV, box 13.)

| **(a)** Name of supported organizations | **(b)** Box number from above |
|---|---|
|  |  |
|  |  |
|  |  |
|  |  |

14 ☐ [0] An organization organized and operated to test for public safety. Section 509(a)(4). (See specific instructions.)

### Support Schedule (Complete only if you checked box 10, 11, or 12 above.) Use cash method of accounting.

| Calendar year (or fiscal year beginning in) ▶ | (a) 1988 | (b) 1987 | (c) 1986 | (d) 1985 | (e) Total |
|---|---|---|---|---|---|
| 15 Gifts, grants, and contributions received. (Do not include unusual grants. See line 28.) . . |  |  |  |  |  |
| 16 Membership fees received . . . . |  |  |  |  |  |
| 17 Gross receipts from admissions, merchandise sold or services performed, or furnishing of facilities in any activity that is not a business unrelated to the organization's charitable, etc., purpose . . . . . . . . . . . |  |  |  |  |  |
| 18 Gross income from interest, dividends, amounts received from payments on securities loans (section 512(a)(5)), rents, royalties, and unrelated business taxable income (less section 511 taxes) from businesses acquired by the organization after June 30, 1975 . . . |  |  |  |  |  |
| 19 Net income from unrelated business activities not included in line 18 . . |  |  |  |  |  |
| 20 Tax revenues levied for your benefit and either paid to you or expended on your behalf . . . |  |  |  |  |  |
| 21 The value of services or facilities furnished to you by a governmental unit without charge. Do not include the value of services or facilities generally furnished to the public without charge . . . . . . . . . . |  |  |  |  |  |
| 22 Other income. Attach schedule. Do not include gain (or loss) from sale of capital assets . |  |  |  |  |  |
| 23 Total of lines 15 through 22 . . . |  |  |  |  |  |
| 24 Line 23 minus line 17 . . . . . . |  |  |  |  |  |
| 25 Enter 1% of line 23 . . . . . . |  |  |  |  | ///////////// |

26 Organizations described in box 10 or 11:
   **a** Enter 2% of amount in column (e), line 24 . . . . . . . . . . . . . . . . . . . . .
   **b** Attach a list (not open to public inspection) showing the name of and amount contributed by each person (other than a governmental unit or publicly supported organization) whose total gifts for 1985 through 1988 exceeded the amount shown in line 26a. Enter the sum of all excess amounts here . . . . . . . . . .

*(Continued on page 3)*

**Part IV**   Support Schedule (continued) **(Complete only if you checked box 10, 11, or 12 on page 2.)**

**27**   Organizations described in box 12, page 2:

  **a**   Attach a list for amounts shown on lines 15, 16, and 17, showing the name of, and total amounts received in each year from, each "disqualified person," and enter the sum of such amounts for each year:

     (1988) ..................... (1987)..................... (1986) ..................... (1985) .....................

  **b**   Attach a list showing, for 1985 through 1988, the name and amount included in line 17 for each person (other than "disqualified persons") from whom the organization received more during that year than the larger of: the amount on line 25 for the year or $5,000. Include organizations described in boxes 5 through 11 as well as individuals. Enter the sum of these excess amounts for each year:

     (1988) _____ (1987) _____ (1986) _____ (1985) _____

**28**   For an organization described in box 10, 11, or 12, page 2, that received any unusual grants during 1985 through 1988, attach a list (not open to public inspection) for each year showing the name of the contributor, the date and amount of the grant, and a brief description of the nature of the grant. Do not include these grants in line 15 above. (See specific instructions.)

**Part V**   **Private School Questionnaire**
             **(To be completed ONLY by schools that checked box 6 in Part IV)**

| | | Yes (1) | No (2) |
|---|---|---|---|
| **29** | Do you have a racially nondiscriminatory policy toward students by statement in your charter, bylaws, other governing instrument, or in a resolution of your governing body? . . . . . . . **29** | | |
| **30** | Do you include a statement of your racially nondiscriminatory policy toward students in all your brochures, catalogues, and other written communications with the public dealing with student admissions, programs, and scholarships? . . . . . . . . . . . . . . . **30** | | |
| **31** | Have you publicized your racially nondiscriminatory policy through newspaper or broadcast media during the period of solicitation for students, or during the registration period if you have no solicitation program, in a way that makes the policy known to all parts of the general community you serve? . . . . . . . . . . **31** | | |
| | If "Yes," please describe; if "No," please explain. (If you need more space, attach a separate statement.) ----------------------------------------------------------------- ----------------------------------------------------------------- ----------------------------------------------------------------- | | |
| **32** | Do you maintain the following: | | |
| **a** | Records indicating the racial composition of the student body, faculty, and administrative staff? . . . . . **32a** | | |
| **b** | Records documenting that scholarships and other financial assistance are awarded on a racially nondiscriminatory basis? . . . . . . . . . . . . . . . . . **32b** | | |
| **c** | Copies of all catalogues, brochures, announcements, and other written communications to the public dealing with student admissions, programs, and scholarships? . . . . . . . . . **32c** | | |
| **d** | Copies of all material used by you or on your behalf to solicit contributions? . . . . . . . **32d** | | |
| | If you answered "No" to any of the above, please explain. (If you need more space, attach a separate statement.) ----------------------------------------------------------------- ----------------------------------------------------------------- | | |
| **33** | Do you discriminate by race in any way with respect to: | | |
| **a** | Students' rights or privileges? . . . . . . . . . . . . . . . . **33a** | | |
| **b** | Admissions policies? . . . . . . . . . . . . . . . . . . **33b** | | |
| **c** | Employment of faculty or administrative staff? . . . . . . . . . . . **33c** | | |
| **d** | Scholarships or other financial assistance? (See instructions.) . . . . . . . **33d** | | |
| **e** | Educational policies? . . . . . . . . . . . . . . . . . . **33e** | | |
| **f** | Use of facilities? . . . . . . . . . . . . . . . . . . . **33f** | | |
| **g** | Athletic programs? . . . . . . . . . . . . . . . . . . **33g** | | |
| **h** | Other extracurricular activities? . . . . . . . . . . . . . . . **33h** | | |
| | If you answered "Yes" to any of the above, please explain. (If you need more space, attach a separate statement.) ----------------------------------------------------------------- ----------------------------------------------------------------- | | |
| **34a** | Do you receive any financial aid or assistance from a governmental agency? . . . . . . . **34a** | | |
| **b** | Has your right to such aid ever been revoked or suspended? . . . . . . . . **34b** | | |
| | If you answered "Yes" to either 34a or b, please explain using an attached separate statement. | | |
| **35** | Do you certify that you have complied with the applicable requirements of sections 4.01 through 4.05 of Rev. Proc. 75-50, 1975-2 C.B. 587, covering racial nondiscrimination? If "No," attach an explanation. (See instructions for Part V.) **35** | | |

Schedule A (Form 990) 1989

**Part VI**   **Lobbying Expenditures by Public Charities** (see instructions)
**(To be completed ONLY by an eligible organization that filed Form 5768)**

Check here ▶ **a** ☐   If the organization belongs to an affiliated group (see instructions).
Check here ▶ **b** ☐   If you checked **a** and "limited control" provisions apply (see instructions).

| Limits on Lobbying Expenses | (a) Affiliated group totals | (b) To be completed for ALL electing organizations |
|---|---|---|
| **36** Total (grassroots) lobbying expenses to influence public opinion . . . . . . . . . | | |
| **37** Total lobbying expenses to influence a legislative body . . . . . . . . . . | | |
| **38** Total lobbying expenses (add lines 36 and 37) . . . . . . . . . . . . | | |
| **39** Other exempt purpose expenses (see Part VI instructions) . . . . . . . . | | |
| **40** Total exempt purpose expenses (add lines 38 and 39) (see instructions). . . . . . . | ░░░░░ | |
| **41** Lobbying nontaxable amount. Enter the smaller of $1,000,000 or the amount determined under the following table— | ░░░░░ | |
| **42** Grassroots nontaxable amount (enter 25% of line 41) . . . . . . . . . . | | |
| **43** Excess of line 36 over line 42 . . . . . . . . . . . . . . . . | | |
| **44** Excess of line 38 over line 41 . . . . . . . . . . . . . . . . | | |

*(table for line 41):*

| If the amount on line 40 is— | The lobbying nontaxable amount is— |
|---|---|
| Not over $500,000 . . . . . . . . . | 20% of the amount on line 40. . . . . . . . . |
| Over $500,000 but not over $1,000,000 . . . | $100,000 plus 15% of the excess over $500,000 . . . . |
| Over $1,000,000 but not over $1,500,000 . . . | $175,000 plus 10% of the excess over $1,000,000 . . . |
| Over $1,500,000 . . . . . . . . . | $225,000 plus 5% of the excess over $1,500,000 . . . |

**(Complete lines 43 and 44. File Form 4720 if either line 36 exceeds line 42 or line 38 exceeds line 41.)**

### 4-Year Averaging Period Under Section 501(h)

(Some organizations that made a section 501(h) election do not have to complete all of the five columns below. See the instructions for lines 45–50 for details.)

| Calendar year (or fiscal year beginning in) ▶ | Lobbying Expenses During 4-Year Averaging Period | | | | |
|---|---|---|---|---|---|
| | (a) 1989 | (b) 1988 | (c) 1987 | (d) 1986 | (e) Total |
| **45** Lobbying nontaxable amount (see instructions) . . . . . . . . . | | | | | |
| **46** Lobbying ceiling amount (150% of line 45(e)) . . . . . . . . | ░░░░ | ░░░░ | ░░░░ | ░░░░ | |
| **47** Total lobbying expenses (see instructions) . . . . . . . . . | | | | | |
| **48** Grassroots nontaxable amount (see instructions) . . . . . . . . | | | | | |
| **49** Grassroots ceiling amount (150% of line 48(e)) . . . . . . . . | ░░░░ | ░░░░ | ░░░░ | ░░░░ | |
| **50** Grassroots lobbying expenses (see instructions) . . . . . . . . | | | | | |

Schedule A (Form 990) 1989                                                                                    Page **5**

**Part VII** **Information Regarding Transfers To and Transactions and Relationships With Noncharitable Exempt Organizations**

| | | Yes | No |
|---|---|---|---|
| **51** Did the reporting organization directly or indirectly engage in any of the following with any other organization described in section 501(c) of the Code (other than section 501(c)(3) organizations) or in section 527, relating to political organizations? | | | |

**a** Transfers from the reporting organization to a noncharitable exempt organization of:

  (i) Cash  . . . . . . . . . . . . . . . . . . . . . . . . . . . . . . . . . . . . . . . . . . . .

  (ii) Other assets   . . . . . . . . . . . . . . . . . . . . . . . . . . . . . . . . . . . . . .

**b** Other Transactions:

  (i) Sales of assets to a noncharitable exempt organization  . . . . . . . . . . . . . . . . .

  (ii) Purchases of assets from a noncharitable exempt organization  . . . . . . . . . . . . .

  (iii) Rental of facilities or equipment   . . . . . . . . . . . . . . . . . . . . . . . . . . .

  (iv) Reimbursement arrangements .  . . . . . . . . . . . . . . . . . . . . . . . . . . . .

  (v) Loans or loan guarantees .  . . . . . . . . . . . . . . . . . . . . . . . . . . . . . .

  (vi) Performance of services or membership or fundraising solicitations   . . . . . . . . . .

**c** Sharing of facilities, equipment, mailing lists or other assets, or paid employees  . . . . . . . . . .

**d** If the answer to any of the above is "Yes," complete the following schedule. The "Amount involved" column below should always indicate the fair market value of the goods, other assets, or services given by the reporting organization. If the organization received less than fair market value in any transaction or sharing arrangement, the column should also indicate the value of the goods, other assets, or services received.

| (a) Line no. | (b) Amount involved | (c) Name of noncharitable exempt organization | (d) Description of transfers, transactions, and sharing arrangements |
|---|---|---|---|
| | | | |
| | | | |
| | | | |
| | | | |
| | | | |
| | | | |
| | | | |
| | | | |
| | | | |
| | | | |
| | | | |
| | | | |
| | | | |
| | | | |
| | | | |

**52a** Is the organization directly or indirectly affiliated with, or related to, one or more tax-exempt organizations described in section 501(c) of the Code (other than section 501(c)(3)) or in section 527?  . . . . . . . . . . . . . ☐ **Yes** ☐ **No**

**b** If "Yes," complete the following schedule.

| (a) Name of organization | (b) Type of organization | (c) Description of relationship |
|---|---|---|
| | | |
| | | |
| | | |
| | | |
| | | |
| | | |
| | | |
| | | |
| | | |
| | | |
| | | |
| | | |

*U.S. Government Printing Office: 1990-245-134

# INDEX

## A

"A Reorganization", 236–37, 249–52, 252–54, 254–56
Acceleration (creditors' remedy), 98, 136
Accounts receivable financing, 99, 113–14
Anchor tenants, 120–21
Annual meetings, 57–62, 324–25
Arbitration, 16, 28, 191
Articles of Incorporation:
    ammendent of, 2, 11, 324
    close corporation, 11–12
    dividend provisions, 9
    forms, 8–14
    indemnification provisions, 9, 175–76
    not-for-profit corporations, 315–16, 318–24
    optional powers in, 2–3, 10
    S Corporation, 7
    stock, 43–44
    transfer restrictions, 12
Assignment for benefit of creditors, 92, 95, 274–79
Auctions, 235

## B

"B Reorganization", 236–37, 256–60
"Battle of the forms," 127

Bankruptcy:
    automatic stay, 269–70
    confirmation of plan, 270
    constituting default, 109, 111
    fraudulent conveyances, 267, 270
    involuntary, 271–72, 292
    preferences, 267
    reaffirmation of debt, 298
    resolutions re, 91
    voluntary, 267–70, 279–94
    wage earner plans, 267
Board of Directors:
    Articles of Incorporation clauses, 6, 8, 319
    bylaw clauses, 16–17
    classification of, 85
    committees of, 59–60, 86–87
    elimination of, 12
    interested directors, 87, 166–67
    meetings of, 11, 85–86, 325
    mergers and acquisitions, 236
    resignation and removal, 87–88
    resolutions of, 68–96
Bonuses, 74–75, 94, 202
Borrowing, limitations on, 12, 13, 108
Business brokers, 240–41
Business judgment rule, 62, 163, 169, 236
Buy-sell agreements, 25, 50–51, 300–301
Bylaws:
    arbitration, 16
    forms, 14–18